MARY WOLLSTONECRAFT IN CONTEXT

Mary Wollstonecraft (1759–1797) was one of the most influential and controversial women of her age. No writer, except perhaps her political foe, Edmund Burke, and her fellow reformer, Thomas Paine, inspired more intense reactions. In her brief literary career before her untimely death in 1797, Wollstonecraft achieved remarkable success in an unusually wide range of genres: from education tracts and political polemics, to novels and travel writing. Just as impressive as her expansive range was the profound evolution of her thinking in the decade when she flourished as an author. In this collection of essays, leading international scholars reveal the intricate biographical, critical, cultural, and historical context crucial for understanding Mary Wollstonecraft's oeuvre. Chapters on British radicalism and conservatism, French *philosophes* and English Dissenters, constitutional law and domestic law, sentimental literature, eighteenth-century periodicals, and more elucidate Wollstonecraft's social and political thought, historical writings, moral tales for children, and novels.

NANCY E. JOHNSON is Professor of English and Associate Dean of the College of Liberal Arts and Sciences at the State University of New York at New Paltz. She is the author of *The English Jacobin Novel on Rights Property and the Law* (2004), editor of *Impassioned Jurisprudence* (2015), and scholarly editor of *The Court Journals of Frances Burney 1790–1, Vol. VI* (2019). She has published widely on literature of the 1790s and the intersections of literature and legal thought in the eighteenth century.

PAUL KEEN is Professor of English at Carleton University, Canada. He is the author and editor of several books, including *The Crisis of Literature in the 1790s: Print Culture and the Public Sphere* (1999), *Literature, Commerce, and the Spectacle of Modernity, 1750–1800* (2012), and *The Humanities in a Utilitarian Age: Imagining What We Know, 1800–1850* (forthcoming).

T0381772

MARY WOLLSTONECRAFT IN CONTEXT

EDITED BY

NANCY E. JOHNSON

State University of New York, New Paltz

and

PAUL KEEN

Carleton University, Canada

CAMBRIDGE
UNIVERSITY PRESS

CAMBRIDGE
UNIVERSITY PRESS

University Printing House, Cambridge CB2 8BS, United Kingdom

One Liberty Plaza, 20th Floor, New York, NY 10006, USA

477 Williamstown Road, Port Melbourne, VIC 3207, Australia

314-321, 3rd Floor, Plot 3, Splendor Forum, Jasola District Centre, New Delhi - 110025, India

103 Penang Road, #05-06/07, Visioncrest Commercial, Singapore 238467

Cambridge University Press is part of the University of Cambridge.

It furthers the University's mission by disseminating knowledge in the pursuit of education, learning and research at the highest international levels of excellence.

www.cambridge.org
Information on this title: www.cambridge.org/9781108404235
DOI: 10.1017/9781108261067

© Cambridge University Press 2020

First published 2020
First paperback edition 2022

A catalogue record for this publication is available from the British Library

ISBN 978-1-108-41699-3 Hardback
ISBN 978-1-108-40423-5 Paperback

Contents

Illustrations	*page*	ix
Notes on Contributors		x
Preface		xxi
Frontispiece		xxviii
Chronology		xxix

PART I LIFE AND WORKS   1

1   Biography   3
Kate Chisholm

2   Correspondence   11
Andrew McInnes

3   Family   21
Julie Carlson

4   Joseph Johnson   29
David Fallon

PART II CRITICAL FORTUNES   39

5   Early Critical Reception   41
Nancy E. Johnson

6   Nineteenth-Century Critical Reception   50
Eileen Hunt Botting

7   1970s Critical Reception   57
Julie Murray

8   Recent Critical Reception   64
Eliza O'Brien

PART III HISTORICAL AND CULTURAL CONTEXTS   73

THE FRENCH REVOLUTION DEBATE   75

9   Writing the French Revolution   77
     Mary A. Favret

10   Radical Societies   87
     David O'Shaughnessy

11   Radical Publishers   95
     Jon Mee

12   British Conservatism   102
     Paul Keen

THE RIGHTS OF WOMAN DEBATE   109

13   Jacobin Reformers   111
     Mary Fairclough

14   Liberal Reformers   119
     Michelle Levy

15   Conservative Reformers   127
     Claire Grogan

PHILOSOPHICAL FRAMEWORKS   137

16   French *Philosophes*   139
     Sylvana Tomaselli

17   Dissenters   146
     Andrew McKendry

18   Jean-Jacques Rousseau   155
     Laura Kirkley

19   Edmund Burke   164
     Frans de Bruyn

20   William Godwin   173
     Pamela Clemit

21 Political Theory   182
    Lena Halldenius

22 Feminist Theory   189
    Jane Moore

LEGAL AND SOCIAL CULTURE   197

23 The Constitution   199
    Ian Ward

24 Property Law   207
    Catherine Packham

25 Domestic Law   215
    Rebecca Probert

26 Slavery and Abolition   222
    Katie Donington

27 The Bluestockings   230
    Betty A. Schellenberg

28 Conduct Literature   238
    Vivien Jones

29 Theories of Education   246
    Frances Ferguson

LITERATURE   255

30 Sentimentalism and Sensibility   257
    Alex Wetmore

31 English Jacobin Novels   264
    April London

32 Anti-Jacobin Novels   273
    Gary Kelly

33 Children's Literature   281
    Andrew O'Malley

34 Gothic Literature   289
    Michael Gamer

35 Travel Writing   297
    Pamela Perkins

36 History Writing   305
    Jonathan Sachs

37 Periodicals   314
    Jacqueline George

38 Translations   323
    Alessa Johns

Suggested Further Reading   332
Index   352

Illustrations

Frontispiece *Mary Wollstonecraft*, by John Opie, c. 1797
Courtesy of the National Portrait Gallery, London   *page* xxviii
1 *Mary Shelley*, by Richard Rothwell, 1840
    Courtesy of the National Portrait Gallery, London   27
2 *Joseph Johnson*, by William Sharp, after Moses Haughton
    the Elder c. 1780–1820
    Courtesy of the National Portrait Gallery, London   32
3 *WOMEN'S RIGHTS, 1792*. Engraved frontispiece from the
    first volume of *The Lady's Magazine*, printed at Philadelphia,
    December 1792
    Courtesy of Granger Historical Picture Archive
    www.granger.com   45
4 *William Godwin*, by James Northcote, 1802
    Courtesy of the National Portrait Gallery, London   176

Notes on Contributors

EILEEN HUNT BOTTING is Professor of Political Science at the University of Notre Dame (USA). Her books include *Family Feuds: Wollstonecraft, Burke, and Rousseau on the Transformation of the Family* (2006), *Wollstonecraft, Mill, and Women's Human Rights* (2016), and *Mary Shelley and the Rights of the Child: Political Philosophy in "Frankenstein"* (2017).

JULIE CARLSON is Professor of English at University of California Santa Barbara. She is the author of *In the Theatre of Romanticism: Coleridge, Nationalism, Women* (Cambridge University Press, 1994), *England's First Family of Writers: Mary Wollstonecraft, William Godwin, Mary Shelley* (2007), and co-editor with Elisabeth Weber of *Speaking About Torture* (2012). Her articles focus on the cultural politics of British Romantic-era writing and mind studies. She is co-editor with Aranye Fradenburg of Brainstorm Books, an imprint of punctum books. Currently she is writing a book on "Creativity and Friendship: A Radical Legacy of British Romanticism."

KATE CHISHOLM is the author of *Wits and Wives: Dr Johnson in the Company of Women* (2011) and *Fanny Burney: Her Life* (1998). She has also written *Hungry Hell: What It's Really Like to Be Anorexic* (2002). A former fellow of the Royal Literary Fund and the Hawthornden Fund, she has taught on the MA course in creative writing (non-fiction) at City University in London. She was the radio critic of *The Spectator* magazine and reviews occasionally for *The Times Literary Supplement.*

PAMELA CLEMIT is Professor of English at Queen Mary University of London and a Supernumerary Fellow at Wolfson College, University of Oxford. She is the author of *The Godwinian Novel* (1993) and has published many essays on William Godwin and his intellectual circle. She has published a dozen or so scholarly and critical editions of William Godwin's and Mary Shelley's writings, including (with Gina

Luria Walker) *Memoirs of the Author of A Vindication of the Rights of Woman* (2001), and *Caleb Williams* (2009). She is the General Editor of *The Letters of William Godwin*, 6 vols. (in progress): *Volume I: 1778–1797*, edited by her, appeared in 2011; *Volume II: 1798–1805*, also edited by her, appeared in 2014. She is currently editing *Volume IV: 1816–1828*.

FRANS DE BRUYN is Professor Emeritus of English at the University of Ottawa. He has written extensively on Edmund Burke, including the monograph *The Literary Genres of Edmund Burke* (1996). He has also authored numerous publications on other subjects in eighteenth-century studies: georgic and agricultural writing, the reception of *Don Quixote*, the cultural impact of financial speculation (the South Sea Bubble), and Shakespeare in the eighteenth century. With Shaun Regan, he recently co-edited *The Culture of the Seven Years' War* (2014).

KATIE DONINGTON is a Lecturer in History at London South Bank University. Her research focuses on the history, legacies, and representation of British transatlantic slavery. In particular, she is interested in the ways in which slavery impacted on the familial and cultural world of the planter–merchant elites in Jamaica and Britain. Her doctoral and post-doctoral work was conducted with the *Legacies of British Slave-ownership* project at University College London between 2009 and 2015. She is a co-author of *Legacies of British Slave-Ownership: Colonial Slavery and the Formation of Victorian Britain* (Cambridge University Press, 2015). She is the co-editor of *Britain's History and Memory of Transatlantic Slavery: The Local Nuances of a "National Sin"* (2016). Her monograph *The Bonds of Family: Slavery, Commerce and Culture in the British Atlantic World* will be published in 2019.

MARY FAIRCLOUGH is Senior Lecturer in the Department of English and Related Literature and Centre for Eighteenth-Century Studies at the University of York, United Kingdom. She is the author of *The Romantic Crowd: Sympathy, Controversy and Print Culture* (Cambridge University Press, 2013), *Literature, Electricity and Politics 1740–1840: Electrick Communication Every Where* (2017), and several journal articles and essays which investigate the intersection of literature, science, and politics in the eighteenth-century and Romantic period.

DAVID FALLON is Senior Lecturer in English Literature at the University of Roehampton, London. He is the author of *Blake, Myth, and Enlightenment: The Politics of Apotheosis* (2017) and co-editor, with Jon Mee, of

Romanticism and Revolution: A Reader (2011). He has published essays on Blake, including "Homelands: Blake, Albion, and the French Revolution" in *Home and Nation in British Literature from the English to the French Revolution* (Cambridge University Press, 2015), and on eighteenth-century book culture, including "Piccadilly Booksellers and Conservative Sociability" in *Sociable Places: Locating Culture in Romantic-Period Britain* (Cambridge University Press, 2017). He is currently writing a monograph on "London Booksellers and Literary Sociability, 1740–1840."

MARY A. FAVRET teaches English and Women and Gender Studies at Johns Hopkins University. She is the author of *War at a Distance: Romanticism and the Making of Modern Wartime* and *Romantic Correspondence: Women, Politics and the Fiction of Letters* (Cambridge University Press) as well as various essays on topics in the field of Romanticism. With Nicola Watson, she edited *At the Limits of Romanticism* (1994), and with Donald Gray, a critical edition of *Pride and Prejudice* (2016).

FRANCES FERGUSON teaches in the English Department at the University of Chicago, where she is Ann L. and Lawrence B. Buttenwieser Professor. She is the author of *Wordsworth: Language as Counter-Spirit*; *Solitude and the Sublime: Romanticism and the Aesthetics of Individuation* (1997); and *Pornography, The Theory: What Utilitarianism Did to Action* (2004), along with essays on various topics in eighteenth-century and Romantic studies and literary theory.

MICHAEL GAMER is Professor of English at the University of Pennsylvania and author of *Romanticism and the Gothic* (Cambridge University Press, 2000) and *Romanticism, Self-Canonization, and the Business of Poetry* (Cambridge University Press, 2017). As a member of the Multigraph Collective, he helped to produce *Interacting with Print: Modes of Reading in the Age of Print Saturation* (2018). He is currently at work on several projects relating to women writers, the gothic, and melodrama.

JACQUELINE GEORGE is Associate Professor of English at the State University of New York at New Paltz. She has published articles about Romantic reading practices and relationships between books and people, including "Confessions of a Mass Public: Reflexive Formations of Subjectivity in Early Nineteenth-Century British Fiction" (*Studies in the Novel* [2014]) and "Avatars in Edinburgh: *The Private Memoirs and Confessions of a Justified Sinner* and the Second Life of Hogg's Ettrick Shepherd" (*Romanticism and Victorianism on the Net* [2012]). She is currently at work on a monograph about genre, the history of reading, and late-Romantic prose fiction.

CLAIRE GROGAN is a full professor in the English Department of Bishop's University, Quebec, Canada. Her research focuses on the politics of British writing in the 1790s and the early nineteenth century. She is editor of scholarly editions – Jane Austen's *Northanger Abbey* (1994/ 2002), Elizabeth Hamilton's *Memoirs of Modern Philosophers* (2000), and Thomas Paine's *Rights of Man, Parts I and II* (2011) – book chapters and articles, and a book-length study entitled *Politics and Genre in the Work of Elizabeth Hamilton, 1756–1816* (2012).

LENA HALLDENIUS is Professor of Human Rights Studies at Lund University in Sweden. With a Ph.D. in Philosophy, she is working in political philosophy and the history of modern political thought. Her research focus is on conceptions of freedom and rights, particularly but not exclusively in the republican tradition. Halldenius is the author of *Mary Wollstonecraft and Feminist Republicanism: Independence, Rights and the Experience of Unfreedom* (2015) and several articles and book chapters on Wollstonecraft's political philosophy.

ALESSA JOHNS is Professor of English at the University of California, Davis. She has published *Bluestocking Feminism and British–German Cultural Transfer, 1750–1837* (2014) and *Women's Utopias of the Eighteenth Century* (2003). She has also edited *Dreadful Visitations: Confronting Natural Catastrophe in the Age of Enlightenment* (1999) and *Reflections on Sentiment: Essays in Honor of George Starr* (2016). Her current research is on the spread of English Studies in eighteenth- and nineteenth-century Germany.

NANCY E. JOHNSON is Associate Dean of the College of Liberal Arts and Sciences and Professor of English at the State University of New York, New Paltz. She is the author of *The English Jacobin Novel on Rights, Property and the Law: Critiquing the Contract* (2004); editor of *Impassioned Jurisprudence: Law, Literature and Emotion, 1760–1848* (2015); and scholarly editor of *The Court Journals and Letters of Frances Burney, 1790–June 1791, Vol. VI* (2019). She is currently working on a volume of Charles Burney's letters and a study of women's concepts of justice in the eighteenth century.

VIVIEN JONES during her academic career as Professor of Eighteenth-Century Gender and Culture in the School of English at the University of Leeds published widely on writing by and about women in the period, with particular interests in instructional literature, Wollstonecraft, and Austen. She contributed the chapter on Austen to the recent *Oxford History of the Novel in English* (2015). From 2006 to 2016 she was Pro Vice-Chancellor for Student Education and now, partly retired, chairs the University's Cultural Institute.

PAUL KEEN is Professor of English at Carleton University. He is the author of *Literature, Commerce, and the Spectacle of Modernity, 1750–1800* (2012), and *The Crisis of Literature in the 1790s: Print Culture and the Public Sphere* (1999). His edited books include *The Radical Popular Press in Britain, 1817–1821* (2003), *Revolutions in Romantic Literature: An Anthology of Print Culture, 1780–1832* (2004), *Bookish Histories: Books, Literature, and Commercial Modernity, 1700–1900* (co-edited with Ina Ferris, 2009), and *The Age of Authors: An Anthology of Eighteenth-Century Print Culture* (2014). His forthcoming book is entitled *A Defense of the Humanities in a Utilitarian Age: Imagining What We Know, 1800–1850*.

GARY KELLY is a Distinguished University Professor at the University of Alberta and author of essays, monographs, and editions on British Romantic literature, especially the novel and women's writing from the Bluestockings to the Revolutionary aftermath. These include an edition of Wollstonecraft's novels; *Revolutionary Feminism: A Literary and Political Biography of Wollstonecraft* (1992); and *Women, Writing, and Revolution* (1993), on several of Wollstonecraft's contemporaries. Other contributions include multi-volume editions of *Bluestocking Feminism* (1999), *Varieties of Female Gothic* (2002), and *Newgate Narratives* (2008), editions of Sarah Scott's *Millenium Hall* (1995), poems of Felicia Hemans, and poems and prose of Lydia Sigourney. He is the General Editor of the ongoing *Oxford History of Popular Print Culture* (2012). Current projects include *Cheap Print* (2012) and a history of *Modern Fun*.

LAURA KIRKLEY is a comparativist with expertise in both English and French literature. She was a College Lecturer in French at The Queen's College, Oxford and a Research Fellow at Trinity Hall, Cambridge before joining the School of English at Newcastle University in 2013 as a Lecturer in Eighteenth-Century Literature. She has research interests in the literature of the French Revolution, literary and cultural translation, cosmopolitanism, and women writers, particularly Mary Wollstonecraft. Her edition of *Caroline of Lichtfield*, Thomas Holcroft's translation of

Isabelle de Montolieu's novel, was published in 2014, and she is currently completing a monograph, *The Cosmopolitanism of Mary Wollstonecraft.*

MICHELLE LEVY is a Professor in the Department of English and Co-Director of the Digital Humanities Innovation Lab at Simon Fraser University. She is a co-author (with Tom Mole) of the *Broadview Introduction to Book History* (2017); co-editor (with Tom Mole) of the *Broadview Reader in Book History* (2014); author of *Family Authorship and Romantic Print Culture* (2008); and co-editor (with Anne Mellor) of a Broadview edition of Lucy Aikin's *Epistles on Women* (2010). She has published extensively on women writers, print and manuscript culture, and digital humanities, and has recently completed a book, entitled *Literary Manuscript Culture in Romantic Britain*. She directs the *Women's Print History Project, 1750–1830*, a comprehensive bibliographical database of women's books.

APRIL LONDON is Emeritus Professor at the University of Ottawa and editor of *The Cambridge Guide to the Eighteenth-Century Novel, 1660–1820* (forthcoming). Her publications include *The Cambridge Introduction to the Eighteenth-Century Novel* (2012), *Literary History Writing, 1770–1820* (2010), and *Women and Property in the Eighteenth-Century English Novel* (1999).

ANDREW MCINNES is Senior Lecturer and Programme Leader in English Literature at Edge Hill University. He researches Romantic-period women's writing, Gothic fiction, and children's literature, and has published on authors including Mary Hays, Charlotte Dacre, and Arthur Ransome. His first book, *Wollstonecraft's Ghost: The Fate of the Female Philosopher in the Romantic Period*, was published in 2016. He recently published "'English Verdure, English Culture, English Comfort': Ireland and the Gothic Elsewhere in Jane Austen's *Emma*" in *Romantic Textualities: Literature and Print Culture, 1780–1840* (Spring 2017) and co-edited "Edgy Romanticism," a special issue of *Romanticism* (July 2018).

ANDREW MCKENDRY is Associate Professor of English at Nord University. His most recent work has appeared in *Eighteenth-Century Studies* and *Studies in Romanticism*, and he has also published essays on eighteenth-century politics and education. His current book project examines the conceptual history of toleration, in particular how seventeenth-century attitudes toward religious difference were inflected by shifting paradigms of disability.

JON MEE is Professor of Eighteenth-Century Studies at the University of York. He edited Wollstonecraft's *Letters Written during a Short Residence in Sweden, Norway, and Denmark* with Tone Brekke. His most recent monographs are *Conversable Worlds Literature, Contention, and Community 1762–1830* (2011) and *Print, Publicity, and Popular Radicalism in the 1790s: The Laurel of Liberty* (Cambridge University Press, 2016).

JANE MOORE is Reader in English Literature in the School of English, Communication and Philosophy at Cardiff University. She is the author and editor of several articles and books on Wollstonecraft and women's writing, including *The Feminist Reader: Essays in Gender and the Politics of Literary Criticism*, co-edited with Catherine Belsey (second edition, 1997). She is also the author of *Mary Wollstonecraft* (1999) and editor of *Mary Wollstonecraft* (2012).

JULIE MURRAY is Associate Professor of English at Carleton University. She has published widely on British women writers such as Mary Wollstonecraft, Joanna Baillie, Mary Hays, and Elizabeth Hamilton in journals such as *Women's Writing, ELH, European Romantic Review, Studies in Romanticism,* and *Eighteenth-Century Fiction.* She is currently completing a book-length study entitled *Mary Wollstonecraft, Modernity, and Feminist Historiography.*

ELIZA O'BRIEN is a Teaching Fellow at Newcastle University. She has published articles on William Godwin, Thomas Holcroft, and sentimental fiction, and is a contributor to *The Cambridge Guide to the Eighteenth-Century Novel, 1660–1820,* edited by April London. She is a co-editor of and contributor to *New Approaches to William Godwin: Forms, Fears, Futures* (forthcoming).

ANDREW O'MALLEY is Associate Professor in the English Department at Ryerson University in Toronto, where his teaching and research focus on children's literature and culture, both historical and current, popular cultures, and comics and child readers. He is the author of *The Making of the Modern Child: Children's Literature and Childhood in the Late Eighteenth Century* (2003) and *Children's Literature, Popular Culture, and "Robinson Crusoe"* (2012). He is also editor of *Literary Cultures and Eighteenth-Century Childhoods* (2018), and is working on a digital archive and exhibit entitled "A Crisis of Innocence: Comic Books and Children's Culture, 1940–1954."

DAVID O'SHAUGHNESSY is Associate Professor of eighteenth-century studies at the School of English, Trinity College Dublin. He is the author of *William Godwin and the Theatre*, editor of *The Plays of William Godwin*, and co-editor of *The Diary of William Godwin* (2010). He has published widely on Godwin and on eighteenth-century theatre studies, with essays in journals such as *Eighteenth-Century Life*, *Journal of Eighteenth-Century Studies*, *Nineteenth-Century Literature*, and *Huntington Library Quarterly*, as well as in a number of essay collections. Most recently, he edited a volume of essays on *Ireland, Enlightenment and the English Stage, 1740–1820* (2019) and is currently working on Oliver Goldsmith.

CATHERINE PACKHAM is Reader in English and Head of English Literature at the University of Sussex. She is author of *Eighteenth-Century Vitalism* (2012) and co-editor of *Political Economy, Literature, and the Formation of Knowledge, 1720–1850* (2018), and she has written many articles on eighteenth-century literature, philosophy, and political economy. She is currently at work on a study of the writings of Mary Wollstonecraft in the context of late eighteenth-century debates over political economy, a project for which she has been the recipient of a Leverhulme Research Fellowship. Her work on Wollstonecraft has appeared in the following journals: *ELH*, *Women's Writing*, and *European Romantic Review*.

PAMELA PERKINS is a Professor in the Department of English, Film, Theatre and Media at the University of Manitoba, where she teaches eighteenth-century and Romantic-era literature. Her publications include a monograph on early nineteenth-century Edinburgh women writers and editions of works by a number of eighteenth- and nineteenth-century authors including Elizabeth Hamilton, Robert Bage, Anne Grant, Elizabeth Isabella Spence, John Moore, and Margaret Oliphant. She is currently working on a study of British travelers in the North Atlantic in the late eighteenth and early nineteenth centuries.

REBECCA PROBERT is Professor of Law at the University of Exeter. Her research focuses on the law and history of marriage, bigamy, divorce, and cohabitation, and she is the author of numerous articles and books, including *Marriage Law and Practice in the Long Eighteenth Century:*

A Reassessment (2009) and *The Legal Regulation of Cohabitation: From Fornicators to Family, 1600–2010* (2012), both published by Cambridge University Press. She has also published a number of guides for family historians, including *Marriage Law for Genealogists (2012) and Divorced, Bigamist, Bereaved? (2015)*, and has appeared numerous times on TV and radio programs, including *Harlots, Heroines and Housewives, A House Through Time*, and *Who Do You Think You Are?*

JONATHAN SACHS is the author of *The Poetics of Decline in British Romanticism* (Cambridge University Press, 2018), *Romantic Antiquity: Rome in the British Imagination, 1789–1832* (2010), and co-author, with the Multigraph Collective, of *Interacting with Print: Elements of Reading in the Era of Print Saturation* (2018). He is Professor of English at Concordia University, Montreal, where he also directs the inter-institutional Interacting with Print Research Group. Sachs has held a fellowship at the National Humanities Center (2014–15) and a membership at the Institute for Advanced Study, Princeton (2017–18).

BETTY A. SCHELLENBERG is a Professor of English at Simon Fraser University. Her interests in the Bluestocking movement, authorship, the print trade, and scribal cultures inform her most recent monograph, *Literary Coteries and the Making of Modern Print Culture* (Cambridge University Press, 2016). Other publications include *Samuel Richardson in Context*, co-edited with Peter Sabor (Cambridge University Press, 2017), *The Professionalization of Women Writers in Eighteenth-Century Britain* (Cambridge University Press, 2005), and *Reconsidering the Blue-stockings*, co-edited with Nicole Pohl (2003). She is currently research-ing the eighteenth-century manuscript verse miscellany.

SYLVANA TOMASELLI is Sir Harry Hinsley Lecturer in History at St. John's College, University of Cambridge. Her recent publications on Wollstonecraft include "Reflections on Inequality, Respect and Love in the Political Writings of Mary Wollstonecraft" in *The Social and Political Thought of Mary Wollstonecraft*, edited by Sandrine Berge and Alan Coffee (2016); "Mary Wollstonecraft" in *Oxford Bibliographies in Philosophy*, edited by Duncan Pritchard (2016); "Mary Wollstonecraft" in *The Stanford Encyclopedia of Philosophy*, edited by Edward N. Zalta (2012); and *"Mary Wollstonecraft: Civil Society, Revolution, Economic Equality"* in *Encyclopedia of Concise Concepts by Women Phil-osophers*, edited by Mary Ellen Waithe and Ruth Hagengruber (2018).

IAN WARD is Professor of Law at Newcastle University. His teaching and research interests are concentrated on the interdisciplinary relation of law, literature, and history. Among his more recent books can be counted *Law and the Brontes* (2011), *Sex, Crime and Literature in Victorian England* (2014), and *Writing the Victorian Constitution,* (2018). He has also edited the fifth volume in the forthcoming *Cultural Histories of Law* series, entitled *A Cultural History of Law in the Age of Reform.* At present he is completing a major new study of English legal history since the Reformation, to be published in spring 2020.

ALEX WETMORE is an Assistant Professor in the English department at the University of the Fraser Valley in Canada. He is the author of *Men of Feeling in Eighteenth-Century Literature* (2013), and his current research focuses on, among other things, intersections of the mechanical and the sentimental in the literature and culture of the 1700s.

Preface

An article that appeared in the April 1797 edition of the *Monthly Magazine* entitled "On Artificial Taste" offered readers a meditation on two of the most widely noted dimensions of this popular theme: "a taste for rural scenes" and the more "natural" quality of poetry that had been "written in the infancy of society." In some ways, both of these were standard topics, frequently discussed in the literary magazines of the day, though the article addressed them with compelling rigor and clarity, and with a refreshing impatience for empty poses and cultural double standards. It was curious, the author suggested, given people's widely professed love of nature, "how few people seem to contemplate nature with their own eyes. I have 'brushed the dew away' in the morning; but, pacing over the printless grass, I have wondered that, in such delightful situations, the sun was allowed to rise in solitary majesty, whilst my eyes alone hailed its beautifying beams."[1] Having offered a no-nonsense reflection on the state of people's real interest in nature beyond the sort of "romantic kind of declamation" that was so much in vogue, the author moved on to offer a fairly standard list of the age's assumptions: poetry is a "transcript of immediate emotions" transfigured by the effects of those "happy moment[s]" in which the poet is enriched by images "spontaneously bursting on him" without the need for any recourse to "understanding or memory."[2] This account of creativity, like the article's definition of the poet as "a man of strong feelings" giving "us a picture of his mind when he was actually alone, conversing with himself, and marking the impression which nature made on his own heart" seemed to converge with William Wordsworth's ideas about poetry in his Preface to the *Lyrical Ballads*. Its related insistence on the higher spiritual worth of those moments when the poet worshipped "in a temple not made with hands, and the world seems to contain only the mind that formed and contemplates it" seemed to echo Pysche's declaration of sublime internalization in Keats's ode.[3] Except, of course, that the article was published in April 1797, well ahead of

Wordsworth's account in the Preface to the 1800 edition of the *Lyrical Ballads* and a full generation before Keats's work.

Published anonymously (it was addressed to the editor and signed W. Q.) in the correspondence section of the *Monthly*, immediately following a letter championing the role of "country banks" in promoting "internal trade and manufactures," the article was only publicly attributed to Wollstonecraft when William Godwin included it in his edition of her *Posthumous Works* a year later.[4] In many ways, it is classic Wollstonecraft, absolutely in step with the themes of her day but a full step ahead of many of the writers who would weigh in on them, intellectually searching but wonderfully critical of empty posturing, philosophically expansive yet grounded in a shrewd sense of the age. But in its original format as an anonymous "letter" (these were often commissioned and paid articles that were included in a letter format) it also highlighted the side of Wollstonecraft that can be easy to forget, the professional writer contributing to a range of periodicals in a number of guises (including her frequent role as a reviewer of the *Analytical Review*), preoccupied not just with groundbreaking questions about democracy and the rights of men and women but also with standard topics that would have struck a chord with mainstream reading audiences.

Five months later she was dead. The "Marriages and Obituaries" section of the October edition of the *Gentleman's Magazine* contained a notice that "Mrs. Godwin, wife of Mr. Wm. G. of Somers-town; a woman of uncommon talents and considerable knowledge, and well known throughout Europe by her literary works, under her original name of Wollstonecraft" had died "in childbed."[5] Having provided a cursory list of her main publications, the *Gentleman's* offered a gracious person tribute. "Her manners were gentle, easy, and elegant; her conversation intelligent and amusing, without the least trait of literary pride, or the apparent consciousness of powers above the level of her sex; and, for soundness of understanding, and sensibility of heart, she was, perhaps, never equalled."[6] Then, having ushered Wollstonecraft gently back into the feminine sphere of duties by insisting that "her practical skill in education was even superior to her speculations upon that subject," it concluded by emphasizing its aversion "to the system she supported in politics and morals, both by her writings and practice."[7] As an obituary, it was balanced and polite, if far less enthusiastic than an obituary three pages earlier for "Elizabeth Neale, better known by the name of *Betty*," who had run a fruit shop at her "house in-St. James's-Street," where "her company was ever sought for by the highest of our men of rank and fortune ... She was a woman of pleasing manners and conversation, and abounding with anecdote and entertainment."[8] Readers of the two obituaries could be forgiven for assuming that the "Queen of Apple women" had the bigger impact on her age.[9]

The *Gentleman's* had not always been so polite. Seven years earlier, it had responded to Wollstonecraft's *A Vindication of the Rights of Men* with "a horse-laugh," reducing her intervention in political debate to the parodic image of a woman riding to the defense of Richard Price "armed *cap-à-pie*," pathetically unaware that jousting was no place for ladies. It mocked her critique of the effects of inequalities in property, scorned the misguided tendency of "our new philosophers" to encourage "millions of people, both of the *great* and *little* vulgar" to use "the free exercise of their reason, whether they wish it or are capable of it or not," and denounced the "stale and shameful tricks" of these "malcontents," who, having "nothing to lose, may lend their names and offer their hands, for any mischief."[10] Then it retreated into disapproving silence, declining to review any of Wollstonecraft's subsequent publications. The review would not be the last example of hostile attention that Wollstonecraft faced, much of which lapsed into personal attacks; nor was she lacking in responses that were equally enthusiastic about the important nature of her interventions, many of which saw in Wollstonecraft's work a vision of a social order that would help to foster genuine moral integrity in both the private and public domains. Whether writers agreed with her ideas or not, she had everyone's attention.

As the *Gentleman's* obituary came close to acknowledging, Wollstonecraft was one of the most influential women of her day in an age that would turn out to be a crucial one in the history of modernity, whether as a revolutionary turning point or (for reformers) a missed opportunity, an extraordinary literary flourishing or a philosophical reconsideration of the most fundamental aspects of the Enlightenment. Wollstonecraft played a central role in all these dynamics. She began writing in the later 1780s, in the wake of the American Revolution, and she came of age intellectually in the early 1790s, in the midst of the French Revolution. In Britain, reform movements were in full force as they debated liberty, rights, and governance; counterrevolutionary sentiments also ran high, and fears that the foundations of British liberty could be destroyed began to spread. Ideas circulated through Britain, America, and France as the political, legal, and economic subject of the monarchy was transformed into the citizen of a social contract. In some ways, though, the sheer intensity of these developments and the high stakes that were involved have helped to overshadow the extraordinary magnitude of Wollstonecraft's achievements in the few years that she worked as a professional author, in terms of the quantity of what she produced, the ambitious scale of the questions she was wrestling with, and, just as impressively, the profound development of her thinking over that decade.

No writer, except perhaps her political foe, Edmund Burke, and her fellow reformer, Thomas Paine, inspired more intense reactions. In her brief literary career before her untimely death in 1797, Wollstonecraft achieved remarkable success in an unusually wide range of genres, from education tracts and political polemics, to novels and travel writing. Just as impressive as her expansive range was the profound evolution of her thinking in the decade that she flourished as an author. Few readers of her 1792 *Vindication of the Rights of Woman* would have anticipated the comment that "[i]f ever there was a book calculated to make a man fall in love with its author, this appears to me to be the book," as William Godwin wrote about her *Letters Written during a Short Residence in Sweden, Norway, and Denmark*. However, Wollstonecraft's *Letters* marked an important extension rather than a departure from her feminist commitments. Her relatively brief but intense career as an author was marked by a constant development in her thinking about the major issues of her day. Running through all of this was the remarkable cultural achievement of a woman with few connections and little formal education who, within a few short years, rose to the pinnacle of the English literary community. In 1787, having traveled to London with almost nothing, like so many aspiring authors before her, Wollstonecraft quickly became a prominent member of the intellectual circle that had formed around the publisher and editor, Joseph Johnson, with whom she found employment as a reviewer and translator.

More than any writer of her generation, Wollstonecraft insisted that the emancipatory efforts associated with the French Revolution be extended to a thorough reconsideration of the rights of women as well. For Wollstonecraft, as for so many Enlightenment thinkers, reformist ideals were bound up with questions of education, but her interest in women's education grew out of personal experience. As an early proponent of female education, she opened a school for girls with her sister Eliza and her friend Frances Blood in Newington Green. She also published an educational treatise, *Thoughts on the Education of Daughters* (1787), and compiled an anthology for young women, *The Female Reader* (1789). As a British radical and political theorist, she wrote one of the first responses to Edmund Burke's widely read condemnation of the French Revolution,

Reflections on the Revolution in France (1790). Her *Vindication of the Rights of Men* (1790) is not only a persuasive endorsement of human rights but also the first comprehensive articulation of political theory by a woman in British history. As a feminist (before the term was in use), she wrote what is often hailed as the first extensive study of women in patriarchal culture, *A Vindication of the Rights of Woman* (1792), and advocated for the advancement of women. Recognizing the power of fiction to integrate political arguments into the practice of everyday life, she wrote two novels that contributed to the development of the novel at the end of the eighteenth century: *Mary: A Fiction* (1788), a sentimental and somewhat autobiographical bildungsroman, and *Maria; or, The Wrongs of Woman* (1798), a narrative study of the legal and political "wrongs" engendered against women. In 1796, she extended her literary talents in a radically new direction in her travelogue, *Letters Written during a Short Residence in Sweden, Norway, and Denmark*, a text whose fusion of haunting interiority, evocative accounts of her surroundings, and sturdy Enlightenment rationalism enabled her to break new ground in her efforts to articulate the problems and possibilities facing women.

Like the 1790s generally, Wollstonecraft's greatest strengths were in some ways her biggest liability. The uncompromising courage of her arguments and the urgency of the topics involved had a polarizing effect that tended, almost immediately, to eclipse the highly nuanced character of her thinking. Whether critics embraced her ideas or denounced them, the popular impression of her work tended to circulate in simplified, sometimes caricatured ways that often failed to appreciate the subtlety of her engagement with the many contending political and intellectual currents of her day. Recent decades, however, have seen a marked shift toward a more sympathetic understanding of these complexities. This volume will contribute to this critical reappraisal in three valuable ways: by emphasizing the sophistication of Wollstonecraft's intellectual preoccupations and influences; by focusing on the material realities of her work as a professional author; and by stressing the remarkable breadth and evolution of her work.

In the latter part of the twentieth century, on the heels of the second wave of feminism, scholars of the eighteenth century made a concerted effort to publish updated editions of Mary Wollstonecraft's works.[11] Recent years have also seen the publication of several valuable works of criticism.[12] However, there are no book-length studies of the wide and very rich context in which Mary Wollstonecraft lived and wrote. This collection is designed to fill that gap. The first eight essays of the volume will provide the reader with biographical information on Wollstonecraft's vibrant and tumultuous life, as well as the publishing and reception history of her controversial work. The thirty essays that follow, under "Historical and Cultural Contexts," are designed to provide the reader with background on the political events to which Mary Wollstonecraft was responding in her work, such as the French Revolution and radical movements in Great Britain, and the intellectual and cultural thought that informed Wollstonecraft's writing and activism. Notably, this includes essays on education, travel writing, fiction, and periodical writing, to provide context for the many genres that Wollstonecraft did so much to shape. Our hope is that these essays will help to provide readers with a broader and more nuanced sense, both of the pressures and opportunities of the age in which Wollstonecraft worked and to which she offered such memorable responses, and of the many different sides of Wollstonecraft herself, as a political activist and a professional writer at a time when this career path remained an uphill battle for women. Wollstonecraft was a polemicist but also a novelist, reviewer, and translator, and most memorably, a pioneering feminist whose groundbreaking work excited powerful responses, the intensity of which has both ensured an enduring appreciation of her unique historical importance and, sometimes, made it difficult to appreciate her work in the nuanced ways that it deserves.

Notes

1 *Monthly Magazine*, 3 (1797), 279.
2 Ibid.
3 Ibid., 279–80.
4 Ibid., 278.
5 *Gentleman's Magazine*, 67:2 (1797), 894.
6 Ibid., 894.
7 Ibid.
8 Ibid., 891.
9 Ibid.
10 *Gentleman's Magazine*, 61:1 (1791), 151–54.
11 The most important of these is the seven-volume *The Works of Mary Wollstonecraft* (1989) edited by Janet Todd and Marilyn Butler; but see also the *Collected Letters of Mary Wollstonecraft* (1979), edited by Ralph Wardle, and a later edition (2003), edited by Janet Todd, as well as multiple biographies including those written by Todd, Claire Tomalin, and most recently Lyndall Gordon.

12 Significant examples include Gary Kelly's examination of Wollstonecraft's radicalism, *Revolutionary Feminism* (1992); Virginia Sapiro's study of Wollstonecraft's political theory, *A Vindication of Political Virtue* (1992); Barbara Taylor's inquiry into Wollstonecraft's feminist theory in *Mary Wollstonecraft and the Feminist Imagination* (2003); Claudia L. Johnson's *Cambridge Companion to Mary Wollstonecraft* (2002); Lena Halldenius' *Mary Wollstonecraft and Feminist Republicanism* (2015); and Sandrine Bergès' and Alan Coffee's *The Social and Political Philosophy of Mary Wollstonecraft* (2016).

Frontispiece: *Mary Wollstonecraft*, by John Opie, c. 1797.
Courtesy of the National Portrait Gallery, London

Chronology

	Mary Wollstonecraft's Life	Historical and Literary Events
1759	MW born April 27 to Edward John Wollstonecraft and Elizabeth Dickson in Spitalfields, London, as eldest daughter and second child.	
1760		Accession of George III.
1761	MW's brother Henry is born.	Jean-Jacques Rousseau's *Julie, ou la nouvelle Héloïse* published.
1762		Jean-Jacques Rousseau's *Émile, ou de l'éducation* and *Du contrat social* published.
1763	MW's sister Elizabeth (Eliza or Bess) is born. Family moves to Epping Forest.	
1765	MW's sister Everina is born. Family moves to Barking.	
1768	MW's brother James is born. Family moves to Beverley, Yorkshire. MW meets Jane Arden.	Royal Academy established in London, with Sir Joshua Reynolds its first president.
1770	MW's brother Charles is born.	Captain Cook reaches Australia and names Botany Bay. Jean-Jacques Rousseau writes *Les Confessions*, published in 1782.
1774	Family moves to Hoxton. MW meets the Reverend and Mrs. Clare, and Fanny Blood, with whom she will open a school.	Donaldson *v.* Beckett decided in the House of Lords, confirming that copyright is of limited duration. Publication of Joseph Priestley's *Experiments and Observations on Different Kinds of Air*, Vol. 1.
1755–83		American War of Independence.
1776	Family moves to Langharne, Wales.	Edward Gibbon's *The Decline and Fall of the Roman Empire*, Vol. 1 and Adam Smith's *Wealth of Nations* published.

(*cont.*)

	Mary Wollstonecraft's Life	Historical and Literary Events
1777	Family moves to Walworth, suburb of London.	Richard Brinsley Sheridan's *The School for Scandal* performed at Drury Lane, to great acclaim.
1778	MW takes position as paid companion to Mrs. Sarah Dawson of Bath.	Frances Burney's *Evelina* published.
1780	Family moves to Enfield, Middlesex.	Gordon Riots in London.
1781	MW returns home to care for ailing mother.	Immanuel Kant's *The Critique of Pure Reason* published.
1782	MW's mother dies April 19. Eliza marries Meredith Bishop October 20. Edward Wollstonecraft remarries and moves to Wales. MW lives with Blood family in Walham Green.	
1783	Eliza gives birth to a daughter Mary on August 10.	Joseph Montgolfier launches the first hot-air balloon in Paris in front of a large crowd that includes Louis XVI.
1784	MW cares for Eliza, who is suffering from post-partum depression. Eliza and Meredith legally separate. Their daughter dies. MW, Eliza, and Fanny, after a false start in Islington, open a school in Newington Green. MW meets Reverend Richard Price and Samuel Johnson.	Charlotte Smith's *Elegiac Sonnets* published. William Pitt elected prime minister.
1785	Fanny Blood moves to Lisbon to marry Hugh Skeys. By March, Fanny is pregnant. MW goes to Lisbon to care for Fanny, but Fanny dies after giving birth, and the baby dies soon after.	William Cowper's *The Task* published.
1786	MW closes school in Newington Green and takes a job as governess to eldest daughters of the Kingsborough family, Mitchelstown, County Cork. MW visits Eton on the way to Ireland.	Robert Burns' *Poems, Chiefly in the Scottish Dialect* published.
1787	*Thoughts on the Education of Daughters* published by Joseph Johnson. MW begins writing *Mary: A Fiction* and "Cave of Fancy." MW is dismissed from position as governess, returns to London, and settles in Blackfriars.	The Society for the Abolition of the Slave Trade founded in London.

(*cont.*)

	Mary Wollstonecraft's Life	Historical and Literary Events
1788	*Mary: A Fiction, Original Stories from Real Life*, and MW's translation of Jacques Necker's *Of the Importance of Religious Opinions* published by Joseph Johnson. MW contributes to the *Analytical Review* published by Joseph Johnson and Thomas Christie. MW supports Everina, who has left her post at Miss Rowden's School, Paris.	Beginning of the impeachment trial of Warren Hastings, governor-general of Bengal. *Analytical Review* established by Joseph Johnson and Thomas Christie.
1789	*The Female Reader* published by Joseph Johnson under pseudonym "Mr. Creswick." MW meets the Swiss artist Henry Fuseli.	Beginning of the French Revolution. Jeremy Bentham's *Principles of Morals and Legislation* published. William Blake's *Songs of Innocence* published.
1790	MW's translations of Maria van de Werken de Cambon's *Young Grandison*, an adaptation of Samuel Richardson's novel, and Christian Salzmann's *Elements of Morality, for the Use of Children* are published by Joseph Johnson. *A Vindication of the Rights of Men* is published anonymously on November 29 and under MW's name on December 18.	Edmund Burke's *Reflections on the Revolution in France* published. Joanna Baillie's *Poems* published. Anna Barbauld's *An Address to the Opposers of the Repeal of the Corporation and Test Acts* published. William Blake's *The Marriage of Heaven and Hell* published. Helen Maria Williams' *Letters Written in France* published. Catharine Macaulay's *Letters on Education* published.
1791	Second edition of *Original Stories* is published with illustrations by William Blake. MW writes *A Vindication of the Rights of Woman*. MW meets *William Godwin* at the home of Joseph Johnson.	Joseph Priestley's house destroyed by an anti-revolutionary mob while Priestley hosts a celebratory dinner on the anniversary of the storming of the Bastille. Priestley emigrates to America. Thomas Paine's *Rights of Man* published. Anna Barbauld's *Epistle to William Wilberforce on the Rejection of the Bill for Abolishing the Slave Trade* published. Erasmus Darwin's *The Botanical Garden*, Part One, published.
1792	*A Vindication of the Rights of Woman* is published by Joseph Johnson. Second revised edition is published later this year. In December, MW travels to France to witness the revolution.	September massacres in Paris. London Corresponding Society founded. Thomas Paine tried *in absentia* and convicted of seditious libel for *Rights of Man*, Part Two. Robert Bage's *Man as He Is* published. Charlotte Smith's *Desmond* published.

(*cont.*)

	Mary Wollstonecraft's Life	Historical and Literary Events
1793	MW meets Gilbert Imlay. In June, MW moves from Paris to Neuilly to escape the violence in Paris. Now pregnant, MW returns to Paris, where she registers as Imlay's wife.	Execution of Louis XVI and Marie Antoinette. France declares war against Britain. Reign of Terror in France. *British Critic: A New Review* established. William Godwin's *Enquiry concerning Political Justice, and Its Influence on General Virtue and Happiness* published. Mary Hays's *Letters and Essays, Morals and Miscellaneous* published. Daniel Isaac Eaton's *The Pernicious Effects of the Art of Printing upon Society, Exposed* published. Hannah Moore's *Village Politics* published. Charlotte Smith's *The Old Manor House* published.
1794	MW moves to Le Havre, where her daughter Fanny Imlay is born in May. *An Historical and Moral View of the Origin and Progress of the French Revolution* is published by Joseph Johnson.	Fall of Robespierre. High treason trials for fourteen members of the London Corresponding Society. William Blake's *Songs of Experience* published. William Godwin's *Things as They Are; or, The Adventures of Caleb Williams* published. Ann Radcliffe's *The Mysteries of Udolpho* published. Erasmus Darwin's *Zoonomia; or, The Laws of Organic Life*, Part One, published. Thomas Holcroft's *The Adventures of Hugh Trevor*, Part One published. Charlotte Smith's *The Wanderings of Warwick* published.
1795	MW moves back to London but discovers Imlay's infidelity and attempts suicide. MW travels to Scandinavia with her daughter and her daughter's nurse on behalf of Imlay's business interests. Returns in September. MW attempts suicide again in October.	Introduction of Pitt's Gagging Acts aimed at curtailing freedom of speech and assembly. William Blake's *The Book of Ahania* and *The Song of Los* published. Maria Edgeworth's *Letters for Literary Ladies* published. Thomas Spence's *Spensonia* published.

(*cont.*)

	Mary Wollstonecraft's Life	Historical and Literary Events
1796	*Letters Written during a Short Residence in Sweden, Norway, and Denmark* is published by Joseph Johnson. MW meets Godwin again; they become lovers. MW begins writing *The Wrongs of Woman; or, Maria*.	Samuel Taylor Coleridge's *The Watchman* published.
1797	MW and Godwin marry on March 29 in Old St. Pancras Church. MW gives birth to her daughter Mary on August 30 and dies on September 10 from complications following childbirth. She is buried in St. Pancras Churchyard.	William and Dorothy Wordsworth move to Alfoxton House, Somerset, just a few miles from Samuel Taylor Coleridge's home in Nether Stowey. William Godwin's *The Enquirer* published.
1798		Godwin's *Memoirs of the Author of A Vindication of the Rights of Woman* published by Joseph Johnson. *Posthumous Works of the Author of A Vindication of the Rights of Woman*, edited by Godwin, published by Joseph Johnson. Irish Rebellion. Joanna Baillie's *Plays on the Passions* (first of three volumes) published. Thomas Malthus's *An Essay on the Principles of Population* published. Richard Polwhele's *The Unsex'd Females* published. William Wordsworth's and Samuel Taylor Coleridge's *Lyrical Ballads* published.
1799		Mary Hays's *The Victim of Prejudice* published. Jane West's *A Tale of the Times* published.
1800		Maria Edgeworth's *Castle Rackrent* published. Mary Robinson's *Lyrical Tales* published.

PART I

Life and Works

CHAPTER I

Biography

Kate Chisholm

On the night of December 26, 1792, Mary Wollstonecraft, alone in her apartment on the rue Meslée in Paris, sat writing a letter to her publisher Joseph Johnson in London. "Once or twice, lifting my eyes from the paper, I have seen eyes glare through a glass-door opposite my chair, and bloody hands shook at me ... I want to see something alive; death in so many frightful shapes has taken hold of my fancy.—I am going to bed— and, for the first time in my life, I cannot put out the candle."[1] She had crossed the Channel to witness the events in France, inspired by the revolutionaries' attempt to create a more equal society along republican lines. But the silent streets as Louis XVI passed by on his way to trial, so dignified in the face of what she knew to be certain death, shocked her. Wollstonecraft was fierce in argument, quick to pass judgment, sensitive to injustice, but always keenly aware of the springs of human action.

Her life was forged in difficult circumstances. The second of seven children, Mary was born on April 27, 1759 in Spitalfields, in the heart of London's silk-weaving business, by which her family made their money. But the settled life of the wealthy and well-educated was not her destiny. Her father Edward soon tired of making handkerchiefs, and by the time Mary was four he had moved his family out of the city to Epping in Essex, where he adopted the lifestyle of a gentleman farmer. Before long the family had moved again, first to Barking, also in Essex, and then to Beverley in Yorkshire, where they settled for six years while Edward ran through what remained of his inheritance (said to have been £10,000, which, if true, would be worth today approximately £600,000).[2] Mary's early years seesawed from moneyed ease to indebted insecurity.

Her mother Elizabeth, vulnerable, unbookish, weak in character, was the kind of woman Mary would later castigate in her writings. She favored her first child, the son and heir, and failed to protect any of her children from the violent excesses of their lazy, alcoholic father. Mary often slept across her parents' bedroom door to ensure Elizabeth was not assaulted by her drunken husband. Denied the education that for her brothers was guaranteed, Mary looked elsewhere for intellectual satisfaction. In Beverley, her school friend Jane Arden's family had a fine library (Jane's father gave lectures on experimental science), of which Mary made far better use than Jane. Later, when the family was suddenly uprooted to Hoxton, she was befriended by their new neighbors the Clares, a reclusive clergyman and his wife, who gave her time and space to read widely. Through the Clares, Mary also met Fanny Blood, in a similar family situation, striving to support her mother and siblings to make up for their father's fecklessness. Mary was impressed by Fanny's "masculine understanding, and sound judgment," allied with "every feminine virtue."[3] Mary knew herself to be clever, but she always doubted her ability to win and keep affection, those feminine qualities she both admired and distrusted. As the portraits of her by John Opie reveal, she took very little care of her appearance; her hair was unkempt, her dress simply made. Her gaze, though, is compelling: thoughtful, intense, far-seeing.

In the spring of 1778, aged nineteen, Mary took the only recourse open to her as the poorly educated daughter of a by then penniless father, leaving home to become the live-in companion of a rich widow. Surprisingly, given the dependent nature of her role, Mary remained with Mrs. Dawson for almost four years, enjoying their visits to Bath, Bristol, Southampton, and Windsor, where she was brought within the orbit of clever, witty, educated women. Only when her mother fell gravely ill, in late 1781, did she leave, summoned home by her two younger sisters, Everina and Eliza.

In spite of her unsatisfactory childhood, or perhaps because of it, Mary was always intensely loyal to her family, continuing to support them, often with money, long after they had all grown up. She needed always to feel that she was useful and necessary to them, as if to justify her desire to outgrow them intellectually. When Eliza, who had married in October 1782, became ill after giving birth (probably with postnatal depression), Mary moved in to care for the baby girl. Soon, though, she became convinced that the problem was Eliza's husband Meredith Bishop. "She seems to think she has been very ill used," Mary told Everina. Whatever the truth, Mary decided that Eliza must be rescued. While Bishop was away from home, she hired a hackney coach to take her and Eliza from Bermondsey, south of the river, across London Bridge to new lodgings in Hackney, leaving behind the baby. Eliza was so distressed, torn by indecision and desperate about her child ("the poor brat," as Mary thought of her), that "she bit her wedding ring to pieces."

Mary feared Eliza's future would be no different from their mother's. She took what she knew to be a "desperate" measure, in spite of its implications for Eliza, her baby, and for Mary and Everina too.[4] Eliza never saw her daughter again (the baby died just before her first birthday), and the sisters were now, all three, tainted by their unconventional behavior. Charles Kegan Paul, who in 1879 attempted to resurrect Wollstonecraft's reputation after a century of neglect, explained this episode as "the first occasion on which any of the great social questions presented themselves to Mary Wollstonecraft: but her rapid mind had no hesitation how this one should be answered."[5]

A couple of years later, Mary stepped into another family crisis, this time to rescue her friend Fanny Blood who was by 1785 living in Lisbon with her husband, an English merchant, and expecting their first child. Mary abandoned her sisters, and the school they had set up in Newington Green, braving the storms of the Bay of Biscay in late November ("the Captain was afraid we should be dismasted") because she feared that Fanny, always delicate, might not survive childbirth. She arrived too late, and Fanny died, as she had feared, along with the baby. Mary could only return disconsolate to London, but the experience showed her how fearless she could be (especially when compared with her fellow travelers) and how much a change of scene could invigorate her spirits.

In her absence, pupil numbers at the school in Newington Green had dwindled, since none of the sisters had turned out to be naturally gifted as teachers, and lack of money forced them to give up the house and find different employment. In October 1786 Mary set off once again, this time to Ireland to become governess to the daughters of Lady Kingsborough, writing to Everina: "I must labor for content and try to reconcile myself to a state which is contrary to every feeling of my soul ... I entered the great gates [of the Kingsborough estate at Mitchelstown] with the same kind of feeling as I should if I was going into the Bastille."[6] Within a year she had freed herself, returning to London after being dismissed for becoming more important to the children in her charge than their mother (two of whom were much later to follow Wollstonecraft's careless respect for convention by abandoning their abusive husbands).

Mary had by then published her first book, in late January 1787. *Thoughts on the Education of Daughters*, written at great speed, was inspired by her own lack of an education and her failed attempt to teach others. It was published by Joseph Johnson, whom she had met while living at Newington Green. Perhaps Mary's chief attribute was her gift for friendship; that "unconquerable greatness of soul" which drew people to her.[7] Earlier, in April 1784, she had been taken to meet Dr. Johnson, the essayist and creator of the *Dictionary*, by the Reverend John Hewlett, another of her new friends from Newington Green. Johnson was approaching death, his body physically decaying, but he treated Wollstonecraft "with particular kindness and affection" and they had "a long conversation."[8] What they talked about, given their apparently opposing views on politics, the law, and the rights of men and women, is not known. Yet Wollstonecraft never forgot their meeting, which may well have encouraged her to become a professional writer.

"Your sex generally laugh at female determinations; but let me tell you, I never yet resolved to do, any thing of consequence, that I did not adhere resolutely to it, till I had accomplished my purpose, improbable as it might have appeared to a more timid mind," she told her publisher in late 1787. Joseph Johnson had stepped in to help her on her return from the Kingsboroughs, providing her with enough money to rent a home of her own in Blackfriars, south of the river, in return for what she could deliver in writing. "Mr Johnson . . . assures me that if I exert my talents in writing I may support myself in a comfortable way," she assured Everina. "I am then going to be the first of a new genus."[9]

As if inspired, the work poured out of her: a novel *Mary; A Fiction* (1788), a collection of short stories "calculated to regulate the affections, and form the mind to truth and goodness,"[10] and countless book reviews, essays, and translations for Johnson's new periodical, the *Analytical Review*. She also, more controversially, in December 1790 published *A Vindication of the Rights of Men*, as a counterblast to Edmund Burke's conservative *Reflections on the Revolution in France*. At first the *Vindication* appeared anonymously but, three weeks later, the second edition announced its author as "Mary Wollstonecraft."

A year later, her companion volume, *A Vindication of the Rights of Woman*, began to appear piecemeal from Johnson's presses. Not all were impressed, the writer and political philosopher William Godwin complaining that it was "a very unequal performance . . . deficient in method and arrangement," and the playwright Hannah Cowley that it was "unfeminine."[11] Wollstonecraft wrote it in just six weeks, pressed by her publisher to get on with it. On reflection she wished she had taken longer, but through the *Vindication* she became famous, attracting some prestigious visitors to her new home in Store Street, Bloomsbury. Talleyrand, bishop of Autun and leader of the aristocratic faction which had ignited the demand for reform in France, wanted to meet the writer who so boldly dedicated her book to him. (Wollstonecraft hoped the compliment would encourage Talleyrand to take an interest in female education; it didn't.)

Her newfound self-belief is evident in a letter to Mary Hays, in which she critiques the manuscript of *Letters and Essays, Moral and Miscellaneous* that Hays sent to her for approval: "I do not approve of your preface—and I will tell you why ... This kind of vain humility has ever disgusted me."[12] Meanwhile she began to experiment with some of the ideas about marriage and relationships she had developed in the *Vindication*, proposing that she should live *à trois* with the artist Henry Fuseli (for whom she had conceived a passionate attachment) and his wife. Mrs. Fuseli proved less than compliant, barring Wollstonecraft from their home.

To escape a situation that had become embarrassing, Wollstonecraft left for Paris, traveling as a "political pilgrim," anxious to see for herself this new French society and promising to provide Johnson with eyewitness reportage.[13] She was soon embedded in the expatriate community, her company sought after because of the *Vindication*. This gave her the bloom of confidence and before long she attracted the attention of Gilbert Imlay, an American army captain who had traveled to Paris ostensibly, like Mary, out of curiosity but secretly hoping to make financial capital out of the revolutionary chaos. Imlay was handsome, a published writer, amusing and flirtatious, and Wollstonecraft fell deeply in love.

They moved in together, leaving Paris, which had become too danger-ous (Mary once stepped in a puddle of blood from the latest victims of the guillotine before realizing what it was), and settling in the rural hamlet of Neuilly, just beyond the city walls. Wollstonecraft believed that at last she had found "her true friend," and by late August 1793 she was pregnant. Imlay, though, was an adventurer, and he soon began leaving her alone for weeks at a time while he traveled to Le Havre to pursue his commercial interests. Wollstonecraft felt abandoned and soon despaired. "I do not want to be loved like a goddess," she told Imlay on January 2, 1794, "but I wish to be necessary to you." Professional success had not cured her emotional fragility and, in spite of her conflicted views on marriage as an institution, she began signing herself as "Mary Imlay." This was in part self-protection: the British had been declared as enemy aliens and Wollstonecraft could have been imprisoned. Imlay, for his part, obtained a certificate from the American ambassador stating that Mary was his wife and *de facto* American. But there is no official record of a marriage.

Pregnant and alone, Mary returned to the French capital and carried on working, finishing *An Historical and Moral View of the Origin and Progress of the French Revolution* just in time for the birth of her daughter, named

Fanny after her friend, on May 14, 1794. John Adams, the second American president, was so impressed he read the book twice. "She seems to have half a mind to be an English woman; yet more inclined to be an American," he remarked.[14] Fanny Imlay's birth united her parents briefly. Imlay talked of moving his family to America, living in the wilds, and establishing a new kind of republican society, but by the end of September he had absconded again, this time to London. "I wish one moment that I had never heard of the cruelties that have been practiced here [in France], and the next envy the mothers who have been killed with their children," Mary told him in a letter and shortly after took a dose of laudanum, enough to cause death.[15] Just in time she was discovered, probably by her maid Marguerite, who urged her to think of Fanny, just one year old.

The shock of realizing that she had almost succeeded in abandoning her daughter galvanized Wollstonecraft, and by the end of May 1795 she was in Hull, awaiting a boat that would take her to Scandinavia. Her mission was to find out what had happened to the ship on which Imlay had sent, in secret, a cargo of silver bullion intended for Gothenburg (the silver would pay for much-needed grain to send back to France). It was a most unusual journey for a young woman, her one-year-old child, and a very reluctant Marguerite, but Wollstonecraft appears to have been in her element. She never found the ship, or the silver, but she created from her uncomfortable adventures at sea and across the rugged northern landscape a new kind of travel writing.

In *Letters Written during a Short Residence in Sweden, Norway, and Denmark* (published in January 1796 and soon translated into German, Dutch, and Portuguese) Wollstonecraft fused a critical examination of her emotional distress with keen observations about the society she was traveling through. The poet Robert Southey remarked, "She has made me in love with a cold climate."[16] Just a couple of months before publication, Wollstonecraft had tried to kill herself for the second time. This time her suicide attempt was no cry for help but a determined effort to end her life (she had discovered Imlay was living openly with another woman, and she could no longer delude herself that he would come back to her). Waiting until late on a cold, wet night in mid-October, she walked beside the river from Battersea Bridge (which she decided was too public) to Putney Bridge, making sure her skirts were thoroughly sodden by the rain and heavy enough to weigh her down. Only when she thought no one was nearby did she jump into the River Thames. Some fishermen, though, had watched her pacing to and fro, and they jumped in after her, bringing her safely back to the riverbank gasping for breath and only semi-conscious.

The horror of trying, and failing, to drown herself purged any remaining suicidal urges and Mary was at last able to tell Imlay, "I now solemnly assure you, that this is an eternal farewell."[17] Thereafter she resolved to look forward. By the following spring, aged thirty-six, she had made a new friend in William Godwin, whom she had met at the house of the novelist, poet, and campaigner Mary Hays (about whose work Wollstonecraft had once been so terse). He was forty and had just written a bestseller, the gothic thriller *Caleb Williams*, in which a poor, self-educated young man is destroyed by a tyrannical neighbor. Godwin, not an overtly emotional man, took some while to adjust to Mary's acutely sensitive response to their developing friendship, but very soon he was writing her love letters.

A year later, on March 29, 1797, they were married in St. Pancras Church, Mary signing herself as "Mary Wollstonecraft, spinster." She was now pregnant with her second child and, anxious "to live as rationally as I can," she began signing her letters "Mary Wollstonecraft, femme GOD-WIN."[18] While she waited for her child to be born, she began writing another novel, never finished, but later published by Godwin in its incomplete state as *The Wrongs of Woman; or, Maria.*

Mary's labor began in the early hours of Wednesday, August 30. Godwin wanted to employ a trained male physician, but Mary insisted all she needed was the services of an experienced midwife, Mrs. Blenkinsop. It was a long and difficult labor, and her child, named Mary Godwin, was not safely delivered until 11:20 that night. Already weakened by severe loss of blood, Mary then had to endure the futile attempts of Mrs. Blenkinsop to remove the placenta, which had not come away naturally. At three in the morning Godwin rushed off to find an obstetrician, but it was too late. The placenta had been damaged and some of it left behind to breed infection in Mary's womb. At first she rallied, but by Saturday afternoon she was suffering from a fever. On Sunday she began shaking uncontrollably as her body succumbed to septicemia.

Godwin later clinically recorded the progress of Mary's decline in his *Memoirs*. Puppies were brought to Mary's breast to suckle her milk, because it was thought too contaminated to give to the baby. Ten days of acute suffering followed, relieved only by small doses of wine, but at twenty to eight on the morning of Sunday September 10, Wollstonecraft died, aged thirty-eight, leaving two motherless daughters.

In her *Letters from Sweden* Wollstonecraft wrote about Fanny, "I dread to unfold her mind, lest it should render her unfit for the world she is to inhabit—Hapless woman! what a fate is thine!"[19] She was not to know that Fanny would kill herself, aged twenty-two. Mary Godwin, born in such terrible circumstances, would live on to create *Frankenstein*, still unsurpassed as the logical endgame of the Romantic imagination.

Notes

1 *The Collected Letters of Mary Wollstonecraft*, edited by Janet Todd (London: Allen Lane, 2003), 216–17.
2 William Godwin gives this figure in *Memoirs of the Author of A Vindication of the Rights of Woman*, edited by Richard Holmes (London: Penguin, 1987), 205.
3 From a letter to Jane Arden, *Collected Letters*, 25.
4 From letters to her sister Everina, *Collected Letters*, 40–50.
5 Mary Wollstonecraft, *Letters to Imlay, with Prefatory Memoir by C. Kegan Paul* (London: C. Kegan Paul, 1879), xi.
6 The letter is dated October 30, 1786, almost three years before the destruction of the Bastille in July 1789. *Collected Letters*, 84.
7 William Godwin in his *Memoirs*, 216–17.
8 Godwin writes about this in the *Memoirs* (216), although the meeting occurred many years before he knew Wollstonecraft.
9 *Collected Letters*, 134, 139.
10 The subtitle of *Original Stories*, published in April 1788.
11 Quoted by Janet Todd in *Mary Wollstonecraft: A Revolutionary Life* (London: Weidenfeld & Nicolson, 2000), 184.
12 *Collected Letters*, 209–11.
13 The phrase is suggested by Claire Tomalin in *The Life and Death of Mary Wollstonecraft* (London: Penguin, revised edn., 1992), 157.
14 Quoted by Lyndall Gordon in *Mary Wollstonecraft: A New Genus* (London: Little, Brown, 2005), 210.
15 *Letters to Imlay*, 103.
16 Quoted by Sylvia Norman in her introduction to *Letters Written during a Short Residence in Sweden, Norway, and Denmark* (Fontwell: Centaur Press, 1970), xii.
17 *Collected Letters*, 339.
18 Ibid., 408–09.
19 *Letters Written during a Short Residence*, 66.

CHAPTER 2

Correspondence

Andrew McInnes

In an early letter to her childhood friend, Jane Arden, Mary Wollstonecraft practices a set of rhetorical techniques which will come to define her epistolary strategies in private and public: powerful expression combined with canny emotional manipulation, emphasizing the writer's sense of singularity. Angry at Jane's perceived preference for another friend, Wollstonecraft berates her:

> —Before I begin I beg pardon for the freedom of my style.—If I did not love you I should not write so;—I have a heart that scorns disguise, and a countenance which will not dissemble...—I am a little singular in my thoughts of love and friendship; I must have first place or none.—I own your behaviour is more according to the opinion of the world, but I would break such narrow bounds.[1]

In its agitated syntax, organized, like Emily Dickinson's verse, around the pointed use of dashes, its aggressive vulnerability, and its flouting of social proscription, this letter acts as a template for how Wollstonecraft will manage both her private epistolary relationships and her public readership: her demand to have "first place or none" in her friendships testifying to Wollstonecraft's extreme – literally all-or-nothing – demands on her readers.

In her introduction to Wollstonecraft's *Collected Letters*, Janet Todd comments, somewhat disapprovingly, on the "eerie consistency of tone" maintained throughout Wollstonecraft's short life from teenage epistles such as the above to the love letters addressed to Gilbert Imlay and William Godwin.[2] Todd implies that Wollstonecraft's letters betray her arrested development – her eerily consistent tone is that of an angry adolescent. In contrast, I argue that Wollstonecraft, very early on, develops a successful strategy for managing her readers' responses to her and her demands: Wollstonecraft divides her correspondents into ideal readers and those who fail to understand her message, manipulating them into responding to her as she desires.

In her letter to Jane Arden, Wollstonecraft cleverly splits her friend into these two different but interrelated, ideal or failing readers. One reader is to understand that she has permanently lost Wollstonecraft's friendship: "I once thought myself worthy of your friendship—I thank you for bringing me to a right sense of myself"; the other, who sees beyond the anger and hurt to an offer of reconciliation, is told in no uncertain terms "I shall expect a written answer to this,—."[3] The 'failing' Jane Arden should understand that she has lost Wollstonecraft's friendship; the 'ideal' friend needs to reply in order to salvage the relationship. By the time she writes *Letters Written during a Short Residence in Sweden, Norway, and Denmark*, Wollstonecraft has moved beyond the manipulation of teenage friendships to the managed promulgation of her political and philosophical aims, through the manipulation of her public readership's desire to get to know the celebrity she had become after the publication of *A Vindication of the Rights of Woman*. But both manipulations are accomplished through Wollstonecraft's careful ordering of her relationships with her readership.

In this chapter, I contextualize Wollstonecraft's manipulation of the letter form in relation to eighteenth-century and Romantic-period epistolary contexts, analyzing how Wollstonecraft's rhetorical strategies play out in both her personal letters to her American lover, Gilbert Imlay, and in her published travelogue, *Letters from Sweden*. Wollstonecraft returned to the letter form throughout her career, including a varied set of personal correspondents, as well as publications presenting themselves as letters, drawing on conventional understandings of the letter's directness and intimacy, as well as using letters to re-present herself, her personal circumstances, and her political philosophy and activism. Wollstonecraft uses both her personal and political letters to forge new imaginative spaces for women's agency.

* * *

There is a tension between epistolary practice and theory in terms of a belief in the direct, personal, and intimate connection forged between letter writer and reader on the one hand and arguments about epistolarity's representational dynamics on the other: theorists of the epistolary form argue that letters are multiply mediated – through the postal network, by epistolary conventions, and by self-conscious self-fashioning on the writer's part. In this section, I review eighteenth-century, Romantic-period, and theoretical models of epistolarity on how letters mediate the self; the changing contexts of epistolary form from the eighteenth century into the Romantic period; and the concept of "epistolary space" as an arena in which new models of self, history, and politics could be imagined, discussed, and enacted.

Responding to a letter from Godwin criticizing her writing style, Wollstonecraft mounts a passionate defense of her intellectual and emotional abilities, drawing on epistolary conventions to make her points:

> And, for I would wish you to see my heart and mind just as it appears to myself, without drawing any veil of affected humility over it, though this whole letter is a proof of painful diffidence, I am compelled to think that there is something in my writings more valuable, than in the productions of some people on whom you bestow warm eulogiums—I mean more mind—denominate it as you will— more of the observations of my own senses, more of the combining of my own imagination—the effusion of my own feelings and passions than the cold workings of the brain on the materials procured by the senses and imagination of other writers—[4]

The idea that the recipient of a letter could "see my heart and mind just as it appears to myself" is an epistolary convention underpinned by a belief in what Amanda Gilroy and W. M. Verhoeven term the "transparency" of the letter form, that letters gift readers with a direct and intimate knowledge of the writer's authentic emotions – and, in Wollstonecraft's case, here, her imaginative and intellectual prowess.

Gilroy and Verhoeven argue that the letter's "transparency" is part of "[t]he most historically powerful fiction of the letter" which is "the trope of authenticity and intimacy, which elides questions of linguistic, historical, and political mediation, and which construes the letter as feminine."[5] For the editors of *Epistolary Histories*, the direct access to selfhood seemingly offered by letters is a troublesome fiction, obfuscating the ways in which epistolarity functions in consumer culture to commodify both letters and, more problematically, women. Critics of eighteenth-century epistolarity from Clare Brant to Susan E. Whyman agree with Gilroy and Verhoeven that letters assume a fiction of authenticity and intimacy, often gendered as feminine, in order to forge a connection between letter writer and reader. These critics provide various, sometimes overlapping, sometimes contradictory, models of epistolarity, from Gilroy and Verhoeven's focus on anxiety, through Brant's more open-ended, playful approach, to James How's mapping of what he calls "epistolary spaces," in relation to the development of the post office from the late seventeenth century onwards.

Gilroy and Verhoeven theorize the eighteenth-century letter as embodying anxieties about female agency, the literary marketplace, and commerce itself in the period. Letters enforce a set of cultural demands on women,

hinging on their essential passivity and domesticity, labeling these precon-
ceptions 'natural'. Focusing on the historical conditions of the production
and reception of letters enables Gilroy and Verhoeven to unpick the
naturalness of the letter's authentic femininity (and women's intimate
epistolarity) in order to reveal these demands as historically determined
rather than natural preconditions of women's position in culture. However, their focus on anxiety, although it usefully deconstructs conservative
mythologizing of epistolarity and femininity, tends to reinforce rather than
question women's passivity, or at least their acquiescence to these cultural
tropes.

Rather than reading eighteenth-century letter writers and readers as
victims of false consciousness, Brant grants the letter writers she studies
with a degree of agency in the shaping of their epistolary 'character',
arguing that the idea of character in the eighteenth century included
an element of performative self-fashioning depending more on various
typologies of identity rather than an assumption of psychological depth.
For Brant, "[l]etters offered a spectrum of performance" in which "[p]art of
character's attraction may have been precisely because it was a kind of
act."[6] In both her private and public letters, Wollstonecraft experimented
with various 'characters': teacher, author, lover, traveler, philosopher,
aesthete. Brant's focus on character as type rather than psyche offers us a
way to read Wollstonecraft's various self-representations between and
within texts as at once a generic feature of epistolarity and as Wollstonecraft's deliberate authorial strategy.

Wollstonecraft is attracted to the letter form because epistolarity offers
her ways to create an imaginative space to explore and develop new models
of female agency, including experimenting with different ideas of character. James How argues that eighteenth-century letters allowed writers and
readers a unique opportunity to imagine new spaces of communication,
conversation, and argument. Connecting these 'epistolary spaces' to
twenty-first-century social media, How argues that letters, like cyberspace
today, offered people new areas "to live and to think, and hence to act."[7]
Focusing on the development of the Post Office in the late seventeenth
century and culminating in a detailed analysis of Samuel Richardson's
1748 *Clarissa*, How's emphasis predates Wollstonecraft's life and work.
However, his focus on space, especially the manipulation of distance in
letters, offers a useful model for analyzing Wollstonecraft's letters, and
their relationship with her travel writing. How argues that "epistolary
spaces are 'public' spaces within which supposedly 'private' writings travel –
at once imaginary and real: imaginary, because you can't really inhabit

them as you can other social spaces . . .; real, because they were policed by a government ever more keen to monitor the letters that passed along the national postal routes."[8] Wollstonecraft's writing career was invested in examining the borderlines between the private and public in terms of both political philosophy and fiction. Focusing on issues of interpretation and interception in *Clarissa*, How argues that "[e]pistolary space . . . becomes an empowering forum within which women can participate in the world of politics and take risks."[9] Wollstonecraft uses 'epistolary spaces' to bridge the fault lines between private and public – her work can be characterized as embodying the feminist dictum to make the personal political and vice versa – and is characterized by risk-taking, including traveling as a single mother across Scandinavia for uncertain goals. Wollstonecraft's major work is concentrated in the 1790s, a revolutionary decade in which eighteenth-century conventions, including those relating to the epistolary form, were being reimagined in the light of the French Revolution and the Romantic movement.

* * *

The French Revolution reshaped every element of social, cultural, political, economic, and spiritual life, on the Continent, in Britain, and around the world, including how both women and letters were read and understood. Wollstonecraft placed herself at the heart of these tumultuous changes, recording her responses in her personal letters, and using the epistolary form in her published writing, from addressing Edmund Burke in *A Vindication of the Rights of Men* and Talleyrand in *A Vindication of the Rights of Woman*, to her *Letters from Sweden*, and including letters from mother to daughter in her unfinished fragment of a novel, *The Wrongs of Woman; or, Maria*. Posthumously, her letters were used by her first biographers, her widower, the political philosopher William Godwin, and her friend and mentee, the novelist Mary Hays, to represent her as a kind of sentimental heroine imbued with Romantic genius. Letters are a key element in our understanding of Wollstonecraft's life, work, and political philosophy.

Mary Favret's *Romantic Correspondence* theorizes both the wider signifi-cance of the letter form in the French Revolution and Romantic period and the specific authorial choices made by Wollstonecraft in her letter writing. Surveying the proliferation of letters in the revolutionary period, Favret argues that letters became "a phenomenally useful political tool, available to anyone with a pen," reading the epistolary form as a

democratic, politically charged form of writing, allowing writers a simulac-
rum of direct address.[10] Like critics of eighteenth-century epistolarity,
Favret analyzes the connection between public and private spheres in
Romantic-period letter writing, stressing, however, "that correspondence
[between public and private] continually revises – and disrupts – fixed
images or narratives."[11] If the eighteenth-century letter imagines an intimate, authentic encounter with individual hearts and minds, even if this
individuality is codified in terms of "character," Romantic correspondence
questions this intimacy and authenticity by providing readers with an
experience based on flux, fluidity, even fragmentation.

Turning to Wollstonecraft, Favret argues that *Letters from Sweden*
offers its readers "a collective and various, rather than an individual and
predictable, 'self.'"[12] Contrasting Wollstonecraft's personal letters to
Gilbert Imlay to the published travelogue, addressed to an unnamed
recipient, Favret argues that Wollstonecraft deliberately changes the tone,
from vulnerable, wronged lover in her private correspondence to a woman
in control of herself, her surroundings, and the form of the letter in her
travel writing. There is a tension here between the fluctuating 'self' in
theory and Wollstonecraft's (self-)control in practice. I want to revisit the
connections, or correspondences, between her private and public letters to
explore Wollstonecraft's shifts from vulnerability to self-control. Although
her letters to Imlay and *Letters from Sweden* are often markedly tonally
different, I argue that they share a rhetorical strategy Wollstonecraft had
practiced and perfected since adolescence.

* * *

Ingrid Horrocks' chapter on Wollstonecraft's *Letters from Sweden* in her
recent *Women Wanderers and the Writing of Mobility, 1784–1814* elegantly
cuts through earlier critical hang-ups about the travelogue's success or
failure on aesthetic, political, and personal grounds. Horrocks' monograph
argues that the wandering subjects of works by Charlotte Smith, Ann
Radcliffe, Wollstonecraft, and Frances Burney are reflected in the
wandering forms of Smith's poetry, Radcliffe's and Burney's novels, and
Wollstonecraft's travel writing in order to reflect upon women's lack of a
stable position in eighteenth-century culture. *Letters from Sweden*, for
Horrocks, enacts a 'Pyrrhic victory' in proving the failure of empirical
models of sympathy to ameliorate either Wollstonecraft's condition or that
of other European citizens at a moment of revolutionary crisis. Horrocks'
chapter movingly concludes:

> In Wollstonecraft, the voice of the woman wanderer becomes the voice of a woman unable to rest, to adequately express her pain, or to safely feel for others, but also a woman continuing to seek a satisfactory way to travel forward – and a way to feel and live.[13]

For Horrocks, Wollstonecraft balances victory in the jaws of defeat. Personal and political failure is partially transfigured into future potential – a partly utopian, partly hopeless belief in futurity which characterizes her writing not only in her *Letters from Sweden* but in *A Vindication of the Rights of Woman* and beyond.

Wollstonecraft's ambivalent faith in futurity finds expression in her rhetorical, epistolary strategies, which are shared between her personal and public letters. Just as she threatened her childhood friend, Jane Arden, that she must take "first place or none" in her friends' affections, Wollstonecraft's letters to Imlay constantly return to a trope which mingles threat and plea: "We live together, or eternally part!"[14] Another letter cajoles Imlay, "we must meet shortly, or part for ever."[15] In an early letter from Scandinavia, Wollstonecraft tells her perfidious lover: "we must live together, or I will be entirely independent."[16] Wollstonecraft's personal correspondence with Imlay combines an intense vulnerability with emotional manipulation which seems to have provoked a series of equally painful responses. She often complains about Imlay's distance, both emotional and physical, embodied in his too-slow responses to her letters, and the unsatisfactory nature of his replies. Her threatened alternative to living with Imlay, to "be entirely independent," both raises the possibility of withdrawing Imlay's access to their child and focuses on what is possibly the key tenet of Wollstonecraft's personal philosophy: the importance of independence of thought and action in her idea of individual agency, also present in her letter to Godwin protesting against his criticisms of her writerly style.

Wollstonecraft weaves this language of parting and independence in relation to her daughter, Fanny, declaring to Imlay "We [Wollstonecraft and Fanny] will part no more . . . I will exert myself to obtain an independence for her" and later she declares that she will refuse his aid and rely on others for support "to obtain the object I have in view, the independence of my child."[17] Again, Wollstonecraft is implicitly threatening Imlay with the withdrawal of access to their child but, at the same time, she is stressing the significance of independence to her and her child – to all women. What Janet Todd represents as Wollstonecraft's "eerie consistency of tone" is present in her letter to Imlay: an all-or-nothing rhetoric which combines an adolescent, emotional, almost violent vulnerability with a cannier manipulation of the letter form. These letters seem to have caused Imlay, as well as Wollstonecraft, considerable pain, but they were ultimately unsuccessful in their aim of convincing him that the couple should live together. Wollstonecraft's *Letters from Sweden* more successfully, if still ambivalently, harness her rhetorical strategies to gain her reader's sympathies.

Throughout her personal letters to Imlay, Wollstonecraft addresses her lover as "my friend," even when she is complaining that he is far from friendly. As Favret points out, Wollstonecraft's shaping of *Letters from Sweden* is strikingly different from her private account of her travels, with the published account excising moments of intense personal vulnerability, such as an early fall and concussion, and focusing instead on questions of aesthetics, politics, and culture. However, she addresses the unnamed recipient of her published letters as "my friend," inviting the readers of her published work to occupy the imaginative space of friendship in a manner which she makes clear that the anonymous narratee of her letters fails to do. Contemporary responses to *Letters from Sweden* suggest that Wollstonecraft's rhetorical strategy here was definitely successful. For example, Wollstonecraft's friend the novelist and poet Amelia Alderson Opie wrote to her: "I remember when my desire of seeing you was repressed by fear – but as soon as I read your letters from Norway, the cold awe which the philosopher has excited, was lost in the tender sympathy called forth by the woman."[18] In his biography of Wollstone-craft, Godwin writes of the travelogue, "If ever there were a book calcu-lated to make a man in love with its author, this appears to me to be the book."[19] These expressions of love for Wollstonecraft align her travel writing with sentimental discourse. However, I find Godwin's emphasis on calculation telling: Godwin detects an element of manipulation in Wollstonecraft's writing, although this does not discourage him from falling in love with her.

In conclusion, Godwin draws on his own correspondence with Wollstonecraft to shape his representation of her "intellectual character" at the end of his controversial *Memoirs*. In a series of philosophical love letters, in which Godwin and Wollstonecraft discuss their deepening feelings for each other as well as differences in their philosophies and writing styles (including the letter in which Wollstonecraft declares she has "more mind" than some of Godwin's favorite writers), he seeks to reassure her about the quality of her imagination, "Upon consideration I find in you one fault, & but one, ... You have the feelings of nature, & you have the honesty to avow them. In all this you do well. I am sure you do. But do not let them tyrannise over you. Estimate everything at its just value."[20] He concludes his conciliatory letter by asking for some comfort himself: "Do you not see, while I exhort you to be a philosopher, how painfully acute are my own feelings? I need some soothing, though I cannot ask it from you."[21] Godwin's mild criticism of the tyranny of Wollstonecraft's feelings prompts her to consider their intellectual differences:

> One word of my ONLY fault—our imaginations have been rather differently employed—I am more of a painter than you—I like to tell the truth, my taste for the picturesque has been more cultivated—I delight to view the grand scenes of nature and the various changes of the human countenance.[22]

Wollstonecraft's account of their differently employed imaginations is echoed in Godwin's later account of her intellectual character in his *Memoirs* in which he contrasts his "attempt at logical and metaphysical distinction" with her "taste for the picturesque."[23] Criticized then for misreading the counterrevolutionary turn in British politics when publishing the revolutionary biography of his late wife, and chastised now for misrepresenting Wollstonecraft's character, Godwin in fact drew on her own correspondence with him to represent her as a radical, Romantic heroine.

Notes

1 *The Collected Letters of Mary Wollstonecraft*, edited by Janet Todd (London: Penguin, 1993), 13.
2 Janet Todd, "Introduction" in *Letters*, ix–xxix, x.
3 *Letters of Wollstonecraft*, 13, 14.
4 *Letters of Wollstonecraft*, 358.
5 Amanda Gilroy and W. M. Verhoeven, "Introduction," in *Epistolary Histories: Letters, Fiction, Culture*, edited by Gilroy and Verhoeven (Charlottesville: University of Virginia Press, 2000), 1.
6 Clare Brant, *Eighteenth-Century Letters and British Culture* (London: Palgrave Macmillan, 2006), 24.
7 James S. How, *Epistolary Spaces: English Letter-Writing from the Foundation of the Post Office to Richardson's "Clarissa"* (Abingdon: Ashgate, 2003), 1.
8 Ibid., 5.
9 Ibid., 17.
10 Mary Favret, *Romantic Correspondence: Women, Politics and the Fiction of Letters* (Cambridge: Cambridge University Press, 1993), 9.
11 Ibid.
12 Favret, 111.

13 Ingrid Horrocks, *Women Wanderers and the Writing of Mobility, 1784–1814* (Cambridge: Cambridge University Press, 2017), 168.
14 *Letters*, 321.
15 *Letters*, 317.
16 *Letters*, 308.
17 *Letters*, 318, 323.
18 Quoted in Claire Tomalin, *The Life and Death of Mary Wollstonecraft* (London: Penguin, 1974), 239.
19 William Godwin, *Memoirs of the Author of A Vindication of the Rights of Woman* (London: Penguin, 1987), 249.
20 *The Letters of William Godwin, Vol. 1: 1778–1797* (Oxford: Oxford University Press, 2011), 173.
21 *Letters of Godwin*, 174.
22 *Letters of Wollstonecraft*, 350.
23 *Memoirs*, 273.

CHAPTER 3

Family

Julie Carlson

> We are soon to meet, to try whether we have mind enough to keep
> our hearts warm.
>
> Mary Wollstonecraft to Gilbert Imlay, August 1793[1]

Affirming the presence of mind in so-called affairs of the heart is a signal
Wollstonecraft achievement. The conviction emerges out of her intense
experiences of the shaping realities of family life. The range of familial
settings in which Mary Wollstonecraft lived play a defining role in her
reflections on what it means to be born into a particular family and how
this beginning affects what follows. The topic informs her life, writing
career, reputation, and legacy for a number of interconnected reasons.
Wollstonecraft comes of age in an era when familial roles and their
connection to civic duties and the rights of men and women are being
hotly contested. The contestation is sharpened by debates about the
revolution occurring in France, but is not synonymous with it. Wollstonecraft enters an unusually wide range of familial arrangements that heighten
her perspectives on the desirability of social and domestic reform. They
include the households she resides in as a child with her biological parents
and siblings, aristocratic households where she works as a lady's companion and governess, residences in Europe as a single woman and then single
mother, and households she occupies as the lover and then wife of William
Godwin along with daughter Fanny Imlay and, for a few days, baby Mary
Godwin. In addition, Wollstonecraft is a sex radical in her practice and
occasionally in her writings. Her legacy is governed by changing estima-
tions of feminism, egalitarian family roles, sexual liberation, and intersec-
tional identity politics. It is also animated by glaring inconsistencies in
what she says, writes, and does as a family member and how these
divergences continue even today to shape the contours of family life.

Born on April 27, 1759, Wollstonecraft is the second child, and first daughter,
of seven children born to Edward John Wollstonecraft (?1737–1803) and

Elizabeth née Dickson Wollstonecraft (d. 1782). Her paternal grandfather, Edward Wollstonecraft (1689–1765), is a master silk-weaver
whose second wife Elizabeth (1716–46) is the mother of Edward John.
The grandfather dies a gentleman with an estate of £10,000, for which
her father is the main legatee and who leaves legacies to all his other
descendants except his then five-year-old granddaughter, Mary.[2] The
Dicksons are a Protestant wine-merchant family in Ballyshannon, Ireland. Her upbringing is marked by multiple changes in residence that
accord with ever-diminishing financial resources on account of her
father's lack of skill or interest in gentleman farming and business. She
begins life on Primrose Street in Spitalfields with a family farm in Essex,
then moves to farms in Barking and Walkington, then to the village of
Beverley, then back to London at Queen's Row, Hoxton, then to
Laugharne in South Wales, and then back near London in Walworth.
At age nineteen Wollstonecraft leaves her parents' household to try life
on her own. Characteristic of this effort, she returns shortly thereafter to
tend to her mother's deteriorating health in the autumn of 1781 and
stays until her mother dies from complications of dropsy in April 1782.
By all accounts, her parents' marriage is unhappy. Her father's fecklessness and reputed tyranny coupled with her mother's docility cause
Wollstonecraft to assume increasing responsibility for the care of her
younger siblings and for protecting her mother from her father's abuse.
Devising arrangements to keep her younger siblings afloat remains a
persistent concern throughout her life. Her father remarries within the
year and moves with new wife Lydia and youngest son Charles back to
Laugharne.

Details of early life with individual siblings influence several domestic
reforms that her writings advocate. First-born Edward Bland (Ned [1757/
8–1807]) is an intimate reminder of how decisive birth order and gender
are to one's prospects. Ned inherits a third of his grandfather's estate as a
young boy, stays his mother's favorite, receives a good education, marries
well, and practices successfully as a lawyer. His trajectory is in marked
contrast to that of second son, and third child, Henry Woodstock
(1761–?). Apprenticed at age fourteen to an apothecary-surgeon while
the family resides in Beverley, he falls out of all family discourse and
records shortly thereafter, leaving biographers to speculate that he is
confined somewhere for insanity. Emily Sunstein suggests that the move
to Hoxton, "synonymous with lunacy," influences the family's relocation,
but Brenda Ayres contends that this remains speculation.[3] Sixth child
James (1768–1806) is sent to sea early on and primarily leads a seafaring

life, though he tries repeatedly to escape from it, enlisting his sister's aid. At one point he is accused of being a spy while in Paris and is forced to leave the country. He acquires the rank of lieutenant in the Royal Navy and dies single at age thirty-six of yellow fever. Youngest child Charles (1770–1817) is articled to brother Ned but does not pursue law. He moves to America in 1792, where he becomes a speculator in Pennsylvania, fails at his calico printing business, and eventually joins the army, acquiring the rank of brevet major. He divorces his first wife, Sarah Garrison, for adultery and remarries the following year.

Wollstonecraft's life is more decisively shaped by concern for her two sisters, though concern does not imply deep affection. The pretty daughter Elizabeth (Eliza, Bess [1763 to late 1820s or 30s]) marries Meredith Bishop, a well-to-do shipwright from Rotherhithe, at age nineteen.[4] Less than two years later, Wollstonecraft engineers her sister's flight from this household, alarmed by Eliza's postpartum depression and Wollstonecraft's assessment of Bishop's overbearingness. Besides her husband, with whom she is never reconciled, Eliza abandons newborn daughter Mary, who dies within the year. This bold act results in Wollstonecraft's first major exposure to the interdependence that defines female independence, a dynamic about which she remains ambivalent. To maintain herself and the absconded Eliza financially, she founds a girls' day school in Newington Green, which she runs for two years with Eliza, youngest sister Everina (1765–1843), and her beloved Fanny Blood (1757–86). Their all-female household is one of Wollstonecraft's ongoing fantasy forma-tions, though it maintains a clear preference for living with friends over blood. The constellation is disrupted when Fanny Blood moves to Lisbon to marry Hugh Skeys in January 1785; late that autumn, Wollstonecraft attends Fanny's childbirth and, a few days later, deathbed. Dwindled enrolment and loss of heart upon her return to London prompt Wollstonecraft to close the school and to situate herself and her sisters otherwise. Everina never marries and supports herself as a governess and schoolmistress in Ireland until her death in the early 1840s.

Wollstonecraft's search for freedom from the confines of paternal households lands her in aristocratic households that deepen her aversion to patriarchal privilege. Between 1779 and 1781 she serves as lady's companion to wealthy widow Sarah Dawson, in Bath and Windsor, and then in 1786–87 as governess to three of the five daughters of Robert and Caroline King, Lord and Lady Kingsborough in County Cork, Ireland. The frivolous behaviors of Lord and Lady Kingsborough little endear her to aristocratic family life with its penchant for balls, dress, lapdogs, and libertinism. She is endeared to her charges, especially to fourteen-year-old Margaret, whose attachment to Wollstonecraft extends well into Margaret's adulthood and occasions Wollstonecraft's dismissal just as the group prepares to embark on a tour of the Continent in June 1788. The experience deepens Wollstonecraft's skepticism regarding the feeling capacities of the rich and is formative for Margaret, who becomes a children's author and lives openly with her lover under the name of the governess featured in Wollstonecraft's *Original Stories from Real Life* (1788). These generally disheartening early observations of family life inform a lifetime of attempts to re-educate daughters and initiate a successful career as a writer.

Wollstonecraft's blossoming radicalism as a published vindicator of the rights of both men and women (1790–92) culminates in a series of domestic experiments in France and Scandinavia that are in no sense domesticated or domesticating. This period of pronounced independence from the conventions of bourgeois femininity coincides with the most excruciating feelings of dependence that she ever experiences – a tension that suffuses *Letters Written during a Short Residence in Sweden, Norway, and Denmark* (1796) and the unfinished *The Wrongs of Woman; or, Maria* (1798). Traveling alone and as a single woman, she arrives in Paris to the home of Aline Fillietaz in mid-December 1792 and moves in the spring to nearby Neuilly-sur-Seine, when the fall of the Girondins makes Paris no longer safe for British citizens or their Parisian hosts. Shortly before moving, she meets Gilbert Imlay (?1754–?1828), an American frontiersman, author, and speculator in land who is in France to capitalize on European desires for less tumultuous environments. Receptive to each other's allure and intelligence, the two become lovers. In order to protect Wollstonecraft from government harassment, in early September Imlay registers her as his wife at the American Embassy, and they live openly together in Paris. Reveling in the heady sensations of heterosexual couple-dom, Wollstonecraft quips to a female friend that she has acquired "the matrimonial phraseology without having clogged my soul by promising obedience &c &c."[5]

This satisfaction is short-lived, tested sorely by Imlay's protracted business dealings in Le Havre and Wollstonecraft's pregnancy. Wearied by both, she joins Imlay in Le Havre in the winter, and they rent a house on the rue de Corderie owned by an English soap merchant. Here daughter Fanny is delivered by a midwife on May 14, 1794 and registered as legitimate in the Maison Commune under the name Françoise Imlay (1794–1816). The couple often refer to Fanny as the barrier-child, her conception presumably having occurred at one of the toll barriers sur-rounding Paris in the period when Wollstonecraft lived in Neuilly-sur-Seine. But Imlay leaves again, this time for London, and Wollstonecraft and Fanny return to Paris, where she hires a young Parisian to replace her now-pregnant Le Havre nurse. Marguerite Fournée proves to be an extremely valuable nursemaid to Fanny and companion to Wollstonecraft for the rest of Wollstonecraft's life. Her competence is wide-ranging, for the three females set sail for Scandinavia when Fanny is thirteen months old and spend close to four months traveling unaccompanied in Sweden, Norway, and Denmark, while Wollstonecraft, acting as Imlay's business envoy, attempts to obtain information about and compensation for the lost cargo of silver and ship that Imlay and associates had backed a Captain Ellefsen to deliver. It further involves seeing Wollstonecraft through periods of serious depression and two suicide attempts while also tending to Fanny. Shortly after the women return from Scandinavia, Wollstone-craft learns that Imlay is living with another woman and, after a second attempt at suicide and brief consideration of a *ménage à trois*, the two part ways.

Definitive for Wollstonecraft's legacy are the familial arrangements that she enters with the radical writer, William Godwin (1756–1836), who becomes her legal husband, first biographer, and editor of her posthumous works. Born in Wisbech in the Cambridgeshire Fens, Godwin is the seventh of thirteen children born to Reverend John Godwin (1723–72), a Dissenting minister, and Ann Hull (1723–1809). Tutored in strict Sandemanian principles, Godwin is educated for the ministry at the Dissenting Academy in Hoxton, enters a position at Stowmarket in 1779, and resigns it in 1782, thereafter living as an atheist and a profes-sional writer. During the period of their relationship, Godwin is one of the most lionized writers in England and a hub of London's radical network. Most striking about the longevity of Godwin's and Wollstonecraft's rela-tionship is that it exists for less than two years. The two meet once in mid-November 1791 at a dinner hosted by radical publisher, Joseph Johnson (1738–1809), to their mutual dissatisfaction. They meet again in January 1796 at a small party given by Mary Hays (1760–1843), who is a friend and admirer of both. Thence commences a complex coordination of two highly developed minds whose articulated principles and practices of independence are not always compatible. Even less symmetric are those relating to sex, Godwin still a virgin at forty and Wollstonecraft increas-ingly attuned to the voluptuousness of ideas. Still, they make their way in ways that underscore the difficulties and productiveness of a shared commitment to sincerity. In July, Wollstonecraft moves with Fanny, Marguerite, and a new maid, Mary, to 16 Judd Place West, close to where Godwin lives on Chalton Street in Somers Town.

The two become lovers in August, pursuing their independent schedules in the day and meeting frequently in the evenings to dine together and "philosophize," their code for sex. Despite Godwin's care in plotting Wollstonecraft's menstrual cycle in his diary, she discovers that she is pregnant in late December 1796. And despite his indictment of marriage as despotism in *Enquiry concerning Political Justice* (1793), they marry on March 29, 1797 at the church at St. Pancras. Godwin's best friend Thomas Holcroft (1745–1809) salutes them as "the most extraordinary married pair in existence," but Wollstonecraft loses several of her female friends now that the marriage gives the lie to her status as "Mrs. Imlay."[6] They move into new quarters at 29, The Polygon, and Godwin rents an apartment for himself nearby. Though Wollstonecraft's letters complain incisively about the unfair caretaking responsibilities women bear even if they work, she too appreciates part-time cohabitation. "I wish you, from my soul, to be riveted in my heart; but I do not desire to have you always at my elbow."[7]

This more reasonable assessment of conjugal domesticity is also cut short, this time by death. Anticipating the same easy labor as she had experienced with Fanny, on the morning of August 30 Wollstonecraft prepares to give birth to the being that the expectant parents hailed throughout the summer as "William." A baby daughter is born a little before midnight after some eighteen hours of labor. When the placenta is not expelled, the midwife Mrs. Blenkinsop requests assistance from Dr. Poignard, who attempts to extract it by hand. The placenta breaks into pieces, some adhering to the womb, resulting in a massive infection and fever. For ten days, physicians and friends rally around both Wollstonecraft and Godwin, but their attentiveness does not save her. Wollstonecraft dies on September 10 at "twenty to eight." No blood family member attends her bedside or funeral.

Not expected to live either, baby Mary is sent to Godwin's friend Maria Reveley to join Fanny. Godwin adopts Fanny that year, and the two daughters grow up together with a father whose evolving household remains sexually unorthodox, though less avowedly feminist, and expands to include a stepmother, Mary Jane Vial Clairmont (?1766–1841), and three half-siblings, Charles Clairmont (1795–1850), Mary Jane (Claire) Clairmont (1798–1879), and William Godwin (1803–32). Fanny's and Mary's lives take very different courses, Fanny the familial caregiver,

Figure 1   *Mary Shelley*, by Richard Rothwell, 1840.
Courtesy of the National Portrait Gallery, London

go-between, and peacemaker until she dies at age twenty-two by suicide, Mary the adventurer who elopes at age sixteen with then-married Percy Bysshe Shelley (1792–1822), moves with Percy all over Britain and the Continent, survives her husband and three of her four children, and authors some dozen texts, most notably her hideous progeny, *Frankenstein*

(1818). Yet both of their life courses bear the discernible imprint of having been born to a woman who spent her life scrutinizing women's thoughts and feelings and trying to get others to take their complexities more seriously.

Wollstonecraft is given a family and inherits a notion of family that her life and writings attempt to re-create so that it better accommodates female passions. The thoughts and feelings that compose her "family" do not cohere, but they are unprecedented, remarkably uncensored, and deeply moving. The forthrightness with which she exposes the lasting effects of beginning life within an environment whose defining challenge is fostering the kind of security that enables cognitive and emotional flourishing is a major gift to aspiring readers. It is why there still "are not many individuals with whose character the public welfare and improvement are more intimately connected than the author of a *Vindication of the Rights of Woman*."[8]

Notes

1 Roger Ingpen, ed., *The Love Letters of Mary Wollstonecraft to Gilbert Imlay* (London: Hutchinson, 1908), 2.

2 Janet Todd, *Mary Wollstonecraft: A Revolutionary Life* (New York: Columbia University Press, 2000), 3.

3 Emily Sunstein, *A Different Face: The Life of Mary Wollstonecraft* (Boston: Little, Brown, & Company, 1975), 35; Brenda Ayres, *Betwixt and Between: The Biographies of Mary Wollstonecraft* (New York, London: Anthem Press, 2017), 105.

4 Todd, *Mary Wollstonecraft*, 43.

5 Wollstonecraft to Ruth Barlow, April 27, 1794, *The Collected Letters of Mary Wollstonecraft*, edited by Janet Todd (New York: Columbia University Press, 2003), 251.

6 Holcroft to Godwin, April 6, 1797, in Charles Kegan Paul, *William Godwin: His Friends and Contemporaries*, 2 vols. (London: H. S. King, 1876), 1: 240.

7 Cited in William St. Clair, *The Godwins and the Shelleys: A Biography of a Family* (Baltimore: Johns Hopkins University Press, 1989), 172.

8 William Godwin, *Memoirs of the Author of A Vindication of the Rights of Woman (1798)*, edited by Pamela Clemit and Gina Luria Walker (Peterborough: Broadview Press, 2001), 1.

CHAPTER 4

Joseph Johnson

David Fallon

During the eighteenth and early nineteenth centuries, the most significant booksellers were both retailers and publishers, financing books and their distribution.[1] In an 1809 *Gentleman's Magazine* obituary, John Aikin honored Joseph Johnson as "the Father of the Trade." Averse to "puffing and parade" and "typographical luxury," his "kindness of heart" was evident and his "house and purse were always open to the calls of friendship, kindred, or misfortune."[2] For Lyndall Gordon, he was "less an employer than a mentor" to Wollstonecraft, fostering her literary career.[3] Their relationship exemplifies the ascendancy of booksellers in eighteenth-century literary culture. As they came to dominate a commercialized cultural marketplace, they appropriated some of the power to shape public taste previously associated with aristocratic patrons. Commercially successful booksellers like Johnson could promote particular interests and causes through publications. His support for Wollstonecraft contributed to a critical project, stimulating public debate on religious and political liberty. John Bugg connects Johnson's commitment to publishing different opinions on contentious subjects to Dissent, as "a specific practice of supporting the collision of opinion," which by the later 1790s could be construed as subversive.[4]

Writing to her sister Everina in 1787, Wollstonecraft announced her determination on a literary career: "I am then going to be the first of a new genus."[5] The bookseller's encouragement was critical: "Mr Johnson ... assured me that if I exert my talents in writing I may support myself in a comfortable way." Wollstonecraft described how "his sensible conversation would soon wear away the impression, that a formality—or rather stiffness of manners, first makes to his disadvantage—I am sure you would love him did you know with what *tenderness* and humanity he has behaved to me."[6] Johnson's complex relationship to Wollstonecraft covered financial support, mentoring, shared investment in sensibility, and intense friendship.

Johnson originated in a family from Everton, on Liverpool's outskirts, connected to local Baptists, dissenters from the Church of England. In 1754, Johnson was apprenticed to the religious bookseller George Keith, working at his shop close to London Bridge until 1761. He soon became an independent trader at Fish Street Hill, by the Monument, a prime site for custom from passing medical students. By 1765, he was at 8 Paternoster Row, the center of the London book trade. In 1765, Johnson co-published Joseph Priestley's *Essay on a Course of Liberal Education*, commencing a long relationship. Johnson acted as Priestley's London bookseller and publisher, issuing his controversial theology, biblical criticism, defenses of Dissent, political pamphlets, education, philosophy, and scientific works, as well as hosting him on London visits. This drew Johnson into Unitarianism. He published work by authors connected with the Warrington dissenting academy and, in 1774, helped Theophilus Lindsey to found the first dedicated Unitarian chapel in England, in Essex Street, off the Strand. Johnson was a member and provided cheap publishing and distribution for Unitarian publications.

In January 1770, Johnson's bookshop was engulfed in a fire. Although the inhabitants escaped, the blaze destroyed the stock. Friends rallied to help him to re-establish his business at 72 St Paul's Churchyard. From here, he issued many significant works. According to Leslie Chard's data, Johnson's 1790s output primarily covered religion, literature, medicine, politics, and poetry, but he also published substantially in science and language.[7] His literary acumen was exemplified by publishing poetry that would significantly shape Romanticism, including Anna Laetitia Barbauld's *Poems* (1773), William Cowper's *The Task* (1785), and Erasmus Darwin's *The Loves of the Plants* (1789) and *The Economy of Vegetation* (1791). Later in his career, Maria Edgeworth's fiction proved lucrative.

It is unsurprising that Johnson supported Wollstonecraft's radical and feminist writing. His commitment to Dissent led him to publish on other causes related to human rights, including the abolition of slavery, support of the American colonists, and political reform.[8] He had already issued texts with a feminist orientation, such as Mary Scott's poem *The Female Advocate* (1774) and *Laws Respecting Women, as They Regard Their Natural Rights* (1777). He would go on to publish Wollstonecraft's protégée Mary Hays' *Appeal to the Men of Great Britain, in Behalf of Women* (1798).

Wollstonecraft's sense of obligation to Johnson and their emotional ties are evident in a letter c. 1790:

You made me very low-spirited last night, by your manner of talking.—You are my only friend—the only person I am *intimate* with.—I never had a father, or a brother—you have been both to me, ever since I knew you—yet I have sometimes been very petulant.[9]

Such was their intimacy that, after traveling together in 1792, she told William Roscoe, "the world, to talk big, married m[e] to him whilst we were away."[10] Wollstonecraft was aware of Johnson's extraordinary generosity, in a business frequently satirized for its mercenary exploitation of writers. Asking him to state her debts in 1788, she distinguished him from the "generality of people in trade": "*you were a man* before you were a bookseller."[11]

According to William Godwin, half way through *A Vindication of the Rights of Men* (1790), Wollstonecraft had a "fit of torpor and indolence, and began to repent of her undertaking." Calling on Johnson in the evening "for the purpose of relieving herself by an hour or two's conversation," she shared her thoughts, and Johnson insisted she could abandon the work "if it would contribute to her happiness." This unexpected response "piqued her pride." She speedily completed the work for publication by November,[12] and a second edition followed before the end of the year. Johnson provided valuable editorial advice, too, though she responded with typical independence. Writing concerning *Original Stories*, she praised his "generally judicious" remarks but "cannot *now* concur with you, I mean with respect to the preface." She stuck to her original, hating "the usual smooth way of exhibiting, proud humility."[13]

Johnson went beyond a bookseller's usual support. He helped to administer Wollstonecraft's father's properties, as he noted "with no little trouble to both of us."[14] He would help with family matters and even settle her tradesmen's bills.[15] She was frequently in debt to him but felt that this did not compromise her independence, assuring Godwin in 1786 that Johnson had "been a gainer" from her writing.[16]

Wollstonecraft may already have known Johnson through Newington Green contacts, but the connection was established in 1786 through Reverend John Hewlett, whose sermons Johnson had co-published. Hewlett encouraged Wollstonecraft to write what became *Thoughts on the Education of Daughters*. He brought the proposal to Johnson, who purchased it for ten guineas, staving off the debts of Wollstonecraft's school. Mary probably met Johnson when delivering the manuscript to his shop.[17] He then proved a valuable connection to London while she was governess for the Kingsboroughs in Mitchelstown. Writing in December 1786,

Figure 2   *Joseph Johnson*, by William Sharp, after Moses Haughton the Elder,
c. 1780–1820.
Courtesy of the National Portrait Gallery, London

Wollstonecraft discussed her activities and ordered spelling books, sermons, Charlotte Smith's poems, and *Thoughts on the Education of Daughters*. She told Everina that "Little Johnson" also sent Hewlett's *Sermons* and Cowper's poems with "a very civil note." After her dismissal, Wollstonecraft told Everina that Johnson "insisted on my coming to his house, and contrived to detain me there a long time—you can *scarcely* conceive how warmly, and delicately he has interested himself in my fate." He found her a home in George Street, where she lived until autumn 1791, when she moved to Store Street. Both locations enabled regular visits to Johnson's shop.

James Raven notes that "Bookshops . . . became important places where people learnt of books and discussed them," hosting "diverse business and amusement."[18] In the shadow of St Paul's, Johnson's bookshop occupied an L-shaped ground floor, with storage and living space above, where he hosted regular dinners and gatherings, renowned for stimulating discussions and lively sociability. According to Alexander Gilchrist, Johnson supplied "plain but hospitable weekly dinners ... in a little quaintly shaped upstairs room, with walls not at right angles."[19] It was reputedly decorated with Fuseli's portrait of Joseph Priestley and *The Nightmare*.[20] The environment was congenial to female intellectuals. Anna Laetitia Barbauld visited Johnson's shop in the 1780s and 90s, enjoying hospitality and "'the feast of reason and the flow of soul,' in a chosen knot of lettered equals," among "dissenters and persons of opposition-politics."[21] In 1784, she recalled "our evenings, particularly at Johnson's, were so truly social and lively, that we protracted them sometimes till ... but I am not telling tales."[22]

Johnson's gatherings attracted thinkers with varied opinions, from many fields. Gerald Tyson identifies a core group: the painter Henry Fuseli, the clergyman George Gregory, the mathematician John Bonnycastle, and the Catholic biblical scholar, Alexander Geddes.[23] Other visitors included the religious of many different persuasions. Dissenters were prominent, but Johnson hosted many shades of opinion, including Anglican clergy as different as James Hurdis and Thomas Malthus, and Evangelicals, such as John Newton. Jon Mee notes in this volume (Chapter 11) that Johnson remained at the respectable end of radicalism. Visitors and contacts included veteran reformers associated with the Society for Constitutional Information (to which Johnson himself belonged), such as Major John Cartwright and John Horne Tooke, but also democrats such as Thomas Paine, Joel Barlow, and Daniel Isaac Eaton. Johnson's medical connections and publications, as well as his work for Priestley, meant he hosted prominent scientists. He published for members of the Birmingham Lunar Society, including Richard Lovell Edgeworth and Erasmus Darwin, and many visited when in London. More familiar literary figures also found their way into his shop and his imprint, including Samuel Taylor Coleridge, Maria Edgeworth, William Hazlitt, and William Wordsworth.

James Knowles recalled Johnson's weekly dinners, admiring "the prudence with which he allayed the occasional contests of his irritable guests" over "conflicting opinions." While "conversation took a free range," Johnson's "placid equanimity ... regulated in some degree its freedom."[24] The gatherings helped attendees make new connections. On November 13, 1791, William Godwin first met Wollstonecraft. His diary records "Dine at Johnson's, with Paine, Shovet & Wolstencraft; talk of monarchy, Tooke, Johnson, Voltaire, pursuits & religion,"[25] exemplifying a lively and dynamic conversational world. Godwin had come to hear Paine, who turned out "no great talker," leaving the discussion "principally between me and Mary." He "heard her, very frequently when I wished to hear Paine."[26]

Johnson described the shop as an emotionally supportive environment, where "she spent many of her afternoons & most of her evenings":

> whatever was the state of her mind it appeared when she entered, & the turn of conversation might easily be guessed; when harassed, which was very often ye case, she was relieved by unbosoming herself & generally returned home calm, frequently in spirits. F[useli]. was frequently with us.[27]

From 1764, the Swiss painter and polymath Fuseli was Johnson's close friend and became a dominant presence in the circle. Johnson had co-published Fuseli's *Remarks on the Writings and Conduct of J. J. Rousseau* (1767), and this enthusiasm for Rousseau was shared by many of Johnson's authors and visitors. Wollstonecraft's engagement with Rousseau in the *Vindications* is likely to have been shaped by discussions at Johnson's, especially with Fuseli.

Fuseli seems to have been competitive in company. On first meeting, Johnson warned Bonnycastle that "if you wish to enjoy his conversation, you will not attempt to stop the torrent of his words by contradicting him."[28] While Johnson's house was a civilized space, Fuseli's "ready wit" often led to friction, especially with Geddes. Both were "impatient of contradiction" and held each other in low estimation. Fuseli frequently amused himself by irritating Geddes to the point at which he had to take a calming walk around the churchyard.[29]

Johnson's networks gave Wollstonecraft wider contacts, such as the Liverpool lawyer William Roscoe, who commissioned her portrait by John Williamson in 1791 and enthused about *Vindication of the Rights of Men*. Wollstonecraft wrote in January 1792, noting "M^r. J. tells me that you make the Liverpool women read my book."[30] In the late 1780s, Johnson encouraged her to study French, Italian, German, and Dutch to produce translations, which included Necker's *On the Importance of Religious Opinions* (1788), Salzmann's *Elements of Morality* (1790), and de Cambon's *Young Grandison* (1790). His extensive trade and continued relationship with Priestley, after his exile in the United States from 1794, gave Johnson global links. M. Laurent, a fashionable bookseller in Paris, was a contact for Everina and Mary Wollstonecraft when they were in

Paris.[31] Johnson's letterbook indicates international reach: contacts and customers extended to Hamburg, Rotterdam, India, Jamaica, and Boston, New York, and Philadelphia.

Aikin's obituary, perhaps defensively, asserts that "turbulence and sedition were utterly abhorrent" to Johnson, who was not a "party man."[32] Johnson was prudent with his publications, preferring public debate over agitation. He often published opposed political or religious texts. Nevertheless, during the later 1790s conservatives waged a campaign to discredit Johnson, his circle, and authors as Jacobins, with the *Anti-Jacobin*'s poem "The New Morality" featuring many Johnson writers, including Wollstonecraft.

During February 1798, an agent called Hancock visited Johnson's shop and purchased Gilbert Wakefield's *Reply to Some Parts of the Bishop of Landaff's Address to the People of Great Britain* (1798). Wakefield attacked clerical support for government war policy and doubted the hard-pressed poor would repel a French invasion. Although published by John Cuthell and sold widely, Johnson and Jeremiah Jordan were singled out by an *ex officio* information from the Attorney General and tried for seditious libel before a special jury.[33] Jordan quickly pleaded guilty, placing Johnson in an invidious position for his trial on July 17, 1798. The jury found Johnson guilty. During the sentencing hearing, the *Analytical Review* and other publications were produced as aggravating evidence. Johnson received six months in the King's Bench prison, was fined £50, and was required to give £700 sureties for future conduct. This was regarded as a blow to opponents of the political and religious establishment. *The Anti-Jacobin Review*, the first issue of which indexed Wollstonecraft under P. for prostitute, rejoiced that "this favourite publisher and friend of the PRIESTLEYS, the DARWINS, the GODWINS, and other *unprejudiced* authors" was prosecuted. After Johnson wrapped up the *Analytical Review* in December 1798, the *Anti-Jacobin* crowed that it had "received its death blow."[34] However, Johnson paid for comfortable quarters and remained busy in confinement. According to Knowles, he hosted regular dinners; visitors included Godwin, Fuseli, and Richard Lovell and Maria Edgeworth.[35]

After his release in August 1799, Johnson became more cautious, largely avoiding political controversy.[36] In ill health, he spent more time at his cottage at Purser's Cross in Fulham, while his assistants, his great-nephew John Miles and Rowland Hunter, led the business until they took over after his death on December 20, 1809. Johnson was a lifelong sufferer from asthma, which probably caused his death. Miles and Hunter ran

"J. Johnson & Co" until 1815, when Hunter took over under his own name. Johnson had generously made provision for Fuseli and for Joseph Priestley's son, and provided £200 for Wollstonecraft's daughter Fanny.[37]

Johnson co-published Godwin's *Memoirs of the Author of A Vindication of the Rights of Woman* with her *Posthumous Works* (1798), taking keen interest in her legacy and advising Godwin while he compiled the edition. Godwin wrote during January 1798, responding to Johnson's corrections to the *Memoirs*, especially the language describing Wollstonecraft's father's violence and Fuseli's character and influence.[38] Johnson seems to have queried Godwin's characterization of Wollstonecraft as a victim of sensibility. His letterbook also reveals continued contact with the Wollstonecraft family, even providing financial support to Mary's wayward brother James.[39]

Johnson provided crucial support for authors in whom he perceived outstanding talent. He recognized Wollstonecraft as the "first of a new Genus," and provided conditions which enabled her to flourish.

Notes

1 James Raven, *The Business of Books: Booksellers and the English Book Trade* (New Haven: Yale University Press, 2007), 4–5.
2 [John Aikin], "Joseph Johnson," *Gentleman's Magazine* (December 1809), 1167–68.
3 Lyndall Gordon, *Vindication: A Life of Mary Wollstonecraft* (London: Virago, 2006), 129.
4 John Bugg, ed., *The Joseph Johnson Letterbook* (Oxford: Oxford University Press, 2016), liii.
5 Janet Todd, ed., *The Collected Letters of Mary Wollstonecraft* (New York: Columbia University Press, 2003), 139.
6 *Collected Letters*, 139.
7 Leslie F. Chard II, "Joseph Johnson in the 1790s," *Wordsworth Circle*, 33:3 (2002), 95–100.
8 See Gerald P. Tyson, *Joseph Johnson: A Liberal Publisher* (Iowa: University of Iowa Press, 1979), 90–91, and Helen Braithwaite, *Romanticism, Publishing and Dissent: Joseph Johnson and the Cause of Liberty* (Basingstoke: Palgrave, 2003), 45–58, 76–78.
9 *Collected Letters*, 166.
10 *Collected Letters*, 208.
11 *Collected Letters*, 148.
12 William Godwin, *Memoirs of the Author of the Vindication of the Rights of Woman*, in Mark Philp, ed., *Collected Novels and Memoirs of William Godwin*, 8 vols. (London: Pickering & Chatto, 1992), 1: 108.
13 *Collected Letters*, 142.

14 Bodleian Library, MS Abinger c. 44, fol. 48.

15 *Collected Letters*, 407.

16 *Collected Letters*, 358.

17 See Gordon, *Vindication*, 109.

18 Raven, *Business of Books*, 6.

19 Alexander Gilchrist, *Life of William Blake*, 2 vols. (London: Macmillan, 1863), 1: 92.

20 Leslie F. Chard, "Joseph Johnson: Father of the Book Trade," *Bulletin of the New York Public Library*, 79 (1975), 63.

21 Lucy Aikin, "Memoir," in *The Works of Anna Laetitia Barbauld*, 2 vols. (London: Longman et al., 1825), 1: xxxii–xxxiii.

22 *Works of Barbauld*, 2: 24

23 Tyson, *Joseph Johnson*, 66.

24 Knowles, *Life*, 1: 301.

25 MS. Abinger e. 4, fol. 5v. godwindiary.bodleian.ox.ac.uk/folio/e.199_0005v [Accessed 14/6/2017].

26 Godwin, *Memoirs*, 113.

27 "A Few Facts," Bodleian Library, MS Abinger c. 44, fol. 48.

28 John Knowles, *The Life and Writings of Henry Fuseli*, 3 vols. (London: Henry Colburn & Richard Bentley, 1831), 1: 59.

29 Knowles, *Life*, 73–74.

30 *Collected Letters*, 197.

31 *Collected Letters*, 151–52, 215.

32 [Aikin], "Biographical Account," 1167–68.

33 See Tyson, *Joseph Johnson*, 134–75, Braithwaite, *Romanticism*, 155–69, and Bugg, *Letterbook*, li–lix.

34 "Prefatory Address to the Reader," *Anti-Jacobin Review*, 1 (1798), iv–v.

35 Knowles, *Life*, 1: 202.

36 Bugg, *Letterbook*, lix.

37 Knowles, *Life*, 1: 302.

38 January 11, 1798, in Pamela Clemit, ed., *The Letters of William Godwin, Volume II: 1798–1805* (Oxford: Oxford University Press, 2014), 7–8.

39 See letters to Charles Wollstonecraft, October 1, 1802 and Everina April 1, 1807, Bugg, *Letterbook*, 87–88, 143–44.

PART II

Critical Fortunes

CHAPTER 5

Early Critical Reception

Nancy E. Johnson

In a span of just over ten years, the reception of Mary Wollstonecraft's work moved from temperate admiration to heightened political controversy, emotional sympathy, and personal condemnation. When Wollstonecraft wrote about female education, her ideas were generally well received. At times her thoughts were dismissed as trite or she was admonished for encouraging young women to be too independent. But she was in safe territory. Predictably, when Wollstonecraft entered into political and cultural controversies, her thoughts were either embraced because they aligned with theories of the rights of man, or they were thought to be revolutionary and a challenge to British stability. Most controversial was Wollstonecraft's suggestion that women actively participate in civil society. In this case, she drew censorious responses from parties at both ends of the political spectrum. Her later publications, including posthumous work published by her husband, William Godwin, elicited starkly personal reactions, ranging from sympathy for her emotional turmoil, and pity because her husband made her intimate life public, to outrage over her sexual behavior and condemnation of her dubious moral conduct. Wollstonecraft's early reception was charged with the controversies of the 1790s and marked by the uncertainty surrounding the place of women in the transformation of civil society.

Thoughts on the Education of Daughters: With Reflections on Female Conduct, in the More Important Duties of Life, published in London by Joseph Johnson in 1787 and reprinted in Dublin by William Sleater in 1788, was Wollstonecraft's first published work. The reviews of *Thoughts* are measured but generally positive, recognizing Wollstonecraft as a new and important public voice. The *European Magazine and London Review* finds little that is new in Wollstonecraft's *Thoughts*, and suggests that she is not always "perfectly just." However, it acknowledges that she writes "with a perspicuity and judgment which we often look for in vain even in the pages of *professional* writers."[1] The *Critical Review* considers *Thoughts* to be

41

"sometimes desultory," "occasionally trite," and "in a few instances, erroneous," but concedes that overall her ideas are "clear, judicious, and correct."[2] The *English Review* concludes that Wollstonecraft has "reflected maturely on her subject" and "recommend[s] these Thoughts as worthy the attention of those who are more immediately concerned in the education of young ladies."[3] The Monthly Review is more effusive in its praise and finds the style of *Thoughts* to be "correct and agreeable," its observations "judicious, and highly worthy of attention," and its author "the voice of wisdom."[4]

The critical attention Wollstonecraft received with her first publication all but disappeared with the publications that immediately followed. Her novel *Mary: A Fiction* (1788), her moral tales, *Original Stories from Real Life; with Conversations Calculated to Regulate the Affections, and Form the Mind to Truth and Goodness* (1788), and her anthology, *The Female Reader: or, Miscellaneous Pieces, in Prose and Verse: Selected from the Best Writers, and Disposed under Proper Heads: for the Improvement of Young Women* (1789), received little notice. *Mary* and *The Female Reader* saw only one edition each in the late eighteenth century. *Original Stories* did slightly better, a new edition appearing in 1791 and another in 1796, both with illustrations by William Blake. It was the publication of *A Vindication of the Rights of Men, in a Letter to the Right Honourable Edmund Burke* that established Wollstonecraft as a political thinker and restored critical attention. *A Vindication of the Rights of Men* was published anonymously on 29 November 1790 by Joseph Johnson, and republished under Wollstonecraft's name on 18 December 1790. It was reviewed by eight periodicals, and one of those reviews – that of the *Gentleman's Magazine* – was reprinted in *Walker's Hibernian Magazine*. As one might expect, its reception fell along political lines. The *Analytical Review*, a periodical that was published by Joseph Johnson, and to which Wollstonecraft contributed, finds much to praise. It highlights Wollstonecraft's attack on Burke's concept of hereditary rights and supports her views on property. It also endorses her critique of game laws and the "pressing" system in which men were forced into military service. The *Monthly Review*, owned by Ralph Griffiths, another liberal publisher, finds Wollstonecraft's style ineffective – "too many ideas" are mixed "too much together" – but concludes that Wollstonecraft makes "many very good and judicious remarks."[5]

Some reviews of *Rights of Men* foreground Wollstonecraft's treatment of Edmund Burke. The *English Review*, published by the progressive John Murray, notes that "where she [Wollstonecraft] keeps to her purpose in answering Mr. Burke, she does it with strength, clearness, and brevity, and as much politeness as his own unqualified language entitles him to."[6] In contrast, the *Critical Review*, published by the more conservative Archibald Hamilton, calls her attack on Burke "personal" and "illiberal," and occasionally comes to Burke's defense.[7] Both reviews also make a point of Wollstonecraft's gender. The *English Review* comments that "[t]he language may be thought by some too bold and pointed for a female pen," but admits that "when women undertake to write on masculine subjects, and reason as Miss Wollstonecraft does, we wish their language to be free from all female *prettiness*."[8] The *Critical Review* acknowledges in a footnote that it was unaware of the author's gender when the article was written, and apologizes for any inadvertent disrespect. The review is actually quite respectful, although it finds little with which to agree. It questions the viability of the "birthright" as a foundation of a social contract, and it considers Wollstonecraft's optimism about the National Assembly to be premature. The *Gentleman's Magazine* foregrounds Wollstonecraft's gender at the very start of its review article. "The *rights of men* asserted by a fair lady!" it begins, "[w]e should be sorry to raise a horse-laugh against a fair lady; but we were always taught to suppose that the *rights of women* were the proper theme of the female sex."[9] The review ends with an assertion that Wollstonecraft and her fellow modern philosophers, strive to "poison and inflame the minds of the lower class of his Majesty's subjects to violate their subordination and obedience," and all are involved in an attempted "ruin of their country."[10]

A Vindication of the Rights of Woman with Strictures on Political and Moral Subjects was published by Joseph Johnson in 1792. A second edition appeared in 1792, and it was reprinted in 1796. *Rights of Woman* was reviewed by eleven periodicals, although the reviews in the *Scots Magazine* and *Sentimental and Masonic Magazine* are abridgements of William Enfield's article in the *Monthly Review*. The reviews are generally positive and, in nearly all cases, they focus on Wollstonecraft's assessment of female education and consequent plans for reform. The *Analytical Review*, for example, explains that while the title, *Rights of Woman*, suggests a discussion of rights, it is "in reality . . . an elaborate *treatise* of *female education*."[11] Its review indicates a general agreement with her views and recommendations for female education. In the *Monthly Review*, Enfield praises Wollstonecraft as an active philosopher, one whose work has "stepped forth into the public walks of men."[12] He embraces her premise of a genderless mind and her goal to transform women and men into rational human beings, devoid of sexual distinction, "except in affairs of love."[13] His review is an overall endorsement of Wollstonecraft's ideas; however, he concedes that "several of her opinions are fanciful, and some of her projects romantic." His most important point of disagreement is over female citizenship. "We do not see," Enfield argues, "that the condition or the character of women would be improved, by assuming an active part in civil government."[14] The *Critical Review* finds many of Wollstonecraft's conclusions to be "absurd." However, it recognizes Wollstonecraft's use of the "rights of man" as the foundation for her arguments about women, and while it considers this premise to be "fallacious," it reads her arguments correctly, and it understands the depth of Wollstonecraft's reasoning.[15] Still, while it agrees that women should not be idolized, nor should they be coerced into domestic conduct, the *Critical Review* rejects Wollstonecraft's proposal that women be "more useful active citizens."[16] Most other periodicals reviewed *Rights of Woman* favorably, offering long quotations preceded by a general endorsement. *Town and Country Magazine* was the exception. It considers *Rights of Women* to be "[a]n indignant invective," in which Wollstonecraft "seems to allude a little too freely to the communication of sexes, and talks of the essence of sensuality, the sexual character, &c. &c."[17]

Outside of Britain, *Rights of Woman* was widely read and particularly well received. Eileen Hunt Botting calls *Rights of Woman* an "international success," citing its positive reception in Spain and Germany, as well as France and America. In America, where it was published in Boston and Philadelphia, it gleaned the attention of women, including Abigail Adams, who were interested in education, abolition, and suffrage.[18] Philadelphia's *Lady's Magazine and Repository of Entertaining Knowledge*, which was published by William Gibbons, who had also published *Rights of Woman* in Philadelphia, ran a long, positive review and used as the frontispiece of its first volume an allegorical image of the Genius of Emulation presenting Liberty with a copy of the *Rights of Women*.[19] In France, Isabelle Bour argues that the response to *Rights of Woman* was not only more favorable, but also "more insightful and less moralistic," than it was in England.[20] She credits the importance of education to the French revolutionary debates for the support of Wollstonecraft's treatise.[21]

Wollstonecraft's subsequent publication, *An Historical and Moral View of the Origin and Progress of the French Revolution; and the Effect it has produced in Europe*, published by Joseph Johnson in 1794, did not meet with the same critical interest as did her *Vindications*, and it saw only one edition. The lack of excitement – both positive and negative – may have been due to the fact that this volume covered only the early part of the Revolution, and it was the first of an anticipated two or three volumes.

Figure 3 *WOMEN'S RIGHTS, 1792.* Allegorical depiction of a woman presenting the
seated figure of Liberty with a copy of Mary Wollstonecraft's *A Vindication of the Rights of
Woman.* Engraved frontispiece from the first volume of *The Lady's Magazine*, printed at
Philadelphia, December 1792.
Courtesy of GRANGER www.granger.com

In addition, by 1794, the egregious violence of the French Revolution was
widely known and even enthusiasts were reticent to offer their unqualified
support. Responses were mildly positive and tended to focus on
Wollstonecraft's intellectual abilities. In a brief review, the *New Annual
Register* acknowledges Wollstonecraft's "vigorous and well informed mind,

habituated to reflection, and to entertain liberal and comprehensive views of policy and morals."[22] In a much longer article, the *Analytical Review* praises her judgment, skills of observation, and enlightened understanding, and it provides extensive excerpts from multiple chapters. The *Monthly Review* considers Wollstonecraft qualified for what it sees as a difficult, if not impossible, task: to offer an accurate and impartial history of the French Revolution. It published lengthy excerpts, often from those parts of Wollstonecraft's analysis that are disapproving of the French.

Other responses were slightly more critical. The *British Critic* takes an evidentiary approach and draws visual comparisons between Wollstonecraft's text and a history of France from the *New Annual Register*. It concludes that *Historical and Moral Views* is a mere "abridgement" of a history given in the *New Annual Register*, "with moral, political, and miscellaneous reflections" by Wollstonecraft.[23] The *British Critic* challenges Wollstonecraft's logic, and uses her observations and arguments to arrive at conclusions that undermine Wollstonecraft's justification of the French Revolution. In the end, it implies that she is an amateur philosopher. The *Critical Review* takes a measured approach. While it suggests that Wollstonecraft does not go far enough in condemning "those scenes of horror and atrocity, which that bleeding country has since witnessed,"[24] it finds "many just remarks and forcible observations" in her history and agrees with her criticisms of the French and their "unfitness for so great a revolution."[25]

Wollstonecraft's final publication during her lifetime, *Letters Written During a Short Residence in Sweden, Norway, and Denmark* (Joseph Johnson, 1796), was based on letters Wollstonecraft wrote from Scandinavia, where she was working on behalf of Gilbert Imlay and his business venture, despite the unraveling of their relationship. The book proved to be a popular travelogue. It was published in America and translated into German, Dutch, Swedish, and Portuguese. A second edition came out in London in 1802, and reviews were favorable.[26] All agree that her *Letters* do not provide a comprehensive study of Scandinavia, but, instead, offer a series of observations presented as sketches of life in Sweden, Norway, and Denmark. About these sketches they are complimentary. The *Analytical Review* finds them "highly picturesque";[27] the *British Critic* praises the emotion that infuses her descriptions; and the *Monthly Review* values her poetical images and heightened sensibility.

All treat Wollstonecraft as an established writer, and most seem relieved that not only has she turned her attention to a subject less controversial than those of her *Vindications* and *Historical and Moral Views*, but she has also written as a woman revealing her melancholic moods and her emotional turmoil. The *British Critic* applauds her for melding those "finer sensibilities of a female" with her "masculine understanding." It is pleased to see Wollstonecraft exhibiting "that delicacy and liveliness of feeling which is the peculiar characteristic of the sex,"[28] and attributes this change to marriage and motherhood. The *Monthly Review* begins its review with recognition of Wollstonecraft's masculine mind, but concludes with admiration for "the happy union" of "refined sense, vigorous fancy, and lively sensibility."[29] The reviews become more censorious when Wollstonecraft veers from her Romantic descriptions and emotional disclosures toward political, philosophical, and theological topics. The *British Critic* faults her for overstepping her "proper sphere" and charges her with "derid [ing] facts which she cannot disprove, and avow[ing] opinions which it is dangerous to disseminate."[30] The *Monthly Mirror* identifies Wollstonecraft as a "*political* traveller" and chastises her for her "skepticism" and "infidelity" to orthodox Christianity,[31] and the *Monthly Review* finds that some of her ideas are "not quite consistent with sound philosophy."[32]

After Wollstonecraft's death in 1797, and Godwin's publication of both *Posthumous Works of the Author of A Vindication of the Rights of Woman* and *Memoirs of the Author of A Vindication of the Rights of Woman*, Wollstonecraft's reputation went into a decline. Nearly every periodical reviewed both works at the same time – they had both been published by Joseph Johnson in January of 1798 – and the reception of her posthumous works was colored by the personal revelations in the *Memoirs*. Wollstonecraft's second novel, *The Wrongs of Woman; or, Maria*, which was published unfinished in Volumes 1 and 2 of *Posthumous Works*, received the most attention. The *Analytical Review* and the *Critical Review* identify the "wrongs of woman" as laws and customs governing marriage; however, the *British Critic* and the *Anti-Jacobin Review and Magazine* interpret "wrongs" as a bad marriage and foolish choices. The *Analytical Review* sees a vindication of Maria's behavior in "the exercise of her natural and social rights," while the *Anti-Jacobin* reduces her natural rights theory to the right to infidelity.[33] The *Monthly Mirror* finds the novel hard to critique because it is unfinished, but concludes that Maria is a character "drawn with considerable truth and freedom."[34] The *Monthly Review* rejects the "moral tendency" of the novel and, like most reviews, defends the institution of marriage.[35] Of the other posthumous writings, little is said. On her letters to Imlay, the *Analytical Review* is complimentary and sympathetic, and the *Monthly Mirror* suggests, as did Godwin in his Preface, that they are akin to *The Sorrows of Young Werther*. But most reviews concentrate on Wollstonecraft's behavior, rather than the literary quality of the letters, and Godwin's audaciousness in publishing them. The *Monthly Review* thought she should have exercised more prudence in her relationship with Imlay, and the *British Critic*, after defending Imlay's behavior, asserts that Godwin, as her husband, should have destroyed rather than published the letters.

Early responses to Wollstonecraft's work reveal that reform of female education was an acceptable change at the end of the eighteenth century, but female participation in civil society – citizenship in particular – was not. Nor was a liberation of women's sexual conduct. Reviewers were most at ease when Wollstonecraft's writing matched their expectations of feminine sensibility and she exposed not her strength but her vulnerability. Reviewers were most disturbed when they had to face Wollstonecraft's cultural and sexual transgressions. Still, despite the condemnations at the end of the 1790s, Wollstonecraft's influence persisted well beyond the 1790s. *Rights of Woman*, in particular, had a lasting impact, and, as Hunt Botting observes, it not only "captured the political spirit of the immediate past" but also "directed the trajectory of women's rights discourse across Britain, Europe, and the United States."[36] The early reception of Wollstonecraft's work was valuable in disclosing the path forward to female agency.

Notes

1 *European Magazine and London Review*, 11 (January–June 1787), 407.
2 *Critical Review*, 63 (1787), 287–78.
3 *English Review*, 10 (1787), 315.
4 *Monthly Review*, 78 (January–June 1788), 258.
5 *Monthly Review*, 4 (January 1791), 96.
6 *English Review*, 17 (1791), 61.
7 *Critical Review*, 70 (1790), 694–96.
8 *English Review*, 17 (1791), 61.
9 *Gentleman's Magazine*, 41 (February 1791), 151.
10 Ibid., 154.
11 *Analytical Review*, 12 (January–April 1792), 248
12 *Monthly Review*, 8 (June 1792), 198
13 Ibid.
14 *Monthly Review*, 8 (June 1792), 209.
15 *Critical Review*, 4 (April 1792), 389.
16 Ibid., 392.
17 *Town and Country Magazine*, 24 (1792), 279.
18 Eileen Hunt Botting, *Wollstonecraft, Mill and Women's Human Rights* (New Haven: Yale University Press, 2016), 170–71.

19 *Lady's Magazine, and Repository of Entertaining Knowledge*, 1 (December 1792).

20 Isabelle Bour, The Reception of the *Vindication of the Rights of Woman* and of the *Wrongs of Woman* in Revolutionary France," *Journal for Eighteenth-Century Studies* 36 (2013), 585.

21 Ibid., 580.

22 *New Annual Register*, (1794), 221.

23 *British Critic*, 6 (July 1795), 29–36.

24 *Critical Review*, 16 (1796), 392.

25 Ibid., 391, 395.

26 Janet Todd, *Mary Wollstonecraft: A Revolutionary Life* (New York: Columbia University Press, 2000), 370, 485 n. 7.

27 *Analytical Review*, 22 (January–June 1796), 230.

28 *British Critic*, 7 (June 1796), 602.

29 *Monthly Review*, 20 (July 1796), 251, 257.

30 *British Critic*, 7 (June 1796), 607.

31 *Monthly Mirror*, 1 (March 1796), 285, 287, 288.

32 *Monthly Review*, 20 (July 1796), 257.

33 *Analytical Review*, 27 (January–June 1798), 241.

34 *Monthly Mirror*, 5 (1798), 154.

35 *Monthly Review*, 27 (November 1798), 326.

36 Hunt Botting, *Wollstonecraft, Mill and Women's Human Rights*, 44.

CHAPTER 6

Nineteenth-Century Critical Reception

Eileen Hunt Botting

It has often been repeated that Wollstonecraft was not read for a century after her death in 1797 owing to the negative impact of her husband William Godwin's *Memoirs of the Author of A Vindication of the Rights of Woman* (1798) on her posthumous reputation. Although the *Memoirs* and post-revolutionary politics everywhere dampened and even drove underground the reception of her persona and ideas in the first decades of the nineteenth century, Wollstonecraft's reception in nineteenth-century continental Europe, as in the United States and Brazil, was more positive and sustained in comparison to the public backlash she faced as a "fallen woman" in her homeland of Britain through the bulk of the Victorian era.

The publication of the *Rights of Woman* in London, Paris, Lyon, Boston, and Philadelphia in 1792 made Wollstonecraft the most famous women's rights advocate of the European and North American Enlightenment. A second London edition, authorized and revised by Wollstonecraft, appeared in 1792.[1] The *Rights of Woman* was published in Dublin and translated into German in 1793. Matthew Carey printed it twice in Philadelphia in 1794, and Joseph Johnson printed the third edition, likely unauthorized by Wollstonecraft, in London in 1796.[2] Substantial excerpts of the *Rights of Woman* were published in Boston and Philadelphia magazines and translated for a Spanish periodical in the 1790s.[3]

The *Rights of Woman* was reprinted, translated, and repackaged with new introductory material many times in Britain, Europe, and the Americas in the long nineteenth century. Wollstonecraft's fame on the issue of women's rights and the public cachet of her name meant that there were even strategic misattributions of texts to her. M. César Gardeton professed to produce a new "loose" French translation of the *Rights of Woman* in Paris in 1826.[4] Comparison of a rare edition of his book at the Bibliothèque Nationale de France with Wollstonecraft's and other Enlightenment feminist works revealed that he actually reprinted a French translation of Sophia's *Woman Not Inferior to Man* (1739) and misattributed it to

"Mistriss Godwin." His additional misrepresentation, in the subtitle, that the book was in its eighth edition, suggests that he thought Wollstonecraft's (married) name would sell copies. Soon thereafter in Brazil, Nísia Floresta translated Gardeton's 1826 book into Portuguese, complete with the (now unwitting) misattribution of the author as "Mistriss Godwin." Given that Floresta's book was printed three times in 1830s Brazil, it seems that Wollstonecraft's married name indeed could sell books on the issue of the inequality of the sexes. Floresta and her works stirred further public reception of Wollstonecraft – as both a theorist and a symbol of women's rights – in Brazil over the remainder of the nineteenth century.

Beyond such intriguing literary fakes (intentional and unintentional), the English text of the *Rights of Woman* was reprinted in London in 1841, 1844, three times from 1890 to 1892 for its centennial, and in 1896. Its popularity continued in the United States, where it was published in New York in 1833, 1845, 1856, plus two times from 1890 to 1891 for its centennial. The second German translation was published in Dresden and Leipzig in 1899, and the first Czech translation was published in Prague in 1904. Although the bulk of its reprinting and retranslation took place in the late nineteenth century, the thousands of copies printed in Europe and America in the 1790s would have continued to circulate in libraries for decades, enabling the readership of the text well beyond its availability at booksellers. In addition, the *Rights of Woman* was excerpted and printed in books, newspapers, and magazines throughout the nineteenth century, in Germany, Britain, and the United States.[5]

Given the robust, early international reception of the *Rights of Woman*, why have scholars often failed to acknowledge Wollstonecraft's influential status in nineteenth-century feminist political thought? There are three main reasons. First, the rise of anti-Jacobin discourse meant that an association with the cause of the French Revolution tainted Wollstonecraft and her works.[6] Anti-Jacobin discourse – or anti-revolutionary discourse in the wake of the radical stage of the French Revolution – prevailed in countries that were enemies with the French republic, especially Britain and the United States. Wollstonecraft was a supporter of the ideals of the French Revolution, and as such, she and her works became seen by the general public as dangerous sources of political instability.

Second, William Godwin published his scandalous *Memoirs of the Author of A Vindication of the Rights of Woman* in January 1798 – the year that was, coincidentally, the apex of anti-Jacobin discourse in Britain and the United States. Godwin composed the *Memoirs* as a tribute to his wife's memory and philosophical legacy, within two months of her untimely death as a result of a childbirth infection in September 1797.[7] Unfortunately, the *Memoirs* damaged Wollstonecraft's posthumous reputation, because it revealed many shocking details about her romantic life, including her tumultuous affair and illegitimate child with Gilbert Imlay and her pre-marital sexual relationship with Godwin. Intellectual historians have argued that after the mixed but generally positive early reception of the *Rights of Woman* in Britain, Europe, and the United States, the publication of the shocking *Memoirs* plunged Wollstonecraft and her feminist philosophy into disrepute.[8]

Third, the *Memoirs* sparked public interest in her life story and autobiographical writings, and, in turn, a shift in the general public's attention from her *Rights of Woman* to her biography. In the context of the reactionary politics of the post-revolutionary era, the widespread reception of these texts meant that Wollstonecraft's life took on more – and typically negative – significance than her ideas, at least for the general reader. Certainly the *Rights of Woman* had notoriety in the context of anti-Jacobin politics, but the *Memoirs* instigated a biographical and politically reactionary turn in the way people read and responded to the *Rights of Woman*.

Seeking to correct – too late – the damage done to his wife's posthumous reputation as a result of his transparent report of her life, Godwin published a second, edited edition of the *Memoirs* in London in 1798. As Lyndall Gordon has argued, Godwin's corrections to the text still did not address the most problematic aspects of his treatment of his wife's romances, and thus did not put an end to salacious and misguided public interest in her love life in the years to follow.[9] Moreover, the *Memoirs* continued in broad public circulation. The book was printed in Dublin in 1798, and three times in Philadelphia between 1799 and 1804. German and French translations appeared in 1799 and 1802 respectively. The *Memoirs* were discussed extensively – and usually critically – in British and American magazines between 1798 and 1818.[10]

Wollstonecraft's autobiographical *Letters Written during a Short Residence in Sweden, Norway, and Denmark* – initially published in London, Delaware, Hamburg, and Altona in 1796 – had as its implicit subject her tragic romance with Imlay. The *Letters* saw a surge of reprinting and translations after the *Memoirs*, probably because of the rise of public interest in Wollstonecraft's unconventional life story. Swedish, Dutch, and Portuguese translations of the *Letters*, a new German translation in Leipzig, and another printing in London, were produced between 1798 and 1806. In this same period, her incomplete novel *The Wrongs of Woman; or, Maria* – initially published by Godwin in London in 1798 – was translated into French, Swedish, and German and published again in English in Philadelphia. The novel was widely read as a semi-autobiographical defense of women's right to sexual freedom and divorce.[11] No new editions of Wollstonecraft's *Rights of Woman* appeared between 1796 and 1826; yet Wollstonecraft remained well known among literary elites in Britain, Europe, and the Americas through the reception of the *Memoirs*, *Letters*, and *Maria* during this time. In fact, it was likely the popularity of Godwin's *Memoirs* and his edition of his wife's posthumous works that led Gardeton and Floresta – across continents – to consider the name "Mistriss Godwin" sufficiently well known within their literary publics to publish apparent translations of her work.

The public salience of her scandalous life story in the first decades after her death shifted the wider public's focus from her ideas on women's rights to her biography. Consequently, a commonly reiterated scholarly view has been that Wollstonecraft failed to have an impact in nineteenth-century political thought, and only began to enjoy a serious following once the leading feminists of the early twentieth century (such as Emma Goldman and Virginia Woolf) revived her memory and celebrated her life and works as part of their own philosophies.[12] In fact, the post-revolutionary reception of the *Memoirs* and Wollstonecraft's autobiographical writings complicated, but did not eliminate, interest in her life and work in nineteenth-century Britain, continental Europe, Brazil, and the United States. While the *Memoirs* certainly tarnished Wollstonecraft's reputation for a general audience during the nineteenth century, her philosophical and iconic significance was far from lost in the century after her death. Even as her persona persisted as a controversial cultural icon of both the dangers and the promises of women' rights, her philosophy navigated an influential course through nineteenth-century literary and political thought. Moreover, women's rights advocates reclaimed her life story as a symbol of their cause, recycling it for their own feminist purposes.

Previous studies have focused on post-revolutionary Britain and the United States, mainly the 1790s, showing Wollstonecraft was more welcome in the rights-based, democratizing culture of America than in her anti-revolutionary, Francophobe homeland.[13] Her longer-term influence in early nineteenth-century Britain is mainly discussed in terms of her impact on Romantic and early Victorian literature, especially women writers[14] and what has been called the "Godwin–Shelley" circle.[15] This long-standing scholarly emphasis on the latter group of Wollstonecraft's "disciples" has filtered Wollstonecraft's legacies through the life and works of her husband Godwin, their daughter Mary Shelley, and the other

British Romantics, such as Percy Shelley and Lord Byron. A Victorian bias developed against the Wollstonecraft–Godwin–Shelley circles, whose transgressive choices in matters of sex and love made them public objects of "obloquy and scorn" in British Victorian society.[16] This Victorian-era scorn filtered into twentieth-century literary criticism, feminist historiography, and histories of political thought, generating the view of Wollstonecraft as taboo, unknown, or unread for the bulk of the nineteenth century.

In a refreshing change of historiography, British historian Arianne Chernock's recent book shows how the male radicals in Joseph Johnson's and Godwin's intellectual circles in 1790s London rallied around Wollstonecraft as a philosophical and symbolic inspiration for their own defenses of the female sex against patriarchal oppression. Their early championing of Wollstonecraft set the stage for later British intellectuals, such as John Stuart Mill, to freely engage the woman question as part of broader theories of republican government and economic justice in the nineteenth century.[17]

Beyond mentioning Wollstonecraft's impact in Britain on radicals, socialists, and chartists such as William Thompson, Anna Wheeler, Frances Wright, and the Owens, most scholarship has leaped forward to the late Victorian era to chart her reception among women writers such as George Eliot and women's suffragists such as Millicent Fawcett.[18] Some attention has been given to Wollstonecraft's legacies for the mid-nineteenth century Unitarians in Britain, especially in the private lives and writings of those interested in women's rights, such as Harriet Taylor.[19] Barbara Caine has influentially argued that Wollstonecraft was more of a "ghost" than a tangible influence in 1850s British feminism, not referenced in public due to the scandal of the *Memoirs* and its dissonance with staid Victorian conventions of feminine propriety and sexual morality.[20] Avoiding the pitfall of generalizing from one case to another, this essay shows that the trend abroad was different than in her homeland of Britain. As in the nineteenth-century United States, where Wollstonecraft enjoyed a steady and increasingly warm reception in both public and private,[21] continental Europeans and Brazilians were comparatively open to receiving and debating Wollstonecraft, both as an icon and a philosopher of women's rights, as part of their responses to the woman question.

Notes

1 Ulrich T. Hardt, "Textual Introduction," in Hardt, ed., *A Critical Edition of Mary Wollstonecraft's A Vindication of the Rights of Woman: With Strictures on Moral and Political Subjects* (New York: Whitston, 1982), 1–3.

2 Hardt, "Textual Introduction," 2–3.

3 Susan Branson, *These Fiery Frenchified Dames: Women and Political Culture in Early National Philadelphia* (Philadelphia: University of Pennsylvania Press, 2001), 39; Sally Ann Kitts, "Mary Wollstonecraft's 'A Vindication of the Rights of Woman': A Judicious Response from Eighteenth-Century Spain," *Modern Language Review*, 89:2 (1994), 354.

4 Eileen Hunt Botting and Charlotte Hammond Matthews, "Overthrowing the Floresta–Wollstonecraft Myth for Latin American Feminism," *Gender and History*, 26:1 (2014), 64–83.

5 Bonnie S. Anderson, *Joyous Greetings: The First International Women's Rights Movement, 1830–60* (Oxford: Oxford University Press, 2001), 14; Eileen Hunt Botting and Christine Carey, "Wollstonecraft's Philosophical Impact on Nineteenth-Century American Women's Rights Advocates," *American Journal of Political Science*, 48:4 (2004), 718; Lyndall Gordon, *Vindication: A Life of Mary Wollstonecraft* (New York: HarperCollins, 2005), 447.

6 Karen M. Offen, *European Feminisms, 1700–1950: A Political History* (Stanford: Stanford University Press, 2000), 77–78.

7 Gordon, *Vindication*, 368.

8 Regina M. Janes, "On the Reception of Mary Wollstonecraft's *A Vindication of the Rights of Woman*," *Journal of the History of Ideas*, 39:2 (1978), 293–302; Marcelle Thiébaux, "Mary Wollstonecraft in Federalist America, 1791–1802," in D. H. Reiman, M. C. Jaye, and B. T. Bennett, eds., *The Evidence of Imagination: Studies of Interactions between Life and Art in English Romantic Literature* (New York: New York University Press 1978), 195–228.

9 Gordon, *Vindication*, 379.

10 Gordon, *Vindication*, 378–79, 389; Thiébaux, "Mary Wollstonecraft," 206–27.

11 Roxanne Eberle, *Chastity and Transgression in Women's Writing, 1792–1897: Interrupting the Harlot's Progress* (New York: Palgrave, 2002), 58.

12 Anderson, *Joyous Greetings*, 55, 69; G. J. Barker-Benfield, *The Culture of Sensibility: Sex and Society in Eighteenth-Century Britain* (Chicago: University of Chicago Press, 1992), 368–95; Barbara Caine, *English Feminism, 1780–1980* (Oxford: Oxford University Press, 1997), 40; Cora Kaplan, "Mary Wollstonecraft's Reception and Legacies," in Claudia L. Johnson, ed., *The Cambridge Companion to Mary Wollstonecraft* (Cambridge: Cambridge University Press, 2002), 249; Jane Rendall, *The Origins of Modern Feminism: Women in Britain, France and the United States, 1780–1860* (New York: Palgrave, 1984), 33; Virginia Sapiro, *A Vindication of Political Virtue: The Political Theory of Mary Wollstonecraft* (Chicago: University of Chicago Press, 1992), 275–77; Barbara Taylor, *Mary Wollstonecraft and the Feminist Imagination* (Cambridge: Cambridge University Press, 2003), 9, 250.

13 E.g., Janes, "On the Reception"; Kaplan, "Mary Wollstonecraft's Reception"; Thiébaux, "Mary Wollstonecraft."

14 E.g., Eberle, *Chastity and Transgression*, 76–135; Susan Manly, "Mary Wollstonecraft and Her Legacy," in G. Plain and S. Sellers, eds., *A History*

of Feminist Literary Criticism (Cambridge: Cambridge University Press, 2007), 47–57; Anne K. Mellor, "Mary Wollstonecraft's *A Vindication of the Rights of Woman* and the Women Writers of Her Day," in *The Cambridge Companion to Mary Wollstonecraft*, 141–59; Taylor, *Mary Wollstonecraft*, 188–92.

15 E.g., Betty T. Bennett, *Mary Wollstonecraft Shelley: An Introduction* (Baltimore: Johns Hopkins University Press, 1998), 9, 10, 19; Gordon, *Vindication*, 330–452; William St. Clair, *The Godwins and the Shelleys: A Biography of a Family* (Baltimore: Johns Hopkins University Press, 1989), 493–94.

16 Charles Kegan Paul, "Prefatory Memoir," in Wollstonecraft, *Letters to Imlay* (London: Charles Kegan Paul, 1879), v.

17 Arianne Chernock, *Men and the Making of Modern British Feminism* (Stanford: Stanford University Press, 2009), 19–21, 69–77.

18 E.g., Barbara Caine, "Victorian Feminism and the Ghost of Mary Wollstonecraft," *Women's Writing*, 4:2 (1997), 261, 263; Adriana Craciun, ed., *A Routledge Literary Sourcebook on Mary Wollstonecraft's A Vindication of the Rights of Woman* (London: Routledge, 2002), 54–61; Barbara Taylor, *Eve and the New Jerusalem: Socialism and Feminism in the Nineteenth Century* (Cambridge: Harvard University Press, 1983), 1–9; Taylor, *Mary Wollstonecraft*, 248.

19 Pamela Hirsch, "Mary Wollstonecraft: A Problematic Legacy," in Clarissa Campbell Orr, ed., *Wollstonecraft's Daughters: Womanhood in England and France, 1780–1920* (Manchester: Manchester University Press, 1996), 43–60.

20 Caine, "Victorian Feminism," 261, 263.

21 Botting and Carey, "Wollstonecraft's Philosophical Impact," 707–22.

CHAPTER 7

1970s Critical Reception

Julie Murray

The critical reception of Mary Wollstonecraft in 1970s Britain and America was almost entirely mediated through biography. Between 1970 and 1976 alone, as Janet Todd noted over forty years ago, six biographies of Wollstonecraft were published in just six years: Margaret George's *One Woman's "Situation": A Study of Mary Wollstonecraft* (1970); Edna Nixon's *Mary Wollstonecraft: Her Life and Times* (1971); Eleanor Flexner's *Mary Wollstonecraft* (1972); Emily Sunstein's *A Different Face: The Life of Mary Wollstonecraft* (1975); Claire Tomalin's *The Life and Death of Mary Wollstonecraft* (1974); and Margaret Tims' *Mary Wollstonecraft: A Social Pioneer* (1976).[1] Such an extraordinary number of biographies were produced in such quick succession that, as Cora Kaplan remarks, "we might cynically see some of them as responding at least as much to a publishing opportunity as to a cause." For Kaplan, "something remains disturbingly hidden in this sudden excess of biography, as if Wollstonecraft's life must be repeated again and again, more like a symptom that conceals a fear, a symptom that must be expressed but not named."[2] The inextricable connection between Wollstonecraft's life narrative and her life's work has a long history. The conflation of her life with her most famous book, *A Vindication of the Rights of Woman,* can be traced, for instance, to the 1798 publication of William Godwin's *Memoirs of the Author of A Vindication of the Rights of Woman*, the very title of which substituted Wollstonecraft's most famous book for the woman herself. Biographies of Wollstonecraft have also tended to appear at high moments of feminist struggle, a seemingly self-evident fact that bears more investigation than it has received thus far. Almost a century after Godwin's *Memoirs* – a century, moreover, during which Wollstonecraft's name was anathema – the 1880s and 1890s saw a new biography by Elizabeth Robins Pennell, and a new edition of *A Vindication of the Rights of Woman* by the prominent suffragist Millicent Garrett Fawcett, coinciding with the height of the women's suffrage movement. Similarly, the 1970s rage for biographies of Wollstonecraft peaked with second-wave feminism, and laid the groundwork for the major works of feminist criticism about Wollstonecraft produced in the 1980s and 1990s, such as Mary Poovey's *The Proper Lady and the Woman Writer* (1984), Joan Landes' *Women and the Public Sphere in the Age of the French Revolution* (1988), Virginia Sapiro's *A Vindication of Political Virtue: The Political Theory of Mary Wollstonecraft* (1992), and Claudia Johnson's *Equivocal Beings: Politics, Gender, and Sentimentality in the 1790s* (1995), among others.

The long-standing image of Wollstonecraft as feminist maverick goes back to the late nineteenth century, when biographers such as Pennell defended her by arguing that because Wollstonecraft "had the courage to express opinions new to her generation, and the independence to live according to her own standard of right and wrong, she was denounced as another Messalina."[3] Writing in a similar vein in a 1924 biography of Wollstonecraft, Madeline Linford displayed the progressive historiography that would come to characterize second-wave liberal feminist celebrations of Wollstonecraft as pioneer:

> Mary Wollstonecraft has her place in history as the great pioneer of the feminist movement. It was she, more than any other one person, who laid the first stones of that rough and painful road that has led to the enfranchisement of women and, among civilized races, an almost universal recognition of their rights as human beings. In her lifetime Mary saw her work scoffed at and shunned: after her death a storm of calumny beat upon her name. But to-day any student reading the history of the women's movement back through the patriotic labours of the Great War, the brave, pathetic struggles of the Suffragettes, the few lone efforts of Victorian days, comes inevitably to Mary Wollstonecraft's name as its founder.[4]

The image of Wollstonecraft that Linford presents here belongs to a historiography of progressive modernity that is itself a product of the work of Scottish historians writing in the era in which Wollstonecraft lived. Late eighteenth-century histories of society, sometimes referred to as conjectural or stadial histories, took the treatment of women as an index of a culture's modernity or civilization, with the result that women were symbolically built into the very fabric of progressive historiographies of the period and were the standard-bearers of a society's relative enlightenment. Women thus functioned in conjectural histories as confirmation of late eighteenth-century Britons' robust sense of their society's polished commercial modernity and enlightened view of women. In Linford's narrative, however, a very different view emerges. From the vantage of the early twentieth century, Wollstonecraft "laid the first stones" of the "rough and painful road" that led to the "enfranchisement of women," a narrative that implicitly sees Wollstonecraft as having lived in dark and unenlightened times, and having juggled, in the words of another early twentieth-century commentator, "the wild joys of the pioneer with the bitter pains of the outcast."[5]

The trope of Wollstonecraft as lonely trailblazer persisted with Wollstonecraft's 1970s reception. Margaret George's 1970 biography began in the spirit of its late nineteenth- and early twentieth-century predecessors with the assertion that "[e]very list of women who have made feminist history in the modern Western world includes if not begins with the name of Mary Wollstonecraft." "Mary," she continued, "is an obvious pioneer."[6] Proceeding by way of the suggestion that there were "possible candidates before her," such as Aphra Behn or Mary Astell, and that Wollstonecraft had "ambitious contemporaries" such as Catherine Macaulay and Olympe de Gouges, George concluded that, even still, Wollstonecraft's pre-eminence was "unchallengeable."[7] The logic of Wollstonecraft's exceptionalism was also amply on display in Emily W. Sunstein's 1975 biography of Wollstonecraft, entitled *A Different Face: The Life of Mary Wollstonecraft*, which opened with an unflattering image of the era in which Wollstonecraft was born and lived: "Mary Wollstonecraft was born in mid-eighteenth-century England into a society that believed women to be inferior morally and intellectually, and into a class whose ideal women were the sheltered, submissive, lifelong wards of fathers or husbands – decorative, domestically useful sex objects."[8] In a gesture typical of biographies of Wollstonecraft from the late nineteenth century on, Sunstein invoked the figure of Wollstonecraft as a prophet and visionary, someone "so far ahead of her time as to be isolated and reviled."[9] Wollstonecraft was modern, that is, in spite of the supposedly barbaric pre-modernity of her historical moment. For her part, Eleanor Flexner opened her 1972 biography by dispensing entirely with George's consideration of other "possible candidates" for the title of feminist pioneer, and asserting with faint praise that "[w]hat is so astonishing about the *Vindication* is not that Mary wrote it, but that she was alone in raising the issues that she did."[10] Entitled *Mary Wollstonecraft: A Social Pioneer*, Margaret Tims' 1976 biography made explicit the logic of historical inevitability and progressive modernity that shaped so much of the work on Wollstonecraft produced in the 1970s. Tims' title lays bare the degree to which second-wave feminists saw in Wollstonecraft a modern and enlightened figure with the tragic misfortune to have lived in dark and unenlightened times, a view that would no doubt have surprised Scottish historians of society at the time.

The figure of Wollstonecraft as feminist pioneer possesses a lingering irony, finally, in that Wollstonecraft herself was no fan of female exceptionalism, or at least not in the hagiographic mode in which she encountered it in the late eighteenth-century genre of collective biographies of women, or "women worthies," as they were known.[11] Wollstonecraft made clear in her *Vindication of the Rights of Woman* that she was not fond of the elitist impulse that shaped biographies of exemplary women, and asserted that she would "not lay any great stress on the example of a few women who, from having received a masculine education, have acquired courage and resolution." In a footnote to this remark, she added, "Sappho, Eloisa, Mrs. Macaulay, the Empress of Russia ... These, and many more, may be reckoned exceptions; and are not all heroes, as well as heroines, exceptions to general rules?" Wollstonecraft preferred instead "to see women neither heroines nor brutes" but rather as "reasonable creatures."[12] And yet, a heroine she unequivocally became for women such as Pennell and Fawcett, who claimed her as feminism's founder more than one hundred years after her death. Perhaps Wollstonecraft's objection to heroines can be specified further by suggesting that she preferred singularity to exemplarity. While she clearly had little time for the exemplary conduct of "women worthies," she did see herself as a lone wolf, as most of her commentators have noted, and thus in some sense helped to fashion the very image of female pioneer that attached to her in the late nineteenth century. One can see this self-conscious fashioning at work, for instance, in a letter she wrote to her sister in which she confided that she was "not born to tread in the beaten track."[13]

Janet Todd's frustration with the publishing industry's appetite for hagiographies of Wollstonecraft was evident in 1976, when in a review of the spate of 1970s biographies, she observed that the histories of many eighteenth-century women who "pleaded" for women's education and rights remained "unwritten." Meanwhile, publishers were "scrambling after each other in their desire to register their involvement in the women's movement" by publishing multiple "biographies of the woman increasingly described in blurbs as its founder."[14] Concerned that the feminist recovery of, and scholarly attention to, other women writers and their work was being sidelined, Todd herself produced in the 1980s several studies of women writers that expanded upon the work begun in the late 1970s by feminist scholars, such as Elaine Showalter in *A Literature of Their Own* (1977). Among many other books, Todd published *Women's Friendship in Literature* (1980) and *The Sign of Angellica: Women, Writing and Fiction, 1660–1800* (1989), both of which included discussions of

Wollstonecraft and her fiction, and situated her in the context of other women novelists at the time.

In her 1970 biography of Wollstonecraft, Margaret George declared that Wollstonecraft made "a stunning contribution to liberal ideology, indeed, to general modern consciousness,"[15] a comment that appears somewhat anachronistic on the other side of the historical turn in Wollstonecraft scholarship that began in the late 1980s and early 1990s. Virginia Sapiro's witty observation that "those who make Wollstonecraft sound like a late eighteenth-century John Locke in drag mistake her," captures the shift in scholars' conception of Wollstonecraft's relationship to political history and historiography that began in the decade following the bicentennial of the French Revolution and the historic events of 1989.[16] The degree to which 1970s biographers and critics relied on the liberal and rights-based frameworks established by Wollstonecraft's late nineteenth-century commentators is also apparent, for instance, in the suggestion by recent feminist critics that "Fawcett and turn-of-the-century suffragists equated Wollstonecraft with their movement for the vote," which, they suggest "contributed to a standard twentieth-century caricature of the *Rights of Woman* as a 'liberal feminist' text naively focused on the salvific power of civil and political rights."[17] Sapiro's book, along with other historically minded books about Wollstonecraft in the 1990s, such as Gary Kelly's *Revolutionary Feminism: The Mind and Career of Mary Wollstonecraft* and Claudia Johnson's *Equivocal Beings*, went a long way toward situating Wollstonecraft in the midst of her intellectual, social, and political contemporaries, and made it possible to see that the reason for the oft-mentioned anemic discussion of rights in Wollstonecraft's two *Vindications* is that her political idiom was that of virtue, drawn from a tradition associated with civic humanism and classical republicanism, far more than it was of rights and the legacy of Lockean liberalism. In a similar vein, Wollstonecraft scholars such as Barbara Taylor have considered the degree to which the image of Wollstonecraft as the standard-bearer of secular liberalism is at odds with clear evidence of what Taylor calls the "religious foundations" of Wollstonecraft's feminism.[18]

The 1970s was without question a crucial turning point in the reception of Wollstonecraft. Bolstered by the energy of second-wave feminism, biographers saw in Wollstonecraft's life – especially in harrowing stories of a young Wollstonecraft defending her mother from her father's violence – a powerful narrative of resistance to established forms of authority.[19] The mid-twentieth century had witnessed, much like the previous century, another "great forgetting." A 1937 biography of Wollstonecraft

by George R. Preedy (a pseudonym for Marjorie Bowen) contained little of
the adulation of late-Victorian admirers like Pennell and Fawcett, and
instead diminished Wollstonecraft's accomplishment with statements such
as these: "Mary Wollstonecraft's fame depended almost entirely on her
sex ... What she said was platitudinous or crude – but a woman said it."[20]
Preedy's biography formed the basis for the egregious treatment Wollstonecraft subsequently received in the post-war period at the hands of two
American ego psychologists. Marynia F. Farnham and Ferdinand Lundberg's *Modern Woman: The Lost Sex*, published in 1947, contained an
extended, hostile analysis of Wollstonecraft. Diagnosing American women
in general and mothers in particular with acute neuroses stemming from
career ambitions that led them away from the stabilizing succor of motherhood, *Modern Woman* charged feminism and feminists with responsibility
for society's ills, and Wollstonecraft herself for feminism as such. On
Modern Woman's view, Wollstonecraft's "childhood had been fearfully
tragic and had left her with a twisted personality." The authors declared
that Wollstonecraft suffered from "penis envy" and that "the shadow of the
phallus lay darkly, threateningly, over every move" she made.[21] Imagine
with what relief, then, a sensitive biography such as Ralph M. Wardle's was
received, published only three years after *Modern Woman*. Entitled *Mary
Wollstonecraft: A Critical Biography*, Wardle's treatment of Wollstonecraft
was widely praised for its even-handed approach to Wollstonecraft's life,
and for its judicious and informed use of her letters. With the exception of
Wardle's biography, however, Wollstonecraft languished in the middle
decades of the twentieth century as an object of serious scholarly interest.[22]
The 1970s reception of Wollstonecraft definitively changed that. Since
then, interest in Wollstonecraft and her work has only increased, and still
shows no sign of abating. Indeed, it is difficult to imagine that she will
languish in obscurity, or suffer neglect, ever again.

Notes

1 See Janet Todd, "The Biographies of Mary Wollstonecraft," *Signs*, 1:3 (1976),
721–34. The biographical interest in Wollstonecraft in the 1970s revived
scholarly interest in *A Vindication of the Rights of Woman*, leading to two
important teaching editions in 1975, one edited by Carol Poston and the
other by Miriam Kramnick. The publication of these editions arguably led to
interest in other works by Wollstonecraft, including her fiction. An edition of
Mary and *The Wrongs of Woman* edited by Gary Kelly appeared in 1976, for
instance.

2 Cora Kaplan, "Mary Wollstonecraft's Reception and Legacies," in Claudia L. Johnson, ed., *The Cambridge Companion to Mary Wollstonecraft* (Cambridge: Cambridge University Press, 2002), 253–54.

3 Elizabeth Robins Pennell, *Life of Mary Wollstonecraft* (Boston: Roberts Brothers, 1884), 1.

4 Madeline Linford, *Mary Wollstonecraft* (London: Leonard Parsons, 1924), 7.

5 G. R. Stirling Taylor, *Mary Wollstonecraft: A Study in Economics and Romance* (London: M. Secker, 1911), 18.

6 Margaret George, *One Woman's "Situation": A Study of Mary Wollstonecraft* (Urbana: University of Illinois Press, 1970), 3.

7 Ibid.

8 Emily W. Sunstein, *A Different Face: The Life of Mary Wollstonecraft* (Boston: Little, Brown & Co, 1975), 3.

9 Ibid., 3.

10 Eleanor Flexner, *Mary Wollstonecraft: A Biography* (Baltimore: Penguin Books, 1972).

11 See Barbara Taylor, "An Impossible Heroine? Mary Wollstonecraft and Female Heroism," *Soundings*, 3 (1996), 119–35.

12 Mary Wollstonecraft, *A Vindication of the Rights of Woman*, in *The Works of Mary Wollstonecraft*, edited by Janet Todd and Marilyn Butler (New York: New York University Press, 1989), 5: 145–46.

13 Quoted in Taylor, "An Impossible Heroine," 121.

14 Todd, "The Biographies of Mary Wollstonecraft," 730.

15 George, *One Woman's "Situation"*, 4.

16 Virginia Sapiro, *A Vindication of Political Virtue: The Political Theory of Mary Wollstonecraft* (Chicago: University of Chicago Press, 1992), xx.

17 Eileen Hunt Botting, Christine Carey Wilkerson, and Elizabeth N. Kozlow, "Wollstonecraft as an International Feminist Meme," *Journal of Women's History*, 26:2 (2014), 13–38.

18 Barbara Taylor, "The Religious Foundations of Mary Wollstonecraft's Feminism" in Claudia L. Johnson, ed., *The Cambridge Companion to Mary Wollstonecraft* (Cambridge: Cambridge University Press, 2002), 99.

19 The theme of familial dysfunction shaped second-wave feminist treatments of Wollstonecraft's life, but was especially pronounced in Margaret George's 1970 biography.

20 George R. Preedy. *This Shining Woman: Mary Wollstonecraft Godwin, 1759–1797* (London: Collins, 1937), 11.

21 Ferdinand Lundberg and Marynia F. Farnham, *Modern Woman: The Lost Sex* (New York: Grosset & Dunlop, 1947), 149–51.

22 For a fuller discussion of Wollstonecraft's reception in the mid-twentieth century, see Todd, "The Biographies of Mary Wollstonecraft," 727–29.

CHAPTER 8

Recent Critical Reception

Eliza O'Brien

Wollstonecraft's life and writings have attracted increasing critical attention in recent years, with a considerable broadening of topics and themes
positioning Wollstonecraft's work in a number of new ways. Certain
patterns have emerged. Critics like Anne K. Mellor, Tilottama Rajan,
Claudia L. Johnson, and Harriet Guest, who first taught us how to
appreciate Wollstonecraft's writing, continue to develop and refine our
understanding of her work. Hundreds of new critics now work with,
around, and on Wollstonecraft. One notable feature of such criticism is
that there are still areas of her work which are relatively under-discussed,
such as *An Historical and Moral View of the French Revolution*, her
reviewing work, and some of her writing on children and education,
though this last area has received some good critical exploration in recent
years. A further notable feature of Wollstonecraft studies is that her life
continues to attract substantial biographical attention, and finally it is
worth noting that there are relatively few recent monographs wholly
devoted to Wollstonecraft, considering the extent of the role she now
plays in Enlightenment and Romantic studies. Meanwhile, articles and
chapters partly or wholly focused on her work have proliferated, discussing
especially the *Vindications of the Rights of Woman*, *The Wrongs of Woman;
or, Maria*, and *Letters from Sweden*. The latter has gained substantial
ground in recent years to become perhaps the most rewarding text for
critical attention. Yet that small number of monographs is steadily increasing, and as the earliest works from the 1990s retain their value, it is with
those that I begin.

Criticism from the early 1990s testifies to the ongoing debt in Wollstonecraft studies to feminist and political theory. With the passing of
time the significance of new historicism has become more apparent,
as its development enabled critical approaches to Wollstonecraft to be
revised rewardingly and expanded in new directions. It allowed critics to
move beyond the early responses to Wollstonecraft as an Enlightenment

philosopher, to a consideration of her as a Romantic-era writer, in tandem with the productive re-visioning of Romanticism itself. Gary Kelly's *Revolutionary Feminism: The Mind and Career of Mary Wollstonecraft* maintains its place for its detailed but accessible exploration of Wollstonecraft's intellectual and philosophical development, especially in relation to his argument that Wollstonecraft's development of mind was inseparable from her experiments in form, to write a female revolution into being.[1] Virginia Sapiro makes a significant contribution with her study, *A Vindication of Political Virtue: The Political Theory of Mary Wollstonecraft*.[2] It presents its analysis from the double perspective of political science and feminist theory, and follows Sapiro's interests in political and social order, allied with gender consciousness, to reveal the coherent and logical development of Wollstonecraft as a political theorist, briskly dismantling the provisional, inconsistent Wollstonecraft visible in other critical arguments from this period and earlier. Each chapter is based on a concept, such as social order or representation in language, and the two final chapters, on "Wollstonecraft and Feminist Traditions" and "Wollstonecraft and the Canon" conclude the study by raising the persistent problems faced by Wollstonecraft, and women more widely, relating to their exclusion from political democracy and the literary canon. Moira Ferguson's work on Wollstonecraft's use of the discourse of slavery in relation to the rights of woman opens new ground for research on colonialism and race in the period. In *Subject to Others: British Women Writers and Colonial Slavery, 1670–1834*, Ferguson's chapter "The Radical Impulse: After the French Revolution" positions Wollstonecraft within a range of white British women authors writing against slavery, and also contains a discussion of Wollstonecraft's inclusion of "Inkle and Yarico" in *The Female Reader* (1788).[3] Wollstonecraft's rhetorical connection of women's dependence with the discourse of slavery is analyzed in greater detail a year later in Ferguson's *Colonialism and Gender Relations from Mary Wollstonecraft to Jamaica Kincaid*, where she demonstrates that Wollstonecraft "introduc[ed] the thematic of colonial and gender relations in tandem, possibly the first woman to do so on a theoretical level."[4]

Syndy McMillan Conger gives an important new framework for reading and understanding Wollstonecraft's paradoxes and contradictions in a fluently written and substantial study of sensibility. *Mary Wollstonecraft and the Language of Sensibility* sets out to critique the broad claim that "her language of sensibility can imprison its speakers," which includes Wollstonecraft herself.[5] Throughout the study, Conger examines the modes, myths, and values of sensibility, which variously limit, warp, express, and enable Wollstonecraft's writing and thought. Of further note here are the chapters on the *Cave of Fancy* and *An Historical and Moral View of the French Revolution*, where these awkward texts are carefully positioned within Conger's overall argument for an analysis of their coherence and their place in Wollstonecraft's oeuvre. In *Equivocal Beings: Politics, Gender and Sentimentality in the 1790s*, Claudia L. Johnson's influential and detailed chapters on Wollstonecraft explore her attack (in the *Vindication of the Rights of Woman* and both novels) upon the codes of chivalric sentimentality of the Burkean model, which dominate gender relations and coerce women into a position of powerlessness and victimhood.[6] In *Rebel Writer: Mary Wollstonecraft and Enlightenment Politics*, Wendy Gunther-Canada continues to develop the field of study on Wollstonecraft as political theorist, examining questions about inclusion and authority within the Revolution debate and its writers more widely as much as she explores such ideas within Wollstonecraft's two *Vindications* and novels, writing persuasively about Wollstonecraft's subversive power throughout.[7] Saba Bahar's *Mary Wollstonecraft's Social and Aesthetic Philosophy: "An Eve to Please Me"* analyzes the pertinent subjects of women readers and civic or "public women," exploring the ways in which women's "aesthetic representation is ... directly related to public and political life" rather than retracing the public-private model.[8] This is a study that is attentive to the ways in which Wollstonecraft revises available models of femininity and selfhood, and provides a good exploration of her perplexed engagement with Rousseau.

Barbara Taylor's *Mary Wollstonecraft and the Feminist Imagination* has become a classic in the field for its substantial, nuanced, and authoritative exploration of Wollstonecraft's mind and work.[9] The best critic on Wollstonecraft's religious thought, Taylor has a profound understanding of the way religion structures and underpins her feminist and political theory, and by desecularizing the critical approach to Wollstonecraft's radical theories, Taylor rehistoricizes both Wollstonecraft's utopian imaginings and her original critics' responses to them. In *Mary Wollstonecraft, Pedagogy, and the Practice of Feminism*, Kirstin Collins Hanley analyzes the ways in which the developing role of the mother–teacher works as a figure of reform across a wide range of Wollstonecraft's writings.[10] Alert to the problems this presents (in terms of overbearing authority and restrictive forms of pedagogical practice), as well as its positive characteristics of self-development and enquiry, Hanley marks out the ways in which Wollstonecraft developed, tested, and refined her educational theory and practice. Lastly, Lena Halldenius has made a notable contribution to the field in her recent study *Mary Wollstonecraft and Feminist Republicanism: Independence, Rights and the Experience of Unfreedom.*[11] Halldenius focuses on the central role that independence plays in Wollstonecraft's philosophical thought, arguing that when the centrality of independence to Wollstonecraft's writings on liberty, society, community and reason is fully analyzed, the coherence and consistency of her ideas come into clearer focus. The desired independence takes the form of both material and intellectual freedom, but not to the point of annihilating duty or society. Halldenius' analysis takes place within a careful exploration of the precise nature and implications of Wollstonecraft's republican thought amidst the varieties of theories of liberty in the eighteenth century, and her work will surely open up new areas of exploration for scholars interested in Wollstonecraft's political and philosophical thought.

The volume *Mary Wollstonecraft's A Vindication of the Rights of Woman: A Sourcebook*, edited by Adriana Craicun, provides an excellent starting point for a reader new to Wollstonecraft, as it gives a rounded introduction to her life, her central text, and her critics.[12] The four sections of the volume are *Contexts* (including some of Wollstonecraft's letters, and extracts from Rousseau and Macaulay), *Interpretations* (nineteenth- and twentieth-century responses, arranged thematically, and a brief essay on Wollstonecraft's critical history), *Key Passages*, and *Further Reading.* A similarly valuable resource is the volume edited by Jane Moore entitled *Mary Wollstonecraft.*[13] This is a collection of some of the most rewarding and influential criticism on Wollstonecraft, from 1855 (George Eliot) to 2006 (Simon Swift). Its three parts are Part 1, "Survey of the Work and Reputation"; the substantial Part 2, "Contexts: History, Politics, Culture," which is arranged thematically with topics such as gender and enlightenment, the French Revolution, and religion; and Part 3, "Texts: Novels, Literary Reviews, Letters," covering articles and chapters on specific writings. Classic works of criticism by G. J. Barker-Benfield, Mary Poovey, Vivien Jones, John Whale, Cora Kaplan, and Barbara Taylor are all present. In *Mary Wollstonecraft and Mary Shelley: Writing Lives*, edited by Helen M. Buss, D. L. Macdonald, and Anne McWhir, the contributors for the Wollstonecraft half of the book cover the significance of Wollstonecraft's pronouns, her poetics of sensibility, autobiography and memoir, and motherhood and desire.[14] The essay collection edited by Maria J. Falco, *Feminist Interpretations of Mary Wollstonecraft* is a deeply political one, examining still-urgent questions of women's freedom and autonomy in its exploration of Wollstonecraft's work and reputation. Contributors include Wendy Gunther-Canada, Virginia Sapiro, Miriam Brody, and

Carol Poston, and among the topics covered are violence, masculine and colonial rhetoric, liberalism, and political theory.[15]

Edited by Claudia L. Johnson, *The Cambridge Companion to Mary Wollstonecraft* represents an important step in the development of a canonical Wollstonecraft.[16] Essays cover her ideas on education and sexuality, religion and the French Revolution, conduct literature, her novels, *Vindications*, and reviewing work, her travel writing, and her fellow women writers. A concluding essay by Cora Kaplan on "Mary Wollstonecraft's Reception and Legacies" gives a valuable and perceptive analysis of Wollstonecraft studies as far as the 1990s. A recent addition to the Cambridge series, *The Cambridge Companion to British Literature of the French Revolution in the 1790s*, edited by Pamela Clemit, features Wollstonecraft in no fewer than three chapters: in "Wollstonecraft, *Vindications* and *Historical and Moral View of the French Revolution*" by Jane Rendall, in "Wollstonecraft and Godwin: Dialogues" by Nancy E. Johnson, and she also features substantially in Gina Luria Walker's "Women's Voices."[17] Increasingly Wollstonecraft is seen as the foundation for any analysis of women's writing in the 1790s, providing the ground upon which other writers can be explored and understood. *Called to Civil Existence: Mary Wollstonecraft's A Vindication of the Rights of Woman*, edited by Enit Karafili Steiner, is an important collection of essays which illustrates this point further.[18] As with Halldenius' monograph mentioned above, this collection promises to stimulate new ways of thinking about Wollstonecraft and political thought. Steiner's introduction takes the 2008 financial crash and the discourse surrounding women's apparent risk-averse behavior as a provocative starting point for a re-engagement with the question of gender and the public sphere: should women seek to be seen as women, or strive for a gender-neutral equality? Each position has its advantages and penalties, each position is one that Wollstonecraft engaged with and considered, each continues to perplex. The essays here examine "the centrality and productivity of paradox in feminist thought"[19] and combine to provide a detailed and nuanced exploration of the *Vindication,* with many leading scholars in the field contributing cutting-edge work (such as Wollstonecraft's debt to Scottish Enlightenment philosophy, once thought to have a negligible presence in her work). Another excellent collection is *The Social and Political Philosophy of Mary Wollstonecraft,* edited by Sandrine Bergès and Alan Coffee, which, while similarly political and current, covers a broader range of writings and topics, including maternity, slavery, and friendship, as well as civic rights and duties.[20]

Early critical biographies are presented by Jennifer Lorch, *Mary Wollstonecraft: The Making of a Radical Feminist*, and Harriet Devine

Jump, *Mary Wollstonecraft: Writer*,[21] both of whom make good use of existing scholarship in their slim volumes covering the length of Wollstonecraft's career and writings. Claire Tomalin's 1974 biography, *The Life and Death of Mary Wollstonecraft* was republished with a revised bibliography and a brief extension of the section discussing *Letters Written in Sweden, Norway, and Denmark*.[22] Jump continues her biographical work by editing Volume 2, on Wollstonecraft, of *Lives of the Great Romantics III: Godwin, Wollstonecraft and Mary Shelley by Their Contemporaries*.[23] This volume gives a very useful overview of the posthumous responses to Wollstonecraft by reprinting facsimile accounts by Joseph Johnson, William Godwin, and Mary Hays, various anonymous antagonists from contemporary magazines and periodicals (many of whom were reviewers of Godwin's *Memoirs* in 1798), a private letter by Anna Seward (1798), and responses from much later in the nineteenth century, including those of Mathilde Blind (1878) and Margaret Oliphant (1882). Of especial note is the anonymous *A Defence of the Character and Conduct of the Late Mary Wollstonecraft Godwin* (London: 1803), a sober and deeply sympathetic account acquitting Wollstonecraft's principles and morality of impropriety, and which describes her as "glowing with piety towards God and benevolence to man."[24] In 2000, Janet Todd, one of Wollstonecraft's most significant editors and critics, published her substantial literary biography, *Mary Wollstonecraft: A Revolutionary Life*.[25] Todd's detailed exploration and scholarship, coupled with the authoritative literary analysis and scholarly tone (at times austere, at times exasperated by its subject), make this essential reading. In *Mary Wollstonecraft: A New Genus* Lyndall Gordon's biography considerably expands our knowledge of Wollstonecraft's Scandinavian journey, courtesy of the painstaking research by Gunnar Molden into the legal intricacies of the case of Imlay's missing ship.[26] This includes a previously unknown letter from Wollstonecraft to the Danish prime minister in September 1795, in which she sets out the case of fraud and deception. Unlike Todd, and with a longer historical perspective than Tomalin, Gordon maintains her focus on Wollstonecraft's intellectual and social legacies after her death, in the final four chapters. A different type of biography is offered by Julie A. Carlson, *England's First Family of Writers: Mary Wollstonecraft, William Godwin, Mary Shelley*.[27] This is a skillful and perceptive analysis of the interweaving of life, writing, influence, and family across the thought and work of the three authors, and Carlson is especially nuanced in her exploration of the often seemingly contradictory roles played by desire, love, and family relations. Finally, the most recent biography, Charlotte Gordon's *Romantic Outlaws: The*

Extraordinary Lives of Mary Wollstonecraft and Mary Shelley is a pacey dual biography with alternating chapters on each writer.[28]

Regarding journal articles, book chapters, and essays, current critical work is continually extending and repositioning Wollstonecraft's place in her historical period and beyond. There is ongoing interest in her place in the Godwin–Shelley nexus of writers, feminist studies, sensibility, politics, nations, rights, and theories of language and rhetoric in the long eighteenth century, as we have seen already. As well as this, Wollstonecraft's work has more recently been discussed in relation to melancholy, memoir, and biographical and autobiographical studies. *Letters from Sweden* has some claim to be Wollstonecraft's most popular work at present, facilitating discussions of the aforementioned topics, but also of travel writing, anthropology, historical progress, maternity, sympathy, and suffering. Other areas of expanding critical interest are children's and educational literature, and Wollstonecraft's place in the wider context of European women's writing (particularly French authors like Manon Roland and Olympe de Gouges), her translations, and her work in translation. Property and law, bodies, sport, mentoring, friendship, female sociability, and commerce are all subjects of recent work. Wollstonecraft as a writer of history is an area that still has much potential, and on the subject of Wollstonecraft as reviewer, one of the most useful accounts is still that of Mitzi Myers, in "Sensibility and the 'Walk of Reason': Mary Wollstonecraft's Literary Reviews as Cultural Critique" in *Sensibility in Transformation*, edited by Syndy McMillan Conger.[29] Here Myers summarizes the history of critical responses to Wollstonecraft's reviewing work, and argues clearly the ways in which such reviews add to our understanding of Wollstonecraft's comprehension of selfhood, readers, and the politics of criticism. Wollstonecraft maintains her place in studies of fictional developments in the 1790s, especially as the quality and interest of her novels has been recognized and reappraised. One early example of this is Eleanor Ty's chapter, "Female Confinement Literalized: *The Wrongs of Woman; or, Maria*" in *Unsex'd Revolutionaries: Five Women Novelists of the 1790s*.[30] Here Ty examines how prison metaphors work within the narrative structure of the novel in an analysis that is well situated within 1790s female-authored novels. As with Elizabeth Dolan's *Seeing Suffering in Women's Literature of the Romantic Era*, where three out of the seven chapters discuss Wollstonecraft's writings, Wollstonecraft's novels work well in broad studies of the form in the 1790s, but their intricacies are often more rewardingly explored when analyzed in relation to her oeuvre as a whole.[31] To follow the development of Wollstonecraft's thought across her own work, and across the numerous critical responses in recent decades, testifies to the ways in which her ideas span the distance between the universal and the particular: across genre, across disciplines, and across history.

Notes

1 Gary Kelly, *Revolutionary Feminism: The Mind and Career of Mary Wollstonecraft* (Basingstoke: Macmillan, 1992).
2 Virginia Sapiro, *A Vindication of Political Virtue: The Political Theory of Mary Wollstonecraft* (Chicago: University of Chicago Press, 1992).
3 Moira Ferguson, *Subject to Others: British Women Writers and Colonial Slavery, 1670–1834* (London and New York: Routledge, 1992).
4 Moira Ferguson, *Colonialism and Gender Relations from Mary Wollstonecraft to Jamaica Kincaid* (Columbia University Press, 1993), 2.
5 Syndy McMillan Conger, *Mary Wollstonecraft and the Language of Sensibility* (London and Toronto: Associated University Presses, 1994), xii.
6 Claudia L. Johnson, *Equivocal Beings: Politics, Gender and Sentimentality in the 1790s* (Chicago: University of Chicago Press, 1995).
7 Wendy Gunther-Canada, *Rebel Writer: Mary Wollstonecraft and Enlightenment Politics* (DeKalb: Northern Illinois University Press, 2001).
8 Saba Bahar, *Mary Wollstonecraft's Social and Aesthetic Philosophy: "An Eve to Please Me"* (Basingstoke: Palgrave, 2002), 7.
9 Barbara Taylor, *Mary Wollstonecraft and the Feminist Imagination* (Cambridge: Cambridge University Press, 2003).
10 Kirstin Collins Hanley, *Mary Wollstonecraft, Pedagogy, and the Practice of Feminism* (New York: Routledge, 2013).
11 Lena Halldenius, *Mary Wollstonecraft and Feminist Republicanism: Independence, Rights and the Experience of Unfreedom* (London: Pickering & Chatto, 2015).
12 Adriana Craicun, ed., *Mary Wollstonecraft's A Vindication of the Rights of Woman: A Sourcebook* (London: Routledge, 2002).
13 Jane Moore, ed., *Mary Wollstonecraft* (Farnham: Ashgate, 2012; reprinted Routledge, 2016).
14 In Helen M. Buss, D. L. Macdonald, and Anne McWhir, eds., *Mary Wollstonecraft and Mary Shelley: Writing Lives* (Ontario: Wilfrid Laurier University Press, 2001).
15 Maria J. Falco, ed., *Feminist Interpretations of Mary Wollstonecraft* (Pennsylvania: Pennsylvania State University Press, 1996).
16 Claudia L. Johnson, ed., *The Cambridge Companion to Mary Wollstonecraft* (Cambridge: Cambridge University Press, 2002).
17 Pamela Clemit, ed., *The Cambridge Companion to British Literature of the French Revolution in the 1790s* (Cambridge: Cambridge University Press, 2011).
18 Enit Karafili Steiner, ed., *Called to Civil Existence: Mary Wollstonecraft's A Vindication of the Rights of Woman* (Amsterdam: Rodopi, 2014).

19 Ibid., xiv.

20 Sandrine Bergès and Alan Coffee, eds., *The Social and Political Philosophy of Mary Wollstonecraft* (Oxford: Oxford University Press, 2016).

21 Jennifer Lorch, *Mary Wollstonecraft: The Making of a Radical Feminist* (New York: Berg, 1990); Harriet Devine Jump, *Mary Wollstonecraft: Writer* (Hemel Hempstead: Harvester Wheatsheaf, 1994).

22 Claire Tomalin, *The Life and Death of Mary Wollstonecraft* (London: Penguin, 1992).

23 Harriet Devine Jump, *Lives of the Great Romantics III: Vol. 2, Wollstonecraft* (London: Pickering & Chatto, 1999).

24 Ibid., 226.

25 Janet Todd, *Mary Wollstonecraft: A Revolutionary Life* (London: Weidenfeld & Nicolson, 2000).

26 Lyndall Gordon, *Mary Wollstonecraft: A New Genus* (London: Little, Brown, 2005).

27 Julie A. Carlson, *England's First Family of Writers: Mary Wollstonecraft, William Godwin, Mary Shelley* (Baltimore: Johns Hopkins University Press, 2007).

28 Charlotte Gordon, *Romantic Outlaws: The Extraordinary Lives of Mary Wollstonecraft and Mary Shelley* (London: Penguin, 2015).

29 Mitzi Myers, "Sensibility and the 'Walk of Reason': Mary Wollstonecraft's Literary Reviews as Cultural Critique," in Syndy McMillan Conger, ed., *Sensibility in Transformation* (London & Toronto: Associated University Presses, 1990), 120–44.

30 Eleanor Ty, *Unsex'd Revolutionaries: Five Women Novelists of the 1790s* (University of Toronto Press, 1993), 31–45.

31 Elizabeth Dolan, *Seeing Suffering in Women's Literature of the Romantic Era* (Farnham: Ashgate, 2008).

PART III

Historical and Cultural Contexts

The French Revolution Debate

CHAPTER 9

Writing the French Revolution

Mary A. Favret

Late in her *Historical and Moral View of the Origin and Progress of the French Revolution* (1794), after recounting the major events of 1789 and the King's removal to Paris, Mary Wollstonecraft pauses to consider the "progress" needed before the French people can properly govern themselves:

> Freedom is a solid good, that requires to be treated with reverence and respect.—But, whilst an effeminate race of heroes are contending for her smiles, with all the blandishments of gallantry, it is to their more vigorous and natural posterity, that she will consign herself with all the mild effulgence of artless charms.[1]

Similar pauses punctuate the *Historical and Moral View*: a people enslaved by their king and court, with "no distinct idea of what is meant by liberty in a practical sense" lack the "wisdom of experience" to step forward into the space of authority (6: 221). "The progress of reason being gradual," such instruction cannot be rushed; it may take decades, perhaps longer (6: 210).[2]

Gradualism, we are told, is the lesson Wollstonecraft takes away from her historical reflections on the Revolution and Terror.[3] The passage about Freedom casts gradualism in the form of generational succession: from courteous gallants to a more vigorous progeny. As she dresses her reflections on the French nation in the guise of gender, Wollstonecraft inserts another lesson, familiar from her attack on Edmund Burke in *A Vindication of the Rights of Men* (1790) and from her *Vindication of the Rights of Woman* (1792).[4] Personification allows her to conflate women with Freedom, and suggest that gallantry (or Burke's cherished "chivalry") respects neither. Nor does gallantry cultivate "vigorous" men: Freedom will offer her gifts to manly sons rather than effeminate fathers. Here Wollstonecraft wants to substantiate a "solid good," yet the scene fuses the prospect of political freedom with codified notions of gender and sexuality: the "naturally" vigorous win the "artlessly charming" (6: 210). As Freedom plays her part in this nominally natural progression, the

passage evokes less history than allegory, less democratic forum than
romantic bower – or commercial marketplace (both *solid good* and *consignment* suggest an economic transaction).

What place does this allegory, and abstract personification more generally,
have in Wollstonecraft's progressive history? It appears to mix historical and
mythical, mortal and immortal actors in a bid to record universal truths. Yet
in taking this "freedom," Wollstonecraft takes serious risks.[5] She reinscribes a
narrative of gender and sexuality she elsewhere repudiates. And she subsumes
historical progress into an Oedipal plot. When Wollstonecraft depicts Freedom in this manner, moreover, women as historical actors – those who
confronted the King at Versailles, for instance – disappear. What freedom can
there be in a feminized allegory of Freedom or an allegorical history?

* * *

The rise of democracy in France required a "revolution in the poetic
structures" of historical knowledge, writes Jacques Rancière.[6] Rancière
traces this revolution through the rise of the profession of History, paying
special care to the legacy of Jules Michelet, the mid-nineteenth-century
historian of the Revolution. Crucially for Rancière, Michelet forged a
poetics "appropriate to democratic historical knowledge."[7] Navigating
between rhetorical historiography (devoted to a logic of exemplary individuals) and empirical historiography (devoted to evidence by documenta-
tion), Michelet devised a "third way": a "republican-romantic" poetics
which "grant[ed] reality to those names that succeeded the name of the
king ... those 'personified abstractions' [e.g. the Nation, Liberty]
denounced by ... the chroniclers" who trusted only empirical methods.[8]
More specifically, Michelet used personified abstractions as well as personified objects (the very stones!) to displace aristocratic heroes with a
people "who represent themselves to themselves" without the need (or
interference) of words, documents, or example. The art of the republican-
romantic historian thus consists in "making the poor speak by keeping
them silent, of making them speak as silent people."[9] Allegorical scenes
thus ask the reader to *see* rather than *hear* the sovereign people, the
democratic nation, speak. (Here, then, personification does not overlap
with prosopopoeia, the device whereby inanimate things are given voice).

Wollstonecraft's allegory of Freedom operates in this mode. It is as if the
"mild effulgence" we behold were the visual equivalent of Freedom's
unvoiced consent. It becomes the historian's task, then, to interpret what
we see. Wollstonecraft grants reality to this abstract personification; with

reality she grants meaning, intention, and desire. The scenario of Freedom's consignment indicates that well before Michelet, British women aiming to provide a history of the French Revolution experimented with a similar poetics, pursuing the elusive voice and will of a not-quite-constituted people.[10] This scenario alerts us to the specifically gendered risks of such historical poetics. Making the desire of the people (Freedom! Liberty!) visible *as* a woman, a woman who need only be seen for her desires to be understood, exposes the gendered costs of freedom, determination, and consent in democratic society.

Wollstonecraft's efforts to recount the struggle of a "people determined to live free" (6: 202) reflect those of other women writing histories of this moment, most prominently Catharine Macaulay and Helen Maria Williams. All three oppose the poetics manifest in Edmund Burke's *Reflections on the Revolution in France* (1790). They critique his allegorical flourishes, yet borrow and transform them – not without political cost. As J. G. A. Pocock noted years ago, collaboration between allegory and history anchored Burke's – and his predecessors' – faith in England's Ancient Constitution.[11] In the sense that it designated a body of law inaccessible and "more ancient" than the Magna Carta of 1215, the Ancient Constitution was a founding myth, called upon as the guarantor of British freedom. That myth – itself wordless – was given expression by the custom and practice of successive generations. In this sense, the myth "appealed to the authority of tradition, but was anti-historical" and effectively allegorical in form.[12]

The image of the Ancient Constitution, with the tradition and political order it sustained, guides Burke's tirades against the revolutionaries in France. Burke's particular use of allegory displays perpetual faith in inherited meaning; at the same time, his *Reflections* register the fragility of the allegorical mode at that historical moment. In Burke's recounting of his first sight of the queen of France, for instance, personal experience surrenders to allegorical vision:

> ... surely never lighted on this orb, which she [Marie-Antoinette] hardly seemed to touch, a more delightful vision. I saw her just above the horizon, decorating and cheering the elevated sphere she just began to move in,— glittering like the morning-star, full of life, and splendour, and joy. Oh! what a revolution![13]

Burke plays here with the astronomical sense of revolution, of planetary bodies – like Venus, appearing on the horizon as the morning star – revolving on their natural course through the heavens. But the figure cannot be sustained: his celestial Venus is brought to earth by a rude, unnatural revolution. For Burke, the revolutionaries deny and thus destroy the power of allegorical meaning. To them

> a king is but a man, a queen is but a woman; a woman is but an animal, and an animal not of the highest order. All homage paid to *the sex in general as such*, and without distinct views, is to be regarded as romance and folly ... [emphasis added][14]

regarded as, in Wollstonecraft's terms, "the blandishments of effeminate heroes." The sacred status of king, parent, and *la France* herself hinges on the capacity to allegorize, and specifically to allegorize "*the [female] sex in general as such*."

* * *

The most eminent woman historian at the time, Catharine Macaulay, in her *Observations on the Right Honourable Edmund Burke's Reflections on the Revolution in France* (1791) meticulously picks apart Burke's style along with his allegiance to the "great mist of words and terms" used to legitimate the British Royal House of Hanover. Macaulay's historical method – developed over two decades in her eight-volume *History of England from the Ascension of James I to the Revolution [of 1688]* (1763–83) – pointedly breaks the collaboration between allegory and history. It introduces political contestation to Burke's tradition-soaked narrative. Likewise, throughout her *Observations*, empirical accounts based on documentary research dismantle the authority of tradition and allegory. These "are indeed facts" with which she counters Burke.[15]

Macaulay's rejection of Burke's chivalric illusions, as of his Ancient Constitution, cannot be disarticulated from what Rancière calls poetics. To Macaulay, Burke's allegorical style exposes both ignorance of history and complicity with tyranny: his "reflections" offer little more than "mechanized sentimental barbarism."[16] She acutely diagnoses the link between allegory and gendered politics: the "high colouring" of Burke's style mirrors the "charms of the Queen of France," charms "adapted rather to *enslave* our affections, than to *lead* our judgement." "Men of cool minds" – like the historian – remain free of such enslavement. For Macaulay, liberty in Britain or in France communicates itself rather through reason and empirical fact.[17] Against "all the *devices* of pride, all the *fond conceits* of vanity, all the train of *pompous* ostentation" that support "the glare of external magnificence" in Burke's account, Macaulay raises fact-based inquiry (she is especially fond of statistics) and the unadorned "simplicity of ... abstract principles."[18]

Nevertheless, as her criticism shows, the republican historian remains fully capable of wielding abstract personification – pride, vanity, pompous ostentation – in a moral-political allegory of her own devising. Macaulay makes this move often when she critiques the *Reflections*, mimicking Burke's tactics by borrowing the sorcerer's wand. It is as if allegory knew its own. The visual pageantry of Macaulay's allegorization of allegorical style, its *devices* and *conceits*, dissolves Burke's poetics in a vision – not unlike Burke's elevation of Marie-Antoinette. Yet where Burke pictures heavenly light, Macaulay sees glare. Macaulay had compared the pleasures of Burke's style with the "charms" of the French Queen; here the historian not only derides Burke's allegorical impulses, she subjects his very writing to allegorization, as if asking him to feel – and her readers to see – its effects. In other words, Macaulay deploys allegory to render Burke seen, not heard.

* * *

The author of the *Observations* died a few months after its publication, and before she had a chance to meet Wollstonecraft.[19] The older writer's clever detachment from the snares of allegory did not pass to her successors. Helen Maria Williams, the Englishwoman most responsible for documenting the ongoing events in France, found herself pulled into allegory, not least because the French revolutionaries themselves summoned "the apotheosis of the feminine allegory" to "represent every imaginable political attribute."[20] Williams' multi-volume *Letters from France*, written in installments from Paris between 1790 and 1796, made her Britain's foremost foreign correspondent. Before arriving in Paris in 1792, Wollstonecraft had reviewed for the *Analytical Review* Williams' early accounts of revolutionary France; Williams' extensive social contacts in the capital, moreover, helped Wollstonecraft in crafting her *Historical and Moral View*.[21]

Williams' early *Letters* pointedly counter Burke's argument from the *Reflections* as well as his chosen poetics; but in place of Macaulay's history lessons she provides on-the-ground happenings in France.[22] In a way, Williams weaves together empiricism and allegory to form a "solid good." In the first volume, the letter writer initially finds liberty in the heard speech of "all ranks of the people." "The enthusiastic spirit of liberty . . . [is] mingled with the gaiety of social enjoyment. When they converse, liberty is the theme of discourse."[23] The words of conversation are filtered out; Williams distills their essential "spirit." Allegory, then, is not distant:

on the next page, "Liberty appears in France adorned with the freshness of youth, and is loved with the ardour of passion." In England, by comparison, "she is seen in her matronly state ... beheld with sober veneration."[24] Uneven political development here takes the benign form of female bodies, to be revered or pursued with passion (take your pick: her appearance *is* her consent). Diffuse popular discourse about liberty precipitates into Liberty's bodily appearance.

As the *Letters* continue, though, Williams tests allegory and its efforts to capture – make visibly silent – the voice and desire of the people. In a scene near the close of the 1790 volume, she seems to accentuate her complicity with allegory. The scene is perhaps the strangest in all six volumes of the *Letters*.[25] At a private party, the company decides to stage a play:

> My sister took a part in the performance, which I declined doing, till I recollected that one of the principal characters was a statue; upon which, I consented to perform "*la beau role de la statue*."* And in the last scene, I, being the representative of Liberty, appeared with all her usual attributes, and guarding the consecrated banners of the nation, which were placed on an altar, on which was inscribed, in transparent letters, "*à la Liberté 14 Juillet 1789*."** One of the performers, pointing to the statue, says, "*Chaque people a decoré cette idole de quelques attribus qui lui font particuliers. Ce bonnet surtout a devenu un emblem éloquent. Ne pourrions-nous pas en ajuter d'autres qui deviendra peut-êtres aussi célébrés?*"*** He then unfolds a scarf of national riband ... and *adds*, "*Cette noble écharpe! —ces couleurs si bien assortis ne sont-elle pas digne de figurer aussi parmi les attrubuts de la Liberté?*"**** The scarf was thrown over my shoulder, and the piece concluded with the Carillon National... *ça ira* hung on every lip, *ça ira* glowed on every countenance! Thus do the French ... appoint [the cause of liberty] not merely to regulate the great movements of governments, but to mould the figure of the dance.

Williams translates the italicized French phrases in footnotes.[26]

The scene compresses and unites the several narratives that precede it. Whatever play is involved, readers never learn: they see only this final tableau, which wavers between the past tense of report and the present of immediate utterance (see underlined verbs). More curiously, the tableau puts forth a provisional poetics, where each mode of figuration prompts supplementation. Liberty is curiously embodied – the *Anglaise* turned statue – and adorned with her "usual attributes." Mute and immobile, she helps the people "represent ... themselves to themselves." And yet these universal attributes are not enough. Liberty must be decked with emblems peculiarly French. "Eloquent" objects speak silently what should go without saying. An altar is imprinted with "transparent letters" – "transparent" suggesting again the elimination of mediation. Self-evident, the letters have no need to be read (why the need for letters at all?) Along with the performers, Williams feels obliged to offer more: Liberty needs a body; the body needs objects; the objects require written and spoken explanation; and the performer's speech requires translation – by Williams. She takes on silence, perhaps, but silence as print is silent, silence as record, as writing; silence where the voices of the people become History.

* * *

Williams *chooses* a Liberty of silence, which grants her the authority to write into English the experience of Revolution. In the following years, she will be imprisoned, exiled, and live under surveillance in Paris; yet she will continue writing. By 1793, when Wollstonecraft begins writing her *Historical and Moral View*, she too watches Robespierre rise, Louis XIV ride off to execution, and Britain declare war on France. (Wollstonecraft escaped arrest by registering with the United States Embassy as the spouse of her American lover, Gilbert Imlay). These events do not appear in *An Historical and Moral View*. Writing under the shadow of Terror, Wollstonecraft recounts only the halting overtures of 1789, culminating in the King's removal to Paris in October, after the march on Versailles. The final event discussed, the July publication of the Declaration of the Rights of Man, appears out of sequence, suggesting her own historiographical switch of focus to writing *as* event. Knowledge of how the Revolution unfolded – the violence of the September massacres, the guillotine, civil wars, and border wars – presses upon the pages Wollstonecraft writes, but remains muffled. Instead, Wollstonecraft closes the book with a philosophical, even anthropological history, charting the cultural causes of France's situation, excusing the generic "ferocity" of the French people, and sketching the prospect for reform. To write thus she abandons allegory. The last chapter leaves behind both personification *and* person, women's bodies *and* the voice of the people (6: 223–34). They sink from view along with the violence of the intervening "years of anarchy," 1790–94 (6: 220).

Macaulay in 1790 saw in the personification of abstraction a failed politics and poetics, serving the myth of aristocratic succession and feminized "charms," alien to a free people. That same year Williams, anticipating Michelet, sought to wed allegory to the will of the people, substantiating – or maybe allegorizing – her historical authority in the process. Such "republican-romantic" poetics, though, prove self-defeating

to Wollstonecraft, writing in the years of terror. We might read Wollstonecraft's allegory of Freedom as reparative poetics, meant to recast the event
that precedes it, the women's march on Versailles. Wollstonecraft had
previously defended the marchers from Burke's claim that they represented
"the vilest of women" (Wollstonecraft, 5: 30). Here, though, she finds
them "the lowest refuse of the street, women who had thrown off the
virtues of their sex without the power to assume more than the vices of the
other" (6: 196–97). The impotence of women, though, runs deeper and
wider. Introducing the march, Wollstonecraft warns that women's freedom can be manipulated by men:

> From the enjoyment of more freedom than the women of other parts of the
> world, those of France have acquired more independence of spirit . . .; it has
> therefore, been the scheme of designing men very often, since the revolu-
> tion, to lurk behind them as a kind of safeguard, *working them up* to some
> desperate act, and then terming it . . . merely the rage of women (6: 196;
> emphasis added).

Then Wollstonecraft cites evidence that the march, where "market
women" stridently voiced their desires, served in fact as cover for the
machinations of the Duc d'Orléans, an aristocratic villain. Later she
explains that many marchers were men in drag, evidence against the
spontaneity and transparency of this display of the people's will (6: 201).
The ugliness of these revelations, that women's freedom to move and
speak is another device in the hands of scheming men, *worked up* through
disguise and exploitation – hardly an expression of popular will – must be
cleaned up in order to preserve the promise of democracy. For a moment,
allegory complies – with a mild effulgence. In doing so, though, it repeats a
disingenuous structure of gender exploitation, silencing and illusion. The
two scenes – the market women and Freedom – short-circuit each other.

In the last chapter, Wollstonecraft's shift to philosophical abstraction
pulls away altogether from the body, empirical or allegorical. "People
thinking for themselves have more energy in their voice, than any government," the last chapter begins (6: 223). Yet the rest of the chapter quickly
strips away even the physical sensation of voice: under Terror, the historian
learns not to experiment with bodies. *Thinking* has primacy; systems
(commerce, law, manners) take the place of persons, mobs, and events.
"Only the philosophical eye" understands, and it studies not the streets but
"the pages of history" (6: 235). There alone, on the silent page, may the
"imperceptible change in things and opinions" that form History be
known (6: 229).

Notes

1 Mary Wollstonecraft, *The Works of Mary Wollstonecraft*, edited by Janet Todd and Marilyn Butler, 8 vols. (London: W. Pickering, 1989), 6: 213.
2 See also *Works*, 6: 45–46, 226–31, and, less optimistically, 163.
3 See e.g. Tom Furniss, "Mary Wollstonecraft's French Revolution," in Claudia L. Johnson, ed., *The Cambridge Companion to Mary Wollstonecraft* (Cambridge: Cambridge University Press, 2002), 69–79.
4 Claudia L. Johnson, *Equivocal Beings: Politics, Gender, and Sentimentality in the 1790s* (Chicago: University of Chicago Press, 1995), 23–46.
5 Wollstonecraft insists that "it becomes more peculiarly the duty of the historian to record truth; and comment with freedom" (*Works*, 6: 467).
6 Jacques Rancière, *The Names of History: On the Poetics of Knowledge*, translated by Hassan Melehy (Minneapolis: University of Minnesota Press, 1995), 42.
7 Ibid., 43.
8 Ibid., 43.
9 Ibid., 45.
10 The first French Constitution, ratified in September 1791, was abandoned a year later when the first Republic was declared.
11 J. G. A. Pocock, "Blake and the Ancient Constitution," in *Politics, Language and Time: Essays on Political Thought and History* (New York: Atheneum, 1971), 207.
12 Steven Blakemore, "Burke and the Fall of Language," *Eighteenth-Century Studies*, 17:3 (1984), 288.
13 Edmund Burke, *Reflections on the Revolution in France*, Vol. 2 of *The Selected Works* (Indianapolis: Liberty Fund, 1999), 169.
14 Ibid., 171.
15 Catharine Macaulay, *Observations on the Right Honourable Edmund Burke's Reflections on the Revolution in France* (London: C. Dilly, 1790), 8. Reprinted by *Online Library of Liberty*, http://oll.libertyfund.org.
16 Ibid., 23.
17 Ibid., 22.
18 Ibid., 22, 33.
19 Bridget Hill, "The Links Between Mary Wollstonecraft and Catharine Macaulay: New Evidence," *Women's History Review*, 4:2 (1995), 177–92.
20 Lynn Hunt, *The Family Romance of the French Revolution* (Berkeley: University of California Press, 1992), 84, 82.
21 Wollstonecraft in *Analytical Review*, 8 (1791), 431–35.
22 Helen Maria Williams, *Letters from France: Written in the Summer of 1790* (London: T. Caddell, 1790), 217–18.
23 Ibid., 70.
24 Ibid., 71.
25 Williams and her sister were attending a party in August 1790, a month after the first anniversary of the fall of the Bastille. See Letter XXIV of Volume 1 of her *Letters from France*.

26 Ibid., 204–06. * "the coveted role of the statue." ** "To Liberty, 14 July."
   ***Each nation has decorated this idol with some peculiar attributes—This
   cap has long been one of her most eloquent emblem.—Can we not add some
   others, which may, perhaps, become no less celebrated?" **** "That noble
   scarf!—are not its auspicious colors worthy of being among the attributes of
   Liberty?"

CHAPTER 10

Radical Societies

David O'Shaughnessy

When Mary Wollstonecraft became a professional writer in 1786 with the publication of *Thoughts on the Education of Daughters*, London debating societies were routinely discussing issues related to female manners such as "Can that Wife be truly said to love a Husband, who frequently disobeys him?" (yes, but only carried by a small majority) and "Whether it was not false Delicacy which forbid the fair sex making the first advances to the man they love?" (a great majority were against the lady doing so).[1] While such societies had previously had a distinct atmosphere of alehouse masculinity, women had been admitted to public debating societies since the late 1770s and began to contribute to debates in 1780, as Mary Thale and Donna T. Andrews have observed.[2] As one might imagine, debate topics with a feminine slant often related to questions around marital decorum and female manners, but were not absolutely limited to these issues. Debates on whether women should have a say in general elections, the compatibility of female nature with politics, and the nature of female education also took place. Women were not only allowed to attend and to participate in most debating societies in the early 1780s, they also established female-only societies such as La Belle Assemblée and the Female Parliament. Progress appeared to be considerable since the failure of Charles Macklin's experiment in the 1750s when he tried to commercialize female participation in his short-lived British Inquisition venture.[3] However, the years 1780–81 were the apex of female involvement in these debate forums as public taste declined for such events (perhaps because of the anxieties about social stability provoked by the Gordon riots) and by the end of the decade attitudes toward displays of female rhetorical agency remained decidedly ambivalent: *The Times* of October 29, 1788 opined that "the debating ladies would be better employed at their needle and thread, a good sempstress being a more amiable character than a female orator."[4] There was considerable resistance to female participation in rational-critical debate, but issues of interest to women were now nonetheless firmly part of public discourse and, as Thale has observed, these debating societies helped create the environment in which Mary Wollstonecraft and her ideas could be taken seriously.[5]

The radical societies that emerged in the 1790s in the wake of the French Revolution were much more decidedly male spaces. Eschewing the broad range of topics that might be found in debating societies, the radical societies were entirely focused on the discussion of political reform and the rights of man. More than talking shops, the radical societies held meetings, corresponded with other membership branches, published pamphlets, and were explicitly concerned with political activism on the basis that the current incarnation of British politics left much to be desired. As one might envisage, the spectrum of political opinion that one might find in these societies was rather broad: "radical" was a sweeping pejorative that was thrown at a broad range of people who would have strongly repudiated any mutual association. To complicate matters, there were relationships that waxed and waned as events unfurled and which depended on the particular forum in which they met. John Thelwall, for instance, a leading member of the London Corresponding Society (LCS), was an associate and sometime friend of William Godwin's. The two met regularly in the early 1790s and both were members of the Philomaths (fully, the Philomathian Society), a select private group that met to discuss philosophical and political issues. While the Philomaths (to whom we shall return) would certainly have come under the bracket of 'radical' for many conservative observers, there was no public element to the group. And it was far removed from the boisterous and animated meetings of the LCS, where Thelwall would speak so passionately and which Godwin found so disconcerting. Godwin and Thelwall would fall out over their approaches to political and societal reform; Godwin's condemnation "Of Political Associations" in *Political Justice* putting him at odds with Thelwall's more robust approach. "The conviviality of a feast may lead to the depredations of a riot," warned Godwin. He continued:

> While the sympathy of opinion catches from man to man, especially in numerous meetings, and among persons whose passions have not been used to the curb of judgment, actions may be determined on, which solitary reflection would have rejected. There is nothing more barbarous, cruel and blood-thirsty, than the triumph of a mob.[6]

Godwin's anxieties about the LCS – of whom he was certainly thinking in this passage – were widespread in the early 1790s. Fears of radical associations might be dated to Edmund Burke's dark mutterings about Richard

Price's sermon *Discourse on the Love of our Country* (1789), delivered to the Revolution Society, an organization dedicated to the memorializing of the "Glorious" Revolution of 1688. And there were other prominent radical societies, such as the Society for Constitutional Information (SCI, established in 1780 and important as a channel of communication to French republicans in the 1790s), the Society of the Friends of the Liberty of the Press (established in late 1792 in response to loyalist attacks on press freedom), the Society of the Friends of the People (established in 1792 by Charles Grey and other Whiggish politicians to prevent extremism by bringing about modest reform), and the Society of United Englishmen (a clandestine and shadowy organization with links to the revolutionary United Irishmen). However, it was the LCS which was the largest, most prominent, and, arguably, the most coherent of all the radical societies and, as the example of Godwin shows, the organization that was most likely to come to mind when the question of popular politics and reform was raised.

The LCS was formed in January 1792, the same month as *Vindication* was submitted to the printer. Thomas Hardy, a shoemaker (his low profession was held up by critics as particularly damning), was the main founder, and he convened its first meeting at the Bell Inn, off the Strand. There were only nine men in attendance, but the membership grew exponentially. By May 1792 there were nine divisions each with at least thirty members. Although the precise number is not known, at its peak the LCS could boast thousands of members, energized by the ideas and example of both the American and French Revolutions. There was a specific remit to recruit those people who would not normally be part of political discussion – shoemakers, weavers, and tailors were particularly prominent – and membership dues of a penny per week reflected this ambition. It was at meetings such as these that of Paine's ideas would circulate, gaining audiences that would not have accessed those texts otherwise. Nonetheless, the LCS also had considerable success in attracting members from the professions, and counted doctors and lawyers among its numbers. A program of educational publication was also part of the LCS's remit. These included pamphlets, lectures, and periodicals, as well as the reprints of Paine's *Rights of Man* and the *The Age of Reason* (1795) in cheap and accessible formats.[7]

To its detractors, the LCS was a virulent cancer at the heart of English society that needed to be eradicated. John Reeves established the loyalist Society for the Preservation of Liberty and Property against Republicans and Levellers, which conducted an aggressive and successful campaign to suppress radical activities. The LCS was vilified and attacked in print and through arrests and legislation for sedition, particularly *after* the early glow of the French Revolution was dimmed for many British observers in the wake of Louis XVI's execution, the declaration of war with France, and the excesses of the Terror. The capacity of the LCS to organize mass meetings and to recruit was severely curtailed after a failed attempt by the government to convict leading members such as Thomas Hardy and John Thelwall of treason further caused conservative consternation. The Treason and Sedition bills – more commonly known as the Two Acts – were passed in 1795 and, as well as tightening up treason law, they prevented crowds gathering without a permit, thus making large LCS meetings illegal. In 1798 further mass arrests hobbled the LCS and it was outlawed by parliament in the following year.

Mary Wollstonecraft never betrayed, in her correspondence and published writings at least, much interest in the radical societies that emerged in the 1790s in the wake of the Revolution debate to which she made such a weighty contribution; nonetheless, the degree to which *A Vindication of the Rights of Woman* encouraged the consideration of female autonomy, political rights, education, and propriety by these societies is an important question. We should also acknowledge that she met many men who would go on to play a part in these societies, including the LCS, at Joseph Johnson's famous weekly dinners during the 1780s (Johnson himself was a member of the SCI). Richard Price, John Horne Tooke, Thomas Paine, Thomas Holcroft, and Joel Barlow were among those who were invited along to dine with the publisher; all were or would go on to be key actors in the political theater of the early and mid-1790s. Johnson's circle also included many prominent Dissenters – Anna Laetitia Barbauld, John Disney, and Joseph Priestley, for instance – and in the period 1787–90 there was a significant period of agitation, in which they were heavily involved, to repeal the Test and Corporation Acts (which denied Dissenting Protestants many civil rights).[8] Wollstonecraft was thoroughly immersed, through her writing for the *Analytical Review* and her mixing with Johnson's acquaintance, in the language and arguments of political and religious reform prior to the provocations of Burke's response to the French Revolution.

As Jon Mee has observed, women were only really present in the "interstices" of LCS activity.[9] Meetings were lubricated by considerable alcohol consumption, associated toasts, and much speech-making. The wives of well-known figures such as Susan Thelwall, Eliza Frost (married to John Frost, convicted of sedition in 1793), and Susannah Eaton (married to Daniel Isaac Eaton, radical publisher) were occasionally known to take part in radical activities (outside of divisional meetings), but none could be described as having an established public reputation for political activity or agency. The tragic death of Lydia Hardy is instructional: the Hardys' house was attacked by loyalists when Thomas was in custody awaiting trial for treason, and the trauma was widely believed to have contributed to her death (and that of her unborn child) in childbirth some weeks later. On his acquittal, a mournful Hardy accompanied by a crowd stood in silence outside their home. The trope of the suffering and pathetic female was reaffirmed even at the moment – the acquittal – that might be considered the apex of radical success. Despite the influential women operating within these radical circles, there was limited progress in terms of perceptions of female agency.

Leaving aside the vilification that Wollstonecraft received on her author-ship of the *Vindication*, there was certainly a strong sense that female participation in popular politics was monstrous and "out of nature," as Burke would have it. His lurid description of the "all the unutterable abominations of the furies of hell, in the abused shape of the vilest of women" in his *Reflections on the Revolution in France* (1790) was only echoed and exaggerated, as conservative anxieties increased, in his later *Letter to a Noble Lord* (1796) when he wrote of "obscene harpies . . . who in reality are foul and ravenous birds of prey (both mothers and daughters) . . . and souse down upon our tables, and leave nothing unrent, unrifled, unravaged, or unpolluted with the slime of their filthy offal."[10] The association of political agitation with the monstrous female can be seen in the visual culture of the period as well: witness the leering women pictured at the center of James Gillray's caricature of the most famous mass meeting of the LCS, *Copenhagen House* (1795), and the grotesque figures of Justice, Philanthropy, and Sensibility on the pedestals watching as a mob of political reformers storm St. Paul's Cathedral in his remarkable *New Morality* (1798). Textual and visual examples corroborate that while women may have been at the periphery of political activity, the representa-tion of their corrupted presence could confirm the horrific unnaturalness of the proceedings.

But questions relating to the participation of women in the public sphere were posed and discussed, and for that Wollstonecraft can take much credit. Jon Mee discusses elsewhere in this volume (Chapter 11), how "female patriots" and the "Rights of Woman" were toasted at LCS meetings and how the *Vindication* was advertised in cheap editions in various LCS publications. Perhaps another useful proxy for her impact on radicalism would be the degree to which female issues resonated with a radical society at the other end of the genteel spectrum (in terms of behavior, if not members) such as the highly selective Philomathian Society.

The major source of information about this club is William Godwin's diary, where he noted his dates of attendance and, crucially, many of the topics of debate.[11] The Philomaths were in existence from at least 1790, and the club met on Tuesday evenings for political discussion and dining. Godwin joined in December 1793, likely because of his indignation at the treatment of Thomas Muir, a reforming lawyer who had read out a provocative address from the United Irishmen at a public meeting in Edinburgh in 1792. Muir was convicted of sedition and was incarcerated in London, where Godwin visited him in December 1793 before he was transported. Godwin's decision may also have been motivated by the fact that he could discuss and debate political ideas with a broad spectrum of radicalism – members of the LCS, the SCI, and even the United Irishmen are among the known Philomaths – but within a safe environment, removed from the incendiary space, as Godwin would have it, of public meetings. Certainly, the one account we have of the meetings suggests a much less raucous affair than a LCS meeting, with Godwin and Holcroft dominating proceedings with long speeches that appear to have tested the patience of their fellow members.[12] Although we cannot know precisely how temperate the "collision of mind with mind" (Godwin's phrase on the necessity of frank and robust conversation for the production of philosophical truths) at these meetings actually was, we do know many of the topics of conversation they discussed thanks to Godwin's records. Subjects were largely to do with political reform and cultural matters, and included "drama," "theatres," "means of reform," "hair-powder" (tax on hair powder was a highly politicized matter), and "legislative power." As one might expect, there were debates around religion ("utility of religion" and "God," the latter discussed three times).[13]

But there is also substantial evidence that this private and exclusive male club (membership was restricted to twenty-one members at any one time) devoted considerable time to the question of how women would fit into their redrawn political landscape. Certainly, the reference to a discussion on May 13, 1794 on "prostitutes vs. parsons" does not give much away in terms of what was actually discussed or argued but further debates on "marriage" (June 3, 1794, February 17, 1795 and December 15, 1795), "sexes" (November 11, 1794), and "love" (December 23, 1794 and January 13, 1795) suggest that these men of reform understood that women needed to be accommodated in any reform program. But that the "sexes" were discussed on November 11, 1794 seems particularly significant.

This meeting took place less than a week after the recently widowed Thomas Hardy's acquittal on the charge of treason and his sad walk to his home on November 5. The Philomaths deciding to discuss the "sexes" while, we must remember, John Horne Tooke and John Thelwall still awaited their trial for treason, indicates that the tragic death of Lydia Hardy, a sad anticipation of Wollstonecraft's fate, may have been understood as more than simply a pathetic spectacle. Rather it appears to have been the catalyst for a serious discussion about the place of women within the radical movement. "Love" was to follow as a debate topic on December 23, 1794 and on January 13, 1795, after the collapse of the Treason Trials. Whether inspired by the memory of Lydia Hardy or not, these discussions indicate that at the very moment of radicalism's most jubilant moment, when plans were being made and ambition was soaring, these men, representing a broad array of political positions and radical organizations, saw that the relationships between the sexes and their mutual love and sympathy needed to be theorized and their force harnessed for the success of their political agenda.

There were other important and influential women in these radical circles, of course, women such as Mary Hays (who would re-introduce Godwin and Wollstonecraft in 1796), Amelia Alderson, and Charlotte Smith, for instance. Yet we cannot divorce Mary Wollstonecraft and her *Vindication* from these radical groups and their songs, debates, and discussions. Women's voices were not heard as directly as they had been in the earlier debating societies of the 1780s but, as Harriet Guest has argued so cogently, their remove from homosociality does not indicate a lack of commitment or zeal.[14] Such commitment bled through to many radical societies, even one as exclusive and diverse as the Philomaths.

Notes

1 "London Debates: 1786," in Donna T. Andrews, ed., *London Debating Societies: 1776–1799* (London, 1994), 176–93. *British History Online* www.british-history.ac.uk/london-record-soc/vol30/pp176-193 [Accessed 19 August 2017].

2 Mary Thale, "Women in London Debating Societies in 1780," *Gender & History*, 7:1 (1995), 5–24 and Donna T. Andrews, "Popular Culture and Public Debate: London 1780," *The Historical Journal*, 39:2 (1996), 405–23.

3 Mary Thale, "The Case of the British Inquisition: Money and Women in Mid-Eighteenth-Century London Debating Societies," *Albion*, 31:1 (1999), 31–48. Peter Clark points out that women were largely excluded from or

participated in a diminished capacity in the associational world of Georgian London: *British Clubs and Societies 1580–1800* (Oxford: Oxford University Press, 2000), 130–31, 198–204.

4 Cited in Jon Mee, *Print, Publicity, and Popular Radicalism in the 1790s: The Laurel of Liberty* (Cambridge: Cambridge University Press, 2016), 56.

5 Thale, "Women in Debating Societies in 1780," 21.

6 William Godwin, *An Enquiry Concerning Political Justice*, in *Political and Philosophical Writings of William Godwin*, edited by Mark Philp, 7 vols. (London: W. Pickering, 1993), 3: 118.

7 See the introduction to Michael T. Davis, ed., *London Corresponding Society, 1792–1799*, 6 vols. (London: Pickering & Chatto, 2002), 1.

8 Helen Braithwaite, *Romanticism, Publishing and Dissent: Joseph Johnson and the Cause of Liberty* (Basingstoke: Palgrave, 2003), 59–90.

9 Mee, *Laurel of Liberty*, 10.

10 *The Writings and Speeches of Edmund Burke*, edited by Paul Langford, 9 vols. (Oxford: Clarendon Press, 1981–2015), 3: 122, 9: 156.

11 *The Diary of William Godwin*, edited by Victoria Myers, David O'Shaughnessy, and Mark Philp (Oxford Digital Library, 2010) godwindiary.bodleian .ox.ac.uk.

12 John Binns, *Recollections of the Life of John Binns: Twenty-Five Years in Europe and Fifty-Three in the United States, Written by Himself, with Anecdotes, Political, Historical, and Miscellaneous* (Philadelphia: Parry & M'Millan, 1854), 45.

13 David O'Shaughnessy, "*Caleb Williams* and the Philomaths: Recalibrating Political Justice for the Nineteenth Century," *Nineteenth-Century Literature*, 66:4 (2012), 423–48.

14 Harriet Guest, *Unbounded Attachment: Sentiment and Politics in the Age of the French Revolution* (Oxford: Oxford University Press, 2013), 2, passim.

CHAPTER 11

Radical Publishers

Jon Mee

There are many senses in which Mary Wollstonecraft was a radical writer and thinker, not least through her association with her publisher Joseph Johnson and his circle. Johnson's bookselling business is often identified as "liberal," partly to distinguish it from the cheaper end of the spectrum of radical publishing that threw its weight behind democratic reform after the publication of the second part of Thomas Paine's *Rights of Man* in 1792. Given her close association with Johnson and her "literary" aspirations, it is no surprise that Wollstonecraft had no direct relationship with popular radicalism, but that does not mean that this movement or the many largely anonymous "female citizens" associated with it were uninterested in Wollstonecraft or her ideas.

In eighteenth-century terms, Johnson was a bookseller, that is, he combined publishing with retailing. By the end of the 1770s, he had become one of "an elite group of liberal, dissenting London booksellers who, sometimes in collaboration, were publishing most of the best writers in English, from poets to physicians."[1] Including these collaborative "congers" in the calculation, Johnson reached an average of more than one hundred titles a year over the course of the 1790s.[2] Johnson published everything Wollstonecraft wrote from *Thoughts on the Education of Daughters* (1787) through to the *Letters from Denmark, Sweden, and Norway* (1796). He also employed her regularly as a reviewer at the *Analytical*, right from its inception in 1788, covering especially educational books, novels, and travel writing. Wollstonecraft was certainly part of the inner circle of Johnson's authors, the coterie that dined above his book-shop, described by David Fallon elsewhere in this volume (Chapter 4), and to whom he gave advice at every stage of the writing and publishing process. Her *A Vindication of Rights of Men* (1790), published rapidly by Johnson in November 1790, was among the earliest responses to Burke's *Reflections on the Revolution in France* (1790), and was part of a larger flurry of responses to Burke published by Johnson.[3] Johnson was also the publisher of Wollstonecraft's posthumous works in collaboration with the brothers George and James Robinson. Dissenters of a similar stamp to Johnson and amiable competitors, the brothers Robinson had also published Godwin's *Political Justice* (1793).

Education was a major publishing field for Johnson, and most of Wollstonecraft's output fell within this specialism. Some contemporaries certainly read *A Vindication of the Rights of Woman* (1792) as part of an ongoing conversation within his publishing list advocating rational improvement for women. Most modern critics now see Wollstonecraft's book less as the work of a lone pioneer and more as part of the broad culture of Enlightenment feminism associated, especially, with Rational Dissent. Johnson published many of the authors involved in this formation, including important women writers like Anna Laetitia Barbauld, Elizabeth Hamilton, and, especially, Maria Edgeworth, and circulated publications from his networks in regional hubs like Manchester and Norwich that had politically active communities of Dissenters.[4] Thomas Cooper, who eventually emigrated from Manchester to join Johnson's friend Joseph Priestley in the United States, advocated female suffrage in a footnote to his response to an attack on him in Parliament by Edmund Burke. His associate in the Manchester Constitutional Society, George Philips, supported voting for women in his *Necessity of a Speedy and Effectual Reform in Parliament* (1793).[5]

My description of Wollstonecraft as part of Johnson's "coterie" of authors is designed to indicate something of the limits to the "liberal" or "literary" sociability of the publisher and his authors. "Literary" here may speak to the polite and respectable nature of the milieu of Johnson's shop, his weekly dinners for his authors, and his publishing list, but it should not suggest any kind of disconnect from practical politics. Johnson was a member of the Society of Constitutional Information (SCI), which played a very active role in the circulation of cheap editions of Paine's *Rights of Man* over 1791–92. Ultimately, however, apart from briefly on some copies of Part 1, withdrawn soon after going on sale, his name did not appear as publisher on the colophon of Paine's book, whose main publisher was to be J. S. Jordan, charged with seditious libel for his troubles. Along with Jordan, James Ridgeway and H. D. Symonds were the two most visible publishers imprisoned for circulating *Rights of Man* in cheap editions early on. Although he occasionally collaborated with them in congers, these booksellers were of a rather different stamp than Johnson. Each came from a different position in the marketplace, but none of them enjoyed the solidity or respectability of Johnson's business.

If Johnson was allied to the SCI, then it was the more inclusive and less genteel London Corresponding Society (LCS) with which these other publishers associated, although the two societies did not differ much on their programs for reform and often collaborated, for instance, on petitioning Parliament or in defense of the liberty of the press. When Johnson was finally arrested and imprisoned at the end of the decade, after Wollstonecraft's death, the shocked response was partly to do with the widely perceived respectability of his business that distinguished him from the many publishers imprisoned earlier in the 1790s.[6] After the trial of Paine and his publishers in 1792–93, Johnson became even more circumspect about the risks involved with publishing radical tracts. He does not even seem, for instance, to have been involved in the broad swathe of opinion, including many publishers, active in the Friends to the Liberty of the Press over 1792–93 before Richard Brinsley Sheridan brought its activities to a close. He also declined to publish the second part of the controversial *Advice to the Privileged Orders* by Wollstonecraft's friend Joel Barlow. It was Daniel Isaac Eaton who finally brought out Part 2 in 1795.[7]

Eaton was one of a second wave of publishers who emerged after Paine's trial with the aim of making the reform agenda more widely available in cheap publications. Although he later seems to have attended dinners at Johnson's and certainly acted as a mediator for him in some contractual disputes, in the early 1790s Eaton was a key member of the LCS and much closer to the popular movement than Wollstonecraft's publisher.[8] With Thomas Spence's cheap weekly *Pig's Meat* (1793–95), Eaton's periodical *Politics for the People* (1793–95) aimed to shake the established order of things by reprinting challenging texts from a range of sources, new and old, but they do not seem to have reprinted anything from Wollstonecraft in this period, despite the fact they often went beyond the LCS and SCI's shared program of annual parliaments and universal male suffrage.

By 1795, Eaton and Spence had been joined by other radical publishers, including Richard "Citizen" Lee, operating from various addresses at the sign of the Tree of Liberty, in circulating cheap penny tracts that Johnson and Wollstonecraft may have regarded as trash. The popular radical movement was and is often imagined in terms of a rough masculine world of the tavern and the pint pot that made women rights seem peripheral, but it did also canvas women's suffrage, especially after 1795, and its publishers showed a measure of interest in Wollstonecraft, although what she thought about them and their interest in her work – if she noticed it at all – is unrecorded. Generally speaking, together with much of the broader associational world of clubs and societies, in eighteenth-century Britain, women seem to have played no official part in the LCS, or even the SCI, which could be equally if not more boozy at its dinners, despite the LCS's publisher–poet–songwriter Robert Thomson printing toasts to "THE RIGHTS OF WOMAN!!!" and "the female patriots of Great Britain" in his *Tribute to Liberty* (1792).[9] The LCS also welcomed "the establishment of a female Society of Patriots" in 1793, but no record of it ever meeting survives. Individual women are to be glimpsed as presences within the interstices of LCS activities, often acting in support of their husband's activities, particularly running shops and businesses, including bookshops, when their husbands were imprisoned. Stella Thelwall, for instance, attended debates with her husband, John Thelwall, and provided commentary to her family on the development of radical opinion in London. Susannah Eaton ran her husband's shop when he was in prison or on the run. Lydia Hardy corresponded with her husband on the evolution of the LCS. More generally, though, the LCS seems to have aspired to the masculinity of most available definitions of citizenship, not least in the singing and toasting that were across eighteenth-century political associations. Lydia Hardy's death after her husband's arrest was generally presented as a deep intrusion into the domestic realm in places like Richard Lee's poem *On the Death of Mrs Hardy, Wife of Thomas Hardy* (1794), sold for 1d each or 7s per hundred to raise money for the families of imprisoned radicals.[10]

Nevertheless, as the work of Donna Andrew and Mary Thale has shown, there were debating societies where women were welcome and even entirely female societies where politics were debated in the 1780s.[11] One of these societies met in the spaces that Stella Thelwall went to see her husband defend freedom of speech in 1793. She wrote to her brother about her new status as a political woman, announced in her first letter: "things are gone to such a length that you see it even makes us women politicians." Stella Thelwall even contemplated imprisonment in the cause: "For my part, Mr T has taken such an active part in them, that I have been in expectation of accompanying him to prison. Well, if it should be so never mind. I think I might accompany him there in a much worse cause." Susannah Eaton took on those risks more directly by running the Cock and Swine bookshop when her husband was in flight, even once ushering her visitor Amelia Alderson in and closing the door to form a circle of radical friends. Alderson's presence in this scene indicates that gender boundaries in popular culture could be porous, but Harriet Guest has pointed out how networks of family and friends provided the unmarried Alderson with a unique kind of passport.[12] There is no record of Wollstonecraft enjoying this kind of experience within the print sociability of popular radicalism. Eaton's shop, in fact, was identified in spy reports as among the more commodious of the popular radical bookshops, certainly in comparison to Spence's premises at the Little Turnstile in Holborn or the changing venues of Lee's Tree of Liberty, associated as they were, at least among polite commentators, with chaos and even filth that would make them dubious spaces for any educated or "rational" woman anxious about her social status to be spotted.[13]

Despite the largely masculine ethos of popular forms of radicalism, there was some awareness of and support for Wollstonecraft's ideas from all these popular radical publishers. One of the most brilliant of the cheap satirical pamphlets published by Eaton was the *Pernicious Effects of the Art of Printing* (1794), which mocks anti-Jacobin outrage at "female productions" on political reform, especially "one in particular, called Rights of Woman, and in which, as one of their rights, a share in legislation is claimed and asserted."[14] Only by 1797 does Thomas Spence seem to have taken seriously the idea of women voting, in his *Rights of Infants*, although it later appears as a part of the republic utopia of Spensonia, but the category of the "female citizen" often appears in earlier publications associated with the LCS. For instance, the account of the large outdoor meeting held by the LCS on October 26, 1795, published by Lee, notes that the event was "crowded with Citizens, both male and female." If the language of invasions of privacy appears in its reference to a victimized cast of "the helpless widow and wretched orphan," in the account of the open meeting itself women were implicitly taken to be part of the more general "persevering efforts of reason."[15] John Gale Jones, who had spoken at the October meeting, embarked on a regional tour to assess support for the LCS in the wake of the passing of the repressive Convention Bills at the end of 1795. He recorded meeting several "female Citizens," one of whom had studied Wollstonecraft's *Rights of Woman* and told him: "A female Legislature, Sir, would never have passed those Convention Bills."[16]

Interestingly, the account of the October 1795 meeting published by Lee ends with an advertisement for a cheap edition of Wollstonecraft's *Rights of Woman*.[17] The advertisement also appears in his edition of the description of the LCS meeting held in November to protest against the government's attempt to navigate the Convention Bills through Parliament.[18] It seems unlikely that Lee ever brought out his cheap edition of Wollstonecraft, not least because he was arrested a few days after the November meeting. William Hodgson, another LCS member, produced a proposal – drawn up while he was in prison – for a treatise called

The Female Citizen, with Ridgeway and Symonds at the head of a conger of radical publishers receiving subscriptions. His address "To the Public" argued that "In a general Struggle for FREEDOM, ... it would be a scandalous Omission to overlook the Injuries of the FAIRER PART OF THE CREATION," but again there is no evidence the tract was ever published.[19] Like the 1793 proposal for a society of female patriots, Hodgson and Lee's advertisements suggest we should be careful of any assumption that the radical movement operated with an exclusively masculine notion of citizenship, predicated on restricting women to a domestic sphere understood as strictly separated from politics. Barbara Taylor points out that by the later 1790s Wollstonecraft's ideas, debated at places like the London Forum in 1797 and 1798, fitfully propagated by radical publishers though they may have been, had become "a widely acknowledged, if highly controversial, element in popular democratic thinking."[20]

Notes

1 John Barrell, "Divided We Grow," *London Review of Books*, 25:11 (June 5, 2003), 8–11: 11.
2 Barrell, "Divided We Grow," 11.
3 See Helen Braithwaite, *Romanticism, Publishing and Dissent: Joseph Johnson and the Cause of Liberty* (Basingstoke: Palgrave, 2003), chapter 4, on Johnson's contributions to the Revolution controversy and Wollstonecraft's place among them.
4 See Arianne Chernock's discussion of this point in *Men and the Making of Modern British Feminism* (Stanford: Stanford University Press, 2000), 2–3. Chernock, ibid., 20–21 and 25 mentions authors published in Manchester and Norwich who were published within Johnson's Unitarian networks, including Cooper and Philips (discussed below). She also looks at his role in encouraging women into print, 68–69.
5 See *A Reply to Mr. Burke's Invective against Mr. Cooper and Mr. Watt* (Manchester, 1792) and George Philips, *The Necessity of a Speedy and Effectual Reform in Parliament* (Manchester, 1793). Both pamphlets were published in Manchester, but Johnson was an important distributor of tracts published there. The third edition of Cooper's tract, in 1793, was "printed for" Johnson at St. Paul's Churchyard. Johnson was also the publisher of other works by Cooper. See Braithwaite, *Romanticism, Publishing and Dissent*, especially 120–21.
6 See G. P. Tyson, *Joseph Johnson: A Liberal Publisher* (Iowa: University of Iowa Press, 1979) and Braithwaite, *Romanticism, Publishing and Dissent* for details.
7 Johnson published the first part of Barlow's pamphlet in 1792, but decided not to print the manuscript of the second. How Eaton came to publish is described in 6–7 of Part II, brought out by Eaton in 1795.

8 See Joseph Johnson, *The Joseph Johnson Letterbook*, edited by John Bugg (Oxford: Oxford University Press, 2016), 104, 136. Godwin's diary records dining with Eaton at Johnson's in 1804 and 1805. See the online diary at godwindiary.bodleian.ox.ac.uk/search.html.

9 Robert Thomson, *A Tribute to Liberty: or, A New Collection of Patriotic Songs; entirely Original to which are added the Most Select Songs which have lately appeared in Public* ... (1793 [1792?]), 91, 93.

10 For details, see the discussions in Jon Mee, *Print, Publicity, and Popular Radicalism in the 1790s: The Laurel of Liberty* (Cambridge: Cambridge University Press, 2016), 57–58.

11 See Donna T. Andrew, "Popular Culture and Public Debate: London 1780," *Historical Journal*, 39 (1996), 405–23; and Mary Thale, "London Debating Societies in the 1790s," *Historical Journal*, 32 (1989), 57–86, and "Women in London Debating Societies in 1780," *Gender & History*, 7 (1995), 5–24.

12 Harriet Guest, *Unbounded Attachment: Sentiment and Politics in the Age of the French Revolution* (Oxford: Oxford University Press, 2013), 145.

13 See the discussion of the descriptions of the different bookshops in Jon Mee, "'Bread & Cheese & Porter Only Being Allowed': Radical Spaces in London, 1792–1795," in Kevin Gilmartin, ed., *Sociable Places: Locating Culture in Romantic-Period Britain* (Cambridge: Cambridge University Press, 2017), 51–69, at 57.

14 Anon. *The Pernicious Effects of the Art of Printing upon Society, Exposed* (1794[?]), 9.

15 See *Account of the Proceedings of a Meeting of the London Corresponding Society, Held in a Field near Copenhagen House, Monday, Oct. 26... 1795* (1795), 4, 5, 8.

16 John Gale Jones, *Sketch of a Political Tour through Rochester, Chatham, Maidstone, Gravesend, &c. Including Reflections on the Tempers and Dispositions of the Inhabitants of Those Places* (1796), 91. Jordan published the pamphlet.

17 Ibid., 16

18 See *Account of the Proceedings of a Meeting of the Inhabitants of Westminster, in Palace-Yard, Monday, Nov. 26, 1795,* where an advertisement for a new sixpenny edition of *Rights of Woman* by "Mrs Wolstonecraft" appears on the final page.

19 *Proposals for Publishing by Subscription ... the Female Citizen* [n.p.].

20 Barbara Taylor, *Mary Wollstonecraft and the Feminist Imagination* (Cambridge: Cambridge University Press, 2003), 177, and Donna T. Andrew, ed., *London Debating Societies: 1776–1799* (London: London Record Society, 1994), *British History Online* www.british-history.ac.uk/london-record-soc/vol30 [Accessed 19 June 2017].

CHAPTER 12

British Conservatism

Paul Keen

For Mary Wollstonecraft, the numerous cultural and political debates that
constituted the public life of British citizens in the final years of the
eighteenth century boiled down to some fundamental choices. As she
put it in her discussion of Rousseau (a philosopher whose blend of
republicanism and misogyny made him an important part of her thinking
about the rights and wrongs of her age), "Rousseau exerts himself to prove
that all *was* right originally; a crowd of authors that all *is* now right; and I,
that all will *be* right."[1] Conservative thinkers would never have endorsed
Rousseau's primitivism, which provided a rationale for wholesale revolution against the ills of modern civilization, and they would likely have
considered it a stretch to say that all *was* right in contemporary Britain.
From the age of Pope and Swift onwards, conservative thinkers tended to
align themselves with a vision of decline that had been hastened by the
effeminizing influence of Britain's consumer revolution. But in the deeply
polarized climate of the 1790s, and in the face of growing demands for
radical democratic reform from an extended public that had never before
presumed to participate in the political process, the present (or at least the
pre-1789 version of it) was looking good.

However much the polarizing effects of tumultuous eras tend to create
an impression of homogeneity on all sides, the real political landscape is
almost always far more nuanced and, in many ways, conflicted. As critics
such as Kevin Gilmartin have emphasized, British conservatism in the
1790s was characterized by a number of competing perspectives, from a
Burkean lament for the death of an age of chivalry to more cautious
thinkers who insisted on the virtues of contemporary Britain, which they
celebrated as the epitome of a polite modern nation energized by commerce and dignified by inherited forms of sociability, to other critics whose
conservatism was infused with reformist energies of its own. Considered
closely enough, most conservatives' thinking included aspects of all three
of these positions. William Pitt himself, who responded to the threats of

radical upheaval with an equally extreme crackdown fueled by an extended network of spies, support for pro-government writers and magazines, draconian legislation designed to curtail people's time-honored rights, and a wave of prosecutions, had originally been elected Prime Minister on a promise to reform Britain's corrupt electoral system. Needless to say, this was no longer on the table in the 1790s.

As the political temperature rose after the outbreak of the French Revolution, however, a growing awareness that differences with reformers greatly outweighed differences among themselves tended to encourage conservatives to coalesce around a group of key stances, all of which would have an enormous influence on the arguments developed by reformers such as Wollstonecraft. On the most immediate level, conservatives insisted that radicals were not only reckless in their thinking in ways that would prove disastrous if they were allowed to succeed, they did not even really support the reforms they claimed to, either because they were too thick to appreciate the full implications of these positions, or, far worse, because they were actively disingenuous, preaching democratic reform in order to promote their own private agendas. Repeated loudly enough and often enough, these became powerful narratives that reformers found difficult to counter. Underlying this, as David Simpson and others have argued, was a broader insistence on Britain's fundamentally traditional character, a position that could best be depicted by contrasting it with the flightiness of the French, who were only behaving like Frenchmen when they threw away the blessings of their monarchical government in favor of a few untried theories. Having spent most of the century at war with each other, this was a predictably popular refrain. Satirical cartoons frequently juxtaposed the sturdy satisfactions of an English farmer and his family, sitting down to a good roast beef dinner, with the haggard image of an emaciated Frenchman salivating over a grotesque plate of frog legs. For those who subscribed to these sorts of contrasts, John Bull, with his gruff but plainspoken character, agrarian roots, distrust of foreign ideas, and disdain for theories that had never been put to the test, had never looked better, however divorced this image may have been from the lived realities of most of those who advocated conservative principles most forcefully in public life. This visceral level of argument, with its blend of personal attack, nostalgia for a past that most Britons had never known, and dark conspiratorial accusations, constituted a major challenge for reformers. On a far more profound level, though, British conservatism was informed by a critique not just of the limitations of reformers, whom they depicted as extremists, but of the Enlightenment itself. This critique, which was both

highly nuanced and longstanding within British thought, raised particularly serious problems for critics such as Wollstonecraft and her fellow
reformers because it rejected Enlightenment assumptions about the inherently progressive force of critical debate altogether.

For conservatives, reformers' claim to the title of philosophers epitomized these various problems. T. J. Mathias was striking a popular chord
when he insisted, in his *Pursuits of Literature*, that "[t]here is one description and sect of men, to whom more than common reprehension is due,
and who cannot be held up too frequently to the public scorn and
abhorrence. I mean the modern philosophers of the French system."[2]
Richard Polwhele, whose satirical poem *The Unsex'd Females* (1798)
borrowed its title from Mathias's poem, echoed Matthias in his denunciation of "[p]hilosophism, the false image of philosophy … a phantom
which heretofore appeared not in open day, though it now attempts the
loftiest flights in the face of the sun."[3] Ironically, conservatives argued,
these self-inflated intellectual pretensions had helped to erode rather than
advance intellectual life. The spirit of self-sufficiency that flowed from
reformers' exaggerated sense of their own capacity for reason and the
arrogance of their collective certainty of the intellectual superiority of the
present day had produced an overweening confidence in their critical
abilities that had, paradoxically, fostered a dangerous sense of
complacency.

For conservatives, a central part of this problem lay in the expanded
public which the reform movement had managed to mobilize, and to
which the protean force of print culture adapted itself all too easily. These
issues emerged in their rawest form in courtroom dramas such as Thomas
Paine's trial for seditious libel for *Rights of Man* Part Two. The political
risk of being seen to be intolerant made prosecuting an author for expressing his or her views a hazardous enterprise, and the Attorney General, Sir
Archibald Macdonald, who argued the case himself, was careful to articulate the government's position in ways that confronted this danger head
on. In doing so, he shone an important light on larger conservative
principles. Far from being an enemy of free speech, he insisted, he was
so deeply in favor of it that he felt compelled to defend it from those
radicals who sought to abuse it. The proof of this, he suggested, was that
Paine had not been arrested for Part One of *Rights of Man*, which had
appeared the previous year:

> Reprehensible as that book was, extremely so, in my opinion, yet it was
> ushered into the world under circumstances that led me to conceive that it

would be confined to the judicious reader, and when confined to the judicious reader, it appeared to me that such a man would refute as he went along.[4]

However offensive the ideas it contained were, it had been published in a standard format, and at a high enough price that it could be counted on to attract an audience that was capable of wrestling with ideas, however inflammatory, without being stirred into action. But Part Two had been published in very different formats, and this new medium changed the message in ways that rendered it criminal by courting the attention of a readership that was wholly incapable of responding critically to dangerous ideas:

> Gentlemen, when I found that another publication was ushered into the world still more reprehensible than the former; that in all shapes, in all sizes, with an industry incredible, it was either totally or partially thrust into the hands of all persons in this country, of subjects of every description; when I found that even children's sweetmeats were wrapped up with parts of this, and delivered into their hands, in the hope that they would read it; when all industry was used, such as I describe to you, in order to obtrude and force this upon that part of the public whose minds cannot be supposed to be conversant with subjects of this sort, and who cannot therefore correct as they go along, I thought it behoved me upon the earliest occasion, which was the first day of the term succeeding this publication, to put a charge upon record against its author.[5]

The point was made repeatedly during this period: publishing a radical text in a cheap format and in an accessible style was a sure sign of its criminality. Left to their own devices, these plebeian readers would never have sought it out. However outrageous reformers may have felt that this class bias was, it reflected a core principle of conservative thought: not everyone was qualified to think in adequately complex ways about the larger issues that affected the good of the nation. Nor, they suggested, was this condescending, since the lower orders, where they understood their true interests, had no desire to meddle in these affairs. Tracts such as Hannah More's *Village Politics* contrasted wise and contented locals, such as Jack the blacksmith, with the disgruntled immaturity of troublemakers, such as Tom, who has discovered his lack of liberty from a radical pamphlet.

This question about the kinds of knowledge that different social groups should engage with extended to women as well, though in this case the prohibition tended to be cultural rather than legal. Women were to be mocked, rather than arrested, for wandering into the kinds of debates for which they were inherently ill-suited. When it came to questions of gender, even writers and magazines that were normally associated with the progressive cause could lapse into chauvinism. In its review of Margaret Bryan's *Letters on Natural Philosophy*, the *Monthly Review* politely but firmly warned that "Politics, Greek, and Analytics, are generally forbidden to the ladies: too much study will spoil their engaging faces and their fascinating manners." These intellectual domains "may be visited for curiosity and amusement," it allowed, "but against a formal inroad and invasion of female Philosophers we shall take arms."[6] In *The Unsex'd Females*, Polwhele expressed his alarm with the fact that "I have, several times, seen boys and girls botanizing together," an activity that could only lead to more serious lapses.[7]

For conservatives, though, it was not just that some women, fired up by the radical energies of the day, had wandered into subjects for which they were not intended. As critics such as Hannah More argued, women's natural fondness for excess reinforced the worst problems of modern literature generally. Protesting against "the swarms of Abridgments, Beauties, and Compendiums, which form too considerable a part of a young lady's library," More warned about women's susceptibility to a vicious cycle that threatened to destroy modern literature.[8] More was relatively progressive in her support for women's access to the kind of "serious study [that] serves to harden the mind for more trying conflicts," especially, she argued, since these examples tended to discourage young readers from any belief that they could imitate them.[9] But too often, she warned, this was not the case. Exposure to the worst kinds of trifling literature fostered a mistaken belief in women's own literary abilities:

> Who are those ever multiplying authors, that with unparalleled fecundity are overstocking the world with their quick succeeding progeny? They are novel writers; the easiness of whose productions is at once the cause of their own fruitfulness, and of the almost infinitely numerous race of imitators to whom they give birth. Such is the frightful facility of this species of composition, that every raw girl while she reads, is tempted to fancy that she can also write.[10]

As critics such as Catherine Gallagher and Catherine Ingrassia have argued, conservative reactions were intensified by what they denounced as a set of mutually reinforcing parallels between the vacuousness and instability of women, commerce, and print culture, with each of these narratives reinforcing the apparent validity of the other two.

These dynamics put women reformers such as Wollstonecraft in a doubly untenable position, caught in the crosshairs of anti-Jacobin and misogynistic denunciations. But it would be a mistake to equate conservatism with a set of purely reactionary postures driven by the revolutionary energies of the decade. At its most profound, eighteenth-century conservatism was ultimately a rejection of the core values of the Enlightenment itself. For reformers, the belief that critical debate among a growing number of informed people would inevitably "dispel those clouds of ignorance, and ... disperse that mass of errour, which have hitherto been so baneful to society" was a philosophical cornerstone.[11] It was a bold recipe for unfettered and energetic debate, whether in print or in the clubs and coffee houses that were hailed as a sign of this new enlightened age. As William Godwin put it in *Political Justice*: "If there be such a thing as truth, it must infallibly be struck out by the collision of mind with mind ... All that is requisite in these discussions is unlimited speculation, and a sufficient variety of systems and opinions."[12]

For conservatives, this was not just wishful thinking; it was an ill-considered delusion that was flawed by several fundamental errors. Not only did it seriously overrate the intellectual quality of the discussions that were going on in these venues, its assumption that people were fundamentally rational – that they were predisposed to be persuaded by the force of the better argument, and capable of wrestling with inflammatory ideas without being roused into action – was dangerously reductive. Just as worrying, its emphasis on the intellectual capacities of each individual overshadowed the received wisdom of past generations. And perhaps most dangerous of all, enthusiastic talk of "unlimited speculation" promoted a gladiatorial atmosphere between antagonists who, having nothing to lose personally and being unencumbered with any of the actual responsibilities of government, were concerned only with making a name for themselves. Every one of these problems was worrying in itself, conservatives warned, but taken together they represented an almost apocalyptic threat to Britain's most valuable achievements.

The most famous declaration of these warnings came in Edmund Burke's *Reflections on the Revolution in France*, which mocked the grandiose ambitions of the Enlightenment reformers whose debates Burke dismissed as the "shallow speculations of the petulant, assuming, short-sighted coxcombs of philosophy."[13] Personalizing these issues in rhetorically powerful ways, Burke insisted that he was "influenced by the inborn feelings of my nature, and not ... illuminated by a single ray of this new-sprung modern light."[14] For Burke, the corrosive effects of "this new conquering empire of light and reason" were fundamentally hostile to the goal of promoting social harmony, but, he warned, these so-called philosophers were not really interested in promoting their country's best interests anyway: "considering their speculative designs as of infinite value, and the actual arrangement of the state as of no estimation, they are at best indifferent about it."[15] Rather than being seduced by these false promises, Burke notoriously insisted, he could take heart in the fact that however foolish the French may be, sensible Englishmen knew better: "we are generally men of untaught feelings ... instead of casting away all our old prejudices, we cherish them to a very considerable degree, and, to take more shame to ourselves, we cherish them because they are prejudices; and the longer they have lasted and the more generally they have prevailed, the more we cherish them."[16] As Burke was well aware, few critiques of the Enlightenment were more powerful in this highly charged atmosphere than the suggestion that, at the end of the day, it simply was not very English. Few arguments would be harder to dislodge, particularly for women reformers such as Wollstonecraft, whose claims to rational argument could be dismissed as a doubly heinous intrusion on this fabled national past anchored in a reassuring sense of gender difference.

Notes

1 Mary Wollstonecraft, *The Works of Mary Wollstonecraft*, edited by Janet Todd and Marilyn Butler (London: W. Pickering, 1989), 5: 84.
2 T. J. Mathias, *The Pursuits of Literature, or What You Will: A Satirical Poem in Dialogue*, 3rd edn., vol. 4 (London, 1797), xxiv.
3 Richard Polwhele, *The Unsex'd Females: A Poem, Addressed to the Author of The Pursuits of Literature* (London, 1798), 10.
4 Quoted in Thomas Erskine, *The Speeches of Thomas Erskine*, compiled by James Ridgway, 2nd edn., 1810 (reprinted London: Garland Publishing, 1974), 2: 47–48.
5 Ibid., 48.
6 *Monthly Review*, 51 (1806), 382.
7 Polwhele, *The Unsex'd Females*, 10.
8 Hannah More, *Strictures on the Modern System of Female Education* (London, 1799), 1: 160.
9 Ibid., 165.
10 Ibid., 169.
11 *Analytical Review*, 22 (1795), 545.
12 William Godwin, *Political and Philosophical Writings of William Godwin*, edited by Mark Philp (London: W. Pickering, 1993), 3: 15.
13 Edmund Burke, *The Works of the Right Honourable Edmund Burke* (Boston: Little, Brown, & Company, 1889), 3: 299.
14 Ibid., 329.
15 Ibid., 332–33, 315.
16 Ibid., 346.

The Rights of Woman Debate

CHAPTER 13

Jacobin Reformers

Mary Fairclough

Barbara Taylor notes that though Mary Wollstonecraft is often seen as an "individual pioneer . . . setting her among her fellow radical literatae, the first coterie of women intellectuals to intervene in British reform politics, gives a truer sense of her historic significance."[1] This chapter investigates how Wollstonecraft's life and professional practice entwined with those of three of her contemporaries, Mary Hays, Mary Robinson, and Charlotte Smith. The reception of reformist causes underwent a sea change during the 1790s, and I analyze how Wollstonecraft, Hays, Robinson, and Smith respond to such change. The first part explores the response to Wollstonecraft's *A Vindication of the Rights of Woman* in 1792–93, when it is possible for Jacobin writers to celebrate and advance the "linked" causes of women's rights and political reform.[2] The second part investigates the period following Wollstonecraft's death, from 1797–99, when anti-Jacobin reaction makes it difficult to advance any reformist cause, and the polemical writings and fiction of Wollstonecraft, Hays, Robinson, and Smith articulate a complication of, and even dissatisfaction with, earlier claims for equality.

Wollstonecraft was acquainted with Hays, Robinson, and Smith, and engaged closely with their work, though the nature of these relationships varied. Her most sustained friendship was with Hays, whom she met in 1792. Wollstonecraft supported Hays' writing career, lent her books and sternly critiqued her work.[3] In early 1796 Hays reintroduced Wollstonecraft to William Godwin. At that time Wollstonecraft also socialized with Mary Robinson, and she reported to Hays that Robinson "has read your novel, and was *very much* pleased with the *main* story but did not like the conclusion."[4] Wollstonecraft and Robinson became distanced in the last months of Wollstonecraft's life, but Robinson sustained her friendship with Godwin until her own death. Wollstonecraft did not know Smith well; they only met once, in July 1797.[5] But she reviewed Smith's work warmly for the *Analytical Review* throughout the 1790s. Wollstonecraft was the central mutual acquaintance in this "coterie," but Smith and Hays later collaborated on a *History of England* published in 1806, though Smith and Robinson never met.[6] Hays, Robinson, and Smith shared a deep admiration for Wollstonecraft, but they explored the ways in which calls for equality, and the supreme confidence with which Wollstonecraft could assert that the mind should "rest" on its own powers, became warped and strained in the late 1790s.

* * *

Wollstonecraft's *Vindication of the Rights of Woman*, published in January 1792, elicited admiration and delight in reformist circles. Despite Wollstonecraft's self-presentation as a pioneer, fellow reformists were quick to group her with her female contemporaries. George Dyer's "Ode on Liberty" (1792) represented liberty urging "Wollstonecraft to break the charm, / Where beauty lies in durance vile opprest." Dyer notes that "the most sensible females, when they turn their attention to political subjects, are more uniformly on the side of liberty than the other sex," and connects the rights of women with reformist causes more broadly, supporting his claims with references to women writers including Smith and Hays.[7] Likewise on December 18, 1792 the British Club at Paris toasted "the Women of Great Britain, particularly those who have distinguished themselves by their writings in favour of the French Revolution," singling out Smith for praise.[8] At this moment of confidence, the impulse to group women writers is a statement of co-operation, though it foreshadows later developments in which these women could be maligned as a body of "unsex'd females."[9]

Smith's novel *Desmond*, published in June 1792, in large part created her reputation as a reformer. *Desmond* painted a sympathetic picture of French revolutionists, and critiqued British conservatives, while connecting the causes of women's rights and political reform. Smith signals her response to Wollstonecraft in her Preface, declaring: "But women it is said have no business with politics.—Why not?—Have they no interest in the scenes that are acting around them, in which they have father, brothers, husbands, sons, or friends engaged!"[10] Though Smith offers women mediated access to the public sphere through their male relations, she shows how writing and publication constitute political acts, echoing Wollstonecraft's claims for the importance of female education in the *Vindication*: "Knowledge, which qualifies women to speak or to write on any other than the most ... trivial subjects, is supposed to be of so difficult attainment, that it cannot be acquired but by the sacrifice of domestic virtues . . . —*I* however, may safely say that it was in the *observance*, not in the *breach* of duty, *I* became an Author."¹¹ Like Wollstonecraft, Smith declares that women's education and participation in political debate is compatible with domesticity.

The broadly positive critical reception of *Desmond* demonstrated that in 1792 "it was still possible in Britain to hear a civil debate," but this changed with the September Massacres in France and the introduction of "rigid censorship" in Britain in early 1793.¹² It was in these months that Hays published her *Letters and Essays Historical and Miscellaneous* (1793). Hays' volume is a confident celebration of the causes advocated by Wollstonecraft, though she notes how political events are making these causes more difficult to espouse: "I almost shudder at the present general diffusion of political knowledge; for however I approve the principles, the desolations in a neighbouring country, make me tremble at the very idea of the dangers . . . attending the practice."¹³ Though "posterity" will see the reward of such diffusion of knowledge, Hays bemoans the turmoil that must precede it.

Such moments of doubt are rare in Hays' *Letters and Essays*, which assert the inevitable success of reform: "The feeble efforts of prejudice and interest must in the end give way to truth, however gradual may be their declining struggles . . . Our nature is progressive, and every thing around us is the same."¹⁴ Hays presents Wollstonecraft's work as an engine of such progressive thought in her Preface, paying "a tribute of public respect in the name of my sex . . . to the virtue and talents of a writer, who with equal courage and ability hath endeavoured to rescue the female mind from those prejudices, by which it has been systematically weakened."¹⁵ Wollstonecraft noted to Hays before publication, "I do not approve of your preface" and advised her to "Rest on yourself—if your essays have merit they will stand alone."¹⁶ Though Hays did not revise the Preface, Wollstonecraft's exhortation becomes a touchstone in her later work.

Hays' essays match Wollstonecraft's *Vindication* in many of their claims. She advocates for women's education, bemoans the immorality of the rich, declares that the present condition of women is bondage, states that learning will not unfit women for domestic life, and emphasizes the importance of genuine rather than apparently virtuous behavior.¹⁷ But Hays places greater emphasis than Wollstonecraft on the practical difficulties that women encounter in earning a living.¹⁸ And though she declares men and women equal, Hays does not follow Wollstonecraft in denying the existence of an essential "sexual character" and in condemning the effects of fashionable sensibility on women.¹⁹ Hays notes that "similarity of mind and principles is the only true basis of harmony," but suggests that the sexes are different but equal. As Miriam Wallace notes, Hays "uses an essentialist move to create a feminine space" that she develops in her fiction, in which sensibility is a catalyst of rational thought.[20] Hays thus celebrates Wollstonecraft while raising issues that she, Robinson, and Smith develop in their fiction and polemical prose.

* * *

Wollstonecraft's posthumous *The Wrongs of Woman* (1798) returns to her calls for "a revolution in female manners" and re-examines the power of these claims in the face of entrenched customs and institutions.[21] In 1797–99 Hays, Robinson, and Smith undertake a similar re-evaluation of earlier claims, and they deal with the vicious reaction to Godwin's *Memoirs of the Author of A Vindication of the Rights of Woman* (1798), which made any assertion of women's rights and any praise of Wollstonecraft a dangerous political act.[22] Hays, Robinson, and Smith all push back against such reaction. Hays exemplifies this courage in her obituary of Wollstonecraft in the *Monthly Magazine* of September 1797. She celebrates Wollstonecraft's "admirable talents," "active humanity," and "exquisite sensibility," and echoing Wollstonecraft's advice of 1793, praises "her ardent, ingenuous, unconquerable spirit . . . [which] rested firmly on its own resources and powers."[23] Robinson and Smith did not write memoirs but paid tribute to Wollstonecraft in their works.

In June 1798 Smith published her novel *The Young Philosopher*, which articulates a remarkable protest against "things as they are" given the repressive environment in which it appeared. She had studied Godwin's *Caleb Williams* (1793) as she composed her novel, but like Hays and Robinson at this period, she also seems to take inspiration from Wollstonecraft's *Wrongs of Woman*. Smith's Preface registers her allegiance to "a Writer whose talents I greatly honoured, and whose untimely death I deeply regret."[24] Smith cites Wollstonecraft twice, but also signals how she is engaged in a common political project to make visible the systematic suppression of women's rights.[25] Smith's heroines, mother and daughter Laura and Medora Glenmorris, both articulate in first-person narratives how they have faced abduction, sexual threat, extortion, and slander, as Laura is powerless to prevent her sufferings being revisited on Medora. The Glenmorrises eventually leave England for America, for as Laura notes, "here I shall be haunted by the images of lawyers, the dread of persecution . . . I shall be incapable of happiness."[26] Though Smith's representation of persecution draws on *Caleb Williams*, like Robinson, Hays, and Wollstonecraft, she demonstrates how persecution "is redoubled in the experience of women."[27] But despite the inept actions of the novel's heroes, the female protagonists of *The Young Philosopher* do have the protection of male companions. In contrast, in 1798 and 1799 Hays and Robinson each produce a novel and a polemical tract exploring the fates of women who are entirely unprotected.

In signs of caution, Hays's *Appeal to the Men of Great Britain in Behalf of Women* (1798) is published anonymously, and Robinson's *Letter to the Women of England, on the Injustice of Mental Subordination* (1799) under the pseudonym Anne Randall. Yet both tracts uphold the principles of Wollstonecraft's *Vindication*, while also emphasizing issues that they increasingly see as pressing, namely practical opportunities for women, and the need for the reform of men's behavior. Hays's Advertisement notes her debt to Wollstonecraft's *Vindication*, but also distinguishes her approach, noting that whereas Wollstonecraft is a "genius; who seldom deigns ... to make new and unexpected truths palatable to common minds," she will undertake the task of "gradual reformation" through appeals to common sense.[28]

Hays follows the *Vindication* in her claims that "woman" is an artificial creation of men, but that through a rational education, women might acquire equality. She names roles in which women might flourish in literature, or even as "a Chancellor, a Bishop, a Judge, or a General."[29] But Hays still differs from Wollstonecraft on sexual characteristics, noting that in their "extreme delicacy" women's character "differs essentially from man's."[30] Despite gendered differences, requiring different social roles, Hays argues for "that equality which holds a people, a nation, a world equipoised."[31] But though Hays concludes that men need only "make women happy ... by considering them as rational beings upon a footing with themselves" she acknowledges that this aim is obstructed by men's self-interest.[32] When they realize "the first step ... [is] the reformation of the moral conduct of the men themselves ... [then] men ... are not ashamed to declare, that they would rather a thousand times take women as they are."[33] For Hays, male vice is an immovable obstacle.

Robinson in her *Letter* notes her debt to Wollstonecraft, but declares that "the same subject may be argued in a variety of ways ... For it requires a *legion of Wollstonecrafts* to undermine the poisons of prejudice and malevolence."[34] Like Hays she focuses on men's repression of the rights of women, and on opportunities for women to support themselves, and she insists on equality of opportunity despite gendered differences.[35] Anticipating her novel *The Natural Daughter*, Robinson assesses the options for women who have lost the protection of husband or family, emphasizing the destitution hinted at by Smith in *The Young Philosopher*. Such a woman "flies to her own sex, they ... avoid her. She talks of punishing the villain who has destroyed her: he smiles at the menace, and tells her, *she* is a WOMAN."[36] Yet the *Letter* also makes claims for equality, declaring "WOMAN is a thinking and an enlightened being!" and naming Wollstonecraft among others as examples.[37] Learning forms the crux of Robinson's argument; she lists scholarly women back to antiquity, and declares that "the press will be the monument from which the genius of British women will rise to immortal celebrity."[38] Robinson catalyzes activism through example, concluding with "names, which, while they silence the tongue of prejudice, will note fail to EXCITE EMULA-TION."[39] Robinson names Hays, Smith, and Wollstonecraft, and herself.

Despite the confidence of Robinson's *Letter*, *The Natural Daughter* (1799) investigates how the "tongue of prejudice" can blight genius. Though light in tone, Robinson's novel chronicles the bleak fate of Martha Morley, who is falsely accused of infidelity and cast out, then dogged by rumor and scandal. Martha finds work as an actress and a writer, but Robinson represents the precariousness of such labor: "The busy metropolis ... presented a variety of roads to independence: but a female without protection ... a being, who seemed alone even in the midst of multitudes, had little to hope for from a world selfish and prejudging."[40] Authorship offers Martha respite, but she is cheated, and even incarcerated in an asylum, until saved by a fortuitous sequence of deaths and marriage. Robinson suggests that a lone woman cannot prevail over such difficulties.

While Martha is only suspected of sexual impropriety, Mary Raymond, heroine of Hays's *The Victim of Prejudice* (1799), is an actual victim of rape. To a greater extent than Robinson, Hays unpacks the difficulties she raises in her *Appeal*: "when we consider ... how difficult the return to virtue is made; we must balance well, before we judge rigorously."[41] Hays returns to this and to the *Appeal*'s censure of libertinism in her Advertisement, noting: "*Man* has hitherto been solicitous ... to indulge his own voluptuousness and to counteract its baneful tendencies: not less tragical than absurd have been the consequences!"[42] Hays's narrative confirms the precarious state of female virtue, given the actions of men. In an echo of Smith's *Young Philosopher*, two generations of women are ruined. Mary's mother relates how her education contributed to her seduction, and disgrace: "I perceived myself the victim of the injustice, of the prejudice, of society, which, by opposing to my return to virtue almost insuperable barriers, had plunged me into irremediable ruin."[43] Sir Peter Osbourne notes after he rapes Mary that "What is called in your sex honour and character, can ... never be restored to you; nor will any asseverations ... obliterate the stain."[44] Mary, like Robinson's Martha, seeks employment at a printer's, but is abused and dismissed. Unlike Robinson, Hays provides no fortuitous marriage to save Mary, who dies in poverty. Rejecting the aid of her faithless sweetheart, she repeats Wollstonecraft's maxim: "to confide in the heart of man is to lay up stores for sorrow; henceforth I rest on myself."[45] Hays never forgot Wollstonecraft's instruction. In her memoir for *The Annual Necrology* (1800), she cites a letter in which Wollstonecraft declares: "I am easy with regard to the opinions of the *best* part of mankind – I *rest* on my own."[46] But for women without Wollstonecraft's extraordinary strengths, Hays, Robinson, and Smith suggest, inveterate prejudices confound their claims to independence and equality.

Notes

1 Barbara Taylor, *Mary Wollstonecraft and the Feminist Imagination* (Cambridge: Cambridge University Press, 2003), 178.
2 Miriam L. Wallace, "Mary Hays's Female Philosopher: Constructing Revolutionary Subjects," in Adriana Craciun and Kari Lokke, eds., *Rebellious Hearts: British Women Writers and the French Revolution* (Albany: SUNY Press, 2001), 233.
3 Mary Hays, *The Correspondence (1779–1843) of Mary Hays, British Novelist*, edited by Marilyn L. Brooks (Lewiston: Edwin Mellen Press, 2004), 307–09.
4 Ibid., 309–10.
5 Stuart Curran, "Charlotte Smith, Mary Wollstonecraft and the Romance of Real Life," in Jacqueline Labbe, ed., *The History of British Women's Writing, Volume 5, 1750–1830*, (Basingstoke: Palgrave Macmillan, 2010), 195.
6 Harriet Guest, "Charlotte Smith, Mary Robinson and the First Year of the War with France," in *History of British Women's Writing*, 207–08.
7 George Dyer, *Poems* (London: J. Johnson, 1792), 36, 37.
8 Amy Garnai, *Revolutionary Imaginings: Charlotte Smith, Mary Robinson, Elizabeth Inchbald* (Basingstoke: Palgrave Macmillan 2009), 22.
9 Richard Polwhele, *The Unsex'd Females* (London: Cadell & Davies, 1798).
10 Charlotte Smith, *Desmond*, edited by Stuart Curran (London: Pickering & Chatto, 2005), 3.
11 Ibid., 3–4.
12 Stuart Curran, "Introduction," in *Desmond*, xvi.
13 Mary Hays, *Letters and Essays, Moral, and Miscellaneous* (London: T. Knott, 1793), 17–18.
14 Ibid., 13.
15 Ibid., v.
16 Brooks, ed., *Correspondence*, 302–03.

17 Hays, *Letters and Essays*, 10, 15, 19–20, 26–27, vii.
18 Ibid., 84.
19 Mary Wollstonecraft, *A Vindication of the Rights of Woman*, in *The Works of Mary Wollstonecraft*, edited by Janet Todd and Marilyn Butler (New York: New York University Press, 1989), 5: 122.
20 Hays, *Letters and Essays*, 22.
21 Wollstonecraft, *Vindication*, 114.
22 Claudia L. Johnson, *Equivocal Beings: Politics, Gender, and Sentimentality in the 1790s – Wollstonecraft, Radcliffe, Burney, Austen* (Chicago: University of Chicago Press, 2009), 8–10.
23 Mary Hays, "Deaths in and near London," *Monthly Magazine*, 4:22 (1797), 232–33.
24 Charlotte Smith, *The Young Philosopher*, edited by A. A. Markeley (London: Pickering & Chatto, 2005), 3.
25 Ibid., 168, 357.
26 Ibid., 429.
27 Markeley, "Introduction," xvi.
28 Mary Hays, *Appeal to the Men of Great Britain in behalf of Women* (London: J. Johnson, 1798), n.p.
29 Ibid., 47, 97, 161–92, 38, 39, 97–98, 95.
30 Ibid., 32.
31 Ibid., 45.
32 Ibid., 293.
33 Ibid., 115–16.
34 Mary Robinson, *A Letter to the Women of England and The Natural Daughter*, edited by Sharon Setzer (Peterborough: Broadview, 2003), 41.
35 Ibid., 48.
36 Ibid., 43.
37 Ibid., 45.
38 Ibid., 82.
39 Ibid., 85.
40 Mary Robinson, *The Natural Daughter*, 207.
41 Hays, *Appeal*, 237.
42 Mary Hays, *The Victim of Prejudice*, edited by Eleanor Ty (Peterborough: Broadview, 1998), 1–2.
43 Ibid., 63, 66.
44 Ibid., 119.
45 Ibid., 130.
46 Mary Hays, "Memoirs of Mary Wollstonecraft," in *The Annual Necrology, for 1797–8* (London: R. Phillips, 1800), 455.

CHAPTER 14

Liberal Reformers

Michelle Levy

In *A Vindication of the Rights of Woman*, Wollstonecraft forcefully contended that sexual inequality was based on a false distinction between the "supposed sexual character" of women and men.[1] Systematically dismantling the assumptions that resulted in the oppression of women, Wollstonecraft placed the blame squarely on men and insisted that patriarchy demeaned both genders. Many scholars have observed that when she entered the rights of women debate in 1792, she did so more directly and forcefully than her contemporaries.[2] Her radicalism also owes its reputation to writing a work devoted to the rights of women, not one that addressed the issue more obliquely through consideration of educational reform. Wollstonecraft believed that a "REVOLUTION in female manners" was necessary before educational reform could be effective;[3] since "[m]en and women must be educated, in a great degree, by the opinions and manners of the society they live in . . . It may then fairly be inferred, that, till society be differently constituted, much cannot be expected from education."[4] Wollstonecraft explicitly situates herself within a masculine political and intellectual tradition, styling herself "a philosopher" expounding "the science of politics."[5] She links the corruption of the monarchy and standing armies to the treatment of women, demonstrating that both belong to the same system of oppression. Adopting a brash, polemical style, she uses the inflammatory rhetoric of degradation, corruption, enslavement, and subjugation to describe the treatment of women, attacking men as tyrants and sensualists who make women into "the toy of man, his rattle, and it must jingle in his ears whenever, dismissing reason, he chooses to be amused."[6] Wollstonecraft did acknowledge her outspokenness: describing how male writers like Rousseau and Dr. Gregory have rendered women "more useless members of society," she notes, "I might have expressed this conviction in a lower key," but she commits herself to "the faithful expression of my feelings."[7]

The three female writers under consideration in this chapter, Anna Barbauld (1743–1825), Maria Edgeworth (1768–1849), and Jane Austen (1775–1817), have traditionally been differentiated from Wollstonecraft (1759–97) as being less uncompromising, and more moderate in their demands. This was a division Barbauld herself articulated in an 1804 letter to Edgeworth, in response to Edgeworth's request that they initiate a lady's magazine. Barbauld demurred, asserting that "[t]here is no bond of union among literary women," and observed that "Mrs. Hannah More would not write along with you or me, and we should probably hesitate at joining Miss Hays, or if she were living, Mrs. Godwin."[8] This placing of women along a continuum, with Wollstonecraft and Hays occupying the radical end of the spectrum, Barbauld and Edgeworth the middle, and More and other socially conservative women the other end, has become an entrenched paradigm for understanding feminism of the Romantic period. None of the women discussed in this chapter addressed addressed the public directly about women's rights; and when they did speak about women, they usually did so in dramatized forms, through literary genres like poetry and the novel. The impact of this generic difference renders exact comparisons difficult. An additional complication noted by many scholars is that, after 1798, any attempt by a female writer to openly identify with Wollstonecraft was highly fraught, with Godwin's revelations about his wife's sexual history and her attempted suicides in his *Memoirs* of her life rendering her essentially unmentionable.[9] The social repudiation of Wollstonecraft was so complete that, in the decades after the *Memoirs* appeared, the only republications of her work were a few editions of *Original Stories* (in London, Dublin, and France) and one further edition of her *Letters from Norway*, in 1802. For decades, none of her political writings were reprinted. The first reprinting of the *Vindication* after Wollstonecraft's death was the third edition in 1844; it was not printed again until the 1890s.

Although Wollstonecraft's scandalous reputation made it difficult for women writers after 1798 to address her by name, her influence can be directly traced in the writing of many women, even those who did not share her tactics. Most scholars now agree that Wollstonecraft's views on women's equal capacities and the education they were entitled to as a consequence were more closely aligned with the women who occupied the middle of the spectrum, including the liberal reformers examined in this chapter.[10] Wollstonecraft moved in similar literary spheres to Barbauld and Edgeworth, with whom she shared a publisher, Joseph Johnson. Johnson created a sociable community for his authors and associated them with each other publicly. In Johnson's *A Catalogue of Books Composed for*

Children and Young Persons, and Generally Used in the Principal Schools and Academies in England, likely dating to the early 1790s, he includes several works by Barbauld, Wollstonecraft's *Original Stories,* and religious works by Sarah Trimmer.[11] Though famous as a publisher of liberal ideas, Johnson published women across the spectrum, from Wollstonecraft and Hays, to Barbauld and Edgeworth, and even, until the French Revolution caused her to break from him, the more conservative writer Sarah Trimmer. Wollstonecraft, whom Johnson mentored throughout her career, was extremely valued by him, even though she died before the others; Edgeworth and Hays were loyal and important to Johnson up until his death.[12]

Notwithstanding their literary connections, in Chapter 4 of *Vindication,* Wollstonecraft launched a direct attack on Anna Barbauld. After citing admiringly two lines from her 128-line poem, "To Mrs. Priestley, with Some Drawings of Birds and Insects"– lines that describe how humans alone are marked for both misfortune and moral virtue – she turns on Barbauld, imploring, "After writing these lines, how could Mrs. Barbauld write the following ignoble comparison?" Lamenting that "even women of superior sense" adopt "the language of men," she then includes the entirety of Barbauld's eighteen-line poem, "To a Lady, with Some Painted Flowers." In this poem, Barbauld describes women as being "to cares unknown," as "born for pleasure and delight ALONE," a claim about sexual character that seems contradicted by the earlier poem.[13] Wollstonecraft attacks this poem by italicizing lines and printing in "indignant capitals" words like "SWEET," "DELICATE LIKE YOU," and so on.[14]

Most scholars have read Barbauld's unpublished and undated poem "The Rights of Women" as an angry response to her treatment by a woman sixteen years her junior. It begins, however, seemingly in sympathy with Wollstonecraft, with the speaker urging "injured Women" to "rise, assert thy right!" It proceeds in similar fashion, to implore women to "Make treacherous Man thy subject." However, the aggressive, militaristic language seems laden with irony, especially when read in light of Barbauld's known anti-war sentiments, a reading seemingly endorsed by the concluding stanza, which stages a withdrawal:

> Then, then, abandon each ambitious thought,
> Conquest or rule thy heart shall feebly move,
> In Nature's school, by her soft maxims taught,
> That separate rights are lost in mutual love.[15]

Many scholars have rejected reading the poem as a final or unambiguous statement of Barbauld's repudiation of Wollstonecraft; for William

McCarthy, the poem "ought to be read … as a working-through of the feelings stirred in her by reading the *Vindication*," emotions that, like the poem itself, were conflicted;[16] for Penny Bradshaw, the poem may not even have been written in response to the *Vindication* at all;[17] and for Elizabeth Raisanen, the poem does not contradict but actually supports the *Vindication*.[18] These scholars further note Wollstonecraft's many approvals of Barbauld's writing, within both the *Vindication* and other writing.[19] Both McCarthy and Bradshaw emphasize that the poem was never published by Barbauld; first published by her niece Lucy Aikin, it does not survive in a single manuscript copy. The apparent lack of social manuscript circulation further seems to support McCarthy's interpretation of the poem as a private exploration.

In her surviving manuscript poems, however, Barbauld is less reticent, speaking directly, and painfully, about the ways in which her unequal education separated her from her brother, precisely the division Wollstonecraft railed against. In an unpublished poem, "To Dr. Aikin on His Complaining That She Neglected Him, October 20th 1768," she addresses her early intimacy with her brother, and explains how for most of her young life her education had been identical to her brother's, until he leaves for medical school, and she is left at home. Barbauld challenges this separation: "Yet sure in different moulds they were not cast / Nor stampt with separate sentiments and taste"[20] – a repudiation of "the supposed sexual character" in explicit terms.

Edgeworth, for her part, often depicts girls learning through example and experience. A comparison of Wollstonecraft's female caregiver, Mrs. Mason, in *Original Stories from Real Life; with Conversations Calculated to Regulate the Affections, and Form the Mind to Truth and Goodness* (1788) and the mother in Maria Edgeworth's "The Purple Jar," a short piece published with *The Parent's Assistant* in 1796, demonstrates their shared, if rather unforgiving, views about how to educate girls. In both stories, female education is depicted as experiential, with the maternal figures allowing the girls under their care to make their own choices, even if they make poor decisions. In *Original Stories*, Caroline spends all of her money on toys, and thus is unable to relieve the horrible suffering of a poor family they subsequently meet in London. The other girl, Mary, has restrained herself and is thus able to supply the wants of the poor, and enjoys the moral satisfaction that comes with it. Mrs. Mason tells Caroline: "I am glad that this accident has occurred, to prove to you that prodigality and generosity are incompatible. Economy and self-denial are necessary in every station, to enable us to be generous, and to act conformably to the rules of justice," and, somewhat cruelly, she remarks that "Mary may this night enjoy peaceful slumbers," implying that Caroline will not.[21] Similarly in "The Purple Jar," Rosamund is faced with a choice between having her worn shoes replaced or buying a beguiling "purple jar." Her mother lays the choice before her, and tells her explicitly that no more money will be forthcoming for shoes, urging her "to think for yourself."[22] Rosamund purchases the jar, only to be immediately disappointed in finding that it is not in fact purple, but merely contains a black liquid. The narrator proceeds by telling us, "Rosamund's disappointment did not end here: many were the difficulties and distresses into which her imprudent choice brought her before the end of the month."[23] She is no longer able to run, dance, even walk; when asked by her parents to go out, she is unable to join them because of her shoes. Not surprisingly, the story ends with Rosamund reaching the inevitable conclusion: "how I wish that I had chosen the shoes! they would have been of so much more use to me than that jar."[24] The chilling didacticism of Rosamund's mother, who allows her daughter to go without rather than rescuing her from the consequences of her bad choice, is matched by Mrs. Mason: for both authors, the female self must learn through rationality to restrain itself, to consider both her own future and the well-being of others. As Megan Norcia notes, both authors seek to teach young women and their caregivers how to "master strategies of consumption."[25]

A consideration of Austen's engagement with questions of female education solidifies this account of Wollstonecraft's powerful influence. *Mansfield Park* might be read as a dramatization of Wollstonecraft's claims about the effects of a "false system of education."[26] *Mansfield Park* is Austen's novel of education, in part because we are introduced to the heroine, Fanny Price, as a ten-year-old girl. Immediately, Austen satirizes the young Bertram girls, aged twelve and fourteen, who mock Fanny for being "ignorant of many things with which they had been long familiar," and "prodigiously stupid: "Dear mama," one of them reports,

> only think, my cousin cannot put the map of Europe together—or my cousin cannot tell the principal rivers in Russia—or, she never heard of Asia Minor—or she does not know the difference between water-colours and crayons!—How strange!—Did you ever hear anything so stupid"[27]

The knowledge of which they boast, the ability to "'repeat the chronological order of the kings of England, with the dates of their accession, and most of the principal events of their reigns!'"[28] offers precisely the kind of meaningless facts, learned by rote and without true understanding, that

Wollstonecraft, and apparently Austen, abhorred. Wollstonecraft had lamented that "in the education of women, the cultivation of the understanding is always subordinate to the acquirement of some corporeal accomplishment,"[29] and Fanny's reluctance to learn either music or drawing, basic accomplishments thought important for pleasing men, is a sign of her intelligence and sensitive resistance to public display. Fanny, upon her arrival at Mansfield Park, can "read, work, and write, but she had been taught nothing more";[30] however, the true education she acquires is neither womanly accomplishments nor book learning but instead what Wollstonecraft would call "conscious virtue."[31] Fanny's rectitude and firmness of mind are narratively endorsed, as her refusal to act in the theatricals proves justified, and as Henry Crawford turns out to be more dangerous than even Fanny imagined.

Austen enacts the false system of education that destroys Maria Bertram, and nearly destroys her sister Julia. Their mother, Lady Bertram, abdicates any role in the education of her daughters:

> To the education of her daughters Lady Bertram paid not the smallest attention. She had not time for such cares. She was a woman who spent her days in sitting, nicely dressed, on a sofa, doing some long piece of needlework, of little use and no beauty, thinking more of her pug than her children ...[32]

Through this characterization, Austen delivers a devastating portrait of one of the "passive indolent women" lamented by Wollstonecraft.[33] By the novel's end, Sir Thomas acknowledges that his primary error was failing to attend to his daughter's moral education: "To be distinguished for elegance and accomplishments, the authorised object of their youth, could have had no useful influence that way, no moral effect on the mind."[34]

In *Lady Susan*, Austen's unpublished novella written more than a decade before *Mansfield Park*, her identification with Wollstonecraft is even more apparent. In this work, Austen uses her eponymous and outrageously immoral anti-heroine, Lady Susan, to endorse, ironically, the very system of education explicitly repudiated by Wollstonecraft. In writing to her intimate friend, Lady Susan explains what she intends for her daughter Frederica's education:

> Not that I am an advocate for the prevailing fashion of acquiring a perfect knowledge in all the Languages Arts, & Sciences;—it is throwing time away;—to be Mistress of French, Italian, German, Music, Singing, Drawing &c will gain a Woman some applause, but will not add one Lover to her list ... I do not mean, therefore, that Frederica's acquirements should be

more than superficial, & I flatter myself that she will not remain long enough at school to understand anything thoroughly.[35]

For Lady Susan, the grand purpose of education is not to allow women "to unfold their faculties"[36] but to empower them to attract a husband. Whereas Wollstonecraft lamented that "what [women] learn is rather by snatches; and as learning is with them, in general, only a secondary thing, they do not pursue any one branch with that persevering ardour necessary to give vigour to the faculties, and clearness to the judgment,"[37] Lady Susan's aim is precisely for her daughter not to "understand anything thoroughly," objecting even to her becoming "mistress" of acceptable female accomplishments. Lady Susan wishes for nothing more than that her daughter gains "grace and manner" as a means of fulfilling the universal truth that Wollstonecraft deeply resented, namely, that "the only way women can rise in the world,—[is] by marriage."[38]

Notes

1 Mary Wollstonecraft, *A Vindication of the Rights of Women*, in *The Works of Mary Wollstonecraft*, edited by Janet Todd and Marilyn Butler, electronic edn. (Charlottesville: InteLex Corp, 2004), 5: 122.
2 See Harriet Guest, *Unbounded Attachment: Sentiment and Politics in the Age of the French Revolution* (Oxford: Oxford University Press, 2013), 92–93 and Anne K. Mellor, "The Debate on the Rights of Woman: Wollstonecraft's Influence on the Women of Her Day," in Enit Karafili Steiner, ed., *Called to Civil Existence: Mary Wollstonecraft's A Vindication of the Rights of Woman* (New York: Rodopi, 2014), 1.
3 *A Vindication of the Rights of Women*, 14.
4 Ibid., 90.
5 Ibid., 103, 106.
6 Ibid., 102.
7 Ibid., 91.
8 Anna Le Breton, *Memoir of Mrs. Barbauld: Including Letters and Notices of Her Family and Friends* (London: Bell, 1874), 87.
9 Guest, *Unbounded Attachment*, 98; Mellor, "The Debate on the Rights of Woman," 6.
10 Penny Bradshaw, "The Limits of Barbauld's Feminism: Re-Reading 'The Rights of Woman,'" *European Romantic Review*, 16:1 (2005), 33–34; Rebecca Davies, *Written Maternal Authority and Eighteenth-Century Education in Britain: Educating by the Book* (Surrey: Ashgate, 2014), 63, 85; Elizabeth Raisanen, "Mary Wollstonecraft, Anna Barbauld, and Equality Feminism," in *Called to Civil Existence*, 27; Marija Reiff, "The 'Fanny Price Wars': Jane Austen's Enlightenment Feminist and Mary Wollstonecraft," *Women's Studies*, 45:3 (2016), 276–77.

11 The catalogue is bound into the British Library copy of *Original Stories from Real Life* (London: Johnson, 1788), N1656; See also Joseph Johnson, *A Catalogue of Books Composed for Children and Young Persons, and Generally Used in the Principal Schools and Academies in England.* (London: J. Johnson [1790]) *Eighteenth Century Collections Online* [Accessed February 14, 2019].

12 Gerald P. Tyson, *Joseph Johnson: A Liberal Publisher* (Iowa City: University of Iowa Press, 1979), 204.

13 Wollstonecraft, *A Vindication of the Rights of Women*, 122, n. 5.

14 "Indignant capitals" is William McCarthy's phrase: see *Anna Barbauld: Voice of the Enlightenment* (Baltimore: Johns Hopkins University Press, 2008), 351–52.

15 William McCarthy and Elizabeth Kraft, *Poems of Anna Barbauld* (Athens: University of Georgia Press, 1994), 121–22.

16 McCarthy, *Anna Barbauld: Voice of the Enlightenment*, 352.

17 Bradshaw, "The Limits of Barbauld's Feminism," 27.

18 Raisanen, "Mary Wollstonecraft, Anna Barbauld, and Equality Feminism," 25–48.

19 Ibid., 33; McCarthy, *Anna Barbauld: Voice of the Enlightenment*, 350.

20 McCarthy and Kraft, *Poems of Anna Barbauld*, 17–19.

21 Mary Wollstonecraft, *Original Stories, from Real Life; with Conversations, Calculated to Regulate the Affections, and Form the Mind to Truth and Goodness* in *The Works of Mary Wollstonecraft*, electronic edn., 4: 445.

22 Maria Edgeworth, *Early Lessons*, Vol. II (London: R. Hunter, 1822), 9.

23 Ibid., 15.

24 Ibid., 16–17.

25 Megan A. Norcia, "The London Shopscape: Educating the Child Consumer in the Stories of Mary Wollstonecraft, Maria Edgeworth, and Mary Martha Sherwood," *Children's Literature*, 41 (2013), 45.

26 Wollstonecraft, *A Vindication of the Rights of Women*, 73.

27 Jane Austen, *Mansfield Park*, edited by John Wiltshire and Janet Todd (New York: Cambridge University Press, 2005), 20.

28 Ibid., 21.

29 Wollstonecraft, *A Vindication of the Rights of Women*, 92.

30 Austen, *Mansfield Park*, 20.

31 Wollstonecraft, *A Vindication of the Rights of Women*, 95.

32 Austen, *Mansfield Park*, 22.

33 Wollstonecraft, *A Vindication of the Rights of Women*, 103.

34 Austen, *Mansfield Park*, 536.

35 Jane Austen, *Later Manuscripts*, edited by Janet Todd and Linda Bree (New York: Cambridge University Press, 2008), 13.

36 Wollstonecraft, *A Vindication of the Rights of Women*, 74.

37 Ibid., 92.

38 Ibid., *A Vindication of the Rights of Women*, 76.

CHAPTER 15

Conservative Reformers

Claire Grogan

The response among British writers to the French Revolution and the debate about the rights of the individual was restricted neither to political and philosophical tracts nor to men. Women writers from all political persuasions used a range of educational, polemical, and fictional works to debate a female's rights – social, political, economic, and legal. Although the debate did not extend to enfranchisement, the call for a decent education, improved legal status, and economic independence was revolutionary enough. Given the disruption that would result from greater rights for women, questions of an appropriate education and suitable expectations about life generally all became matters of public concern.

Views among women writers ranged from the traditional conservative acceptance that "there is a different bent of understanding in the sexes"[1] to the revolutionary English Jacobin assertion which "denies the existence of sexual virtues" because there is no sex in the soul.[2] Those women who most vehemently opposed Wollstonecraft and her views were known as conservative reformers. As supporters of the established system, these women limited their claims to moderate reforms in the area of female education. The difficulty facing female conservative reformers was how to participate in the revolutionary debate and enhance the female's role without overstepping by claiming political or legal rights currently designated male and masculine. They negotiated this thin line between appropriate and inappropriate behavior by claiming a Christian duty to act. They looked to the Bible as a source of inspiration rather than of oppression, providing a corrective to the self-serving males who "misread" scripture. They also worked assiduously to carve out a space of significant value for women in an enhanced and considerably more voluminous domestic sphere. They effectively depicted the domestic sphere as a microcosm of larger society and so invested it with political and national significance. An improved female education then became a necessary first step to producing better wives, daughters, and mothers. Claiming the domestic sphere also excused (in their own minds) their incursions upon topics outside the home, such as slavery, since they bemoaned the slave trade as a disruption of the family unit rather than on philosophical, intellectual, or even economic grounds.

But conservative reformers were neither a monolithic nor a homogeneous group. They disagreed among themselves on the most appropriate form of a female education and indeed the purpose for it. Consideration of Hannah More, Jane West, and Elizabeth Hamilton, three of the most influential conservative reformers, will show the range of opinions they held about female rights. Hannah More, who had enjoyed the company and support of the leading figures of the Blue Stockings while a young poet, by the late eighteenth century held conservative views on the topic of women's rights. Her *Essays on Various Subjects, Principally Designed for Young Ladies* (1777) and *Strictures on the Modern System of Female Education* (1799) voice her strong opposition to revolutionary principles. Both of More's works were immensely popular; the *Strictures* went through thirteen editions, selling 19,000 copies, while *Essays* appeared in numerous educational compendiums. More celebrates Britain as the "land of civil and religious liberty" where "there is as little despotism exercised over the minds, as over the persons of women."[3] She reiterates the sentiments of conservative male educationalists when she claims "Nature, propriety, and custom have prescribed certain bounds to each sex; bounds which the prudent and the candid will never attempt to break down."[4] It is the "different bent of the understanding of the sexes" that determines a male's public role and a female's private one. Females are "the porcelain clay of human kind" and their "greater delicacy ... implies greater fragility; and this weakness natural and moral, clearly points out the necessity of a superior degree of caution, retirement and reserve."[5]

Though women are "instrumental to the good order of society" and have "useful stations to fill, and important characters to sustain,"[6] they are singularly domestic creatures: "domestic life is to women the proper sphere."[7] In order to distance herself from pro-revolutionary sentiment, she houses any educational reform firmly within the feminized domestic sphere. While she invests this sphere with greater moral worth, she falls well short of claiming political rights or liberties for her sex, noting females "already have more liberty than is good for them."[8] "Why will women of sense" she opines "defeat their providential destiny? Why desert their proper sphere, in which they were intended to benefit, to please, even to shine, at least as stars of the *second* magnitude?"[9]

More's fellow conservative reformer Jane West, a Londoner who married a yeoman farmer in Northampton, espouses an even more staunchly conservative position. West's two volumes of educational letters, *Letters Addressed to a Young Man* (1801) and *Letters to a Young Lady* (1806), ridicule the New Philosophy and most claims for greater rights. Though revolutionary fervor hardly remained a threat to national security or values by the late 1790s, West writes as though it is a virulent contagion against which the British must inoculate themselves. Despite her claim to be "a staunch advocate for all the rights of my sex" she is not interested in tracing social behavior to its roots so much as accepting it as "part of the Almighty's ordained plan."[10] Thus in her praise of More's *Essays* and *Strictures*, she concurs with Fordyce, Gregory, and Gisborne that "true penitence will not wish to exceed those bounds" for "women are more happily circumstanced than the other sex."[11]

West's criticisms are not leveled at the social order but at the female's shortcomings within that order. She challenges her readers to perform their gender-specific duties more efficiently. West argues that since a female's duties are domestic she has no need to develop or explore her intellectual potential. Instead she endows the female's position and duties with special significance by arguing that "the customs of society give us advantages not highly valuable of themselves, but capable of being converted to real benefit."[12] West ascribes political power to females through this enhanced domestic sphere: "Although we are not entitled to a place in the senate, we become legislators in the most important sense of the word, by impressing on the minds of all around us the obligation which gives force to the statute."[13] Both West and More present the domestic sphere as a micro-cosm of the larger world in which every mother or wife has a patriotic duty to run an efficient household, as in so doing she "upholds the morals of the nation." For in this way the female has "a power wide in its extent, indefinite in its effects, and inestimable in its importance."[14]

Our third conservative reformer, Elizabeth Hamilton, presents a slightly more moderate position on the issue of women's rights. Born in Ireland but raised in Scotland, Hamilton published many educational works (*Letters on Education* [1801], *Letters Addressed to the Daughter of a Noble-man* [1806], *Exercises in Religious Knowledge* [1809], *Series of Popular Essays* [1813], *Hints to the Patrons and Directors of Schools* [1815]) through her lifetime. Initially, Hamilton concurred that females "experience the double disadvantage arising from original confirmation of mind, and a defective education."[15] But over time she increasingly advocated for equality for women, not only in the eyes of God but also in society at large. In this respect she advocated a more tolerant or liberal position than her fellow conservative reformers "not having been as yet convinced, that there is any subject within the range of human intellect, on which the capacity of any intelligent Being of either Sex, may not be profitably, or at least, innocently employed."[16]

Another major difference between Hamilton and her more conservative peers lies in her insistence that one should not passively or fatalistically accept one's social lot and wait for the rewards in the hereafter. She uses her fiction to model how God-given abilities should be used to improve life in the here and now. Her fictional heroine Mrs. Mason singlehandedly reforms the Scottish cottagers, modeling new methods of domestic economy in *Cottagers of Glenburnie*. Unlike More and West's heroines, who only model exemplary behavior, Hamilton's heroines mature as they learn from their experiences and mistakes and "extend the sphere of [female] usefulness."[17]

Conservative reformers recognize the crucial role that reading plays in educational reform and argue that "there is to women a Christian use to be made of sober studies."[18] But they despair of the wide availability of unsuitable publications and the female reader's ability to discern. They aim to convince the reader to work within the existing system, which is quite distinct from Wollstonecraft's professed goal: "Rousseau exerts himself to prove that all *was* right originally: a crowd of authors that all *is* now right: and I, that all will *be* right."[19] West laments the dangers of increased literacy and access to reading material:

> How can we glory in the general propensity for reading, if the tendency of what is most read proves, that the time so employed is lamentably misspent? Give me the boy at plough, and the girl at her spinning wheel, rather than master learning metaphysics, and miss studying life and manners in the pages of Wollstonecraft and Godwin.[20]

To counteract the recognized allure of fiction, they themselves publish novels. Like many contemporaries, they blame novel-reading for much female foolishness because of content, the misdirected use of time, and the passive reading habits it encourages. However, since "the rage for novels does not decrease [and] while the enemies of our church and state continue to pour their poison into unwary ears through this channel, it behooves the friends of our establishments to convey an antidote by the same course."[21] West published numerous novels, often narrated by the garrulous Prudentia Homespun, who interjects opinions and commentary to guide her impressionable readers: *The Advantages of Education* (1793); *A Gossip's Story* (1796); *A Tale of the Times* (1799); *The Refusal* (1810). More published just one novel, entitled *Cælebs in Search of a Wife* (1809), in which she educates her female reader to be the perfect partner. Hamilton published several successful fictional works in which her mixing of genres introduced her readers to more challenging topics than the simple romance plot.

Generally, novels by conservative reformers eschew the Jacobin's first-person narrative, memoir, or letter format that invited the reader to personally experience the dilemmas facing the heroine. Instead they opt for third-person narratives and authorial interjections, not only to guide or shame readers into compliance but also to remind them that they are reading fiction and not real life. Conservative novelists make full use of fictional death-bed scenes to allow characters to renounce their dabbling with the New Philosophy and subsequent transgressive behavior (usually sexual) prior to dying (West's Geraldine in *Tale of the Times*, Julia Delmont in Hamilton's *Memoirs of Modern Philosophers*.) For West and More the overtly didactic message of their fiction mirrors the patronizing and admonitory tone of their educational treatises, since all aspects of courtship and marriage reaffirm the female's necessary subordination within a patriarchal order. Hamilton slightly challenges this order through her depiction of respected and successful single women. But all three depict characters whose embracing of the New Philosophy ends disastrously. The goal is to dissuade impressionable young readers from emulating radical figures. Even women who assume masculine learning are ridiculed through their actions and other characters' responses.

A shared trait of these conservative reformers is the obligatory attack upon pro-revolutionary sentiment and those "bold assertors of the rights of the weaker sex."[22] Their criticisms are aggressive and bitter. More describes how the "cool, calculating, intellectual wickedness" of the English Jacobins "eats out the very heart and core of virtue, and like a deadly mildew blights and shrivels the blooming promise of the human spring."[23] West characterizes English Jacobins as "describing [the established order] as an excrescence springing out of the body politic, and draining every useful member of its vital juices, in order to swell its own putrid mass into a most hideous and most dangerous deformity."[24] She "attack[s] many of the false dangerous opinions" presented by the "diabolical . . . propagators of the New Philosophy," the "ale-house reformers and barber-shop politicians" who "contrive to wage an alarming war against the cause of order and morals."[25] Hamilton ridicules the foolish pretensions of New Philosophers in *Translation of the Letters of a Hindoo Rajah* but devotes the main plot of her *Memoirs of Modern Philosophers* to describing the devastating effects these ideas have on her small English village. She mocks the New

Philosophers who abandon their families and businesses to participate in the harebrained scheme to join the Hottentots in Africa.

Conservative reformers not only distance themselves and their ideas from pro-revolutionary sentiment in general but from Mary Wollstonecraft in particular. This is especially true after the grieving widower Godwin's 1798 publication of the *Memoirs of the Author of A Vindication of the Rights of Woman* in which he revealed her repeated suicide attempts and two children conceived out of wedlock. The subsequent yoking of revolutionary sympathies with loose sexual proclivities and immoral behavior meant conservative women writers had to clearly differentiate their reforms from those of Wollstonecraft. More purports to have never even read Wollstonecraft's *Rights of Woman*, claiming there was "something fantastic and absurd in the very title with its metaphysical jargon," though this does not prevent her attacking Wollstonecraft for her "promulgation of corrupt morals." Anxious to distance herself from Horace Walpole's description of Wollstonecraft as "a hyena in petticoats,"[26] More argues that her "zeal for [a woman's] true *interest* leads her to oppose" Wollstonecraft's "imaginary rights."[27] West describes Wollstonecraft as a "professed courtesan,"[28] "who has obtained a lamentable distinction" for "affecting a sort of philosophical air" and using terminology and language that "no decent woman would adopt even in the most confidential intercourse."[29] She denounces Wollstonecraft as an example of a revolutionary woman who has "cast off all the characteristics of her sex; who speak[s] with contempt of every feminine virtue, who banishe[s] pity and gentleness from [her] bosom, and with unblushing effrontery, glorying in [her] share, dare[s] to *talk* of *virtue* while she *practice*[s] the deeds of *vice*."[30] Like Richard Polwhele in *The Unsex'd Females* (1798), West unsympathetically describes Wollstonecraft's death shortly after childbirth as the "terrible" termination of her "guilty career" and states that "her posthumous writings shew, that her soul was in the most unfit state to meet her pure and holy Judge."[31] Hamilton alone of these three writers avoids criticizing Wollstonecraft's person. The hero Henry Sydney in *Memoirs of Modern Philosophers* actually defends *A Vindication of the Rights of Woman*, arguing that the "sensible authoress has sometimes permitted her zeal to hurry her into expressions which have raised a prejudice against the whole."[32] But it is significant that it is the hero and not the heroine who has the strength of character to defend Wollstonecraft.

Difficulties arise for conservative female reformers because they subscribe to a set of rules that they themselves transgress, ridiculing learned women as masculine or "unsex'd" despite their own intellectual capabilities and prowess. To explain this, they position themselves as supporters of a practical, rational education but strongly oppose learning that leads a female to appear masculine. A "masculine woman" is "the bold and independent beauty, the intrepid female, the hoyden, the huntress, and the archer, . . . with swinging arms, the confident address, the regimental, and the four-in-hand."[33] An example is Miss Sparkes in *Cœlebs in Search of a Wife*: "a neighboring lady, whom the reputation of being a wit and an Amazon, had kept single at the age of five and forty."[34] Miss Sparkes, who is "remarkable for her pretention to odd and opposite qualities . . . is something of a scholar, a huntress, a politician and a farrier."[35] West has Lord Glanville's overly educated daughter commit suicide in his arms (*Infidel Father*), while the heroine Geraldine in *Tale of the Times* comes to grief after pursuing topics and schemes inappropriate to her sex. Hamilton's Miss Ardent, Bridgetina Botherim, and The Goddess of Reason are all chastised for aping learning and mistaking a smattering of knowledge for real intelligence. According to More the true test of intelligence is invariably domestic in nature:

> A philosophical lady 'may read Mallebranche, Boyle, and Locke:' she may boast of her intellectual superiority; she may talk of abstract and concrete; of substantial forms and essences; complex ideas and mixed modes, of identity and relation; she may decorate all of one sex with all the rhetoric of the other; yet if her affairs are *delabres*, if her house is disorderly, her servants irregular, her children neglected, and her table ill arranged, she will indicate the want of the most valuable faculty of the human mind, a sound judgment.[36]

West takes this one step further to propose "No woman should be permitted to publish an essay on industry, till she can produce a written certificate that her own wardrobe is kept in perfect order; or to dress out fictitious character, unless she can prove . . . that she has clothed her household with the labours of her hands."[37] But arguing that there is no place for female action outside the domestic sphere is problematic since they themselves clearly move and speak from outside that sphere. Expanding the domestic sphere only deflects some of the criticism.

Indeed, though these conservative reformers entered the public fray to support the established order, they often found themselves accused of overstepping the mark. Their willingness to work within the status quo required their loyalty to a male value system that failed to recognize their worth. West was dismissed as the embodiment of her chatty, busybody narrator, while Hamilton was criticized for her ambitious mixing of genres. More's *Village Politics* was commendable, but the moment "she preached to people of fashion she [became] a bishop in *partibus infidelium.*"³⁸ Critics of her Sunday school program accused her of radicalizing the working classes. Unlike the radical writers who understood the perils of challenging the established order, these conservative reformers anticipated acceptance and even praise for strengthening the social order. As female agents of patriarchy, they believed they were "exceptions to the rule" of female inferiority. Though they often strenuously denied other women similar freedoms, publishing opportunities, or intellectual capabilities, they were chagrined to discover that their support hardly protected them from personal attack.

Notes

1 Hannah More, *Essays on Various Subjects, Principally Designed for Young Ladies* (London: J. Wilkie & T. Cadell, 1777), 11.
2 Mary Wollstonecraft, *A Vindication of the Rights of Woman: With Strictures on Political and Moral Subjects* (1792), edited by D. L. Macdonald and K. Scherf (Ontario: Broadview, 1997), 165.
3 More, *Essays*, 21.
4 Ibid., 3.
5 Ibid., 3–4.
6 Ibid., 21, 35.
7 *Strictures on the Modern System of Female Education: With a View of the Principles and Conduct Prevalent among Women of Rank and Fortune*, 2 vols. (London: T. Cadell & W. Davies, 1799), 2: 152.
8 *Memoirs of the Life and Correspondence of Mrs. Hannah More*, 2 vols., ed. William Roberts (New York: Harper, 1836), 2: 372.
9 More, *Strictures*, 2: 165.
10 Jane West, *Letters to a Young Lady, in Which the Duties and Character of Women Are Considered*, 3 vols. (London: Longman, Hurst, Rees, & Orme, 1806), 2: 403.
11 Ibid., 1: 256, 2: 416.
12 Ibid., 1: 127.
13 Ibid., 2: 424.
14 More, *Strictures*, 1: 59–60.
15 Elizabeth Hamilton, *Letters on the Elementary Principles of Education*, 2 vols. (London: G. & J. Robinson, 1801), 1: 2.
16 Elizabeth Hamilton, *A Series of Popular Essays Illustrative of Principles Essentially Connected with the Improvement of the Understanding, the Imagination, and the Heart*, 2 vols. (London: Manners & Millar, Longman, Hurst, Rees, Orme, & Brown, 1813), 1: xxxi.
17 Elizabeth O. Benger, *Memoirs of the Late Mrs. Elizabeth Hamilton*, 2 vols. (London: Longman, Hurst, Rees, Orme & Brown, 1819), 1: 135.
18 More, *Strictures*, 2: 2, 180.

19 Wollstonecraft, *Vindication*, 121.
20 Jane West, *Letters Addressed to a Young Man, on his First Entrance into Life*, 3 vols. (London: T. N. Longman & O. Rees, 1801), 1: 107–08.
21 Jane West, *The Infidel Father*, 3 vols. (London: T. N. Longman & O. Rees, 1802), 1: ii.
22 Gisborne, Thomas, *An Enquiry into the Duties of the Female Sex* (London: Cadell & Davies, 1797), 22.
23 More, *Strictures*, 1: 49.
24 West, *Letters to a Young Lady*, 1: 197.
25 West, *Letters Addressed to a Young Man*, 1: 101, xxiv.
26 Horace Walpole, *Horace Walpole's Miscellaneous Correspondence*, 3 vols., edited by W. S. Lewis and John Riely (New Haven: Yale University Press, 1980), 15: 337–38.
27 More, *Strictures*, 2: 24.
28 West, *Letters Addressed to a Young Man*, 3: 321.
29 Ibid., 3: 343–44.
30 Ibid., 3: 321–22.
31 Ibid., 3: 343.
32 Elizabeth Hamilton, *Memoirs of Modern Philosophers*, 3 vols. [1800], edited by Claire Grogan (Ontario: Broadview, 2000), 101.
33 More, *Strictures*, 1: 75.
34 Hannah More, *Cœlebs, in Search of a Wife: Comprehending Observations on Domestic Habits and Manners, Religion and Morals*, 2 vols. (London, 1809), 2: 84.
35 Ibid., 284.
36 Ibid., 104.
37 West, *Letters to a Young Lady*, 2: 419.
38 Walpole, *Miscellaneous Correspondence*, 11: 214.

Philosophical Frameworks

CHAPTER 16

French Philosophes

Sylvana Tomaselli

Though a reader, reviewer, and translator of contemporary French works, Mary Wollstonecraft was primarily engaged with the writings of British authors. The most notable exception to this is, of course, Jean-Jacques Rousseau, the Genevan, with whose thought she had a complex relationship, as is discussed in Chapter 18 of this volume by Laura Kirkley. Rousseau wrote on subjects that concerned Wollstonecraft most particularly: education, morality, political economy, and the progress of civilization. He was obviously not unique in so doing among writers in French or within the *philosophes'* circles. What marked him out, apart from his phenomenal success in Britain, especially as the author of *Emile*, was his stance on religion, to which he appeared to be open or at least not as staunchly critical as authors such as Voltaire (1694–1778) and Diderot (1713–84) were taken to be. This is not to say that the ideas debated in Parisian *salons* and the *philosophes'* literary output were irrelevant to her. She engaged with some of these through the work of British authors, such as Edmund Burke (1729–97), David Hume (1711–76), and Adam Smith (1723–90). Moreover, if we cast our net a little more widely, it becomes clear that she took an interest in the work of the *physiocrates* and constitutional writers of the period, notably, the Abbé Emmanuel Joseph Sieyès (1748–1836). Moreover, Wollstonecraft read Montaigne (1533–92), François Fénelon (1651–1715), and other canonical French authors, who shaped mid-century and subsequent generations of thinkers. Thus it would be wrong to say that Wollstonecraft was not affected by at least some of the *philosophes'* deliberations and even more so that she was ignorant of them. Her awareness of intellectual life in eighteenth-century France was evident from her earliest publications, but especially so following her stay in the years of its Revolution. However, as the *philosophes* were a very diverse group of thinkers and the Enlightenment is now recognized to have been not only a cosmopolitan enterprise but so multifaceted as to be a questionable historical category, it would be misleading to seek to produce a single homogenous French philosophical context to Wollstonecraft's own thoughts. Instead what follows will give a glimpse of some of the points of intersection between the two, more particularly, those with Montesquieu, Voltaire, Necker, and the *économistes*.

The most important French political theorist and writer who does not feature prominently in Wollstonecraft's intellectual landscape is Charles de Secondat, Baron de Montesquieu (1689–1755). The celebrated author of *De l'Esprit des loix* (1748) became identified with the theory of the separation of powers and what was an idealized account of the English Constitution, describing England as a republic masquerading as a monarchy. David Hume called the work "the best system of political knowledge that, perhaps, has ever yet been communicated to the world." His *Lettres persanes* (1721) had made him famous overnight, the tale of Persian travelers to Europe and their correspondence with their wives and the keepers of their harems providing not only mildly salacious entertainment but also the background to his critical comments on political events, social and political issues, and the mores of his age. His *magnum opus* considered government under three types, republican (democratic and aristocratic), monarchical, and despotic, but its main purpose, as its title indicates, was to argue that all legislative endeavors and political reforms had to be in conformity with the spirit of the countries concerned. To gain a sense of that spirit, legislators and political commentators had to appreciate fully the physical nature of the land, its climate, its history, its legal, social and political characteristics, and the culture and religion of its people. This understanding had to encompass a comprehension of the causal relations among these various features. It is this aspect of Montesquieu's many pronouncements and insights that is of most relevance here.

While Aristotle had stressed the importance of geographical factors in relation to the appropriateness of forms of governments, the theory that the latter had to befit the all-inclusive circumstances of the people became identified with Montesquieu in the eighteenth century. Partly through other authors, such as Edmund Burke and Rousseau, Wollstonecraft was conscious of the need to grasp the spirit of a people in a comprehensive manner as *An Historical and Moral View of the French Revolution; and the Effect It Has Produced in Europe* (1794) demonstrates, for while it did not extend to climatic conditions, it did seek to capture the spirit of the French institutions, culture, and people. As she remarked in a prefatory note, the work went beyond relating facts and opinions to encompass, among other things, descriptions of manners. She sought to capture these and the nature of the French further in her *Letter on the Present Character of the*

French Nation, the first of what she hoped would be a series on the subject, which she wrote from Paris in February 1793. However, it is in her *Letters Written during a Short Residence in Sweden, Norway, and Denmark* (1796) (which was to shape travel literature as a genre) that she sought to relate most markedly climate and landscape to considerations on the nature of mores and the progress of civilization more generally, thereby reflecting the new trend of social analysis that was developed several decades earlier, and that watermarked the humanities, not least history.

Long before her own efforts in that field, historical writing had changed on both side of the Channel in the course of the century. Voltaire's *Essai sur l'histoire générale et sur les mœurs et l'esprit des nations* (1756) was a prime example of a highly polemical historical work that sought to trace the development of European civilization from Charlemagne to the age of Louis XIV. Not confined to Europe, it encompassed much of the globe, apart from Africa, highlighting the antiquity of Chinese culture and countering prevailing prejudices about the Muslim world. Although Wollstonecraft did not follow Voltaire in rejecting the bigotry of the age against Islam, she was to share his interest in mores. She also partook of his notorious anti-clericalism, though hers was born of a typically post-Reformation English anti-popery. We do not know how extensively she read Voltaire, but there is no doubt that she was very familiar with some of his writings directly, including what she referred to as "that justly celebrated work," *L'Ingénu* (1767) and his satirical work on fiscal legislation, *L'Homme aux quarante écus* (1768), which she cited in a letter to her lover, Gilbert Imlay.[1] She remembered the nobility of its American hero, and Voltaire seems to have been associated in her mind with that part of the world. Indeed, *The Female Reader: or Miscellaneous Pieces, in Prose and Verse: Selected from the Best Writers, and Disposed under Proper Heads: for the Improvement of Young Women. By Mr Creswick*, which appeared in 1789 and she authored, included "The Discovery of America," a section of Voltaire's famous history.

Voltaire's influence on her was also mediated through the work of others. In *A Vindication of the Rights of Woman*, she cited a passage of his *Siècle de Louis XIV* (1751) from Adam Smith's translation in *The Theory of Moral Sentiments* (1757). It explained what made the Sun King remarkable, namely, the unsurpassed gracefulness of his deportment and the beauty of his features and voice. The account is important to her argument, as she used it to illustrate that women, like the King, enthralled in her society, not by genuine talents and virtues, but through "frivolous accomplishments," appearance, and artifice.[2] The reign of the magnificent

King had ushered a pleasure-seeking and superficial age, one in which those who did not have to labor were only eager for adventure and shunned their duties. Though he was by no means the only source of her reflections on modernity and the nature of the luxury society of her times, Voltaire's analysis of the age and the development of European civilization permeated her understanding of social reality.

Through Rousseau's biographical works, Wollstonecraft became acquainted with a number of other major figures of eighteenth-century Paris, such as Diderot. She knew of the latter's friendship with Rousseau and of his encouragement behind the latter's composition *Discours sur l'origine et les fondements de l'inégalité parmi les hommes* (1755), but she did not otherwise mention him. Yet, she became the instrument of the propagation of a critique of his purported views on the dispensability of religion for the maintenance of morality in society and hence its reproduction over time. Diderot was not alone among the Parisian intellectual coterie in questioning the purpose of religion, Christianity in the first instance, quite apart from challenging its veracity. Voltaire, Helvétius (1715–71), the Baron d'Holbach (1723–89), and others debated this issue in person and on paper. Among the reactions this generated was Jacques Necker's (1732–1804) *De l'importance des opinions religieuses* (1788), which Wollstonecraft translated and published in the same year. While she was to say in a review that its style was belabored, and would later ridicule Necker's philosophical pretensions in *A Historical and Moral View*, she and he had in fact much in common, and the process of rendering the work into good English prose seems to have had an effect on her own.

The Geneva-born statesman had settled in Paris when eighteen. Besides establishing a bank, he became involved in the Compagnie des Indes (1763–73), wrote in its defense, along with a number of other works on legislation and economics, and was in and out of ministerial office under Louis XVI until his final resignation in 1790. His treatise on religion was a new departure. In the words of Wollstonecraft's review, "he ably proves that the wisest laws would not be sufficient to retrain men within the bounds of morality without those powerful motives, which religion offers to interest the affections, and enlighten the understanding."[3] Like Wollstonecraft, Necker believed religion could uniquely capture the imagination "and counter the allurements of the senses," and that it banded together society as nothing else could. Although she thought his chapter on the effect of religion on sovereigns "not generally useful," and while she was to criticize Madame de Staël, Necker's famous daughter, in a review of a work on Rousseau for her extravagant praise of her father, Wollstonecraft was unusually positive in her long account of *De l'importance des opinions religieuses*, praising its author's virtue, and concluding that few of its readers would fail to perceive "the simple, yet sublime harmony of that system which unites men to each other, and to that Being who is the source of all perfection."[4] However, by the time she came to write *A Historical and Moral View*, she identified him with the *ancien régime*'s tragic mismanagement and was to be very critical of Necker's performance as finance minister and what she saw as his vanity and self-righteousness.

Next to, and arguably more than, anti-clerical debates and discussions of the necessity of religion to morality and order in society, it was developments in French economic theory and plans for economic reforms with which Wollstonecraft seemed to have been most taken. She spoke of the *économistes* (or *physiocrates*), who sought to reorganize the country's financial system and that of its taxation in particular, as "the first champions of civil liberty," of their founder, François Quesnay (1694–1774), first physician to Louis XV, as "the humane M. Quesnai," and of his treatise (presumably, *Tableau économique* [1758]) as "profound." He contributed the entries "Évidence," "Fermiers," and "Grain" to the *Encyclopédie*. While the first considered the relationship between the mind and the body which, in the wake of René Descartes' (1596–1650) famed mind/body dualism, predominated French philosophical debates the other two provided a sketch of his economic views, with their critique of luxury, their argument in favor of the liberty of the grain trade, and their emphasis on the wealth creation of agriculture. That the poor were ground down by taxation in France as well as England was one of Wollstonecraft's repeated complaints. Similarly, while in Scandinavia she took a particular interest in the systems of taxation of the Northern monarchies, and although she thought no perfectly just structure of taxation had yet been invented and might never be achieved, she thought it essential that the tax burden be distributed as evenly as possible. The manner of its collection was also of great importance to her, as it was within French political and philosophical circles, and *A Historical and Moral View* made it clear that she thought this as well as their nature and excessiveness, not to mention their inequity, was a major cause of the Revolution. This view was both informed by her understanding of the *économistes'* efforts and explains her admiration for them.

It was not principally their advocacy of *laissez-faire*, with which they were identified throughout Europe and America, but their endeavors to transform the economy that she applauded. She commended "the enlightened administration of the comptroller general Turgot, a man formed in this school [physiocracy]" for bringing a "glimpse of freedom" to France during his period in office, when he tried to reform the economy and curb feudal privileges.[5] She referred to him as "clear headed, unaffected Turgot."[6] Like Quesnay, whose economic work he refined, Anne Robert Jacques Turgot (1727–81) published a number of influential articles to the *Encyclopédie*. His appointment by Louis XVI in the summer of 1774 was welcomed by the *philosophes*, as was his program of ill-fated reforms to free trade in grain and flour and to abolish artisanal corporations. Necker succeeded him when he fell from power in 1776. In *A Historical and Moral View*, Wollstonecraft gave a sympathetic and relatively detailed account of the resistance Turgot had met from an ignorant and self-interested court, whose selfish extravagance and machinations were in fact undermining the monarchy.

More generally, she thought that the gradual diffusion of the *philosophes'* ideas "to every class of society" had softened the administration in France and made for the progress of political sciences. "A confederacy of philosophers," she argued, "gave a turn for instructive and useful reading to the leaders of circles, and drew the attentions of the nation to the principles of political and civil government." She believed this had been achieved by evading censorship: "Whilst by the compilation of the Encyclopedia, the repository of their thoughts, as an abstract work, they eluded the dangerous vigilance of absolute ministers; thus in a body disseminating those truths in the economy of finance, which, perhaps, they would not have had sufficient courage separately to have produced in individual publications."[7]

She thought of the *économistes* as independently minded, though working for a common purpose, namely demonstrating "that the prosperity of a state depends on the freedom of industry; that talents should be permitted to find their level; that the unshackling of commerce is the only secret to render it flourishing, and answer more effectually the ends for which it is politically necessary; and that the imposts should be laid upon the surplus remaining, after husbandman has been reimbursed for his labor and expenses."[8]

However, this dedicated and upright group of *philosophes* and political economists did not reproduce itself. The next generation of writers exploited "the fashion to talk of liberty" and "to dispute on hypothetical and local points of political economy," with the consequence that truth was disseminated and Paris saw an unprecedented number of demagogues. Thus, while Wollstonecraft showed that the causes of the French Revolution were complex and their roots reached far back into the country's history, it is noteworthy that she believed that the unintended consequences of the spread of what were originally laudable ideas about government and political economy were part of the multifarious contributory mix.

Wollstonecraft respected the *philosophes'* reforming endeavors and esteemed some of its individuals more particularly, especially among the political economists and, as subsequent chapters will show, constitutional writers. Even if it had been one single party with one single ideology, she would not have embraced it, as she very much was her own woman intellectually and because her own religious, philosophical, and political background and her battles differed so markedly from even those thinkers whose ideas she most valued. She also came to see that ideas and political languages, once released, could be as dangerous as their origins had been benign.

Notes

1 *Analytical Review*, 24 (1796), in *The Works of Mary Wollstonecraft*, edited by Janet Todd and Marilyn Butler (London: W. Pickering, 1989), 7: 478. *Letters to Imlay*, in *Works*, 6: 378.
2 *A Vindication of the Rights of Woman*, in *Works*, 5: 128.
3 *Analytical Review*, 3 (1789), in *Works*, 7: 60.
4 Ibid., 7: 66.
5 *A Historical and Moral View*, in *Works*, 6: 19.
6 Ibid., 6: 42.
7 *A Historical and Moral View*, in *Works*, 6: 225.
8 Ibid., 6: 226.

CHAPTER 17

Dissenters

Andrew McKendry

Joining the parade of childish wives, tyrannical husbands, and frivolous dog-moms, the character that concludes Mary Wollstonecraft's *A Vindication of the Rights of Woman* (1792) seems strangely out of place; "were not Dissenters," she ponders, "like women, fond of deliberating together, and asking advice of each other, till by a complication of little contrivances, some little end was brought about?" We are not accustomed to thinking of Dissenters – those, like John Milton and John Bunyan, who refused to conform to the Anglican Church – as small-minded. Wollstonecraft, however, argues that just as women had been made "cunning" by the "tyranny of man," Dissenters were stamped with a "prim littleness" by the tyranny of the state.[1] Wollstonecraft owed much, both personally and intellectually, to Dissenters, but the parallel with Nonconformity is more flattering and generative than it might appear; in denouncing what Dissenters had once been (in the age of Samuel Butler's Puritan-bashing *Hudibras* [1663–78]), Wollstonecraft presents the implicit "progress" of Nonconformity, above all its renunciation of insular sectarianism, as a model for the transformation of female character.

Originating in the Act of Uniformity of 1662, which effectively ejected roughly 2,000 ministers by requiring conformity to Anglican rites, Dissent began as a legal category but became a substantial (albeit heterogeneous) political and cultural identity. By virtue of the set of laws that came to be known as the Clarendon Code, Dissenters were excluded from civil and military office, as well as from English universities, and while the 1689 Toleration Act permitted worship outside the Established Church, Dissenters remained significantly disabled until 1828, when the Corporation and Test Acts were repealed. By 1773, after a period of some decline, "Old Dissenters" (in contradistinction to Methodists) constituted approximately 5 percent of the English population,[2] though historians have determined that their economic and political clout exceeded their numbers. Their cultural influence has now been recovered by scholars like Neil Keeble and Daniel

White, who have demonstrated that Nonconformists featured importantly in histories of literary culture, sociability, and even visual arts.

While not a Dissenter herself, Wollstonecraft was immersed in the world of Nonconformity, in particular that of "Rational Dissenters," a group that included her closest friends and mentors. Rational Dissent describes a (relatively small) subset of Nonconformity defined theologically by their rejection of Calvinism and methodologically by their willingness to privilege personal inquiry over orthodoxy. Joseph Priestley, the foremost figure in this tradition, conceives of this practice as a "perfect freedom of inquiry,"[3] though it was variously conceptualized, sometimes as "impartial debate" or as open-minded "candour." Applied to Scripture, this attitude furnished the provocative Unitarian tendencies with which Rational Dissent became associated, but such incisively free inquiry was extended to all subjects, often with subversive effects. Wollstonecraft's first novel, *Mary: A Fiction* (1788), demonstrates how such an extension could work, as the imperative "to examine the evidence on which her faith was built" not only makes her "a Christian from conviction," but also equips her to interrogate conformity in every guise – to "propriety," to "ceremonies" (social and religious), and even to marriage.[4]

Wollstonecraft initially became involved in the culture of Dissent in 1784 when she moved to Newington Green, an area with a large Dissenting population that had supported prominent Dissenting academies for more than a century. James Burgh, whose *Thoughts on Education* (1747) is considered an influence on Wollstonecraft's pedagogical writings, was schoolmaster at the Stoke Newington Academy, and his widow Hannah helped Wollstonecraft open her own school nearby. The pre-eminent Richard Price, famed for his spirited defense of the American rebels, ministered to the local Dissenting congregation, and Wollstonecraft attended his sermons, establishing a friendship that was to have a decisive impact on her literary career. Through her publisher Joseph Johnson, her connections with the Dissenting community proliferated; both as a publisher and as a dinner host, Johnson was an important hub in a network of leading Dissenters, and Wollstonecraft, who admired his "humanity" and "friendly heart," often visited his home for conversation with these uncommonly "sensible men" – not only Price and Priestley, but men like the Unitarian abolitionist William Roscoe and her future husband William Godwin.[5] Her aversion to "vanity" and "luxury" (including drinking) found an analogue in the abstemiousness of Dissent (she boasted that Price "in his whole life never dreamt of struggling for power or riches").[6] And the principled separation of Dissenters exemplified the kind of intellectual independence that she endorsed for women. Her own "unbending principles" brought her into conflict with sexual rather than religious regulations, but the precocity of her political writing nonetheless owed a good deal to the oppositional discourse cultivated within the Dissenting tradition.[7]

Though in the strictest sense Dissenters had "nothing in common but a dissent from the established church,"[8] they had long been defined by their liberal sympathies. Their republican heritage, regularly flaunted in relation to the 1688 revolution, made them amenable to schemes of popular sovereignty, while their subjection to the penal laws animated the anti-authoritarian inflections of natural law and Christian scripture in their polemics – so much so that Dissent was frequently considered a political faction. They were hardly the only "friends of freedom" in such an expectant age,[9] but there was some truth to the claim that they held a distinctive (if self-consciously politicized) "love of liberty,"[10] one that manifested in their vocal support for the American rebellion, for parliamentary reform, and for the French Revolution. Wollstonecraft's response to the Revolution was mediated by this religio-political tradition, her first foray into political writing, *A Vindication of the Rights of Men* (1790), emerging as a defense of Price, whose sermon *On the Love of Our Country* (1789) had elicited Burke's *Reflections on the Revolution in France* (1790). Though she distances herself from the unseemly "zeal" which was often charged to Dissenters, her portrait of Price suggests how centrally he figured in her conception of that moral character she sought for women; a man "whose talents and modest virtues place him high in the scale of moral excellence," Price appears as a paragon of "unaffected piety" – "personified virtue."[11] The filiation with Rational Dissent is most immediate in the value Wollstonecraft assigns to "free" religious enquiry, but the broader Dissenting tradition is present in the way she positions religious liberty: "the birthright of man," she asserts, "is such a degree of liberty, civil and religious, as is compatible with the liberty of every other individual with whom he is united in a social compact."[12]

We don't usually think of Wollstonecraft as a champion of religious freedom, but her pairing of "civil" with "religious" liberty reflects the concept's ancestry in long-standing debates about "liberty of conscience," a legacy that acuminated her feminism. Conceived as "the natural right every man possesses, of framing his system of religious faith, and choosing his form of worship for himself,"[13] liberty of conscience was foundational to the identity of Dissent; though they formulated the principle in diverse (and sometimes divisive) ways, Dissenters necessarily shared a conviction that the imperatives of conscience were sacred and inviolable. But liberty of conscience was also increasingly presented as a value in itself, abstracted from specific scruples and controversies – so consistently that it would admit even the "most violent enemies" of Nonconformity.[14] As Anthony Lincoln puts it, during this period "Christian liberties became merged into 'natural' liberties and the particular privileges claimed in virtue of Christian conscience and Christian salvation came to be transformed into the rights belonging to all men."[15] While the confrontation between the conscientious Christian and the civil magistrate still figured prominently in political theory, the submersion of sectarian "prejudices" was a common move among liberal Dissenters,[16] one that made their tenets relevant to a writer like Wollstonecraft who grappled with different but not unrelated kinds of oppression and coercion.

The apparently desultory analogy with Dissenters that closes *Rights of Woman* can thus be seen as a culmination of the text's abiding appeal to the prerogatives of conscience. Conscience had always borne potentially feminist implications, and if Wollstonecraft's attachment to Rational Dissent turned her to a masculine reason (rather than to the trenchant "spirit" of a Dissenting prophetess like Katherine Chidley), the resultant critique is nonetheless of a kind with earlier expressions of Dissenting feminism. In a work like *The Wrongs of Woman* (1798) this critique emerges pointedly, Maria asserting her authority to "consult her conscience" in the face of oppressive marriage laws,[17] while in *Rights of Woman* it dismantles the conceptual infrastructure of sexual difference; under a regime that demanded reasoned belief from all "rational beings," the intellectual and social conformity imposed on women becomes inseparable from that mode of "conformity" against which Dissenters had fought for more than a century. In this framework, the constriction of a woman's choice, whether directly or through a negligent education, is a matter not simply of earthly fulfillment but of eternal salvation, since if, as Dissenters averred, "a being capable of immortal life" is enjoined to "to diligently use [his] reason, in order to make [himself] acquainted with the will of God,"[18] then woman – if she "be allowed to have an immortal soul" – was required to do the same.[19] Though this exacting schema subtends the entire *Rights of Woman*, Wollstonecraft occasionally leverages this discourse quite emphatically, as when she facetiously suggests that a wife must be "conformed, as a dependent creature should, to the ceremonies of the church which she was brought up in, piously believing that wiser heads than her own have settled that business."[20] Such a statement is aimed to affront all Protestant readers, for whom such "blind obedience" was anathema, but it could do so because Dissent had imbued conscience with an enduring urgency and authority.[21]

While the hard-fought status of conscience offered Wollstonecraft a means of sanctifying the rights of women, her attraction to denominational disinterestedness also sometimes entailed a disregard for the more immediate ramifications of contemporary debates on Nonconformity. There was certainly much at stake during Wollstonecraft's lifetime, when Dissenters were campaigning vigorously for the repeal of the Test Act, which required civil and military office holders to receive Anglican Communion. Though the Indemnity Acts and the practice of occasional conformity had softened the impact of the penal laws, the Test Act still held considerable power, marking the second-class status of Dissenters and making their position provisional and precarious. The controversy rekindled the inveterate antipathy to Dissenters that persisted long after toleration had become "fashionable";[22] Priestley's house, along with a number of Dissenting homes and chapels, was burned down during the 1791 Birmingham riots. Wollstonecraft's perspective on the penal laws was complex. She duly endorses toleration on various occasions, but her concerns about religious liberty are understandably less pronounced than those of Dissenters. Wollstonecraft was raised in an Anglican household and attended services (without prohibitive scruples) for more than half her life, and while her anti-clerical and non-Trinitarian leanings put her at odds with Anglican orthodoxy, she usually subsumes the particularities of religious compulsion into larger arguments about politics and morality. In *Rights of Woman*, for instance, she condemns the "blind submission imposed at college to forms of belief" because it is "injurious to morality," but the pains of persecution are substantially diluted.[23]

Eschewing the specifics of sectarian suffering was arguably consistent with the liberality of Dissent, but this posture could generate adverse discrepancies with the political realities of Nonconformity, as it did on the topic of education. Responding to the deficiencies of female instruction, Wollstonecraft's recommendation of government-managed day schools (which would involve classes on "the elements of religion") disregarded the anxieties of many Dissenters that such a system would be used first and foremost to impose doctrinal uniformity.[24] Touting the curricular freedom that had helped raise Dissenting academies to esteem, Priestley articulates what such a system felt like for Nonconformists: "to drag [children] from the asylum of their natural guardians, to force them to public places of education, and to instil into them religious sentiments contrary to the judgment and choice of their parents," he shudders, "would be as cruel as obliging a man to make the greatest personal sacrifice, even that of his conscience, to the civil magistrate."[25] In broad strokes Wollstonecraft's views on education are informed by the pedagogical priorities of Dissent, focused as they were on achieving the intellectual independence that a conscientious life demanded, but they are nonetheless inspired by a different set of cultural memories – for Wollstonecraft that of the oppressed woman, for Dissenters that of the persecuted man.

Wollstonecraft, of course, was not oblivious to the concerns of Dissent, but her experience of these issues was distinctively inflected by her own position and priorities. This disjunction is apparent in her response to Dissenting accounts of domesticity, a topic as important for Dissenters as it was to Wollstonecraft herself. Domesticity played an integral role in the way that Dissenters conceived of their identity; the proscriptions against public worship situated domestic space not only as a necessary alternative to the Established Church, but correspondingly as a conceptual locus of religious subjecthood, godly community, and even political opposition. The especially close relationship between Dissenting family and faith took an array of discursive and practical forms, the meeting-house (in some cases a house or cottage) serving to forge intergenerational ties and the Dissenting academy (often imagined as a "family") figuring as an extension of domestic dynamics. For Wollstonecraft, this configuration of power was at once appealing and problematic, since the political and pedagogical potential of domestic space was readily pre-empted by sensuality and sexual tyranny. Thus she clashes with Dissenting writers over those scenes in which domestic sentiments function as the foundation of Christian society. She returns repeatedly to Milton's representations of prelapsarian harmony, finding in the accord between Adam and Eve not a model of Christian liberty but an example of patriarchal discourse – those phrases and images by which men, even before the Fall, impelled women to abrogate their rational capacities.[26] Unable to fully embrace the millenarianism that colored the political visions of Dissent, Wollstonecraft feuded with Anna Laetitia Barbauld on similar grounds, despising her suggestion that wives, like the flowers of the prelapsarian garden, were called "to please" and to "cheer the sense";[27] "so the men tell us," Wollstonecraft scoffs, "but virtue, says reason, must be acquired by rough toils, and useful struggles with worldly cares."[28]

Yet Wollstonecraft was not always so hostile to sentiment and domestic feelings, and her own attempts to account for the religious role of sensibility reflect broader debates that internally divided Dissent. The devotional practices of Nonconformity, particularly Rational Dissent, were defined substantially in opposition to affective dynamics, most sharply the ever-suspect "enthusiasm" that was ascribed to Methodism. The impact of this attitude is patent in much of Wollstonecraft's writing, whether in the precedence she grants to "rational" belief in *Thoughts on the Education of Daughters* (1787),[29] or in her denigration of "weak enthusiasts," whose "fanatical spirit" she represented as vitiating and embarrassing.[30] From this perspective, Wollstonecraft's recuperation of "sacred emotions" (in works like *Letters Written During a Short Residence in Sweden, Norway, and Denmark* [1796] and "On Poetry") seems to mark a movement away from the influence of Nonconformity,[31] and she does admittedly criticize the austerity of Dissenting meeting-houses, for "whilst men have senses, whatever sooths them lends wings to devotion."[32] But Dissent compre-hended an affective tradition, one that proved needful as a means of tempering or "domesticating" its inhospitably cold rational modes – and thus facilitating the non-sectarian benevolence that Wollstonecraft valued.[33] Affiliated with the Aikin–Barbauld circle of Warrington Academy, the spiritual value of sensibility (often carefully distinguished from "enthusiasm") was recognized by some of the most decisively "rational" Dissenters, even Priestley occasionally arguing that "social pas-sions" and sensibility constituted the foundation of devotion.[34] Thus we should be skeptical when Godwin, in his *Memoirs*, ascribes Wollstone-craft's disengagement from organized religion, including Dissent, to her preference for "the sublime and the amiable" elements of faith.[35] Woll-stonecraft not infrequently connects Nonconformity with deep feeling, and the parameters and language of eighteenth-century Dissent provided a framework through which these feelings could be given social and political articulation. In *Mary*, for instance, the heroine's unwavering love, con-ceived as the shadow of divine love, is reified when it prevents her from "conform[ing]" to worldly expectations and unconscionable vows, and in the *Rights of Woman* it is against the indolent orthodoxy of enforced worship (personified in the lazy clergyman) that the emotional power of faith – the "purest effusions of benevolence" – comes into view.[36] This association between Dissent and devotional feeling also perhaps explains why Wollstonecraft was generally indifferent or averse to Methodism; however much she came to appreciate the potential of "enthusiasm," her relationship to Old Dissent affirmed, maybe even generated, a sense that a scrupulous adherence to principles, even those founded on emotion, would manifest as a difficult confrontation with the agents of "conformity" – not simply monarchs and magistrates, but men.

Notes

1 Mary Wollstonecraft, *A Vindication of the Rights of Woman* in *The Works of Mary Wollstonecraft*, edited by Janet Todd and Marilyn Butler (London: W. Pickering, 1989), 5: 265–66.
2 James Bradley, *Religion, Revolution, and English Radicalism: Nonconformity in Eighteenth-Century Politics and Society* (Cambridge: Cambridge University Press, 1990), 93.
3 Joseph Priestley, *A View of the Principles and Conduct of the Protestant Dissenters* (London, 1769), 80.
4 Wollstonecraft, *Mary: A Fiction*, in *Works*, 1: 29, 33–34.
5 Mary Wollstonecraft to Everina Wollstonecraft, November 7, [1787], in *The Collected Letters of Mary Wollstonecraft*, edited by Janet Todd (New York: Columbia University Press, 2003), 139; Wollstonecraft to William Roscoe, February 14, [17]92, in *Letters*, 196.
6 Wollstonecraft, *A Vindication of the Rights of Men*, in *Works*, 5: 18.
7 Wollstonecraft to Joseph Johnson, [1790], in *Letters*, 172.
8 Priestley, *A Free Address to Protestant Dissenters* (London, [1769]), iv.
9 Richard Price, *A Discourse on the Love of Our Country* (London, 1789), 31.
10 Anna Laetitia Barbauld, *An Address to the Opposers of the Repeal of the Corporation and Test Acts* (London, [1790]), 22.
11 Wollstonecraft, *Rights of Men*, in *Works*, 5: 8–9.
12 Ibid., 9.
13 William Enfield, *The Principles and Duty of Protestant Dissenters Considered* (London, [1778]), 8.
14 Priestley, *Address*, vi.
15 Anthony Lincoln, *Some Political & Social Ideas of English Dissent, 1763–1800* (Cambridge: Cambridge University Press, 1938), 1–2.
16 Price, *Country*, 16.
17 Wollstonecraft, *The Wrongs of Woman; or, Maria: A Fragment*, in *Works*, 1: 180.
18 Priestley, *An Essay on the First Principles of Government*, 2nd edn. (London, 1771), 140.
19 Wollstonecraft, *Rights of Woman*, in *Works*, 5: 132.
20 Ibid., 118.
21 Ibid., 153.
22 Priestley, *First Principles*, 236.
23 Wollstonecraft, *Rights of Woman*, in *Works*, 5: 86.
24 Ibid., 240.
25 Priestley, *First Principles*, 98–99.
26 Wollstonecraft, *Rights of Woman*, in *Works*, 5: 124.
27 Barbauld, "To a Lady, with Some Painted Flowers," in *Poems* (London, [1773]), 96.
28 Wollstonecraft, *Rights of Woman*, in *Works*, 5: 123.
29 Wollstonecraft, *Thoughts on the Education of Daughters*, in *Works*, 4: 37, 41.

30 Wollstonecraft to George Blood, March 3 [1788], in *Letters*, 48; Wollstone-craft, *Letters Written in Sweden, Norway, and Denmark*, in *Works*, 6: 287.
31 Wollstonecraft to Gilbert Imlay, July 3, 1795, in *Letters*, 310.
32 Wollstonecraft, *Sweden*, in *Works*, 6: 307.
33 Daniel White, *Early Romanticism and Religious Dissent* (Cambridge: Cambridge University Press, 2006), 69.
34 Priestley, *Two Discourses* (London, [1782]), 2: 47.
35 William Godwin, *Memoirs of the Author of A Vindication of the Rights of Woman* (London, 1798), 33.
36 Wollstonecraft, *Mary*, in *Works*, 1: 46; *Rights of Woman*, in *Works*, 5: 232.

CHAPTER 18

Jean-Jacques Rousseau

Laura Kirkley

It is difficult to overstate the influence of Jean-Jacques Rousseau on the works of Mary Wollstonecraft. Writing to Gilbert Imlay from France in 1784, she contemplated buying their daughter a sash "to honour J. J. Rousseau ... and why not?—for I have always been half in love with him."[1] Half in love, indeed – and half infuriated. Wollstonecraft's excoriating attack on Rousseau's gender politics in *A Vindication of the Rights of Woman* (1792) is well documented, as is the seemingly pernicious role played by *Julie, or, The New Heloise* (1761) in the fate of Wollstonecraft's literary alter ego, Maria, whose Rousseauvian fantasy of romantic love ends in abandonment. Recently, however, critics have begun to give more nuanced accounts of Wollstonecraft's Rousseauism, delineating a complex pattern of enthrallment, identification, and antagonism which not only shapes her political, pedagogical, and philosophical convictions but also her literary self-construction.[2] Her oeuvre suggests a broad and detailed knowledge of Rousseau's corpus, acquired from primary texts and secondary sources. His natural and political philosophy informs her *Historical and Moral View of the French Revolution* (1794), where she refers explicitly to the *Second Discourse* (1754) and *The Social Contract* (1762), and her *Letters Written during a Short Residence in Sweden, Norway, and Denmark* (1795). In her *Original Stories from Real Life*, she strives to adapt the pedagogical theory of *Emile, or On Education* (1762) to a practical educational text for children of both genders. Her reviews and private letters also imply some acquaintance with the *Letter to D'Alembert* (1758); the *Letters Written from the Mountain* (1764); the unfinished *Emile and Sophie* (1780); the infamous *Confessions* (1782); and the melancholic *Reveries of the Solitary Walker* (1782).[3] Given the breadth of her knowledge, a comprehensive account of her Rousseauism is impossible in this short chapter, but the two sections that follow offer brief insights into two relatively neglected areas. The first identifies Rousseau's penchant for paradox as a defining influence on Wollstonecraft's oeuvre, exemplified by her enigmatic literary self-portraiture. The second examines how this fascination with paradox informs her reading of Rousseau's *Heloise* and her portrayal of the connections between authentic expressions of female desire and the creative imagination.

* * *

The crux of Rousseau's paradoxes often lies in the disjunction between what Wollstonecraft calls his "*chimerical* world" and the flawed society of his lived experience.[4] As Michèle Crogniez explains, because paradoxes fly in the face of "common sense," they might be nonsensical, or they might reveal an ostensibly improbable truth – a "chimera" that political or social change could make a reality. This latter sense stems from the Greek root of the word, which signifies a polemical position counter to the orthodox view. Morellet's *Théorie du paradoxe* (1775), which defines paradox as "*une opinion contraire à l'opinion générale*" (an opinion contrary to popular opinion), suggests that eighteenth-century readers were cognizant of the double meaning.[5] As Crogniez observes, paradoxes are a signature part of Rousseau's rhetoric because they advance "*une apparente contradiction qui pousse l'auditeur à remettre en cause ses certitudes*" (an apparent contradiction that impels the listener to question his own certainties).[6] Wollstonecraft's use of the word "paradox" veers between the two definitions of the term, especially when she is referring to Rousseau. In *The Rights of Woman*, she condemns him for letting "reason give way to his desire of singularity, and truth to a favourite paradox"; yet a letter to her sister, Everina, confirms her pleasure in the latter: "I am now reading Rousseau's Emile, and love his paradoxes."[7] Wollstonecraft enjoyed what she called "concentering seeming contradictions,"[8] the process of discerning the complex truth at the heart of a paradox, and in her review of the *Confessions*, she derides narrow-minded readers who "rudely laugh at inconsistencies as if they were absurdities."[9]

One of Rousseau's most famous paradoxes is his claim, in *The Social Contract*, that man is born free but is everywhere in chains, which posits that each of us has an inherently independent (but benevolent) natural self that is warped and imprisoned by social constraints. In different ways, his various textual alter egos represent determined adherence to the truth of an inner self at odds with the established order. As Christopher Kelly points out, Rousseau's transparent self-portraiture transforms the raw material of his personal experience into moral fables representing the philosophical principles that underpin his account of human nature.[10] Each "Rousseau" in his oeuvre is a self-conscious construction, designed to represent a particular aspect of the author's philosophical vision. Depicting himself by turns as an authoritative pedagogical innovator and a guilt-ridden, intensely sensitive malcontent, he sets up an intertextual tension between imagined ideals and corrupt "reality" that is personified in his paradoxical self-portraits.

Rousseau's vision of thwarted Natural Man encapsulates the tension between imagined ideals and lived reality that pervades Wollstonecraft's oeuvre. In her two *Vindications* and her *View of the French Revolution*, she depicts enslavement as a state of mind whereby constraint and dependence are accepted as the immutable and even desirable order of things. By contrast, she constructs herself, both in her works and in her private letters, as a maverick gifted with the capacity to perceive, and suffer acutely from, her own disenfranchisement. Her many alter egos often allude to their counterparts in the works of Rousseau: in *Original Stories*, the formidable Mrs. Mason recalls Emile's Tutor; the eponymous heroine of *Mary: A Fiction* (1788) has a Rousseauvian commitment to personal authenticity and exquisite sensibility that also recalls the heroine of *Heloise*; in *The Wrongs of Woman; or, Maria* (1798), Maria is a Woman of Sensibility who describes the formation of her character in a confessional narrative. Wollstonecraft also describes her affinity with the "strange inconsistent unhappy clever" persona of the *Confessions* – "he rambles into that ... *chimerical* world in which I have too often [wand]ered"[11] – and calls herself a "*Solitary Walker*," one "destined to wander alone."[12] Ironically, the figure of the Solitary Walker inspires Wollstonecraft to a defiant political and stylistic avant-gardism, which Rousseau epitomized himself but discouraged in women. In her private and in her published letters, she draws on his life writing to invest her feelings of alienation with ideological significance, portraying them as symptoms of oppression.

Wollstonecraft's alter egos are also distinctly Rousseauvian because they are at once transparently autobiographical and expedient partial fictions designed to communicate her ideas. Thus she translates one of the paradoxes at the heart of Rousseau's philosophy into her own works: although wedded to his ideal of absolute fidelity to one's authentic self, she articulates her beliefs and experiences through personae whose fictional elements are always apparent. The section that follows focuses on one such persona, the heroine of *Mary*, to explore Wollstonecraft's response to Rousseau's paradoxical attitudes to female desire and romantic love.

* * *

Rousseau's Everywoman, Sophie, embodies a vision of women as innately power-hungry, vacuous, over-sexed, and incurably delicate. In *Heloise*, however, he laments the female condition that *Emile* strives to perpetuate, creating in his heroine, Julie d'Étange, a woman whose traditionally feminine virtues – modesty, compassion, tenderness – co-exist with transgressive and proactive desire for her tutor, Saint-Preux. Having consummated their love affair, Julie repents and enters an arranged marriage with the benevolent aristocrat, Wolmar, redirecting her finely tuned sensibility toward conjugal devotion and maternal duty. Yet Rousseau also hints persistently that she never truly overcomes her love for Saint-Preux and that her ultimate death is arguably a release from inauthenticity.

In many of Wollstonecraft's works, *Heloise* is the unacknowledged template for her analysis of the role erotic love might play in the lives of women struggling against patriarchal hostility to female desire. Her response to Rousseau in general and to *Heloise* in particular is perhaps exemplified by her attack on Germaine de Staël's *Letters on the Writings and Character of J. J. Rousseau* (1788) in an article for the *Analytical Review* in 1789. Staël seemed able to stomach not only Sophie, but also the paranoid misogyny of the *Letter to D'Alembert*, and Wollstonecraft identifies, at the root of this uncritical enthusiasm, the pre-eminence of love in Rousseau's portrayal of female destiny. Her ire can also be explained by her belief that Staël plays down Rousseau's complexities in order to "rescue" his texts for conventional morality. Where Staël sees inconsistencies, Wollstonecraft sees characters that are intricately and compellingly human:

> How little, indeed, do they know of human nature, who by their injudicious candour labour to destroy all identity of character; endeavouring to root out the tares, to soften apparent defects, they may seem to rub off some sharp corners, rude unsightly angles; but could they really succeed in their childish attempt, they would only level original prominent features, and stupidly active, transform a sublime mountain into a beautiful plain.[13]

As Mary Seidman Trouille puts it, for Wollstonecraft, Staël's *Lettres* have "a bulldozer effect on Rousseau's writing, flattening out and burying the most salient features of his thinking."[14] Staël argues that Julie's exemplarity as a wife and mother has a didactic function that redeems her sexual misconduct, but Wollstonecraft refuses to elide the moral complexities of the novel. Whereas she condemns Sophie outright, she draws on certain aspects of *Heloise* and rejects others in the process of developing her feminist voice.

After her marriage to Wolmar, Julie writes a letter to Saint-Preux in which she expresses skepticism about the durability of even the most beguiling love affair, and in several passages of *The Rights of Woman*, Wollstonecraft expresses a similar view: "Love, from its very nature," she claims, "must be transitory."[15] Her concern is that women educated only to excite desire will struggle to establish more durable bonds of friendship with their husbands. Instead of fulfilling their duties as mothers and useful members of society, such women will pine for the worship they have been taught to expect. In *Heloise*, Rousseau furnishes a counter-model in the Wolmars' marriage, described by Julie in terms of a mutual and clear-sighted commitment to the common good, which is possible only because their union is unclouded by passion.[16] Similarly, Wollstonecraft suggests that "a master and mistress of a family ought not to continue to love each other with passion. I mean to say, that they ought not to indulge these emotions which disturb the order of society, and engross the thoughts that should be otherwise employed."[17]

If such love can "disturb the order of society," though, it is obviously powerful while it lasts. Rousseau connects its capacity to conjure illusions of perfection with the imaginative faculty, extolled in many of his works as an avenue to moral enlightenment and emotional solace. Barbara Taylor explains that, in the eighteenth century, the imagination was often under-stood as "a fount of true selfhood" and, in religious discourse, "a psychic pathway between humanity and the divine."[18] Conceiving of the imagin-ation as a "sacred faculty, linking the fantasising mind to its Maker,"[19] Wollstonecraft argues that women should be educated, not only to exercise their reason, but also to strive for some partial knowledge of the divine, glimpsed through "transcendent fantasy."[20] In *The Rights of Woman*, she relates this transcendent imagination to the "genius" of Rousseau, for it "draws the picture of love" in "glowing colours."[21] The image of a glowing or heated imagination appears several times in Wollstonecraft's corpus; the metaphor alludes to her classical conception of the imagination as Prome-thean fire, a creative element, which, in certain privileged human psyches, transforms sensory impressions into divinely inspired insights. A Promethean imagination gives the subject access to visions of sublime virtue and heavenly bliss. She describes Rousseau as "a mind, condemned in a world like this, to prove its noble origin by panting after unattainable perfection; ever pursuing what it acknowledges to be a fleeting dream."[22] Love is fuel to the Promethean fire of his genius. Although she quotes Milton, Wollstonecraft also appears to have *Heloise* in mind when she claims that "an imagination of this vigorous cast can . . . imagine a degree of mutual affection that shall refine the soul, and not expire when it has served as a 'scale to heavenly'; and, like devotion, make it absorb every meaner affection and desire."²³ On one hand, Wollstonecraft responds sardonically to this blissful vision, commenting that Rousseau's "paradise would soon be violated by the entrance of some unexpected guest."²⁴ On the other, she sees in "the delusions of passion" some evidence of "the eager pursuit of the good which every one shapes to his own fancy."²⁵

As the idea of the transcendent imagination gained intellectual and cultural currency, it was compared unfavorably with "the lower-order fictions of the merely fanciful mind," such as daydreams, delusions, and onanistic fantasies.²⁶ The boundary between the two was considered perilously unstable. Wollstonecraft is struck by the fact that Rousseau's Promethean imagination could also generate "wild chimeras," the Sophie-like women of his "lascivious" fantasies.²⁷ In *The Rights of Woman*, she is torn between skepticism about the rewards of love and indignation at the misogyny that curbs and demonizes female desire: both women and men, she argues, should be free to express "the common appetites and passions of their nature."²⁸ In her novels, she persistently returns to the tension set up, in *Heloise*, between female virtue and erotic love. *Mary* exemplifies her exploration of the difficulties women faced in accommodating desire to a life of social utility.

Mary is an heiress forced into an arranged marriage at a young age but granted a period of respite from her marital duties. Like Wollstonecraft, she travels to Portugal to care for a sick friend. There she meets and falls in love with the (entirely fictional) Rousseau-like Henry. Gauche and flawed, he has "genius" that has been prone to the errors of an over-heated imagination.²⁹ He is also terminally ill. Describing Mary's voyage home, Wollstonecraft uses a violent sea-storm to characterize her heroine in terms of the sublime: "The vessel rose on a wave and descended into a yawning gulph—Not slower did her mounting soul return to earth, for—Ah! her treasure and her heart was there. . . . In a little vessel in the midst of such a storm she was not dismayed; she felt herself independent."³⁰ The passage aligns Mary's feelings for Henry with the power of the storm, evoking a depth of feeling that elevates her "mounting soul" but also intensifies the pain and pleasure of her sublimated erotic love. In comparison to her fellow passengers, her relative calm in the face of danger gives her a grandeur which, Wollstonecraft implies, transcends earthly concerns and rises toward the divine. As Taylor observes, "Mary knows that love, illusory and unrealisable in its earthly form, will transmute into the verities of eternal bliss."³¹

Another aspect of Mary's sublimity, however, is her Rousseauvian pursuit of authentic self-realization in the face of a hostile social order.

Since passion is integral to her character, this pursuit entails sincerity in love. Despite Wollstonecraft's emphasis on a transcendent eroticism, Mary struggles to contemplate "solitary happiness," and is drawn back, in consequence, to earthly love.[32] Indeed, her conception of the divine seems dependent on her experiences of fellow feeling: "In a state of bliss, it will be the society of beings we can love, without the alloy that earthly infirmities mix with our best affections, that will constitute great part of our happiness."[33] Like Julie, Mary "cannot live without loving,"[34] and in *Henry*, she appears to find an earth-bound form of salvation – with the caveat, of course, that the relationship cannot last. She contemplates adultery, albeit of the mind rather than the body, and this reaction to her arranged marriage implicitly condemns Julie's decision to renounce love in favor of a dutiful marriage: for Mary, it is immoral to "promise to love one man, when the image of another was ever present to her."[35] The women she meets in Portugal function as foils for her free-spiritedness, their minds "shackled with a set of notions concerning propriety, the fitness of things for the world's eye, trammels which always hamper weak people."[36] Pitting her divinely inspired conscience against "the maxims of worldly wisdom," she makes romantic love the inspiration for authenticity in defiance of social norms: "can I listen to the cold dictates of worldly prudence, and bid my tumultuous passions cease to vex me, be still, find content in grovelling pursuits, and the admiration of the misjudging crowd, when it is only one I wish to please—one who would be all the world to me."[37] For Wollstonecraft, then, Mary's sublime virtue arises not from resistance to love but from courageous opposition to a society that denies women an authentic experience and expression of it.

Wollstonecraft draws on the works of Rousseau to create multiple autofictional personae marked by their determination to live authentically in the face of a hostile social order. These personae are designed to invite intertextual reading: recurring traits and narrative positions delineate a recognizable, if protean, "Wollstonecraft" who is also distinctively Rousseauvian. Each persona represents one aspect of her philosophical vision, which takes some of its complexity from her belief that paradox can offer insight into otherwise elusive truths. As this essay demonstrates, although Wollstonecraft rejects the gender politics of *Emile*, the feminist perspective of *The Rights of Woman* and of Wollstonecraft's novels is partially informed by Rousseau's paradoxical portrait of romantic love as simultaneously dangerous, doomed to extinction, and the sublime brainchild of a Promethean imagination capable of divine insights. In short, Wollstonecraft's fraught admiration for Rousseau makes his influence on her oeuvre complex and profound. She is a resisting reader of his works, at once captivated and critical, and a critical study that fully explores her engagement with them is long overdue.

Notes

1 Mary Wollstonecraft, *The Collected Letters*, edited by Janet Todd (London: Penguin, 2004), 263.
2 Barbara Taylor, *Mary Wollstonecraft and the Feminist Imagination* (Cambridge: Cambridge University Press, 2003), chapters 1–2; Mary Seidman Trouille, *Sexual Politics in the Enlightenment: Women Writers Read Rousseau* (Albany: SUNY Press, 1997), chapter 5.
3 Mary Wollstonecraft, *The Works of Mary Wollstonecraft*, edited by Janet Todd and Marilyn Butler (London: W. Pickering, 1989), 7: 228–34.
4 *Collected Letters*, 115.
5 Cited in Michèle Crogniez, *Rousseau et le paradoxe* (Paris: Honoré Champion Éditeur, 1997), 21.
6 Crogniez, 30.
7 Wollstonecraft, *Works*, 5: 111; Wollstonecraft, *Collected Letters*, 114.
8 Wollstonecraft, *Works*, 7: 229.
9 Ibid., 229.
10 See Christopher Kelly, *Rousseau's Exemplary Life: The Confessions as Political Philosophy* (Ithaca: Cornell University Press, 1987), 16–19.
11 Wollstonecraft, *Collected Letters*, 115.
12 Wollstonecraft, *Collected Letters*, 349; Wollstonecraft, *Works*, 6: 298.
13 Wollstonecraft, *Works*, 7: 136.
14 Trouille, 221.
15 Wollstonecraft, *Works*, 5: 98.
16 See Jean-Jacques Rousseau, *Julie, or, The New Heloise: Letters of Two Lovers Who Live in a Small Town at the Foot of the Alps*, translated by Philip Steward and Jean Vaché, edited by Roger D. Masters and Christopher Kelly (Hanover: University Press of New England for Dartmouth College, 1997), 306–07.
17 Wollstonecraft, *Works*, 5: 99
18 Taylor, *Mary Wollstonecraft and the Feminist Imagination*, 58, 60.
19 Ibid., 21.
20 Ibid.
21 Wollstonecraft, *Works*, 5: 142, 143.
22 Ibid.
23 Ibid.
24 Ibid.
25 Ibid.
26 Taylor, *Mary Wollstonecraft and the Feminist Imagination*, 61.
27 Wollstonecraft, *Works*, 5: 108; ibid., 160.
28 Ibid., 200.
29 Wollstonecraft, *Works*, 1: 28.

30 Ibid., 50.
31 Taylor, *Mary Wollstonecraft and the Feminist Imagination*, 115.
32 Wollstonecraft, *Works*, 1: 46.
33 Ibid., 46.
34 Ibid., 68.
35 Ibid., 42.
36 Ibid., 30.
37 Ibid., 46.

CHAPTER 19

Edmund Burke

Frans de Bruyn

Mary Wollstonecraft's writings reveal a mind keenly interested in the politics of her day and well-read in the works of prominent political theorists of her time – Locke, Rousseau, "commonwealth men," Scottish Enlightenment thinkers – whose ideas helped shape her political thought. Among these writers, none had quite the catalytic, galvanizing effect that Edmund Burke did in spurring her to articulate her political convictions and her feminist principles. Burke's writings on the French Revolution, especially his *Reflections on the Revolution in France* (1790) and his early aesthetic treatise, *An Enquiry into the Origin of Our Ideas of the Sublime and Beautiful* (1757, 1759), challenged Wollstonecraft to formulate her views on key issues in eighteenth-century political thought, such as the basis of political virtue; the origins of political society (social contract theory); the existence of natural rights or "rights of men" (as human rights were then called); and the place of women in the social and political order.

The publication of Burke's *Reflections* on November 1, 1790 provoked a hurried reply on Wollstonecraft's part, which appeared on November 29 as *A Vindication of the Rights of Men, in a Letter to the Right Honourable Edmund Burke*. Among the very first of numerous responses to Burke's *Reflections*, it shows signs of the haste with which it was composed. Despite this, the *Rights of Men* is a subtle engagement with Burke that, in the view of David Bromwich, surpasses the better-known rejoinders of Thomas Paine, Joseph Priestley, and James Mackintosh. "The steadiness of Wollstonecraft's engagement with Burke," argues Bromwich, "gives her book its special authority as an act of moral imagination": her recognition that Burke's political argument is fundamentally one about morality "holds the germ" of her most famous work, *A Vindication of the Rights of Woman* (1792).[1] Bromwich's opinion about the importance of Wollstonecraft's response to Burke is shared by other recent scholars of her political thought.

In light of this, a chapter devoted to Burke's political ideas is entirely pertinent in a collection of essays designed to contextualize Wollstonecraft's writings. The person who unwittingly brought the two together in political debate was the Reverend Richard Price, a Dissenting clergyman and political reformer whom Wollstonecraft met at Newington Green, where she and her sisters had established a school for girls and where he was the minister at the Presbyterian (Unitarian) chapel. On November 4, 1789, Price was invited to address the London Revolution Society, which met annually to celebrate the anniversary of the 1688 Glorious Revolution, when the Catholic king James II had been overthrown and the crown had passed to the Protestants William of Orange and Mary. Price's address to the Society, published as *A Discourse on the Love of Our Country* (1789), extolled the French Revolution as a victory in France for political principles established in England a century earlier by the Glorious Revolution.

Though it appeared a full year after Price's *Discourse*, Burke's *Reflections* was a vehement reaction to Price's interpretation of the political significance of the Glorious Revolution. Price lauded the events of 1688–89 as having established three key political rights in England: (1) liberty of conscience in religion, (2) the legitimacy of resistance to abuses of power, and (3) the right "to chuse our own governors; to cashier them for misconduct; and to frame a government for ourselves."[2] These principles, Price enthusiastically maintained, had now manifested themselves in the American and French Revolutions of 1776 and 1789. His *Discourse* ends, accordingly, with a joyful vision of the light of liberty, newly kindled in France "into a blaze that lays despotism in ashes."[3]

As a Whig, Burke accepted Price's first two statements without argument, though, like many of his fellow Whigs, he inclined to the view that the right to resist tyranny (Price's second point) was a last resort that the nation had not in fact been forced to exercise in 1688, since James II had, by his actions, effectively left the throne vacant. But Burke took vigorous exception to the third point (actually a trinity of three distinct principles). The Glorious Revolution, he took great pains to argue, was not the grand rupture in English political continuity that Price took it to be, nor had it enshrined the political rights enunciated in Price's omnibus third statement. In response, Burke laid out an elaborate history of English constitutional continuity over the centuries, representing the constitution as an "entailed inheritance," like an estate passed on through a family from generation to generation with restrictions (legally known as "entails") on what successors could do to alter or sell off their inheritance.[4]

On a personal level, Wollstonecraft's rapid reply to Burke evinces her loyalty to Price, a friend and mentor whom Burke has, in her view, treated with "indecent familiarity and supercilious contempt."[5] In the process, however, she subjects Burke to some *ad hominem* thrusts of her own, albeit milder in tone than was usual in controversies of this kind. Personal attacks were, indeed, a stock-in-trade of eighteenth-century political debate; in this instance, as will appear, a perceptive insight into Burke's political thought lies behind Wollstonecraft's gendered characterization of him as a sentimental and effeminized man who feebly weeps in the *Reflections* for Marie Antoinette but is unmoved by the distresses of the poor and the "hungry cry of helpless babes."[6]

The response and counter-response dynamic of the political debate among Burke, Price, Wollstonecraft, and others over the French Revolution should alert us to the rhetorical and polemical character of their texts, which can make it difficult to distinguish the underlying political philosophy espoused by the various parties from the rhetorical points they make in the heat of debate. Wollstonecraft, for example, polemically dismisses Burke's emphasis on the continuity of the British constitutional order as an advocacy of political stasis. To insist on a set of constitutional practices sanctioned by history and prescription (uninterrupted use or long-standing custom) is to "reverence the rust of antiquity" and "to remain forever in frozen inactivity, because a thaw, whilst it nourishes the soil, spreads a temporary inundation."[7] Yet, despite Burke's emphasis in the *Reflections* on hereditary succession and the value of continuity, he is well aware, as his writings elsewhere amply testify, that a "state without the means of some change is without the means of its conservation."[8]

Burke was, in other words, no advocate of political immobility, and he was sharply critical of the old order in France, which he regarded as "full of abuses." When the Americans rebelled in the 1770s against the arbitrary measures of the British crown and parliament, he had supported their cause because he regarded their struggle as a reassertion of ancient liberties that they had previously enjoyed, in the face of encroachments from London, the center of the empire. Wollstonecraft and other critics of Burke saw a stark inconsistency in his refusal now to extend his approval to the French Revolution as well – they detected, in fact, an apostasy on his part from his previously held Whig political convictions. But Burke saw an entirely different process of change at work in France: ideologically driven and based on theoretical or abstract principles, rather than the actual historical circumstances of French society and politics. So when

Wollstonecraft alleges that Burke prefers "frozen inactivity" because he fears a "temporary inundation," she both exaggerates his opposition to reform and underplays his apprehensions at the consequences of radical change.

Nonetheless, points of real difference between Burke and Wollstonecraft became apparent under the pressure of debate. Wollstonecraft voices repeatedly her faith in the power of reason and in social progress, enlightenment values she shared with rational Dissenters such as Price and Priestley. All rational creatures have as their "birthright" God-given natural rights. "The birthright of man," she affirms," is such a degree of liberty, civil and religious, as is compatible with the liberty of every other individual with whom he is united in a social compact."[9] In many respects this is a statement that Burke could agree with. As a Whig, he accepts the view that political society is in principle the product of a social compact, but he was always doubtful of political schemes and arguments built on abstract principles rather than the experience of generations. For Wollstonecraft "the eternal foundation of right" is "immutable truth," but Burke sees in humanity little of the rationality necessary to discern such truth abstractly, and he is equally skeptical of any belief in human perfectibility. Burke's orthodox Christian view of human nature precludes Wollstonecraft's optimism about the accessibility of reason.

Consequently, prudence is for Burke a cardinal political virtue. Prudence dictates that because any one person's "private stock of reason" is very small, "individuals would do better to avail themselves of the general bank and capital of nations and of ages"[10] Given the limitations of human reason, time-honored habits and customs, in accordance with our "natural feelings," furnish a more reliable guide for the politician and statesman than abstract principles. Burke calls these customs "prejudices" (a term not meant pejoratively in this context): "Many of our men of speculation, instead of exploding general prejudices, employ their sagacity to discover the latent wisdom which prevails in them." His use here of the possessive adjective "our" contrasts English thinkers with French enlightenment philosophes who seek to reconstruct human nature and society from the ground up, on theoretical assumptions. "We are not the converts of Rousseau," he asserts: "we are not the disciples of Voltaire; Helvetius has made no progress amongst us."[11] Price and Priestley, maintains Burke, do not speak for the English nation.

What especially exercised Wollstonecraft about Burke's position is the specific content of the prejudices or customs he cherishes, particularly deference to rank and hierarchy: from fear of God and awe for kings to reverence for the clergy and respect to nobility. These are *natural* feelings; "all other feelings are false and spurious."[12] At the root of this defense of hierarchy and social subordination, in Wollstonecraft's view, is the need to justify by some pretext or other the unequal distribution of property in society. "[T]he demon of property," she declares with indignation, "has ever been at hand to encroach on the sacred rights of men, and to fence round with awful pomp laws that war with justice."[13] Burke regarded inequality of property as an inevitability, however regrettable, and in such circumstances it was necessary, as he emphasizes near the end of the *Reflections*, for people to "respect that property of which they cannot partake ... and be taught their consolation in the proportions of eternal justice." To Wollstonecraft, who cites this passage at length in *Rights of Men*, Burke's doctrine is nothing but "contemptible, hard-hearted sophistry."[14]

At issue in this stark difference between the two authors is much more than the question of how much wealth the economy could generate in the eighteenth century and how this might be distributed. For both Wollstonecraft and Burke, the nature and possession of property in society is ultimately a question of political and individual virtue, and this question, in turn, takes us to the heart of their opposing texts. Essential to English constitutional stability, in Burke's view, is the fact that political power is entrusted by the rules of parliamentary representation to male landowners, both in the House of Lords and in the Commons. (The rules of inheritance, especially primogeniture, ensured that land normally passed in the male line from father to son.) Because landed property is immovable, it was assumed that men of landed property would have a natural stake in the well-being of their society and on this basis could be presumed to possess political virtue and to take an impartial, "comprehensive, connected view" of the competing interests that compose the state.[15] By contrast, individuals whose wealth is based in money (which is volatile and portable) or who are trained in specific professions (such as medicine and the law) cannot be deemed have the same disinterestedness or equally broad horizons, and are therefore likelier to act from self-interested or partial motives.

Burke is thinking here of virtue in a political rather than a personal sense, a civic virtue that individuals are presumed to have on the basis of their familial lineage and landed wealth, a heritage that gives them the leisure and disinterestedness to exercise active citizenship. He contrasts this "presumptive" virtue with the "active" virtue of those who have achieved wealth or prominence through their own active efforts, such as merchants, manufacturers, and professionals.[16] To Wollstonecraft, Burke has it precisely backwards. Hereditary property and hereditary honors have transformed the nobility and gentry into "artificial monsters" made decadent by their wealth and privilege. How can "a man of rank and fortune ... discover that he is a man when all his wants are instantly supplied, and invention is never sharpened by necessity?" It is folly to impute, as Burke does, a modicum of virtue to such individuals on the basis of their possession of property. Virtue must be earned and striven for, but the "man of rank" has nothing to spur him on: "Will he labour, for every thing valuable must be the fruit of laborious exertions, to attain knowledge and virtue ... when the flattering attention of sycophants is a more luscious cordial?"[17] The other ranks of society, meanwhile, are either, as in the case with the poor, driven to vice out of sheer necessity, or, as in the case of "the middle class of people," subjected to "all the vice and misery that arise in society from ... aping the manners of the great."[18] For Wollstonecraft, the measure of a rational, just society is how effectively it promotes the personal virtue of all its citizens.

In an important sense, Burke and Wollstonecraft argue from the same premise – that a civilized polity is one in which moral and political virtue flourishes – but they reason from this premise to radically different conclusions. Burke regards moral conduct as habitual or even instinctive, guided by inculcated manners and tastes. In Europe, the manners that guide us have their historical roots in "the spirit of a gentleman, and the spirit of religion," which together produced a "system of opinion and sentiment" called chivalry. As a system of manners, chivalry mediated the destructive potential of political power, social and economic inequality, and selfish human passions: "it subdued the fierceness of pride and power; it obliged sovereigns to submit to the soft collar of social esteem, compelled stern authority to submit to elegance, and gave a domination vanquisher of laws, to be subdued by manners."[19]

But this decency of manners, which prescribes due consideration on the ruler's part and due submission on the part of the ruled, entails a measure of hypocrisy that Wollstonecraft finds insupportable. She reacts fiercely to Burke's elegiac expressions of regret at the loss of a chivalric "sensibility of principle" that "inspired courage," "mitigated ferocity," and "ennobled whatever it touched" – all this at the expense of moral clarity, for under chivalry, Burke acknowledges, "vice itself lost half its evil, by losing all its grossness."[20] Wollstonecraft quotes these words back at him, adding scornfully, "What a sentiment to come from a moral pen!" She then proceeds to dismantle his paradox: "Stealing, and whoring, and drunkenness, are gross vices, I presume, though they may not obliterate every moral sentiment . . . but over-reaching [fraud], adultery, and coquetry, are venal offences, though they reduce virtue to an empty name, and make wisdom consist in saving appearances."[21] The poor, at least, can plead necessity in being driven to theft and prostitution, yet their moral transgressions bear a much greater weight of opprobrium than do the equivalent acts when they are euphemistically renamed "over-reaching" and "adultery" to designate the refined vices of the upper classes.

Wollstonecraft finds the same class bias at play in Burke's feminization of natural feeling. In perhaps the best-known passage of the *Reflections*, he laments the violence visited upon the queen of France by a Parisian mob that stormed the palace of Versailles in October 1789: "little did I dream that I should have lived to see such disasters fallen upon her in a nation of gallant men, in a nation of men of honour and of cavaliers. I thought ten thousand swords must have leaped from their scabbards to avenge even a look that threatened her with insult."[22] Burke's tears are reserved "for the downfall of queens" not the "distresses of industrious mothers, whose *helpmates* have been torn from them." As many of her readers have noted, she presents Burke as an effeminized man of sensibility, and she links this gendered characterization with Burke's early and influential presentation, in *A Philosophical Enquiry*, of the aesthetic experiences of sublimity and beauty as starkly gendered and hierarchical categories, with sublimity the more powerful, grand, and masculine of the two, and beauty a subordinate, feminine, pleasurable experience aroused by vulnerability and imperfection.[23]

In condemning Burke's response to the "affecting spectacle" of the attack on the king and queen at Versailles, Wollstonecraft does not condone the actions of the Parisian mob who seized the royal pair, as she made clear in her subsequent *Historical and Moral View of the French Revolution* (1794), in which she describes the events of October 1789 as depraved and atrocious.[24] But she objects to Burke's elevation of a particular class of emotional responses – those aroused by scenes of well-born women in situations of distress – to the status of a universal moral touchstone. In a telling take-down of the moral premises of sensibility, she imagines "fair ladies" who exercise their "tender feelings by the perusal of the last imported novel" but turn away with unconcern from "the sight of a flagellation" inflicted on an African slave.[25] These same women, instructed by Burke's treatise on the sublime and beautiful, have been convinced that "*littleness* and *weakness* are the very essence of beauty" and have abandoned the cultivation of "moral virtues that might chance to excite respect" for fear that this would "interfere with the pleasing sensations they were created to inspire." Her dismay at Burke's gendered conception of moral virtue, accessible in full only to the figure of masculinity, became an impetus for the composition of her best-known political work, *A Vindication of the Rights of Woman* (1792). There she was to interrogate and comprehensively reject the implications of Burke's position: that women ought "not to cultivate the moral virtues that might chance to excite respect" for fear this might "interfere with the pleasing sensations they were created to inspire"; that truth, justice, wisdom, and fortitude are "manly morals"; and that women exist only to rouse men to the exercise of such manly virtue.[26]

Notes

1 David Bromwich, "Wollstonecraft as a Critic of Burke," *Political Theory*, 23 (1995), 619, 620.
2 Richard Price, *A Discourse on the Love of Our Country* (London, 1789), 34.
3 Ibid., 50.
4 Edmund Burke, *Reflections on the Revolution in France*, in *The Writings and Speeches of Edmund Burke*, edited by L. G. Mitchell (Oxford: Clarendon Press, 1989), 8: 83.
5 Mary Wollstonecraft, *A Vindication of the Rights of Men*, in *The Works of Mary Wollstonecraft*, edited by Janet Todd and Marilyn Butler (London: W. Pickering, 1989), 5: 18.
6 Wollstonecraft, *Rights of Men*, 15.
7 Ibid., 10.
8 Burke, *Reflections*, 72.
9 Wollstonecraft, *Rights of Men*, 9.
10 Burke, *Reflections*, 138.
11 Ibid., 137.
12 Ibid., 137–38.
13 Wollstonecraft, *Rights of Men*, 9.
14 Burke, *Reflections*, 290; Wollstonecraft, *Rights of Men*, 55.
15 Burke, *Reflections*, 95.
16 Burke introduces these terms in *Reflections*, 101.
17 Wollstonecraft, *Rights of Men*, 10, 42.
18 Ibid., 23.
19 Burke, *Reflections*, 130, 127.
20 Ibid., 127.
21 Wollstonecraft, *Rights of Men*, 24–25.
22 Burke, *Reflections*, 126–27.
23 Burke, *A Philosophical Enquiry into the Origin of Our Ideas of the Sublime and Beautiful*, in *The Writings and Speeches of Edmund Burke*, edited by T. O. McLoughlin and James T. Boulton (Oxford: Clarendon Press, 1997), 1: 270–72 (part 3, sections 9–11).

24 Wollstonecraft writes, "they were strictly speaking a mob, affixing all the odium to the appellation it can possibly import; and not to be confounded with the honest multitude, who took the Bastille." See *An Historical and Moral View of the French Revolution*, in *The Works of Mary Wollstonecraft*, edited by Janet Todd and Marilyn Butler (London: W. Pickering, 1989), 6: 201–09.

25 Wollstonecraft, *Rights of Men*, 45.

26 Ibid.

CHAPTER 20

William Godwin

Pamela Clemit

The philosophical anarchist William Godwin (1756–1836) has long been celebrated and excoriated for what Charles Lamb later dubbed "the famous fire cause."[1] Lamb refers to one of the most audacious propositions in *An Enquiry Concerning Political Justice* (1793), Godwin's major philosophical work. Suppose you were given the choice of saving Archbishop Fénelon or his chambermaid from a burning palace. (Fénelon was the author of *Les aventures de Télémaque* (1699), a thinly veiled attack on the French monarchy.) According to Godwin, the truly benevolent individual would save Fénelon because of his superior value to humanity—even if the chambermaid were one's wife or mother: "What magic is there in the pronoun 'my,' to overturn the decisions of everlasting truth?"[2]

Godwin's was an extreme position, even among supporters of the French Revolution. Opponents linked his early rejection of the private affections with what Edmund Burke called "the homicide philanthropy of France."[3] As conservative reaction set in toward the end of the 1790s, Godwin was widely caricatured as an embodiment of abstract reason—a view which has continued to shape opinions of his life and writings.

Yet Godwin's letters, which are being published in six volumes, show him to be a more complex figure than his published writings suggest. They reveal a man of strong feelings who reflected intensively on his own experiences. He was not an inflexible rationalist who was unable to form a just estimate of the affections, but was always reassessing his ideas of what it meant to be human. When he made a belated public declaration of the value of the private affections, in the preface to *St. Leon: A Tale of the Sixteenth Century* (1799), his fellow novelist Elizabeth Inchbald, a correspondent since 1792, advised against it:

> "Let the reader rather wonder at that versatile Genius that can write so differently on different occasions—Let Readers wonder at the writer's *art* rather than at his inconstancy—Let them not suppose your principles

changed, but that the Public never knew what these principles were. Let them merely talk of your different productions un[der] the title of 'Godwin's Head' and 'Godwin's Heart'."[4]

* * *

Godwin rose to fame in the 1790s as a kind of English Voltaire or Rousseau. Following *Political Justice*, which became an immediate success among revolutionary sympathizers of all persuasions, he published in 1794 the novel *Caleb Williams*, a gripping suspense narrative, and the pamphlet *Cursory Strictures*, a defense of twelve radicals charged with high treason in October 1794. He later wrote five more full-length novels, works of educational theory, children's books, plays, philosophical biographies, essays, political pamphlets, and a four-volume history of the English Commonwealth. Sociable on principle as well as by disposition, he knew or corresponded with almost everyone of note on the political left from the era of the French Revolution to the 1832 Reform Bill. His circle of friends included nearly all the major literary figures of his age. Godwin's greatest impact was in the debates following the French Revolution, but his influence has been through several revivals, and is currently rising again among scholars and political thinkers.

Inchbald was right to emphasize the protean quality of Godwin's intellect. He did not revise his texts as compulsively as Wordsworth, but he revisited the same preoccupations throughout his writing life. He worked out what he wanted to say during the process of composition, and sent installments of his works to the printer before completion. Individual works do not provide definitive statements of his philosophy, but represent what he thought and judged it possible to say at a particular historical moment—*Political Justice* and *Caleb Williams* each went through two rounds of authorial revisions during the political ferment of the 1790s. Any reader approaching Godwin's writings is confronted by the ambiguities and apparent inconsistencies, which Inchbald regarded as a strength.

There are two main reasons for these changes of heart. Godwin's career did not follow a traditional cycle of rise and fall, but went through different phases. Until recently, critics tended to focus exclusively on the books he wrote in the 1790s. These are his most important works, but they do not represent the whole of his career. His literary acolyte Edward Lytton Bulwer, writing in 1830, described Godwin as "a man, endowed with a mind as various and accomplished as it is inquiring and profound," and drew attention to his diverse achievements as "an historian, an essayist, a biographer, a novelist, a dramatic writer, a philosopher."[5] Such versatility may be attributed to Godwin's upbringing and education in eighteenth-century English religious nonconformity, which held to an ideal of universal knowledge. His writings do not conform to modern disciplinary categories.

Godwin's diversity was also a matter of intellectual outlook. In *Thoughts Occasioned by the Perusal of Dr. Parr's Spital Sermon* (1801), he wrote: "The human intellect is a sort of barometer, directed in its variations by the atmosphere that surrounds it."[6] He was alluding to those who originally welcomed *Political Justice*, and later changed their minds—but the statement is also an instance of his own mental flexibility. In the second and third editions of *Political Justice*, Godwin modified the rational and individualistic doctrines of the first edition, placing a new emphasis on the role of sympathy and feeling in moral judgments. Godwin's politics, too, could seem unstable. In *Political Justice*, he criticized monarchy, aristocracy, priesthood, marriage, and inequality of property. But he did not aim to overturn these institutions, only to suggest their eventual dissolution. His politics were reformist and gradualist. He preached truth and sincerity to an educated elite, not revolution to the masses. A justification for such flexibility may be found in the dissenting belief in the duty of ceaseless enquiry. To commit oneself to following truth, "whithersoever thou leadest,"[7] was to embark on an open quest for moral and spiritual enlightenment. In cases in which further exploration or insight reveals the inadequacies of one's professed views, revision becomes a moral duty.

* * *

In *Political Justice*, Godwin set out to enquire into how government could make us virtuous. But he ended up arguing that government was an obstacle to virtue, and should be done away with. As an Enlightenment thinker, he started from first principles and followed a chain of reasoned deduction. One argument seemed to him to follow seamlessly from another, until it reached an inevitable conclusion. He began with the view that reason could become the sole determinant of human action. Men and women are all equally "perfectible," or capable of moral and intellectual improvement. If people applied reason to every action of their lives, they would gradually free themselves from the constraints of government. Institutions would become redundant, and would slowly wither away. Existing political society, with all its divisions and inequalities, would be replaced by a community of rational men and women, seeking the good of all.

Figure 4   *William Godwin*, by James Northcote, 1802.
Courtesy of the National Portrait Gallery, London

Godwin understood the possible objections to this idea. He acknowledged that some elements in human nature and society obstructed moral
progress (while also insisting that such elements would, in time, be
governable by reason). He examined the psychological effects of inequality
under different forms of government: monarchy, aristocracy, and democracy. He argued that the indirect effects of government may be even more

powerful than its explicit policies: "Politics and modes of government . . . educate and infect us all. They poison our minds, before we can resist, or so much as suspect their malignity."[8] Government impeded freedom of thought, which would otherwise lead to the improvement of human nature.

As a political program, *Political Justice* was far from radical. For Godwin, "The true instruments for changing the opinions of men are argument and persuasion."[9] The best forum for moral progress was private discussion:

> Shew to mankind by a few examples the advantages of political discussion undebauched by political enmity and vehemence, and the beauty of the spectacle will soon render the example contagious. Every man will commune with his neighbour. Every man will be eager to tell and to hear what the interest of all requires them to know. The bolts and fortifications of the temple of truth will be removed . . . Knowledge will be accessible to all.[10]

Godwin insisted on the inward nature of a just revolution. He envisaged political change as a peaceful process, a matter of thoughtful deliberation and growing consensus taking place outside institutions.

Godwin's rational understanding of human nature could lead to extreme conclusions, sometimes in defiance of common sense. He deliberately pushed his ideas as far as they would go—and then a little further. He argued that "marriage is an affair of property, and the worst of all properties." In its control of women's destinies, it was the "most odious of monopolies."[11] Hence marriage as an institution should be abolished, and replaced by relationships based on mutual choice and affection. Godwin further speculated that humanity would gradually acquire the power to defeat physical illness and prolong human life. In his imagined future society, "the men . . . will perhaps be immortal. The whole will be people of men, and not of children . . . There will be no war, no crimes, no administration of justice as it is called, and no government . . . Every man will seek with ineffable ardour the good of all."[12]

There is a utopian cast in Godwin's thought—but he rejected the criticism that his views were impractical. The fact that society could not be transformed immediately did not devalue the vision. The practical significance of Godwin's theory was never far from the surface in *Political Justice*. When he talks about truth and sincerity, the concepts are brought home to the reader through examples of moral dilemmas in everyday life. Should we tell a dying woman that her husband has met with a fatal accident? Should we conceal our political opinions when speaking the truth would lead to imprisonment, or worse? Should we say we are not at home when a troublesome visitor calls? All this gives *Political Justice* something of the air of a self-help book. Godwin was concerned with "the improvement of every hour."[13] He urged his readers to be alert to the possibilities for moral growth in their daily lives, offering a new model of political and social engagement.

Political Justice was published in 1793 in two quarto volumes, priced thirty-six shillings (two to three weeks of a laborer's wages). It was a luxury item, and its intended readership was the educated middling and upper classes. Among these readers, it was a great success, and it was read by the lower classes too. They had access to pirated editions or attended reading groups, where a single copy (bought by subscription) would be read aloud and the ideas debated. Radical publishers helped to spread the word by printing extracts (notably, Godwin's criticisms of different forms of government) in cheap periodicals for working people.

The ideas of *Political Justice* trickled down in other ways as well. Readers took up Godwin's invitation to engage in frank and open debate, and wrote him letters setting out their views. Often they wanted to meet him as well, and some became friends and disciples. For the next few years, Godwin, who had been trained as a dissenting minister, acted as mentor, adviser, and agony aunt to many talented men and women who wrote to him on a wide variety of subjects. They brought problems—practical, ethical, or psychological—for Godwin to solve. He responded with letters that "radiate moral philosophy in action,"[14] encouraging correspondents to put his moral principles into practice in the real world. The letters also show a capacity for empathy and insight into human psychology, as he dispensed advice to young women committed to self-improvement, melancholy students who had lost their way, and aspiring writers of all ages.

* * *

This capacity for empathy should not surprise us, because Godwin never was the extreme rationalist his critics imagined. In his writings of the second half of the decade, he turned his forensic eye on human emotion as an agent of reform. This shift in Godwin's thinking is often attributed to the influence of Mary Wollstonecraft, whom he courted in 1796. But his relationship with her was a stimulant for a change that was already under way. In *Caleb Williams*, begun ten days after the publication of *Political Justice*, he used a confessional narrative to dramatize the workings of sympathy, compassion, loyalty, and love.

The novel is a study of power relations between master and servant: Ferdinando Falkland, a wealthy, cosmopolitan country gentleman (who has secretly killed a man), and his servant Caleb Williams. When Caleb discovers his master's crime, he is cast into a world of fear and uncertainty. Falkland hunts him down in order to buy his silence. But Caleb remains loyal for other reasons: he is emotionally paralyzed by the discovery that "it was possible to love a murderer."[15] The power of emotion in the novel undermines the rational self-sufficiency promoted in *Political Justice*. It is the start of a quest for virtue derived from feeling and sympathy. This quest motivates not only the revisions to *Political Justice* in two subsequent editions, but also a shift of attention to "education, manners, and literature"—the subjects of Godwin's 1797 collection of essays, *The Enquirer*.

By this time Godwin was deeply engaged with Wollstonecraft's "culture of the heart."[16] The pair had first been introduced in 1791, and had quarreled. When they met again in January 1796, it was on different terms. Godwin was in the midst of reassessing his political and philosophical views. Wollstonecraft was not only famous as the author of *Vindication of the Rights of Woman* (1792), but had just published *Letters Written during a Short Residence in Sweden, Norway, and Denmark* (1796), a mixture of travel narrative, sociological analysis, and heartfelt personal reflection. It was a synthesis of reason and feeling—just what Godwin was looking for. He read the book and fell in love with the author.

In April they began to see each other, and in mid-August they became lovers. Their letters bear witness to their enlightened intimacy, with up to three exchanges a day, as they acted as each other's mentor and student, and tried to reconcile their principles with their feelings. They lived and worked apart, read and criticized each other's works in progress, and "woo[ed] philosophy" together—for, Wollstonecraft declared, "I do not like to lose my Philosopher even in the lover."[17] After she became pregnant, they married in March 1797. She died on September 10, shortly after giving birth to their daughter Mary.

Godwin's *Memoirs of the Author of a Vindication of the Rights of Woman*, begun a fortnight after her death, completed his transformation into a man of feeling. The book was in part an act of mourning, in part a love letter, and in part a justification (and celebration) of Wollstonecraft's unconventional life. He struggled to capture the impact of Wollstonecraft's sensibility and the growth of their affection, and described how her love had initiated him into new modes of thinking and feeling. This became the basis of a shared "experiment" in living, untrammeled by legal institutions:

The partiality we conceived for each other, was in that mode, which I have
always regarded as the purest and most refined style of love. It grew with
equal advances in the mind of each . . . I am not conscious that either party
can assume to have been the agent or the patient, the toil-spreader or the
prey, in the affair . . . It was friendship melting into love . . . We did not
marry.[18]

The *Memoirs* may not be an entirely accurate depiction of Wollstonecraft.
But the text is important for the light it sheds on Godwin's changing moral
sensibility toward the end of the 1790s. Reason alone was no longer
sufficient. Human relationships were infused with politics, and political
relationships were in turn underpinned by emotion and personal bonds.
The relationship between Godwin and Wollstonecraft showed that the
personal and the political could be harmonized. His portrayal of their
experimental mode of living made them agents of the gradual social
transformation they both sought to further, in their lives as well as in their
writings.

The publication of Godwin's *Memoirs of the Author of a Vindication of
the Rights of Woman* in January 1798 inflamed a reaction against the "new
philosophy" that was already under way. The book was used by the
conservative press to attack principles "such as Godwin has taught, and
Mrs. Wollstonecroft taught and practised."[19] This hostility may help to
explain why the philosophical writings of Godwin and Wollstonecraft
underwent a temporary eclipse. Nonetheless their ideas entered the literary
imagination, particularly in the next generation of the Godwin/Shelley
family and their associates. They used Godwin's and Wollstonecraft's
writings to legitimate their own experiments in living, and followed the
trail they had blazed as social and cultural critics.

Notes

1 Charles Lamb to Thomas Manning, December 27, 1800, *The Letters of
   Charles and Mary Lamb*, edited by Edwin W. Marrs, Jr. (Ithaca: Cornell
   University Press, 1975–78), 2: 263.
2 *Enquiry Concerning Political Justice*, in *Political and Philosophical Writings of
   William Godwin*, general editor Mark Philp (London: W. Pickering, 1993),
   3: 50.
3 *Letters on a Regicide Peace*, in *The Writings and Speeches of Edmund Burke*,
   general editor Paul Langford (Oxford: Oxford University Press, 1981–2016),
   9: 303.
4 Elizabeth Inchbald to Godwin, December 24, [1799], Bod. MS Abinger c. 5,
   fos. 46v–47r, Bodleian Library.

5 [Edward Lytton Bulwer], "The Lounger, No. I," *New Monthly Magazine*, 28 (1830), 365.
6 *Political and Philosophical Writings*, 2: 70.
7 Ibid., 6: 173, 219.
8 Ibid., 4: 26.
9 Ibid., 3: 115.
10 Ibid., 121–22.
11 Ibid., 453.
12 Ibid., 465.
13 Ibid., 116.
14 Kenneth R. Johnston, Review of *The Letters of William Godwin, Volume I: 1778–1797,* ed. Pamela Clemit (Oxford: Oxford University Press, 2011), *Review 19* (2011), www.nbol-19.org/view_doc.php?index=141.
15 *Caleb Williams,* in *Collected Novels and Memoirs of William Godwin,* general editor Mark Philp (London: Pickering & Chatto), 3: 17.
16 Preface to *St. Leon,* in *Novels and Memoirs,* 4, 11; Godwin quotes Wollstonecraft, *Vindication of the Rights of Woman,* in *The Works of Mary Wollstonecraft,* edited by Janet Todd and Marilyn Butler (London: W. Pickering, 1989), 5: 121.
17 Wollstonecraft to Godwin, [September 15, 1796], in *The Collected Letters of Mary Wollstonecraft,* edited by Janet Todd (London: Allen Lane, 2003), 365.
18 Godwin, *Memoirs of the Author of a Vindication of the Rights of Woman,* in *Novels and Memoirs,* 1: 128–29.
19 Review of Godwin, *Memoirs of the Author of a Vindication of the Rights of Woman* (1798), *Anti-Jacobin Review and Magazine,* 1 (1798), 99.

CHAPTER 21

Political Theory

Lena Halldenius

Is there a political theory in Mary Wollstonecraft's writings? The question is relevant since Wollstonecraft's main preoccupation was moral rather than political: the duty of every thinking person to strive to make themselves as good as they can be. This is a complex duty, involving independent thought, acting on principles of reason, and making oneself useful to others. The challenge involved in this endeavor is a recurrent theme in most of what she wrote. Under what circumstances is it legitimate to lay this expectation on people? How could it be fair to expect of the poor to regard independence of mind as a primary concern, when they can hardly feed their children?

The link between morality and politics is tight in Wollstonecraft's thought, where individual persons' struggles and failures to act morally are understood against the character of the political society they live in, the institutions and norms that determine their standing, and whatever resources they have at their command. An unequal society is detrimental to the morality of everyone within it; on this Wollstonecraft consistently insists. Poverty and humiliation stunt moral and intellectual growth, but so does the pampered existence that comes with wealth. She goes as far as to claim that "among unequals there can be no society,"[1] only masters and servants.

Wollstonecraft's political theory is not a theory of government – even though she had decided views on that – as much as a theory of politics as a circumstance of life. Political society is a set of institutions, but it is also the messy world we live in.

In some ways, Wollstonecraft was a typical eighteenth-century republican. Like other republicans in her intellectual circle – such as Richard Price and Thomas Paine – she believed in man's natural right to equal liberty, that this natural right limits and conditions political power, and that the purpose of political society is to protect the natural rights of all men and women. She also believed that this had implications for political organization: institutions must be representative and accountable, privileges earned and not inherited, and wealth and status fairly dispersed. She supported the principles of the French revolutionaries on this ground.

Freedom, or liberty, is a crucial concept in republican thought of this period. Personal freedom stood for freedom from subordination to arbitrary power and was in that sense inherently political. Richard Price put it in a way that reflects Wollstonecraft's position well: "Individuals in private life, while held under the power of masters, cannot be denominated free however equitably and kindly they may be treated."[2] Coercion infringes freedom, but a person can be unfree also if there is no coercion. If she is vulnerable to the arbitrary will of another, with no means or ways of contesting the other's hold over her, she is in their power and unfree because of it, even if in actual fact she is able to do most of what she wants. This conception of personal freedom has logical implications for government, since an absolute ruler represents just such arbitrary power.

The idiosyncrasies of Wollstonecraft's political theory are partially a reaction to republican principles but from within republican commitments. We will look at some of the features that make her republicanism distinctive: the moral ends of government, her suspicion of the republican trope of "the people," and her conflicted views on revolution. We will conclude with her critique of hierarchies of privilege and wealth.

* * *

In her book on the French Revolution, Wollstonecraft notes that men are unequal by nature in terms of "bodily and mental powers."[3] This natural inequality is a fact but also a moral problem since the strong will exploit their superiority to keep the weak subordinated. Sheer strength is a fact of nature but easily takes on the appearance of rightful dominion. Depending on how political society is organized and on what principles it works, it will either support or counteract such inequalities of powers. Wollstonecraft's main thesis in *The French Revolution* is that the purpose of government is to protect the weak, not only against the effects of natural inequality, but by destroying it. Politically protecting the weak is not a matter of handing out charity or placing limits on how harshly a master may discipline his servants; it is a matter of societal structure, of institutions and norms that equalize the relationships that people are in. Only a republic can do that and so it is the only form of political society worth the name: "a fair representation, to meet at standard periods, without depending on the caprice of the executive power" is a "universal demand"[4] of reason or (which amounts to the same thing) justice.

It is worth noting that Wollstonecraft does not use social contract arguments for the legitimacy of republican government, either historically or hypothetically. In *The Rights of Men* (published in 1790) she states that "[i]t is not, perhaps, of very great consequence who were the founders of a state; savages, thieves, curates, or practitioners in the law."[5] There are no answers to be had by looking backwards or by engaging in counterfactual reasoning about what people might have found acceptable had they only been different than they are. The battle is over what justice requires. Here we arrive at one point at which Wollstonecraft's republicanism challenges a deeply held republican commitment: the unity of the people.

* * *

On the kind of republicanism that we are concerned with, individual persons cannot be free unless political power is under popular control. Under despotic rule everyone is enslaved, regardless of what privileges they enjoy. In a republic, the People – in the singular form – is the highest source of authority and the bearer of sovereignty, and exercises this authority through its representatives.

This People is of course an idealization, a trope for national unity beyond sectarian interests, and can, for that reason, be properly represented only by such persons as are capable of keeping their eye on the good of the national union itself. In the words of the American Federalists, representatives should be those men

> whose wisdom may best discern the true interest of their country, and whose patriotism and love of justice will be least likely to sacrifice it to temporary or partial considerations.[6]

The gritty reality, however, was that possessing such capacity to look beyond sectarian interest turned out to be the same thing as being economically independent, educated, white, and male. Wollstonecraft points out that on such arrangements the universal human interest will be the interests of the privileged in disguise and representation "a convenient handle for despotism,"[7] republican in name only.

If a person is believed fit to represent the nation on the strength of just such inequalities of power that government is supposed to counteract, then the common people – "for whom chiefly government was instituted, and who chiefly deserve consideration"[8] – will be represented by their masters. Are we supposed to think that an "established inequality of rank and property" will secure "the liberty of the whole community, instead of rendering it a sounding epithet of subjection"?[9] If a wife is bound by and powerless under the will of her husband, how can it be right that she be politically represented by men who are just like him?

Even under a republican constitution, politics is conducted by ordinary, flawed, self-serving human beings. Anyone with a seat in parliament or government is more likely to use their status to make their own benefits look rightful than to dismantle them for the sake of others. Their "chief merit is the art of keeping himself in place."[10]

Wollstonecraft's view is that representation *will* be representation of class interests, even in a republic, as long as inequalities of wealth and status remain. For women and the poor, this is a trap. That is why women and the laboring classes who "pay for the support of royalty" but cannot feed their children, need their own representatives: "I really think that women ought to have representatives, instead of being arbitrarily governed without having any direct share allowed them in the deliberations of government."[11] All else is "shuffle and trick," allowing tyranny to continue under an "empty shew" of unity.[12] This is what happened in France after the revolution, when the "same desire of power" turned into a new kind of tyranny with a republican alibi. As Wollstonecraft put it upon her arrival in blood-stained Paris in 1793: "names, not principles, are changed."[13]

* * *

Considering that Wollstonecraft is famous for defending the French revolution, one might expect more revolutionary zeal in her writings than there is. Her position on revolution was complex, and attending to it is worthwhile to see how challenging she found political change to be.

Political change is a practical problem, not only a philosophical one, so how can it be made to work for the good? Power is unstable, that is why political change is possible, but political change for the good will always be change *against* power since the privileged have an interest in maintaining the status quo. As Wollstonecraft puts it in *The Rights of Men*, it is more pleasant for the rich "to justify oppression than correct abuses."[14] Consequently, abolishing privileges will require "the work of men who had no titles to sacrifice."[15]

Remember that hierarchies of status and wealth oppress the minds of all. The vices of the rich may be "polished" and those of the poor "gross,"[16] but slavish dependence under others and absolute power over others equally degrade the human character. So, political change for the good will be change against power, but also change initiated by men and women whose minds are at least partially warped by the injustice they are rising against and by hate and envy for their superiors.

The progress of civilization is arduous, non-linear, and sometimes violent. When the commoners in France rose "from the state of servility" they ran from one extreme to the other, using their new "unbridled liberty" in retaliation against the nobles.[17] The fact that revolutions turn into aggression is predictable, but the blame must fall on the old tyrannical regime. In a system so deeply corrupted that it is beyond ordinary reform, revolt is "politically just"[18] even if the cost is high.

That corruption creeps back in, as it did in France, is the danger of sudden change, but a revolution can be successful in different ways. Slaves who are so habituated to their subordination that they see it as part of the natural fabric of the world will not ask for justice. Only when the lower orders no longer feel a "blind reverence"[19] for their masters, will they find reason to complain. In *Letters Written During a Short Residence in Sweden, Norway, and Denmark* – published in 1796 – Wollstonecraft notes (rightly or wrongly) a pride among the Scandinavian peasants, a sense of themselves as persons of equal worth. She attributed this to the revolution in France, which, by instilling moral stamina in the minds of ordinary people also in the far North, served progressive change indirectly.

"Every great reform requires systematic management," Wollstonecraft reports in *The French Revolution*, adding that peaceful progress depends on "moderation and reciprocity of concessions."[20] But what is progress? What does it require? Wollstonecraft's political theory stays close to the experiences of those living without status and resources. Representation under a republican constitution is necessary but will be insufficient if inequalities of wealth and social standing remain, with women and the laboring majority having a right to nothing.

* * *

Wollstonecraft explicates liberty in terms of independence. Intellectually, independence is a reason-based self-reliance, but socially and politically it is better described as equal interdependence. Our independence in relation to others is not hampered by our need of their affection or assistance; we need each other – we must all "mix in the throng."[21] Independence is, however, hampered by subordination, by *un*equal dependence and vulnerability to coercion. Social and political dependence – unfreedom – has psychological and moral consequences (it fosters envy, contempt, cunning, and self-censorship) but there is nothing intangible or mysterious about it. It is a materially robust function of legal status and economic circumstances. Importantly, unfreedom is not politically contingent; it is maintained and sanctioned by "the partial laws and customs of society."[22]

The oppression of women and the poor is *comprehensive*; it affects them in all they do: "the man who lives by the sweat of his brow has no asylum from oppression ... when was the castle of the poor sacred?"[23] Their oppression is also *strategic*: "as blind obedience is ever sought for by power, tyrants and sensualists are in the right when they endeavour to keep women in the dark, because the former only want slaves, and the latter a play-thing."[24] Lastly, their oppression is *institutionally sanctioned*; it is an integrated part of the fabric of society. Charity and benevolence only sharpen dependence: "If the poor are in distress, they [the rich] will make some *benevolent* exertions to assist them; they will confer obligations, but not do justice."[25] The rectification of oppression requires radical (though gradual) change toward equality of citizenship and legal status and equalization of wealth.

The importance that Wollstonecraft attributes to citizenship and equality before the law – "a civil existence in the state"[26] – needs to be understood in relation to her political theory as a whole. The moral ends of government – destroying natural inequalities of power – requires political equality but also rectification of material inequalities. In the French revolution she hoped more than anything for a "mighty revolution in property."[27]

Being poor, bowing and scraping before the splendors of the rich, deadens the mind. Being rich, envied and gawped at for doing nothing, instills indolence and "blind self-love."[28] The dire consequences of inequality do not, however, take place only in the minds of individual people. It is a structural phenomenon. A "cast-like division" of wealth – a "wall of separation"[29] – sets classes preying upon each other, dividing the rich and the poor into "bands of tyrants and slaves."[30]

Wollstonecraft is famous for insisting that "the distinction of sex [must be] confounded in society,"[31] but this is not an isolated claim about the situation of women. Her main political claim is that the moral purpose of living in society and the reasonableness of expecting people to strive to be virtuous and useful are dependent upon the equalization of representation, status, and wealth.

Notes

1 Mary Wollstonecraft, *A Vindication of the Rights of Men* (1790), in *The Works of Mary Wollstonecraft*, edited by Janet Todd and Marilyn Butler (London: W. Pickering, 1989), 5: 39.
2 Richard Price, *Two Tracts on Civil Liberty, the War with America, and the Debts and Finances of the Kingdom* (1778), *Political Writings*, edited by D. O. Thomas (Cambridge: Cambridge University Press, 1991), 77.

3 Mary Wollstonecraft, *An Historical and Moral View of the French Revolution* (1794), in *The Works of Mary Wollstonecraft*, 6: 17.

4 Wollstonecraft, *The French Revolution*, 6: 39.

5 Wollstonecraft, *The Rights of Men*, 5: 40.

6 A. Hamilton, J. Madison, and J. Jay, *The Federalist Papers* (Oxford: Oxford University Press, 2008), no. 10.

7 Mary Wollstonecraft, *A Vindication of the Rights of Woman* (1792), in *The Works of Mary Wollstonecraft*, 5: 217.

8 Wollstonecraft, *The Rights of Men*, 5: 12.

9 Ibid., 41.

10 Wollstonecraft, *The Rights of Woman*, 5: 214. Compare Edmund Burke, *Reflections on the Revolution in France*, edited by C. C. O'Brien (London: Penguin Books, 1968), 192, on office as a "holy function."

11 Wollstonecraft, *The Rights of Woman*, 5: 217.

12 Ibid., 5: 214; see also 211, and *The Wrongs of Woman; or, Maria. A Fragment* (1798), in *The Works of Mary Wollstonecraft*, 1: 119, 153.

13 Mary Wollstonecraft, "Letter on the Present Character of the French Nation" (1798), in *The Works of Mary Wollstonecraft*, 6: 446.

14 Wollstonecraft, *The Rights of Men*, 5: 52.

15 Ibid., 47.

16 Ibid., 58.

17 Wollstonecraft, *The French Revolution*, 6: 60–62.

18 Ibid., 46.

19 Mary Wollstonecraft, *Letters Written during a Short Residence in Sweden, Norway, and Denmark* (1796), in *The Works of Mary Wollstonecraft*, 6: 255 (Letter 3).

20 Wollstonecraft, *The French Revolution*, 6: 144.

21 Wollstonecraft, *The Rights of Woman*, 5: 181.

22 Wollstonecraft, *The Wrongs of Woman; or, Maria*, in *The Works of Mary Wollstonecraft*, 1: 83.

23 Wollstonecraft, *The Rights of Men*, 5: 15.

24 Wollstonecraft, *The Rights of Woman*, 5: 93.

25 Wollstonecraft, *The Rights of Men*, 5: 52. See also "It is justice, not charity, that is wanting in the world!" (*The Rights of Woman*, 5: 140) and "I have always been an enemy to what is termed charity, because timid bigots endeavouring thus to cover their *sins*, do violence to justice" (*The French Revolution*, 6: 337).

26 Wollstonecraft, *The Rights of Woman*, 5: 219.

27 Wollstonecraft, *The Rights of Men*, 5: 48.

28 Wollstonecraft, *The French Revolution*, 6: 46; also *The Rights of Woman*, 5: 221, and *The Rights of Men*, 5: 2.

29 Wollstonecraft, *The Rights of Men*, 5: 58.

30 Wollstonecraft, *The French Revolution*, 6: 230, 234.

31 Wollstonecraft, *The Rights of Woman*, 5: 126.

CHAPTER 22

Feminist Theory

Jane Moore

To write of feminist theory in the 1790s is a complex undertaking. Even amidst the enthusiasm of the sexual revolution of the 1970s when feminist scholarship in academia homed in on the 1790s in the project to retrieve past women for the establishment of a female history and tradition to rival that of men, a certain unease began to be apparent about usage of the term feminist theory in relation to pre-nineteenth-century culture. It was not until the late nineteenth century that "feminism," in the Oxford English Dictionary's common definition of the word, emerged as a political movement advocating the "equality of the sexes and the establishment of the political, social, and economic rights of the female sex." Hence the charge, in Regina Janes' words, that "To speak of eighteenth-century feminism is to commit a vile anachronism, for there was no movement, no concerted demand for change in the political or economic sphere."[1]

If feminism did not exist in the eighteenth century, strictly speaking, what then can be said of what we now think of as feminist theory in the period? The question can be asked because, as Janes herself recognizes in her appraisal of Mary Astell's seventeenth-century text, *A Serious Proposal to the Ladies* (Part I, 1694), feminist thought has a long history. When Astell proposed the establishment of a "Retirement" where "ladies" might serve God and improve their minds (the two aims have a radical interchangeability) she was practicing a form of feminist theory.[2] Her religious convictions are the crux of her desire to recognize women as rational human beings, pre-empting Mary Wollstonecraft's similar appeal to God in her argument in *Vindication of the Rights of Woman* that women are "human creatures, who, in common with men, are placed on this earth to unfold their faculties."[3]

Nevertheless, with Wollstonecraft feminist theory entered a new phase, moving from an emphasis on the individual's capacity for rational self-improvement and spiritual reflection to an Enlightenment rights-based argument for a wider social change in the position of women. "The

language of rights provides her [Wollstonecraft] with something Astell did
not want," writes Janes, "an argument for change not only in women, but
also in the world."[4] Since that time feminist theorists have returned
repeatedly to Wollstonecraft to assess and debate the various schools of
thought that proved important intellectual influences in the social and
political history of women, from Astell's blueprint for female seminaries in
the seventeenth century to the more culturally mainstream salons operated
by the intellectually and socially privileged bluestocking women of the
eighteenth century to the "revolutionary feminism," to borrow a phrase
from Gary Kelly, of the Wollstonecraft circle in the 1790s.[5] What they
found was less a coherent narrative of feminist progress or even a set of
distinct schools of thought on the condition of women than a constellation
of overlapping voices from both ends of the political spectrum. On some
points, particularly those concerning the education of women, it is difficult
to separate the strands of feminist narrative from the theoretical and
practical activities of the bluestocking scholars, such as Elizabeth Carter
and Elizabeth Montagu, or even the conservative Evangelical moralizing of
Hannah More.[6]

The view that eighteenth-century women were entirely excluded from
the public realm has been significantly revised by modern female historians
who have demonstrated their influence in civic and domestic life in ways
that influenced debates on politics and rights.[7] We can now recognize that
there was considerable participation by women across different political
and class spheres in the public domain, whether this was exhibited in the
individual intellectual achievements of elite bluestocking women or
through the involvement in philanthropic and humanitarian activities
(for example through the anti-slavery movement of the late eighteenth
century or the advocates for missionary work in India in the early nineteenth century) or through British women's activity around parliamentary
politics (aristocratic female influence was a fact of public life, exemplified
by the Duchess of Devonshire's campaigning for Charles James Fox in the
1784 Westminster election) or through the debating societies, originally
founded to prepare men for professional careers but which later included
societies formed by women, or through the work of female novelists and
poets who intervened in debates about marriage, domesticity, education,
and human rights (the latter preoccupation evidenced in the influential
anti-slavery poetry of Hannah More).[8] Although these different pockets of
interest set the stage for Wollstonecraft's advancement of women's social
and political rights in the radical decade of the 1790s, they did not in

themselves constitute theoretical schools of feminism that envisioned widespread social and sexual reform based on female rights.

The battle conducted by Wollstonecraft in *Vindication of the Rights of Woman* (1792) to see women recognized as human beings with an entitlement to human rights was hard fought: while bluestocking women, novelists and artists testified in practice to the participation of women in the cultural sphere, women remained excluded from the official language of parliamentary rights and citizenship. Hence Wollstonecraft's awareness that she "may excite laughter" by proposing that "women ought to have representatives, instead of being arbitrarily governed without having any direct share allowed them in the deliberations of government."[9] It is important, therefore, to differentiate Wollstonecraft's advancement of feminist theory through the call for female rights and political representation from the more general extension of women's role in branches of education, philanthropy and literature. While historical developments in these fields were important and necessary steps toward building a feminist theory of rights, they did not establish such a theory. The term feminist theory has a specificity that might be seen in this regard as unhelpful, as too exclusive in its meaning, for modern historians of gender. Indeed, it is notable that one of the most important modern books on women and Enlightenment culture, Sarah Knott and Barbara Taylor's *Women, Gender, and the Enlightenment*, published in 2005, largely avoids the term feminist theory. Running to over 700 pages, this comprehensive collection of essays does not have an entry for "feminist theory" in the index, although it does include the broader term "feminist discourse." The avoidance of the word "theory" says something about the haziness surrounding the concept in the context of various eighteenth-century social and intellectual movements. Against the polyphony of voices debating the condition of women Wollstonecraft's stands out in her crystallization of a feminist rights-based theory of social and sexual reform.

Still the question remains of what might be called feminism in Wollstonecraft's age. The various literary, philosophical, political, and religious contexts from which her thought emerged are addressed in detail elsewhere in this book. Rather than repeat that material, my approach in the rest of this chapter is to put the term feminist theory itself under scrutiny, to examine how it is put into operation by both Wollstonecraft and her detractors. I want to begin that process by exploring the proposition that in the eighteenth century feminist theory becomes an issue of style as well as one of content. In doing so, I compare the rhetorical strategies of *Rights of Woman* with those of Richard Polwhele's well-known verse satire *The*

Unsex'd Females (1798), a Juvenalian attack on those of Wollstonecraft's contemporaries considered to transgress political and sexually conservative norms.

The *modus operandi* of *Rights of Woman* is to define feminist theory in terms of the negative formulation of that which has not happened, that which is yet to be. In her opening chapter Wollstonecraft declares:

> Rousseau exerts himself to prove that all *was* right originally: a crowd of authors that all *is* now right: and I, that all will *be* right.[10]

Defined in this way, the realization of Wollstonecraft's rights-based version of feminist theory exists in the limbo temporality of the potential rather than the actual. From the opposite side of the political coin, the version of feminist theory to emerge from Polwhele's satire, as behooves the oppositional critical perspective of the genre, is also shaped by negative observations. The very title "Unsex'd Females" has a negative logic, where "unsex'd" means *not* feminine. "'Woman' is then what is not feminist."[11] In this formulation, feminism emerges from Polwhele's satire, as "nothing more than the operation of a woman who desires to be a like a man,"[12] to cite Jacques Derrida on Friedrich Nietzsche, whose negative trope of feminist theory as being "nothing more" than a desire not to be like a woman. Nietzsche's provocative formulation, reproduced in Derrida's *Spurs*, a book published at the peak of second-wave feminism in the 1970s, has a proleptic relevance to another key moment of militant female activity two hundred years earlier, in the 1790s.

Targeted at Mary Wollstonecraft, "whom no decorum checks,"[13] Polwhele's satire puts the issue of style center stage. He attacks Wollstonecraft for flouting a purportedly natural feminine style, casting her as the leader of

> A female band despising NATURE's law,
> As "proud defiance" flashes from their arms,
> And vengeance smothers all their softer charms.[14]

"Proud defiance" versus "softer charms": the terms of the debate are realized as a stark contrast of styles with gendered and national connotations. Unsex'd females are associated with "Gallic freaks," whose "crane-like neck, as Fashion bids, lay bare."[15]

The title "Unsex'd Females" can also be read ironically as a negative echo of Wollstonecraft's earnest wish "to see the distinction of sex confounded in society";[16] Polwhele and Wollstonecraft inhabit the same "unsex'd" orbit albeit from radically different political standpoints. Their works also share the same rhetorical structure of praise and censure. Although in Wollstonecraft's case even the praise she heaps on Catharine Macaulay, author of *Letters on Education* (1790), one of the very few women of her time whose style and judgment she commends (Hester Chapone, who wrote *Letters on the Improvement of the Mind* [1773], is another) is couched as a negative formulation. Wollstonecraft compliments Macaulay for her "style of writing [in which] no sex appears, for it is like the sense it conveys, strong and clear."[17] A writing style stripped of gender markings is the ideal that is promoted here, but it is one that is simultaneously put under erasure by Wollstonecraft's confrontation with the cultural impossibility of escaping a gendered binarism. She falls back, therefore, on a kind of double-negative maneuver in proclaiming as a positive the stylistic power of Macaulay's work:

> I will not call hers a masculine understanding, because I admit not of such an arrogant assumption of reason; but I contend that it was a sound one, and that her judgement, the matured fruit of profound thinking, was a proof that a woman can acquire judgement, in the full extent of the word.[18]

The solution to the impasse created by the culturally negative stereotypes of femininity that Wollstonecraft wishes to oppose at every turn in her argument is to invoke and then swiftly to revoke the only gendered precedent available for describing rationality, that of a "masculine understanding." In her effort to contest the cultural inscription of gender, Wollstonecraft seeks to dismantle the binary code of sexual difference. This is the revolutionary aim of feminist theory that she sees Macaulay striving for and which she attempts to meet in her own style.

That goal was defeated in the relative short term by the conservative backlash against radical reform at the end of the 1790s to which Polwhele's satire made a significant contribution. It is ironic, then, as Susan Wolfson points out, that Polwhele, like Wollstonecraft, professes to be an "egalitarian in the republic of letters."[19] He takes pains in his notes to the poem to assert that in the present age when women writers abound it is no longer necessary for male critics to treat them gallantly: "waving [*sic*] all complimentary civilities" it is for "their judges" to "decide upon their merits with the same rigid impartiality as it seems right to exercise towards the men."[20] Once again, feminist theory is defined through an effort to divest sex of gender; that the proposal comes from the satirical pen of a political reactionary is a further indication of the complex interweaving of voices that represent feminist theory in the eighteenth century.

The historical trajectory, therefore, of feminist theory, far from being linear, is characterized by overlapping temporalities, by interleaved moments of defeat and victory that break up the onward march of progress. In 1798, when Polwhele's satiric poem was published anonymously in London, female reform in Britain, in theory and practice, was under the threat of the conservative backlash against revolutionary ideals. Taking fright at the French Revolution, conservatives like Polwhele took advantage of the sexual revelations in William Godwin's *Memoirs* of Wollstonecraft about her love affairs and illegitimate pregnancies to discredit proponents of sexual reform through ridicule and satire. The site of battle in the 1790s is remarkably similar to that in the 1970s, when the women's liberation movement took up the slogan "the personal is political" in recognition of the ways in which the political permeated women's private lives. In a paradoxical twist, it is precisely on the understanding that the personal is political that Polwhele denounces Wollstonecraft's disciples, foremost among them Mary Robinson, whose well-publicized affair with the Prince of Wales made her a figure of scandal. Polwhele takes advantage of Robinson's personal notoriety to criticize her public works of literature, particularly her novel-writing:

> In Mrs. Robinson's Poetry, there is a peculiar delicacy: but her Novels, as literary compositions, have no great claim to approbation—As containing the doctrines of Philosophism, they merit the severest censure.[21]

Satire is rarely fair, of course, nor does it need to manifest considered critical judgment, but in terms of its separation of "unsex'd females" from the list of socially approved women, led by Hannah More, Polwhele's poem is remarkably un-nuanced and confused. The artist Emma Crewe, for example, is included in Wollstonecraft's group, while the illustrator Diana Beauclerk, who knew Crewe and worked with her, and who had a scandalous personal life to boot, is positioned in More's respectable ranks. The satire also betrays ignorance, as here, in praising the "peculiar delicacy" of Mary Robinson's poetry in contrast to her incendiary fiction, given the explicit pro-Revolutionary radicalism of poetry such as *Ainsi va le Monde* (1790).

The confessional narrative used in fiction by Robinson and other female novelists of the eighteenth century, not least Wollstonecraft, proved a powerful medium for the expression of women's issues. An emphasis on the politics of the personal is manifested formally in the epistolary opening and ending, and in the confessional, often sentimental, narrative of Robinson's 1797 novel *Walsingham; or, The Pupil of Nature*. The heroine of the story, Sir Sidney Aubrey, a girl who is passed off by her mother as a boy for inheritance reasons, falls in love with Walsingham and he with her. Only when Sidney's identity is eventually revealed do the couple declare their love and marry.

Under Robinson's hand this improbable plot is also a tool for satirizing conventional norms of femininity and aristocratic male behavior. A fusion of confessional narrative with satirical social critique in a novel where the true sexual identity of hero/heroine goes undetected for an unlikely length of time creates a world that is precisely fictional, but one that conveys messages deemed sufficiently dangerous to the status quo to merit Polwhele's acerbic attention. In the sense that fiction is evidently not real, it offers another example of what I have been discussing in general terms as the negative formulation of feminist theory. Paradoxically, however, it might be said that the *raison d'être* of feminist theory lies its non-realization, which is something Wollstonecraft acknowledges at the very start of her thesis. To cite her words once more:

> Rousseau exerts himself to prove that all *was* right originally: a crowd of authors that all *is* now right: and I, that all will *be* right."[22]

Notes

1 Regina M. Janes, "Mary, Mary Quite Contrary, Or, Mary Astell and Mary Wollstonecraft Compared," *Studies in Eighteenth-Century Culture*, 5 (1976), 121–39, 121.

2 Mary Astell, *A Serious Proposal to the Ladies. In Two Parts* (London: R. Wilkin, 1697), Part I, 34.

3 Mary Wollstonecraft, *Vindication of the Rights of Woman* (London: Joseph Johnson, 1792), in *The Works of Mary Wollstonecraft*, edited by Janet Todd and Marilyn Butler (London: W. Pickering, 1989), 5: 74.

4 Janes, "'Mary, Mary," 136.

5 See Gary Kelly, *Revolutionary Feminism: The Mind and Career of Mary Wollstonecraft* (Basingstoke: Macmillan, 1992).

6 See Harriet Guest, "The Dream of a Common Language: Hannah More and Mary Wollstonecraft," *Textual Practice*, 9:2 (1995), 303–23; Bridget Hill, "The Links between Mary Wollstonecraft and Catharine Macaulay," *Women's History Review*, 4:2 (1995), 177–92.

7 See Amanda Vickery, "Golden Age to Separate Spheres: A Review of the Categories and Chronology of English Women's History," *The Historical Journal*, 36 (1993), 383–414; see also Vickery's *The Gentlewoman's Daughter: Women's Lives in Georgian England* (New Haven: Yale University Press, 1998); Elaine Chalus, "'My Minerva at my Elbow': The Political Roles of

Women in Eighteenth-Century England," in Stephen Taylor et al., eds., *Hanoverian Britain and Empire* (Rochester: Boydell Press, 1998), 210–28.

8 See Anna Clarke, "Women in Eighteenth-Century British Politics," in Sarah Knott and Barbara Taylor, eds., *Women, Gender and Enlightenment* (Basingstoke: Palgrave Macmillan, 2005), 570–86.

9 Wollstonecraft, *Rights*, 217.

10 Ibid., 84.

11 Janet Todd, *Feminist Literary History: A Defence* (London: Polity, 1988), 127.

12 Jacques Derrida, *Spurs: Nietzsche's Styles* [1976], translated by Barbara Harlow (Chicago: Chicago University Press, 1979), 65.

13 Richard Polwhele, *The Unsex'd Females; A Poem* ([1798] New York: W. M. Cobbett, 1800), 16.

14 Ibid., 7.

15 Ibid., 8.

16 Wollstonecraft, *Rights*, 126.

17 Ibid., 175.

18 Ibid.

19 Susan J. Wolfson, *Borderlines: The Shiftings of Gender in British Romanticism* (Stanford: Stanford University Press, 2006), 16.

20 Polwhele, *Unsex'd Females*, 21.

21 Ibid.

22 Wollstonecraft, *Rights*, 84.

Legal and Social Culture

CHAPTER 23

The Constitution

Ian Ward

There is a familiar problem that attaches to any attempt to survey the English constitution at pretty much any moment in history. And it comes down to this: was there one? The reason for the confusion is of course just as familiar. Whatever passes for an English constitution is "unwritten." The same question might be asked in other jurisdictions. But the presence of a document that claims to be a "constitution" at least prejudices the response. However, in England there is no written constitution, just what the later Victorian commentator Mountstuart Grant Duff would term a "strange abstraction."[1] The problem was given famous expression by Alexis de Tocqueville in his *Democracy in America*, published in 1840. In England, he observed, "the Constitution can change constantly, or rather it does not exist at all."[2] Tocqueville rather evidently preferred the American way, a written constitution enumerating lots of rights. In this he was not alone. Successive revolutions, in America and then France, at the end of the eighteenth century had stimulated considerable debate as to how best to reform and perhaps write an English constitution. It was a conversation that Mary Wollstonecraft entered with a characteristic vigor. We will shortly take a closer look at what she had to say. But first we need to set the scene, to revisit the larger conversation.

* * *

Like any conversation, that which moved around the nature of the English constitution in 1790 was sequential. We might start at the Old Jewry meeting-house in the City of London on November 4, 1789. It was here that the dissenting preacher Richard Price gave a sermon entitled *A Discourse on the Love of Our Country*. Price had something of a reputation as a firebrand. His meeting-house, and its congregation, was notorious. As the title of his sermon suggested, the animating theme was patriotism. And it was because Price loved his country so much that he

199

strongly recommended another revolution. France provided the immediate inspiration. But Price was really interested in the English revolution of a century earlier. It wanted completion, for "though the Revolution was a great work, it was by no means a perfect work, and that all was not then gained which was necessary to put the kingdom in the secure and complete blessings of liberty."[3] Price's closer concern was to broaden religious toleration, most obviously by means of repealing the Test Acts. But that was not the only need. There was the "idolatry" of monarchy too, and the "inequality of our representation," as well as the "vice and venality" that pervaded English political culture.[4]

Fortunately it was all about to change. Price closed his *Discourse*, printed within days of the sermon, with a call to arms:

> What an eventful period this is! ... I have lived to see a diffusion of knowledge which has undermined superstition and error. I have lived to see the rights of men better understood than ever, and nations panting for liberty, which seemed to have lost the idea of it ... Be encouraged all ye friends of freedom and writers in its defence! The times are auspicious. Your labours have not been in vain.[5]

Price's sermon captured a mood of momentary exuberance among London radicals in late 1789. It also spread fear. More significantly, in the history of English constitutional thought at least, it impelled Edmund Burke to write his *Reflections on the Revolution in France* as a rebuttal. And it was of course as a counter-rebuttal that Mary Wollstonecraft wrote her two *Vindications*, on the "rights of men" and the "rights of woman."

Burke had initially welcomed the French revolution. It was a "wonderful spectacle," and "what actors."[6] But he quickly changed his mind. The title of his response to Price's sermon was of course famously disingenuous. *Reflections* might have purported to be about the French Revolution, and much of the first part did indeed treat readers to a suitably thrilling account of the incipient "terror."[7] But Burke's greater purpose was to defend the constitutional settlement which Price had impugned, that of the "Glorious" Revolution of 1688. The creed of the Jacobins, and their admirers in London, was to turn "over the principles" of this "constitution."[8] Ultimately Burke does in *Reflections* what Tocqueville would do half a century later: engage his readers in an exercise in comparative constitutionalism.

The shape of the revolutionary constitution in France was still uncertain as Burke began to write in late 1789. But the shape of the English constitution was very clear, and commendably so. It was a "happy" constitution reflecting the "cautious and deliberate spirit" of consequentially "happy" people.[9] The settlement prescribed in the Declaration of Right is a "most wise, and considerate document, drawn up by great lawyers and great statesmen"; in contrast with the kinds of imagined "bills of rights" being recommended by "warm and inexperienced enthusiasts" such as Price.[10] The Declaration contains "real" rather than "abstract" rights, most important among which are the "right to justice," to "property," and to "good government."[11] And they are "real" rights because they have existed in law for centuries. The Declaration did not invent anything new. It merely reinvested the "ancient" constitution of the common law. As Burke had famously affirmed in Parliament in 1782, the English constitution is a "prescriptive constitution," the "authority" of which "has existed time out of mind."[12] The English constitution in sum represents the "collected reason of ages." It is an "entailed inheritance," the expression of a "partnership not only between those who are living, but between those who are living, those who are dead, and those who are born."[13]

Turning to the more concrete juridical expressions of this settlement, Burke identified all the familiar "revolution principles"; the convention of separate powers which preserves the "balance" of the constitution; the sovereignty of Parliament; the "fundamental excellence" of an independent judiciary; and the rule of law without which there can be "nothing stable" in the political life of the nation.[14] All his Whig readers would have nodded their sober approval. And so would his Tory readers, for Burke then proceeds to say just as many nice things about the Church and the Crown, institutions rightly held in "glory and emulation."[15] The English were a people defined by the "healing voice of Christian charity." The monarchy sets the "frame to the commonwealth," guarding against the ravages of "party tyranny."[16] Burke famously deploys sacramental imagery. The "constitution of our country" is inextricably bound to "our dearest domestic ties," and described in the shared semiotics of English commonwealth, "our state, our hearths, our sepulchres, and our altars."[17] And so it all comes together beautifully; in the shape of a "manly, moral, regulated liberty" which is "combined" with the virtues of practical and effective "government," and an appropriate "veneration" for God and King.[18] It was all very different from the situation in France, where government has been passed to an Assembly of "country curates" and "stock-jobbers," and the task of writing a new constitution vested in a gang of "intriguing" philosophers.

Reflections was an immediate publishing sensation, selling seven thousand copies in its first week. The King recommended "a very good book; every gentleman ought to read it." Gibbon "adored" its "chivalry." Fanny

Burney thought it the "noblest" and most "exalted work that I think I have
ever read."[19] But there were others who were much less impressed. It
ended Burke's friendship with Charles James Fox. The *Monthly Review*
expressed its distaste for history written like a "popular harangue."[20] And
the London radicals were predictably enraged. In time, Tom Paine would
compose his *Rights of Man* in response, devoting much of the first part to a
pointed critique of Burke's work, a "pathless wilderness of rhapsodies."[21]
The people of France, Paine countered, had "brought their" constitutional
mythologies "to the altar, and made of them a burnt-offering to reason,"
and in their place could now be discerned an emergent jurisprudence of
universal rights, written in a plainer "common-sensical" language for the
benefit of the "living, not the dead."[22] And it was an example, Paine
suggested, that the English should do well to follow. It was time to strip
away the "mythologies" of the "ancient" constitution, to tear down the
"idol" of Church and Crown, to lay bare the deceit of the "glorious"
revolution and its "bill of wrongs."[23] The constitution recommended by
Burke is a "burlesque," the obscenity of which is barely shrouded by "the
fog and time of antiquity." And the bright "morning of reason" has
arrived.[24] The *Reflections* had sold well. But it did not sell like Paine's
Rights of Man. By the end of the decade two hundred thousand copies had
been printed and sold, on both sides of the Atlantic.

* * *

It was, according to the *Annual Register*, the defining intellectual conflict
of the age, reinvesting a "rage and animosity equal to that which had
characterized our ancestors during the civil wars."[25] But Paine was not the
first to respond to Burke and his *Reflections*. The first published reply was
Mary Wollstonecraft's *Vindication of the Rights of Man*, which appeared on
November 29th, less than a month after Burke's essay, which had come
out on November 1. It was published anonymously. A second edition
arrived three weeks later on December 18. This time the author's name
was given. It was not a long essay, much shorter indeed than the second
Vindication. But speed was of the essence. Wollstonecraft had been persuaded by the radical publisher Joseph Johnson, for whose journals she was
already working as an editor and reviewer. It was clearly a pressured
situation. In his *Memoir of the Author of A Vindication of the Rights of
Woman*, Godwin would later attest to a sudden "fit of torpor and indolence" midway through the month, most likely a consequence of nervous

exhaustion and a momentary crisis of confidence. Otherwise, he confessed, it was perhaps too "marked" with the "indignation" of the author.[26]

The rapidity has, nevertheless, persuaded some to surmise that Wollstonecraft was aware of what was coming in Burke's *Reflections*, and had begun to write her rebuttal in anticipation. She was certainly aware of Price's *Discourse*, as was all of radical London. Couched as a "letter" to Burke, the *Vindication* assumed the customary personalized tone; it was the "indignation" of the author "aroused." In truth, despite Godwin's later reservations, it was not as vitriolic as some, including Paine's *Rights of Man* or indeed Joseph Priestley's *Letters to the Right Honourable Edmund Burke*, which would also appear in early 1791. The tone was nevertheless acerbic. In terms of substantive argument, Wollstonecraft concentrated her attack on an aligned front: on the relation of political morality and reason. The strategy was hardly surprising. The contestation between sense and sensibility lay at the very heart of the English intellectual Enlightenment. In his *Reflections* Burke had preferred an historical reason in order to justify the constitutional and political state, and had then burnished this state in terms of its "moral" suitability. The English constitution felt right, and had done for centuries.

But it did not feel right to Wollstonecraft, who took issue with both the feeling and the history. A fierce critic of the "cult of sensibility," not least for its gender connotation, it is unsurprising that Wollstonecraft's "indignation" would be raised by the idea that a constitution might just feel right.[27] She closes the first *Vindication* with a rather pointed analogy, at once familial and literary:

> Your real or artificial affection for the English constitution seems to me to resemble the brutal affection of some weak characters. They think it a duty to love their relations with a blind, indolent tenderness, that will not see the faults it might assist to correct, if their affection has been built on rational grounds. They love they know not why, and they will love to the end of the chapter.[28]

Unsurprisingly she took particular exception to the notorious "rape" of Marie Antoinette at the center of the *Reflections*, the consequence of a "debauched" imagination.[29] Countering Burke's distinctively Whiggish species of historical rationality, Wollstonecraft turned to earlier Tory historians such as Hume. Rather than somehow working itself pure over the centuries, the English constitution had been cobbled together from one chance event to another, "a preponderance of inconsistencies" and "pressing necessities."[30] As a consequence there was nothing especially "glorious" about the revolution of 1688, which had in fact changed little. In a curious sense, Burke had recommended the revolution for much the same reason.

Against reason derived from the "rust of antiquity," Wollstonecraft advanced a reason derived from nature.[31] The political consequence of this is a conception of "inalienable rights" that are likewise derived from nature.[32] Paine would of course say much the same. Rights attach to the individual, not the community. But for Wollstonecraft they are also "sacred," expressions of the "justice of God."[33] Much of the first *Vindication* dwells on matters of religion, which is unsurprising given the depth of Wollstonecraft's faith. Her defense of the Reverend Price is passionate and personal.[34] Her critique of the rights and "rapacity" of the established Church is unrelenting.[35] The Church is a parasite on a decaying constitution. Much the same accusation is leveled against the House of Commons. It too exists only to preserve its own interests, and those of the propertied few it represents.[36] The critique of property is definitive. Time and again Wollstonecraft returns to the theme; the "demon of property has ever been at hand to encroach on the sacred rights of man"; it "is only the property of the rich that is secure."[37] The latter aspersion gestures toward the Declaration of Right, so esteemed by Whig historians such as Burke. The Declaration only secures the rights of those who own things, for which reason everyone else is kept in an "abominable" state of servile obedience.[38] If the English are to be free and equal they must first tear down their constitutional idols, the Crown, the Church, and Parliament.

Perhaps understandably the first *Vindication* has paled in critical comparison with the second, the *Vindication of the Rights of Woman*, which appeared in January 1792. The "indignation" appears to overwhelm, too many ideas, too little structured argument. The moment, as Godwin attested, was heated and there was little time for editorial reflection. Samuel Kenrick was impressed nevertheless, appraising a "handsome drubbing of Mister Burke."[39] And he was not alone. The first *Vindication* clearly energized radical London in the closing months of 1790 and then into 1791. And it energized Wollstonecraft too. In a prosaic sense much of the argumentation would be adapted for the second *Vindication*, most obviously perhaps the attack on the "cult of sensibility" and the critique of property. But we can also conjecture something more; that it was perhaps while she raced through drafts of the first *Vindication* in the November of 1790 that Wollstonecraft realized that there was something else that had to be written, something bigger, more radical, more personal. And then we can venture a second conjecture: that if the Reverend Price had not stood in his pulpit at Old Jewry on November 4 and surmised that it was time for another revolution in England, Mary Wollstonecraft might never have written her first *Vindication*, or indeed her second.

Notes

1 M. G. Duff, "Walter Bagehot," in *The Collected Works of Walter Bagehot*, edited by Norman St. John Stevas (Oxford: Oxford University Press, 1986), 148.
2 Alexis de Tocqueville, *Democracy in America* (London: Fontana, 1994), 101.
3 Richard Price, *Political Writings*, edited by D. Thomas (Cambridge: Cambridge University Press, 1991), 191.
4 Ibid., 184–85, 191–92, 194.
5 Ibid., 195–96.
6 Frans de Bruyn, "Edmund Burke, the Political Quixote: Romance, Chivalry and the Political Imagination," *Eighteenth Century Fiction*, 16 (2004), 722.
7 At the heart of this account can be found the famous account of the imagined "rape" of Marie Antoinette in the early hours of October 6, 1789, forced to "fly almost naked" through the corridors of Versailles, chased by rampaging Jacobins intent on piercing her with their "poniards." See Edmund Burke, *Reflections on the Revolution in France* (New York: Penguin, 1986), 164.
8 Ibid., 241.
9 Ibid., 86; James Boyd White, *When Words Lose Their Meaning* (Chicago: University of Chicago Press, 1984), 192–95.
10 Burke, *Reflections*, 100.
11 Ibid., 150–51.
12 Rodney Kilcup, "Burke's Historicism," *Journal of Modern History*, 49 (1977), 400–02.
13 Burke, *Reflections*, 116–19, 194–95.
14 Ibid., 193, 320–21, 325–29.
15 Ibid., 137, 181.
16 Ibid., 94–96, 111, 189, 229, 319.
17 Ibid., 120.
18 Ibid., 89–91, 303–04.
19 Isaac Kramnick, *The Rage of Edmund Burke*, (New York: Basic Books, 1977), 39.
20 James Hodson, *Language and Revolution in Burke, Wollstonecraft, Paine and Godwin*, (Aldershot: Ashgate, 2007), 48, 51.
21 Thomas Paine, *The Rights of Man*, (New York: Penguin, 1985), 64.
22 Ibid., 45.
23 Ibid., 192–93.
24 Ibid., 78, 91, 174.
25 Edward Royle, *Revolutionary Britannia? Reflections on the Threat of Revolution in Britain 1789–1848* (Manchester: Manchester University Press, 2000), 15–16.
26 William Godwin, *Memoirs* (New York: Penguin, 1986), 230. For commentaries on Wollstonecraft in November 1790, see Claire Tomalin, *The Life and*

Death of Mary Wollstonecraft (New York: Penguin, 1985), 124–26 and Diane
Jacobs, *Her Own Woman: The Life of Mary Wollstonecraft* (New York: Simon
& Schuster, 2001), 94–95.

27 The "Advertisement" to the first *Vindication* made reference to the author's
"indignation."

28 Mary Wollstonecraft, *A Vindication of the Rights of Men and A Vindication of
the Rights of Woman*, edited by Sylvana Tomaselli (Cambridge: Cambridge
University Press, 1995), 63–64.

29 Wollstonecraft, *Vindication*, 14, 26, 50. It has been suggested that it was this
passage which inspired Wollstonecraft's initial "indignation." See David
Bromwich, "Wollstonecraft as a Critic of Burke," *Political Theory*, 23
(1995), 620–23, also noting that Mary was herself indignant at the treatment
of Marie Antoinette.

30 Wollstonecraft, *Vindication*, 10, 19. The idea of a constitution working itself
"pure" over time is a centerpiece of Ronald Dworkin's *Law's Empire* (Cambridge: Harvard University Press, 1986).

31 Wollstonecraft, *Vindication*, 8, 30.

32 Ibid., 33.

33 Ibid., 34, 55.

34 Price, nearing death, wrote a brief note of appreciation by return: "particularly
happy in having such an advocate." See Jacobs, *Woman*, 96.

35 Wollstonecraft, *Vindication*, 37–40.

36 Ibid., 43–45.

37 Ibid., 7, 13.

38 Ibid., 53. The inference to the "abominable mischief of slavery" would have
resonated sharply in radical London in 1790.

39 Gary Kelly, *Women, Writing and Revolution 1790–1827* (Oxford: Oxford
University Press, 1993), 17.

CHAPTER 24

Property Law

Catherine Packham

In her author's Preface to *The Wrongs of Woman; or, Maria*, Wollstonecraft declares that her aim is to expose "the misery and oppression, peculiar to women, that arise out of the partial laws and customs of society."[1] From her first major work, the *Vindication of the Rights of Men*, and throughout her writings, Wollstonecraft attacked the property system, upheld by numerous laws, which structured British society in the late eighteenth century, and where the dependent state of women was enshrined. The "prejudices of mankind" which, as Maria reflects in *Wrongs of Woman*, made women the "property of their husbands" was not merely a consequence of socially dominant ideologies of gender, but was formally instituted by property laws which, through the common-law notions of coverture and primogeniture, neither recognized the independent existence of a married woman, nor regarded daughters as equal in status and expectation to sons.[2] This essay explores, first, the significance of property in eighteenth-century Britain; secondly, the complex legal landscape of property law; and finally the repeated and detailed criticisms, often of particular laws and their effects, which Wollstonecraft offered in her writing.

* * *

Property, and the laws which upheld property rights, was fundamental to eighteenth-century political thinking about society and the state, both for those who upheld the status quo and those, including Wollstonecraft, who contested it. Property theory formulated in the previous century by Hobbes, Grotius, Pufendorf, and Locke rejected the earlier notion of a "community of goods" stemming from God's gift of the earth to all mankind as recounted in Genesis.[3] Instead, modern European states were understood to be founded on property, with state power, through the law, serving the crucial function of securing the ownership of property – in land, wealth, and other assets – on which capitalist trade in turn depended. Property, and property law, was thus bound up with the sovereign state, as the ultimate basis of legitimate property ownership, as well as with the individual economic and political rights associated with property.

Political and legal theories of property were strongly informed by the "paradigm" of property in land, a crucial early form of property.[4] James Harrington's classic civic humanist text, *Oceana* (1656), showed how no government was thought to exist without a founding agrarian (a legal determination of the distribution of land ownership), and in François Fénelon's immensely influential political work, *Telemachus* (1699), property in Salentum was regulated by an agrarian limiting the amount of land possessed by any one family. Thomas Paine's *Common Sense* (1776) reiterated the notion that government began in the act of distributing property rights in land; his later *Agrarian Justice* (1797) presented itself as an adaptation of agrarian law. The idea of having rights in property, such as land, through improving and exploiting it by labor, was foundational to Locke's theory of property; meanwhile, political economy, as theorized by the French physiocrats and developed by Adam Smith, has been described as a "property-based model of human improvement."[5] Finally, given that property in land was the basis of political representation, land ownership was also yoked to notions of independence, citizenry, autonomy, and self-possession.[6]

But at the end of the eighteenth century when Wollstonecraft was writing, many voices contested any "normative" account of the "place of property in human affairs."[7] Jean-Jacques Rousseau's *Discourse on Political Economy* (1755) and *Emile* (1762) had contended that any regime founded on private property led to dispossession and alienation, and arguments about the place of property, its relations to the state, and the problem of inequality, were at the heart of French revolutionary debate.[8] Gracchus Babeuf, whom Wollstonecraft admired, argued for a republic based on a system of common property; Robespierre was in favor not of communal ownership, but "communal limits to private property."[9] Property redistribution had of course been an early act of the revolutionary National Assembly, which in 1789 had confiscated church property and abolished feudal property. Scandinavia offered alternative models of property distribution; Mably's *De la legislation, ou, principes des loix* (1774) had praised the strict limits on amounts of property which members of each of Sweden's four estates could own, and Wollstonecraft herself later praised the farmers of northern Norway for their customary division of inherited property among all children, a practice which, preventing the accumulation of property, maintains "the balance of liberty."[10]

In Britain, property theory was countered by the persistence of popular notions of the moral right to shared property; claims of the communal character of property persisted in "innumerable sermons, moral treatises, and courses of jurisprudence throughout the eighteenth century."[11] The limits of private property, and the assertion of a "moral economy," were voiced most strongly in relation to food distribution and especially the grain trade, an issue at the heart of early events in the French Revolution, and which was foregrounded in Wollstonecraft's Revolutionary history.[12] Hannah Barker has shown that the idea of a moral economy in the distribution of property by testators also informed wills in this period.[13] She also argues that the notion of property owners as custodians, rather than independent agents, does much to explain patterns of property inheritance as demonstrated by wills at this time. The most well-known celebration of property held in trust or "mortmain" to be passed through a family from one generation to the next is of course that in Edmund Burke's *Reflections on the Revolution in France* (1790), a work fiercely protesting the French National Assembly's act of property revolution.[14] Not simply the reality of property and property law, then, but also the rhetoric of private property, was freighted with significance in the larger political debates of Wollstonecraft's time.[15]

Among British thinkers attempting to redress the inequalities consequent on property laws were William Ogilvie, whose *Essay on the Right of Property in Land* (1781) called for the nationalization of land, and William Godwin, whose *Political Justice* (1793) looked to a world beyond nation states, where property would revert to individual use.[16] Wollstonecraft herself, among other attacks on the property system, linked accumulated property in land to inequality and poverty, calling in her *Vindication of the Rights of Men* for the division of large estates into small farms.[17] But, in general, Wollstonecraft's writing represents less an attempt to formulate a new property regime than to focus attention on the abuses and injustices of the existing one. In this, she exploited and extended the discourse of human rights, which, as Brewer notes, emerged to counter a political establishment founded on private property.[18] Here, she was not the first: *Hardships of the English Laws in Relation to Wives* (1735) asserted that British laws put married women "in a worse Condition than *Slavery* itself."[19] In an era when civic and political identity were founded on property ownership, women's inability in common law to own separate property constituted a "Wrong" to be repeatedly protested.

* * *

Eighteenth-century property law presents a complex field, with common law (based on case law) supplemented by at least three other bodies of law regulating property ownership: the equity courts, ecclesiastical or civil law, and Parliamentary statutes.[20] The dominant notions governing property and inheritance in common law, namely primogeniture and coverture, did not necessarily operate in other legal systems: civil law (based on Roman law) was more egalitarian than common law, advocating a form of community property within marriage and equal division of parental wealth among all children in inheritance.[21] However, by the end of the century when Wollstonecraft was writing, an ongoing process of legal "rationalization" had made common and statute law dominant, with the decline of ecclesiastical courts.[22] Reforms of inheritance law at the end of the previous century, designed to concentrate wealth in families, had also reduced rights women had previously held to their father's or husband's assets at their deaths.[23] Barker's study of trading families in north-east England in this period shows that it was common even for people of very little or modest wealth to use premarital settlements or the freedom of the testator to avoid the common-law obligations of coverture or primogeniture, two of the key targets in Wollstonecraft's attacks on property law, and the primary mechanisms through which, at marriage or death, property was transferred between persons.[24] But this very recourse to alternative legal provisions demonstrates the vulnerability of women in and to the law, and Wollstonecraft shows herself alert to how, even where at times precarious legal provisions existed, women could be subject to physical and emotional abuse by men whose power, including legal power, was greater than theirs. It is this broader picture of how their inequality in law affected the lived experience of women before, in, and after marriage that Wollstonecraft addressed in her work.

Wollstonecraft had intended to write a second volume to her *Vindication of the Rights of Woman*, addressing women's legal inequities, but while this never appeared, the multiple narratives of the unfinished *Wrongs of Woman* foreground the "rigid laws which enslave women" when the "master-key" is property.[25] Darnford's description of Maria's memoirs as demonstrating the "absurdity of the laws respecting matrimony, which, till divorces could be more easily obtained was ... the most insufferable bondage," is an interpretative guide to their main themes.[26] The "bondage" of matrimony points to the common-law notion of coverture and its consequences. Stemming from medieval times and designed to secure dynastic wealth in families, it was defined by legal commentator Sir William Blackstone as the suspension in marriage of the "very being or legal existence of the woman," who becomes "one person in law" with her husband, "under whose wing, protection, and *cover*, she performs every thing."[27] No married woman – or "feme covert" – could contract, sue, or be sued independently from her husband, and any property not protected by premarital settlement, such as a "separate estate," passed to her husband.[28] Wollstonecraft's gloss on this was that a wife is "as much a man's property as his horse, or his ass, she has nothing she can call her own. He may use any means to get at what the law considers his, the moment his wife is in possession of it, even to the forcing of a lock," as Venables does, seeking money given to Maria by her uncle.[29] Wollstonecraft further observes that coverture enables a husband to spend the "property" of his wife in "dissipation and intemperance"; and that a mother cannot "*lawfully*" take money from a "gambling spendthrift, or beastly drunkard."[30] The story of Maria's second landlady, during her flight from Venables' house, shows how this pertains even when a wife has separated from a husband: income earned by the woman through work undertaken after having left her feckless husband is claimed by him with impunity.[31] At a time when divorce was rare, and the only ground for legal separation was cruelty and adultery (Maria reflects she has "no protection . . . unless she have the plea of bodily fear"), coverture's erasure of the married woman's legal identity thus carried far-reaching consequences.[32] Legal controls held by husbands also extended to their children. As Wollstonecraft observed in a letter to Gilbert Imlay, "it is sufficient for man to condescend to get a child, in order to claim him"; as "femes covert," mothers had no legal status or recognition, and a father would be within his rights to send his wife to prison if she refused to release his child to him.[33] In this context, Maria's act of breastfeeding her daughter might be read as a political intervention in a world where women, wives, and mothers are "*outlaws*."[34] Viewed as an act of labor, which, following Locke, Wollstonecraft had elsewhere observed gives rights "to enjoy the acquisitions" attained through industry, the mother's breastfeeding might constitute a claim for property in her child through assertion of maternal labor.[35]

Wollstonecraft also attacks the inequities of inheritance, another significant area of operation for property law. Her first novel, *Mary*, demonstrates the consequences of the common-law practice of primogeniture, by which the eldest son was the privileged inheritor of an estate. In addition to the evident inequity, and the tendency of primogeniture to accumulate rather than distribute wealth, it is clear that it also debases family relations, evident both in the neglect of Mary by her parents during her elder brother's lifetime, and in her subsequent arranged marriage, designed to secure the acquisition, through any offspring to the union, of a neighboring estate. In *Wrongs of Woman*, Maria's appointment as (apparently) the sole trustee of her daughter's inheritance from Maria's uncle represents an attempt to circumvent the usual patterns of inheritance, and would appear to be without much historical precedent; even where married women nominally owned "separate estates," they were most often controlled by (usually male) trustees. Yet Wollstonecraft is clear how vulnerable Maria as trustee and her daughter as beneficiary are to a mobilization of legal means to strip them of their assets. While the text's climactic and devastating court scene stages the trial of Darnford, in his absence, for adultery, and does not strictly address property law, it is clearly motivated by Venables' attempt to access the wealth inherited by Maria's daughter, enabling Wollstonecraft to illustrate how interconnected legal systems, including property laws, constituted a web of power in which women were caught. That Maria's fortune is thrown into chancery, the court which dealt with claims for possession of property and contested inheritance, at the conclusion of the scene, only underlines this. Even had the trial for adultery not resulted in the loss of Maria's fortune, she might have suffered the very fate from which Darnford had only just escaped: namely, incarceration as a lunatic to enable his estate to be seized. Further, Venables' successful attack on the uncle's bequest is prefigured by that of Maria's elder brother, who disinherits Maria by finding a "flaw" in their mother's will, which had settled money on all her children.[36] Even where (as Barker suggests was indeed common), a parent sought to act equitably to her offspring through her will, female inheritance was vulnerable to a superior male ability to have recourse to a system of law already strongly biased – "partial," in Wollstonecraft's words – in their favor.

Notes

1 Mary Wollstonecraft, *The Wrongs of Woman; or, Maria*, in *The Works of Mary Wollstonecraft*, edited by Janet Todd and Marilyn Butler (London: W. Pickering, 1989), 1: 83.
2 Ibid., 1: 139.
3 Michael Sonenscher, "Property, Community and Citizenship", in Mark Goldie and Robert Wokler, eds., *The Cambridge History of Eighteenth-Century Political Thought* (Cambridge: Cambridge University Press, 2006), 465–94, at 467.
4 John Brewer and Susan Staves, "Introduction," in Brewer and Staves, eds., *Early Modern Conceptions of Property* (London: Routledge 1995), 2.
5 Sonenscher, "Property," 469.

6 Brewer and Staves, "Introduction," 1–2.
7 Sonenscher, "Property," 466.
8 See Patrick Coleman, "Property, Politics and Personality in Rousseau," in *Early Modern Conceptions of Property*, 254–74.
9 Sonenscher, "Property," 469, 468. For Wollstonecraft's admiration of Babeuf, see Barbara Taylor, *Mary Wollstonecraft and the Feminist Imagination* (Cambridge: Cambridge University Press, 2003), 173, 289.
10 Sonenscher "Property," 486. Mary Wollstonecraft, *Letters Written during a Short Residence in Sweden, Norway, and Denmark*, in *Works*, 6: 273.
11 Sonenscher "Property," 467.
12 The classic essay on the moral economy is E. P. Thomson, "The Moral Economy of the English Crowd," *Past & Present*, 50 (1971), 76–136. See also Catherine Packham, "'The Common Grievance of the Revolution': Bread, the Grain Trade, and Political Economy in Wollstonecraft's *View of the French Revolution*," *European Romantic Review*, 25:6 (2014), 705–22.
13 Hannah Barker, *Family and Business during the Industrial Revolution* (Oxford: Oxford University Press, 2017), 50–51.
14 Edmund Burke, *Reflections on the Revolution in France*, edited by Conor Cruise O'Brien (London: Penguin, 1968), 274.
15 On the political importance of the rhetoric of private property, see Brewer and Staves, "Introduction," 18.
16 See Brewer and Staves, "Introduction," 3; Sonenscher, "Property," 493.
17 Mary Wollstonecraft, *A Vindication of the Rights of Men*, in *Works*, 5: 57.
18 Brewer and Staves, "Introduction," 18.
19 [Sarah Chapone], *Hardships of the English Laws in Relation to Wives* (London: W Bowyer for J. Roberts, 1735), 2. On this text see Gillian Skinner, "Women's Status as Legal and Civic Subjects: 'A Worse Condition Than Slavery Itself?'" in Vivien Jones, ed., *Women and Literature in Britain 1700–1800* (Cambridge: Cambridge University Press, 2000), 91–111, at 99.
20 Amy Louise Erickson, *Women and Property in Early Modern England* (London: Routledge, 1993). A further body of law, manorial or borough law, was largely in decline by Wollstonecraft's time.
21 Ibid.
22 Ibid., 6. See Skinner, "Women's Status" for discussion of one such "rationalization", Hardwick's Marriage Act (1753), by which marriage by verbal contract, recognized in church but not common law, was no longer legal.
23 Ruth Perry, "Women in Families: The Great Disinheritance," in Jones, *Women and Literature*, 111–13, at 112, 119.
24 Barker, *Family and Business*. Trusts and settlements set up under Equity made it possible for married women to own property: see Skinner, "Women's Status," 94.
25 Wollstonecraft, *Wrongs*, in *Works*, 1: 178, 148.
26 Ibid., 1: 172.
27 William Blackstone, *Commentaries of the Laws of England, 1771* (London: Reeves & Turner, 1896), 97. Quoted in Skinner, "Women's Status," 92.

28 Erickson, *Women and Property*, 24; on separate estate see Erickson, *Women and Property*, 103, and Susan Staves, *Married Women's Separate Property in England, 1660-1833* (Cambridge: Harvard University Press, 1990).
29 Wollstonecraft, *Wrongs*, in *Works*, 1: 149.
30 Ibid., 145, 149.
31 Ibid., 164–65.
32 Ibid., 149.
33 Susan C. Greenfield, *Mothering Daughters: Novels and the Politics of Family Romance: Burney to Austen* (Detroit: Wayne State University Press, 2003), 102, 97. It was not until the 1839 Infant Custody Bill that, under some conditions, a separated mother could visit and, in rare cases, retain custody of her children.
34 Wollstonecraft, *Wrongs*, in *Works*, 1: 146. Greenfield, *Mothering Daughters*, argues that, by impeding or delaying any subsequent conception, maternal breastfeeding challenged the "aristocratic property system" and its desire for women to produce male heirs.
35 In the *Vindication of the Rights of Men*, Wollstonecraft asserts that "the only security of property that nature authorizes and reason sanctions is, the right a man has to enjoy the acquisitions which his talents and industry have acquired." *Vindication*, in *Works*, 5: 24.
36 Wollstonecraft, *Wrongs*, in *Works*, 1: 140.

CHAPTER 25

Domestic Law

Rebecca Probert

In the eighteenth century there was no formal category of "domestic law." The terminology of "domestic relations" emerged in the nineteenth century, and the modern concept of "family law" only in the twentieth. The eminent lawyer William Blackstone, following the Continental model, included the relationships between husband and wife, parent and child, and master and servant, within the "law of persons" in his groundbreaking *Commentaries on the Laws of England*, but other contemporary writers tended to focus on specific relationships. Nonetheless, the term "domestic law" remains a useful shorthand for the various ways in which the law – whether contained in legislation, or in the decisions of the ecclesiastical, common-law, or criminal courts – regulated family relationships.

Chief among these was the relationship of husband and wife. Although the percentage of births outside marriage had doubled over the course of the eighteenth century, it had barely reached 5 percent of all births by its close. While a few elite men might maintain mistresses in separate establishments or, more rarely, live with them openly, the vast majority of couples who set up home together were married. Even in the 1790s, it was difficult to put any radical ideas about alternatives to marriage into practice, especially since the consequences were borne by any children of the relationship, who would be stigmatized as illegitimate. So it is unsurprising that even Mary Wollstonecraft and William Godwin should have chosen to go through a ceremony of marriage before the birth of their daughter in 1797.

The fact that they married in church – at St. Pancras parish chapel in Camden – reflected the limited options available to them. The Clandestine Marriages Act 1753 had required all marriages to be celebrated according to the rites of the Church of England, with exceptions only being made for Quakers and Jews. The option of marrying in a civil ceremony was not to become available for another forty years. Marriages according to Anglican rites had to be preceded by the calling of banns or the obtaining of a license, and celebrated in the church of the parish where either the bride or groom was resident. Marrying by license was the slightly more expensive option but gave the parties a little more privacy as it removed the need for the intended marriage to be announced in church on the three preceding Sundays.

The act of marrying fundamentally changed a woman's status. As Blackstone famously commented, "[b]y marriage, the husband and wife are one person in law: that is, the very being or legal existence of the woman is suspended during the marriage, or at least is incorporated and consolidated into that of the husband, under whose wing, protection and cover, she performs everything."[1] While the doctrine of coverture very clearly signaled who was to be responsible for legal transactions within the marriage, it did not mean that a wife became her husband's property. Nor did the doctrine of coverture preclude a wife from playing an active role in the running of the household, including entering into transactions with tradesmen for the provision of household goods. While a wife could not contract on her own behalf, she could do so as her husband's agent and pledge his credit for necessities. Tradesmen then looked to the husband for payment of the bills.

Nor did the doctrine of coverture relieve married women of responsibility for their crimes; in that context at least, as Wollstonecraft noted in a *Vindication of the Rights of Woman*, wives did have "a civil existence."[2] Coverture was relevant only in that where a wife was charged with a crime that had been committed in the presence of her husband and there was a presumption that she had done so under his coercion and should therefore be acquitted. This was attributed by the barrister Williams Hawkins to the "Power and Authority which her husband has over her."[3] Even so, there were some offenses too serious for the defense to excuse a wife obeying her husband, namely robbery, murder, and treason. And a wife who killed her husband was regarded as more than a murderess: she was guilty of petty treason, underscoring the hierarchical nature of the relationship. Upon conviction, she was liable to be sentenced to death by burning. Such verdicts were admittedly rare in practice: over the entirety of the eighteenth century only four women who had killed their husbands received such a sentence at the Old Bailey, and the last of these who was burned alive – rather than being strangled in advance – was Catherine Hayes, in 1726. In 1790 hanging was formally substituted for burning, and although the actual offense of petty treason remained on the statute book until 1828, no more wives were convicted of the offense. Even so, the very existence of this crime, and this sanction, on the statute books at the end of the eighteenth century illustrates how far from equal the relationship between husband and wife was.

Similarly, there was no question of a wife having an equal say in the upbringing of the children: as Blackstone noted, "a mother, as such, is entitled to no power, but only to reverence and respect."[4] This was a little misleading in that a *widowed* mother might well enjoy and exercise certain legal powers, such as that of consenting to a child's marriage, at least as long as her husband had not appointed a guardian. But during her husband's lifetime it was he who had the legal power to decide on the way in which children should be educated and to administer correction if they behaved in a way of which he disapproved. If the relationship between the parents broke down, it was the father who was regarded as having the "natural right" to the care of the children. Nonetheless, the courts were far from regarding paternal power as absolute and without limits; it was always subject to the limitations imposed by the law. In *Re Blisset's case*,[5] a father had threatened to remove his six-year-old daughter from her mother's care by force unless the child was delivered up to him. The judge refused to grant a decree of habeas corpus delivering up the child, and told the father that he would be committed if he forcibly removed her. Lord Mansfield supported this outcome, noting that a court would not think it right for a child to be with a father who was a bankrupt, and unable to support her, or who was likely to give the child an "improper" education. In two later cases, fathers without the means to support their children were specifically restrained from interfering with the education of those children; in both cases it was the mother who had directed how the children should be educated and the effect was to uphold her decisions.[6] Even so, no reference was made to maternal rights, the decisions being based on the welfare of the children.

The extent to which the law permitted a husband to exercise more direct control over his wife was also a matter of some debate. Blackstone had suggested that "by the old law" a husband might "give his wife moderate correction," on the basis that he would be the person answerable for her misbehavior. But he quickly added that "this power of correction began to be doubted" in the late seventeenth century and pointed out that a wife was now able to swear the peace against her husband. This might result in the husband's committal to prison: as one late eighteenth-century case noted, the husband's cruel behavior to his wife "had compelled her to exhibit articles of the peace against him, upon which he had been arrested and confined in Newgate for want of bail."[7] In 1782 the cartoonist Gillray lampooned one of the judges of the King's Bench, Francis Buller, for apparently suggesting that a husband could chastise his wife with a stick, as long as it was no thicker than his thumb. "Judge Thumb," as Buller was dubbed, was shown carrying a set of "Patent Sticks for Family Correction: warranted Lawful!" Behind him a wife being beaten by her husband cries "murder," while the husband retorts "It's Law you Bitch! It's not bigger than my Thumb!" While historians have been unable to trace any record of Buller having made any such claim, there are certainly contemporary references to it. But despite the wide circulation of the concept, it certainly did not represent the law at this time. Later editions of the *Commentaries* did not regard it as being necessary to refute such an absurd idea, and wives continued to be able to seek legal protection from violent husbands – although just as today, the number who actually sought such protection was considerably smaller than the number who experienced violence.

Nonetheless, the law did "still permit a husband to restrain a wife of her liberty, in case of any gross misbehaviour,"[8] and a husband who forced his wife to have sex could not be prosecuted for rape. The justification offered for this immunity in Hale's *History of the Pleas of the Crown* was that "by their mutual matrimonial consent and contract the wife has given up herself in this kind unto her husband, which she cannot retract."[9] Yet this was not the only possible reading of the existing authorities. It had its roots in the medieval view that a man would not be guilty of rape if he had previously had consensual sexual intercourse with the woman, but it was noted that "this is no exception at this day" and any woman other than a wife would be protected if the man disregarded her subsequent refusal. Yet despite the weak basis, the marital exemption was to remain part of the law for centuries. The difficulties faced by any woman in seeking to show that she had been the victim of rape offered little hope to wives that they would be able to successfully challenge their husbands' immunity.

The law did not, however, go so far as to order wives to submit to sexual intercourse with their husbands. If one spouse refused to live in the same house as the other, the latter could seek a decree of restitution of conjugal rights from the ecclesiastical courts to compel their return, but while Sir William Scott in *Forster* v. *Forster* referred to matrimonial intercourse as one of the "duties that belong to the very institution of marriage," he acknowledged that such intercourse could not be compelled by the court, and that the law provided no remedy for the spurned spouse. The only sanction in cases of continued refusal on the part of the recalcitrant spouse to return home was that of excommunication. Moreover, insofar as there was a duty to engage in sexual intercourse within marriage, it applied to both spouses. In *Forster* it was the husband who had withdrawn from his wife's bed some time before she had committed adultery, and while Scott held that it could not "justify a wife, in a resort to unlawful pleasures, that lawful ones are withdrawn," the husband's withdrawal could not "be considered as a matter perfectly light" and "if he has so done, he ought to feel less surprise if consequences of human infirmity should ensue."

In that case the husband – who had himself committed adultery – was refused the remedy of a divorce *a mensa et thoro* that would have permitted him to live separately from his wife and relieved him of responsibility for her maintenance. The ecclesiastical courts would authorize such separations in the case of adultery or cruelty. Both husbands and wives could petition on either ground, although in practice husbands were more likely to rely on adultery and wives on a combination of adultery and cruelty. The adultery of a husband, in this context, was viewed as seriously as that of a wife, but the test for establishing legal cruelty was set at a high level. In *Evans* v. *Evans*, Sir William Scott justified the requirement that a spouse seeking a separation be able to demonstrate that they had been subjected to physical harm, suggesting that once spouses understood "that they must live together, except for a very few reasons known to the law, they learn to soften by mutual accommodation that yoke which they know they cannot shake off; they become good husbands and wives from the necessity of remaining husbands and wives; for necessity is a . . . master in teaching the duties it imposes."[10]

This was the optimistic view. In practice, those unable to obtain a legal separation often resorted to other options. Where both wished to live separately they might draw up a private agreement setting out the terms on which they would live apart. Since they were still, in law, one person, trustees had to be interposed in order for the contract to have any effect, and even then the courts were reluctant to allow their agreements to be binding. It was not possible, for example, for the spouses to promise each other that they would be free to remarry, or to bind themselves not to pursue legal remedies afresh. Those prosecuted for bigamy when they made use of their supposed freedom quickly found that the agreement did not protect them from punishment, and the ecclesiastical courts never recognized the validity of contracts barring the right of either spouse to seek legal remedies, whether seeking the return of the other spouse or a formal separation. Others simply deserted, although the authorities regularly pursued and prosecuted husbands who had abandoned wives and children to the support of the parish.

For the vast majority of the population, marriage was a union for life with no option of escape. At this time there was no judicial process for ending a marriage and the only means of terminating a marriage was to obtain a private Act of Parliament. At the time Wollstonecraft was writing, no woman had ever been granted a divorce in England and Wales and fewer than a hundred divorces had been granted to men. The only matrimonial offense recognized for these purposes was the adultery of the wife. In addition, before petitioning Parliament to pass such an Act, a husband had to have already obtained a divorce *a mensa et thoro* and successfully sued his wife's lover for "criminal conversation" in the common-law courts.

The action for criminal conversation reveals much about the way in which the marital relationship was conceptualized. While the standard allegation in a "crim con" suit was that the wife's lover "with force and arms" made an assault upon her and "seduced, debauched, deflowered, lay with and carnally knew her," the true victim was seen as being the husband. Central to his argument was that as a result of the adultery, he had lost his wife's "service and society, comfort, conversation, affection, aid and assistance," a list that summed up both the practical and emotional elements of marriage. The amount of damages was the jury's judgment on what the husband's pain and suffering were worth and varied widely, from a few shillings to many thousands of pounds. Aristocratic husbands tended to receive higher damages, on the basis that they were thought to suffer more from the humiliation of their wife's adultery, especially if the wife's lover was of lower status. The happiness of the marriage was another key factor, with counsel often expatiating on the beauty, accomplishments, virtue, and loving nature of the wife before she committed adultery. Their rhetoric suggests that women were valued for far more than their physical beauty, and that the ideal marriage was seen as involving a degree of reciprocity. Husbands who neglected their wives and allowed them to spend time with other men could expect to receive a lesser award. Tellingly, though, there was no equivalent action for a wife to sue her husband's lover.

Blackstone concluded his account of the legal effects of marriage with the observation that "even the disabilities, which the wife lies under, are for the most part intended for her protection and benefit. So great a favorite is the female sex of the laws of England."[11] That the position under English law is very different today is in no small part due to the women who followed Wollstonecraft's lead in challenging the status quo.

Notes

1 William Blackstone, *Commentaries on the Laws of England, 1765–69* (Chicago: University of Chicago Press, 1979), 1: 430.
2 Mary Wollstonecraft, *A Vindication of the Rights of Woman* (London: Joseph Johnson, 1792), 426.
3 William Hawkins, *A Treatise of the Pleas of the Crown* (London, 1716), 1: 2.
4 Blackstone, *Commentaries*, 1: 441.
5 (1767) Lofft 748; 98 ER 899.
6 *Creuze* v. *Hunter* (1790) 2 Cox 242; 30 ER 113; *ex p Warner* (1792) 4 Bro CC 101; 29 ER 799.
7 *ex p Warner* (1792) 4 Bro CC 101; 29 ER 799.
8 Blackstone, *Commentaries*, 1: 433.
9 Matthew Hale, *History of the Pleas of the Crown* (London: E. & R. Nutt, R. Gosling, 1736), 1: 629.
10 *Evans* v. *Evans* (1790) 1 Hagg Con 35 at 36–37.
11 Blackstone, *Commentaries*, 1: 433.

CHAPTER 26

Slavery and Abolition

Katie Donington

"I'd rather be a rebel than a slave" read the slogan emblazoned on the
T-shirts worn by the cast of *Suffragette* (2015) during a promotional shoot
for the magazine *Time Out*. The quote came from a speech given by
Emmeline Pankhurst on July 14, 1913 at the London Pavilion; she went
on to add "I would rather die than submit ... my challenge to the
Government is: 'Kill me or give me my freedom.'" Pankhurst adopted
the linguistic dichotomy of slavery and freedom to make a political point
about the circumscription of what she perceived to be her inalienable right
to full democratic citizenship. The reaction to the *Time Out* advertising
campaign was swift and critical; Kirsten West Savali stated "When I see
smiling white women effortlessly reject the label 'slave,' as if it solidifies
their feminist credentials, I think about the daughter descendants of
slaves ... and my legacy of both rebel and slave, knowing that they are
not mutually exclusive." She argued that this instinct within Western
feminism was "not a new tradition; it is time-honored and tested."[1] The
incident underscored the complicated and uncomfortable relationship that
feminism has sometimes shared with the history of race, class, and empire.

The interconnections between antislavery and the campaign for
women's rights have been explored in both the British and American
contexts. Women – both free and enslaved – played a unique role within
transatlantic abolitionism as writers, speakers, and activists. They formed
their own antislavery committees, petitioned, and fundraised. While it is
tempting to posit antislavery campaigning in Britain "as a prelude to the
women's suffrage movement," it does not necessarily follow that all of the
women involved in the movement, or who intervened in the debates, saw
antislavery as bound up in the cause of women's emancipation.[2] From the
socially conservative Hannah More to the radical Mary Wollstonecraft,
individuals with incredibly diverse opinions on the role of women contributed to the dialogue on colonial slavery. Women's participation in
antislavery has usually been understood through the framework of

222

philanthropy – as an extension of the domestic realm. Clare Midgley has argued that this characterization fails to recognize the ways in which involvement within the abolition campaign challenged the distinctions between the private and public worlds. She has argued that "extra-Parliamentary political activities in support of anti-slavery were a key means by which both women and men developed the arena of civil society through the late eighteenth and early nineteenth century."[3] Motivated by a complicated web of intersecting interests, antislavery offered those on the margins of British political life – women, dissenters, the middle and working classes – an opportunity to participate in what became one of the first popular mass political mobilizations.

Up until the advent of organized abolition in the late 1780s, slavery had been considered "a public benefit rather than a public issue."[4] Participation in different aspects of the slavery business provided individuals with a route to wealth and respectability, as well as contributing to the national coffers through the payment of taxes on colonial goods. The British public enjoyed the fruits of enslaved labor through its consumption of slave-produced commodities. How then did abolition come to occupy such a central place in British political culture during the closing decades of the eighteenth century? The development of the British antislavery movement has been the subject of extensive historiographical debate. Traditional accounts of the history of abolition have failed to include African-led activism; however, free and enslaved Africans employed a variety of strategies to resist and undermine the system. Their protests spanned from ship to shore with on-board rebellions, plantation uprisings and everyday forms of resistance among the strategies they used to erode the system. Some of the earliest legal challenges to slavery in Britain were instigated following enslaved people's decision to run away. Initially histories of the movement were produced by the men who were involved in the parliamentary campaigns, or those close to them. They created a distinctly masculine metropolitan narrative that focused almost exclusively on themes of Christian duty, humanitarianism, and benevolence in Britain. In 1944 Trinidadian historian Eric Williams published *Capitalism and Slavery*, a work that has continued to provoke debate on both the impact of slavery in Britain and the causes of its abolition. Rejecting earlier hagiographic histories, Williams argued primarily for an economic account of abolition. He suggested that it was a combination of economic decline in the Caribbean, the turn toward the East Indies, and the rise of free trade that sealed the fate of the mercantilist system that underpinned the slave economy in the West Indies. This thesis was repudiated, most famously, by

Seymour Drescher, who argued instead for the continued prosperity of the sugar islands suggesting that the dismantling of slavery was an altruistic act of "econocide."[5] The complex factors leading up to the emergence of abolitionism as a political force take in both economic and cultural shifts. Antislavery became one of *the* most hotly contested and engaging popular political debates of the day, its iconography and rhetoric permeated across a range of contemporaneous issues.

The second half of the eighteenth century was a period of reformist and revolutionary zeal. Radicalism found its ultimate expression in the seismic changes brought about by the American, French, and Haitian Revolutions. Taken together, these Atlantic Revolutions each engaged in their own way with the issue of slavery. In 1791, Toussaint L'Ouverture led the only successful slave revolt leading to the self-emancipation of the enslaved people of what was then the prized French colony of Saint-Domingue (later renamed Haiti). In 1794, under the revolutionary leadership of Maximilien Robespierre, the French abolished slavery; however, they later tried to reinstate the system in 1802 under Napoleon. While the specter of revolutionary violence, particularly in France and Haiti, delayed the cause of abolition in Britain, these events signaled a break with the past – a fundamental reconfiguration of power, tradition, and hierarchy.

This was also a period in which Enlightenment thinkers created a critical culture in which issues of tyranny and liberty were discussed broadly in relation to a number of pressing political, social, and imperial concerns. The limits of an Enlightenment vision of freedom can be read in its complicated relationship with the history of race and empire. Thinkers like David Hume, John Locke, and Immanuel Kant all expressed views that cast the African as intellectually and culturally inferior to the European. As well as acting as Secretary to the Council of Trade and Plantations and investing in the Royal African Company, in his *Second Treatise on Government* Locke set out a defense of slavery. Nevertheless, for writers like Wollstonecraft, this was an exciting and febrile environment in which it seemed that real change was not only thinkable but practicable.

The appeal of the abolitionist cause was broad-based; it attracted radical thinkers, working people, and those in possession of a "middle-class reform complex."[6] With the rise of Evangelicalism in the latter half of the eighteenth century, religion and reform enjoyed a mutually reinforcing relationship that encouraged believers to engage not only in more serious and committed forms of religiosity but also in benevolent acts of improvement. The eighteenth century saw an increase in the wealth, influence, and charitable activities of the middling sort, particularly the commercial and emerging industrial classes. The reformation of social ills became a tool by which the middle classes could forge an identity separate to what they perceived as both the excesses and luxury of the aristocracy and the uncivilized brutishness of the working classes. It also served a more practical role in defining social relations for the dawning of the industrial era. As David Brion Davis has suggested, antislavery "opened new sources of moral prestige for the dominant social class, helped define a participatory role for middle-class activism, and looked forward to the universal goal of compliant, loyal, and self-disciplined workers."[7] In 1787, the drive to improve the condition of the lower orders in society manifested itself in the foundation of the Society for Effecting the Abolition of the Slave Trade, as well as the Society for Carrying into Effect His Majesty's Proclamation against Vice and Immorality. Antislavery, particularly in later years, was bound up with the project of civilizing and Christianizing the enslaved and, to a degree, the corrupted planter class whose despotism had degraded them.

Improvement in both the metropole and the colonies was in part a reflection of Britain's imperial aspirations. Following the loss of the Thirteen Colonies, the 1780s was a key period in the debates surrounding the nature of the British empire – would it be ruled by the sword or would the civilizing mission shape Britain's imperial world? The impeachment of Warren Hastings and the abolition of the slave trade formed two important strands of this discussion. Christopher Leslie Brown has argued convincingly for the centrality of the reconfiguration of national and imperial identity in the rise of British abolitionism. He has suggested that the American Revolution played a pivotal role in the development of what he has termed the "moral capital" of antislavery.[8] American demands for emancipation from the yoke of British tyranny encouraged the emergence of abolitionism as a national concern. Samuel Johnson, an early supporter of antislavery, articulated this position in his remark "We are told, that the subjection of Americans may tend to the diminution of our own liberties ... If slavery be thus fatally contagious, how is it that we hear the loudest yelps for liberty among the drivers of negroes?"[9] In the wake of the humiliating loss of the American War of Independence, the adoption of antislavery became a useful pivot for the vanquished British to regain the moral high ground.

Religious nonconformity was also influential in the development of abolitionist thought. The dominance of the Quakers can be seen in the religious make-up of the Society for Effecting the Abolition of the Slave Trade – of the twelve founding members, nine were Quakers. In 1761 the London Yearly Meeting made the trading of enslaved people a breach of

Quaker discipline, thus enshrining the idea of antislavery within their religious culture and practice. For Rational Dissenters, "Universal tolerance and enlightenment were indissolubly linked," and their "attachment to fundamental natural rights" included "freedom from enslavement."[10] Excluded by the Test Acts from participation in formal politics, dissenters of all varieties were heavily involved in the campaigns for abolition. In 1784 Wollstonecraft moved to Newington Green, a hotbed of radical dissent and an important center for antislavery activism. Two of the founding members of the Society for Effecting the Abolition of the Slave Trade, Joseph Wood senior and Samuel Hoare junior, as well as many of the key campaigners from the later years of antislavery lived in and around Newington Green.[11] Wollstonecraft's mentor and friend Richard Price ministered to the local congregation. Price supported abolition in both Britain and America, stating that "the abolition of the Slave trade would be truly honourable to the present times and worthy of Example to other enlightened Nations."[12] Despite his public sympathy for antislavery, Price's activism was perhaps tempered by the presence of powerful proslavery families, including the Vaughans and the Boddingtons, within his congregation. Given the relative paucity of writing by Price addressing the subject of slavery, it has been suggested that abolition was peripheral to his central concern with religious freedom and political slavery. Whether in relation to nonconformity, women's rights, or American independence, there can be little doubt that the issue of colonial slavery was being debated within the radical circles of Newington Green.

This period of radicalism and reform also coincided with the rise of sentimentality and the rhetoric of sensibility. One of the key features of the antislavery campaign in Britain was its expression through literary and visual culture. From Josiah Wedgewood's "Am I Not a Man and a Brother" medallion to William Cowper's *The Negro's Complaint*, the visual and linguistic symbolism of abolition was rooted in a sentimental plea for pity, empathy, and compassion that appealed directly to the cult of feeling. Antislavery writing was an area that women took a particular interest in, and their productions included political pamphlets, tracts, and poetry. Poetry in particular, with its tradition of female authorship, gave women "a way to voice social and political criticism through the acceptably 'feminine' means of poetic sentiment and appeals to the emotion."[13] Abolitionist literary productions also included a number of narratives written by formerly enslaved people; Ottobah Cugoano, Mary Prince, Ignatius Sancho, and perhaps most famously Olaudah Equiano. In 1791 Equiano's work was reviewed by Wollstonecraft in the *Analytic Review*.

Questioning hierarchies of civilization based solely on "whom the sun-beams more directly dart" she argued that Equiano's "intellectual powers" were "sufficient to wipe off the stigma" of his skin in a society that had assigned it as "a mark of slavery."[14]

Wollstonecraft's own interventions in the slavery debates can be read in her direct remarks on the practice, her engagement with abolitionist writings, and her use of the language of slavery within her own work. Wollstonecraft produced both *A Vindication of the Rights of Men* (1790) and *A Vindication of the Rights of Woman* (1792) during a key period in the abolition debates. The parliamentary select committee was hearing evidence from both pro and antislavery supporters, which the newspapers were widely reporting on. Two significant public petitions were submitted in 1788 and 1792 – an indication of the popular clamor over the slave trade. Wollstonecraft's framing of her arguments in *A Vindication of the Rights of Men* around notions of human rights and justice, including a specific rejection of slavery as a natural human condition, is indicative of the influence of abolitionist discourse within the text. Following the Haitian Revolution in 1791, rhetorical references to slavery took on an immediate and pressing political meaning. The intensity with which the language of slavery appears in *A Vindication of the Rights of Woman* (1792) was a departure from earlier works. Moira Ferguson has documented over eighty instances in relation to "sensation, pleasure, marriage, patriarchal subjugation" and less frequently "the specific condition of colonized slaves."[15] In one of her direct references to colonial slavery Wollstonecraft questioned whether women were to be eternally subjected to "blind propriety" rather than acting according to reason and virtue. Drawing parallels with the injustices meted out to the enslaved she went on to ask "Is sugar always to be produced by vital blood? Is one half of the human species, like the poor African slaves, to be subject to prejudices that brutalize them, when principles would be a sure guard, only to sweeten the cup of man."[16] The comparison of women's position, particularly within marriage, to the institution of slavery was nothing new, as Laura Nym Mayhall has stated: "Slavery and tyranny operate by analogy . . . to limit and expand the domain inhabited by women."[17] Wollstonecraft's use of this specific lexicon at this particular moment enabled her to fuse the issue of women's rights with the question of colonial slavery, creating an urgency and a relevance for her work. This allowed her to tap into the popular political discourse of anti-slavery at a time when the issue was at the forefront of British political life.

Wollstonecraft was writing during a period in which discussions about the nature of liberty and tyranny infused public consciousness. Her use of the language of slavery, with all its connections to a tortured history of race and empire, makes her work an essential part of unpicking the historic relationship between feminism, imperialism, and racism. As Vron Ware has outlined, these interconnections require further analysis in order to account for the

> deceptively straightforward questions: why have black people *and* white women been dominated in different ways as a result of racist and masculinist hierarchies in British/European history? What are the connections between racism and the subordination of women, black and white? What, then, are the connections between the politics of black liberation, whether from slavery, colonialism or the racism of post-industrial society, and those of different strands of feminism?[18]

These questions of intersectionality continue to have meaning and resonance, as a new generation of activists and scholars continue to build on, and learn from, the unfinished emancipatory movements of the past.

Notes

1 Kirsten West Savali, "Sister Suffragette: Slave T-Shirts Highlight Feminism's Race Problem," *The Root*, 10 July 2015, www.theroot.com/sister-suffragette-slave-t-shirts-highlight-white-fe-1790861323 [Accessed 8 May 2017].

2 Clare Midgley, *Women Against Slavery: The British Campaigns, 1780–1870* (London: Routledge, 1992), 5.

3 Ibid., 5.

4 Sridhya Swaminathan, "Developing the Proslavery Position after the Somerset Decision," *Slavery & Abolition*, 24:3 (2003), 43.

5 Seymour Drescher, *Econocide: British Slavery in the Era of Abolition*, second edn. (Chapel Hill: University of North Carolina Press, 2010).

6 David Turley, *The Culture of English Antislavery, 1780–1860* (London: Routledge, 1991), 108–54.

7 David Brion Davis, *The Problem of Slavery in the Age of Revolution, 1770–1823* (New York: Cornell University Press, 1975), 385.

8 Christopher Leslie Brown, *Moral Capital: Foundations of British Abolitionism* (Chapel Hill: University of North Carolina Press, 2006).

9 Samuel Johnson, *Taxation No Tyranny: An Answer to the Resolutions and Address of the American Congress* (London: T. Cadell, 1775), 89.

10 Turley, *The Culture of English Antislavery*, 113–14.

11 These included Anna Laetitia Barbauld, her brother Dr. John Aiken, James Stephen and his wife Sarah Wilberforce, William Allen, Reverend Thomas Burchell, Reverend Samuel Oughton, and Reverend Joseph Kelly.

12 Price quoted in Anthony Page, "'A Species of Slavery': Richard Price's Rational Dissent and Antislavery," *Slavery & Abolition*, 32:1 (2011), 54.

13 Midgley, *Women Against Slavery*, 34.

14 Mary Wollstonecraft, "Review of The Interesting Narrative of the Life of Olaudah Equiano, or Gustavus Vassa, the African," *Analytic Review*, vol. IV (London: J. Johnson, 1789), 27.

15 Moira Ferguson, "Mary Wollstonecraft and the Problematic of Slavery," *Feminist Review*, 42 (1992), 87.

16 Mary Wollstonecraft, *Vindication of the Rights of Women* (London: J. Johnson, 1792), 330.

17 Laura Nym Mayhall, "The Rhetorics of Slavery and Citizenship: Suffragist Discourse and Canonical Texts in Britain, 1880–1914," *Gender and History*, 13:3 (2001), 482.

18 Vron Ware, *Beyond the Pale: White Women, Racism and History* (London: Verso, 1992), 235.

CHAPTER 27

The Bluestockings

Betty A. Schellenberg

In her stinging critique of eighteenth-century writers on women's education for "render[ing] women objects of pity, bordering on contempt,"
Mary Wollstonecraft singles out Hester Chapone's *Letters on the Improvement of the Mind Addressed to a Young Lady* as an exception, paying the
work a "tribute of respect" for its "good sense, and unaffected humility,
and ... many useful observations."[1] Chapone's *Letters*, first published in
1773 and republished or reprinted at least seventy times through to the
middle of the nineteenth century,[2] arose materially and intellectually out
of her participation in the collective that has come to be called the
Bluestockings. This chapter begins with brief sketches of three "first-
generation" Bluestocking women as a means of identifying characteristic
features of this eighteenth-century movement. I then review the Bluestockings' influential model of sociability and their commitments to a rational
and benevolent social order and to female education, before suggesting
their complicated contribution to the British imagination of womanhood
as the nation moved into the contested political territory of the end of the
century. Chapone's Bluestocking life and her resulting *Letters* serve as
useful orientation points to this important context for Wollstonecraft's
thoughts on the nature of woman, women's societal role, and the ideal
education for that role.

* * *

Hester Mulso, later Chapone (1727–1801), was the daughter of a
gentleman farmer. Although apparently discouraged from wide reading
by her mother, she pursued a broad grounding in literature, theology, and
philosophy with the support of her father and four well-educated brothers.
A precocious writer, Mulso became, at the age of twenty-one, part of the
novelist Samuel Richardson's intimate circle. Within this coterie circle her
manuscript writings, including several odes and a lengthy epistolary debate

with Richardson on the subject of a daughter's freedom of marriage choice, circulated widely. But the break-up of this coterie, the death of her husband John Chapone in 1761, and her resulting straitened financial circumstances set Chapone's course in another direction, bringing her into the orbit of the socially prominent Elizabeth Robinson Montagu (1718–1800), later known as "Queen of the Blues."

Montagu's own trajectory began with an informal education: her father was a gentleman landowner, her mother had been educated by Bathsua Makin, and the Robinson household of seven brothers and younger sister Sarah, later the novelist and historian Sarah Scott, was known for lively debate. Montagu built on this foundation through the deliberate cultivation of male and female acquaintances whom she could offer witty correspondence and lively conversation in exchange for intellectual improvement and guidance in reading. Entering the Duchess of Portland's circle while still a teenager, Montagu gained significantly in status, wealth, and independence through her 1742 marriage to a grandson of the first Earl of Sandwich. In the 1750s she formed close friendships with the poet Gilbert West, and through West, with George, Lord Lyttelton, who became her greatest mentor. Meanwhile, Montagu was gaining increasing notice as a hostess whose entertainments offered conversation guided by a shared taste for the world of letters, in distinction to the perceived norm of assemblies stifled by formal etiquette or devoted to the dissipated pastimes of fashion-chasing, card-playing, gossip, and political wrangling. The term "blue stockings" emerged in this context, first to describe male friends dressed in the rough wool hose of the lower orders, and then the gatherings that central members of the group called, half-jokingly, the "bluestocking philosophers."

The bridge between Chapone and Montagu was Elizabeth Carter (1716–1806), who had formed a friendship with the younger Hester Mulso in the Richardson years and brought the needs of the newly widowed Chapone to the attention of Montagu. The middle-class Carter had herself gained recognition in the 1730s for her unusually wide and deep learning in the classical as well as modern languages, nurtured under the tutelage of her clergyman father and first displayed in the pages of the *Gentleman's Magazine*. Her achievements became a matter of national pride, however, with the 1758 subscription publication of her translation of the Greek Stoic philosopher Epictetus – a feat which not only earned the unmarried Carter a modest financial independence but also prompted Montagu to actively solicit her friendship.

* * *

Thus the Bluestocking movement coalesced from small, relatively egalitarian, mixed-gender groupings of friends; its publications in turn emerged organically out of a belief in the possibility of contributing to the general good. The case of Chapone's *Letters on the Improvement of the Mind* illustrates the effective mentoring inherent in the model: originating in the domestic sphere, as familiar letters addressed to her niece, the work was ushered into print with the countenance, encouragement, and practical assistance of the Montagu coterie. Carter provided Chapone with the model of female friendship she recommended in the *Letters*: "if you are fortunate enough to meet with a young woman eight or ten years older than yourself, of good sense and good principles, to whom you can make yourself agreeable, it may be one of the happiest circumstances of your life. She will be able to advise and to improve you" (*Letters*, 5: 293). For her part, Montagu offered Chapone a friendship that cut across the inequalities of patron and dependent; after accompanying Montagu on a summer tour to Scotland, Chapone was able to report to Carter that "I am grown as bold as a lion with Mrs. Montagu, and fly in her face whenever I have a mind; in short I . . . find my love for her takes off my fear and awe, though my respect for her character continually increases." Montagu's ability to put Chapone at ease recalls her strategy with Carter some years earlier, when she wrote to establish their friendship: "I may be accused of ambition in having always endeavourd to ally my mind to its superiors, but I assure you vanity is not the motive, it is much more the happiness than the honour of Miss Carters friendship that I desire."[3] Not only did Montagu promote Chapone's writings in her private correspondence and assist with editing, she also lent her name as dedicatee: Chapone acknowledges "the partiality of [Montagu's] friendship" in believing the letters "capable of being more extensively useful" through publication (*Letters*, "To Mrs. Montagu").

Meanwhile, the interconnected Bluestocking circles gradually achieved the numbers, cultural prominence, and sense of an institution that brought the term into common usage and feminized it through association with its leading hostesses. Fundamental features of this feminized sociability were the ease and politeness that women were seen to contribute to mixed-gender gatherings. In addition to her ability to fashion a social space in which a woman of Chapone's talent and accomplishment was not prohibited by modest status from operating on a level with birth and fortune, Montagu was also recognized for her power to create harmony in times of political tension: "George the third does not know how much he is indebted to the chearful and Classic Assemblies of your Chinese Room," writes John Macpherson from India to Montagu on October 15, 1772 (mo 1506). Montagu in turn describes Elizabeth Vesey as creating a social space that "assembles all the heterogeneous natures in the World, & indeed in many respects resembles Paradise, for there ye Lion sits down by the Lamb, ye Tyger dandles the Kid; the shy scotchman & ye ... Hibernian, the Hero & the Maccaroni, ... the Mungo of Ministry and the inflexible partizans of incorruptible Patriots, Beaux esprits & fine Gentlemen all gather together ... & are soothed into good humour." Tellingly, if Vesey were to "withdraw her influence a moment," all would descend into "discord" (Montagu to Carter, September 4, 1772, mo 3304). Such millennial iconography is not accidental; it signifies a conviction that the Bluestockings were creating what Harriet Guest has described as a new social sphere between the extremes of the political or aristocratic and the domestic or private.[4]

* * *

Elizabeth Eger has characterized Montagu's "bluestocking philosophy" as "the social expression of an Enlightenment belief in freedom of enquiry," accompanied by "a Christian attention to practical virtue and social benevolence, which emphasised the importance of friendship and a rational adherence to duty."[5] Bluestocking sociability as I have described it above reflects this emphasis on mind over body and on the duties accompanying the privileges of enlightenment, status, and wealth. Numerous critics, particularly Karen O'Brien, have noted the personal ties and intellectual debts of many of the core Bluestocking women and men to the Latitudinarian Anglican thought of writers such as Samuel Clarke and Samuel Butler, who emphasized the accessibility of the truths of Christianity to human reason, including to women as rational beings.[6] Chapone's *Letters* take such rational capacity for granted: "You are now in your fifteenth year, and must soon act for yourself; therefore it is high time to store your mind with those principles, which must direct your conduct, and fix your character" (1: 261). The Latitudinarian commitment to tolerance also enabled the Bluestockings to find a degree of common cause with those of the Dissenting tradition, such as Anna Laetitia Barbauld, or a more evangelical cast, such as Hannah More (although they were uncomfortable with skeptics and unbelievers such as David Hume).

But the Bluestocking belief in a reasonable Christianity was most fully expressed not in abstract theological debates, but in a mutual urging to benevolence and charity. Again, Chapone's vigorous prose embodies the emphasis on a female agency that is called upon to enact rational principles:

> You must *inform your understanding* what you ought to *believe*, and to *do*. You must *correct* and *purify* your *heart*; ... You must *form* and *govern* your *temper* and *manners*, according to the laws of benevolence and justice; and quality yourself, by all means in your power, for an *useful* and *agreeable* member of society. All this you see is no light business, nor can it be performed without a sincere and earnest application of the mind. (*Letters*, 1: 262)

Believing in a loving God who desired his creatures to find joy in this world despite the inevitability of suffering, the Bluestockings sought to bring comfort and pleasure to others not only through the expected rounds of elite social life, but also through such efforts as seeking an honorary doctorate and royal pension for the Scottish writer James Beattie to reward his critique of Hume's skeptical philosophy; promoting the subscription publication of Sarah Fielding's translation of Xenophon's *Memoirs of Socrates*; employing the shoemaker-poet James Woodhouse as estate steward; and sponsoring annual dinners for estate tenants and the chimney sweeps of London. As these examples of Montagu's own endeavors indicate, charity entailed active engagement.

The individual lives I have already sketched demonstrate the Bluestocking women's characteristic diligence in pursuing education as a good for themselves, as well as the significant roles played by male encouragers, promoters, and admirers of female intellectual accomplishments. Bluestockings female and male shared a belief in the importance of raising the standard of elite and middle-class women's education as the best means of enabling them to fulfill their social duties. It was this kind of "improved mind" that Chapone sought to produce: one possessing an enlightened, tolerant, and charitable understanding of the Christian faith; the historical and geographical knowledge required of a citizen (if not an enfranchised one) of the growing British empire; the skills necessary to govern a middle-class, gentry, or aristocratic household; and the polite accomplishments necessary to performance of the social duties of hostess, guest, and domestic companion.

* * *

Thus "Bluestocking philosophy" posits a sociable self, defined in terms of relative duties to God, country, neighbor, and family, rather than the emergent liberal notion of an individual in possession of certain natural rights. Similarly, while Montagu's correspondence shows a willingness to go to significant lengths to assist those in need and to extenuate the moral errors of servants and the poor, it is also clear that the objects of such charity were expected to amend those faults and to respond with a gratitude and humility in keeping with their station. In other words, the Bluestocking understanding of a reasonable and benevolent practice of social duties tended to be conservative in its commitment to broad social distinctions and to the existing political order. This conservatism could be complicated in the specific case of female independence. Like her women friends, Montagu was well aware of how thin the line was between the freedoms she enjoyed as a mid-eighteenth-century woman of privilege and the lot of many of her recent forebears and even her peers – including the beloved sister who struggled against the entrenched patriarchalism of her father and the fallout of a bad marriage. This sense of precarious gains arguably disposed Montagu and other Bluestocking women to acquiesce in their own legal and social subordination. At any rate, Montagu was very willing to play – or play at – the feminine roles of muse, courtly mistress, hostess, or country housewife when called upon to do so by her intimates; an illustrative example is Lyttelton's response to her feelings at General Wolfe's death in the conquest of Quebec: "And yet you read Epictetus and converse with Miss Carter. What signifies your Philosophy unless it can teach you to harden your Heart? But would not that make you less amiable? I own it would—You must therefore go on and suffer till you die, and I will preach no more to you that text" (Lyttelton to Montagu, [1761], mo 5042). JoEllen DeLucia has noted the implicit endorsement by Bluestocking women of Scottish Enlightenment theories about gendered qualities of refinement and sensibility as civilizing forces. Such arguments, of course, ultimately co-opted these women in support of systemic structures that restricted them to the domains of sentiment and domesticity, and, in DeLucia's view, ultimately led to Wollstonecraft's repudiation of the movement along with writers such as the Edinburgh doctor (and Montagu's friend) John Gregory.[7]

In her private correspondence with women, Montagu displays moments of resistance; celebrating the somewhat anomalous autonomy she shares with Carter, she writes of the two of them:

> We are not so perfectly the rib of Man as Woman ought to be[.] We can think for ourselves, & also act for ourselves. When a Wife, I was obedient because it was my duty, & being married to a Man of sense & integrity,

obedience was not painful or irksome, . . . but it seems to me that a new
Master, and new lessons, after one's opinions & habits were form'd, must
be a little awkward, & with all due respect to the superior Sex, I do not see
how they can be necessary to a Woman unless she were to defend her Lands
& Tenements by Sword or gun. (July 11, 1782, mo 3530)

These apparent contradictions can perhaps be explained as a limited form
of collective consciousness on the part of the Bluestocking women – one
based on the principles I have described, as well as on their gender and the
cultural function that was mirrored back to them by their contemporaries,
but not extending to woman as a category that encompassed all female
positions in the familial and hierarchical orders of the day. As the Bluestocking movement became simultaneously identified with female action
in the public sphere and with social and political conservatism, it became
the target of both conservative reactionaries and liberal reformers. This
vicissitude of history should nevertheless not blind us to the affinities
between the eighteenth-century Bluestockings and Mary Wollstonecraft –
affinities that she signaled in her inclusion of excerpts from Carter, Talbot,
and Chapone in her 1789 *Female Reader*, but even more significantly in
her "tribute of respect" to Mrs. Chapone.

Notes

1 Mary Wollstonecraft, "A Vindication of the Rights of Woman," in *Mary
    Wollstonecraft: Political Writings*, edited by Janet Todd (London: W. Picker-
    ing, 1993), 157, 188.
2 See the bibliography compiled by Rhoda Zuk, Chapone's modern editor, in
    Rhoda Zuk, ed., *Bluestocking Feminism: Writings of the Bluestocking Circle,
    1738-1785, Vol. 3: Catherine Talbot & Hester Chapone* (London: Pickering &
    Chatto, 1999), 195–99. Zuk also identifies eighteen editions of the letters in
    company with other works of instruction in the nineteenth century. Quota-
    tions from the *Letters* are taken from this edition and cited in the text; the
    dedication is cited from the 1773 London edition.
3 Chapone to Carter, August 19, 1770, *The Posthumous Works of Mrs Chapone*
    (London, 1807), 1: 152–53; Montagu to Carter, [December] 28, [1758],
    Montagu Collection, Huntington Library, San Marino California, mo 3023.
    Further references to the Montagu Collection will be indicated in the text.
4 Harriet Guest, "Bluestocking Feminism," in Nicole Pohl and Betty A. Schel-
    lenberg, eds., *Reconsidering the Bluestockings* (San Marino: Huntington
    Library, 2003), 63–78; see also Emma Major, "The Politics of Sociability:
    Public Dimensions of the Bluestocking Millennium," in *Reconsidering the
    Bluestockings*, 175–92.

5 Elizabeth Eger, *Bluestockings: Women of Reason from Enlightenment to Romanticism* (Basingstoke: Palgrave Macmillan, 2010), 13.
6 Karen O'Brien, *Women and Enlightenment in Eighteenth-Century Britain* (Cambridge: Cambridge University Press, 2009), 44–67.
7 JoEllen M. DeLucia, "A Delicate Debate: Mary Wollstonecraft, the Bluestockings, and the Progress of Women," in Enit Karafili Steiner, ed., *Called to Civil Existence: Mary Wollstonecraft's "A Vindication of the Rights of Woman,"* (Cambridge: Cambridge University Press, 2014), 113–30.

CHAPTER 28

Conduct Literature

Vivien Jones

Mary Wollstonecraft was both a writer and a fierce critic of what we now loosely define as "conduct literature." In one of the most powerful chapters in *A Vindication of the Rights of Woman*, her searing "Animadversions on Some of the Writers Who Have Rendered Women Objects of Pity, Bordering on Contempt" focus particularly on two of the most popular advice texts of the period, James Fordyce's *Sermons to Young Women* (1766) and John Gregory's *A Father's Legacy to his Daughters* (1774). But her first publication, *Thoughts on the Education of Daughters* (1787), was in many respects an orthodox piece of advice writing. Indeed, some passages in *Thoughts* strongly echo Gregory's views, and Wollstonecraft included several excerpts from his writings in her anthology *The Female Reader* (1789). These perhaps unexpected continuities are a valuable reminder of the wide spectrum of texts and writers offering guidance on girls' and women's education and behavior in the eighteenth and early nineteenth centuries, and of the danger in making ahistorical assumptions about their identity and effects. At the same time, the shifts in Wollstonecraft's engagement with Gregory indicate her increasingly sophisticated alertness to the workings of textual politics and provide insight into the radicalizing effects of French Revolutionary ideas on her intellectual development.

Publications offering advice and instruction, for every conceivable situation and for men as well as women, were bestsellers throughout the eighteenth century, one of the staples of a rapidly expanding print culture which catered enthusiastically for an equally fast-growing reading public with a keen appetite for self-improvement. And as booksellers' records and the numbers of surviving editions show, instructional texts aimed at women were a particularly popular subset within this wider literature of social aspiration. But though the Wollstonecraft of *Rights of Woman* would no doubt have quickly grasped the implications of the modern terms "conduct literature" or "conduct book," these were not labels that she would have used. Brought into common critical currency with the emergence of feminist critical historical analysis in the last third of the twentieth century, they describe content rather than form, ideology rather than genre. Texts, by both men and women, which would now be identified confidently as conduct books include a wide variety of genres including sermons, letters, histories, poems, and narrative fictions. In her chapter in *Rights of Woman*, Wollstonecraft introduces the objects of her critique as simply "some modern publications on the female character and education."[1] As we shall see, she recognizes significant differences between her chosen texts, but her broad introductory description nevertheless anticipates something of the modern critical application of "conduct literature." These are texts which, in ostensibly addressing the question of women's education, are characterized primarily by what is assumed to be their effect on young female readers: the definition and inculcation of a particular female "character."

In its original mid-nineteenth-century usage, a "conduct book" held the record of the behavior and achievement of a (male) scholar, public servant, or member of the armed forces.[2] The feminist appropriation of the term to indicate a particular kind of instructional writing aimed at women thus carries with it overtones of a training regime and associated judgments on the performance of those undergoing its disciplinary program. Whether these texts are addressed explicitly to young women themselves or to their parents or other influencers, their ultimate object is the impressionable female who is invited to know herself as in need of direction and restraint. Successful fulfillment of their instructional regime thus depends, crucially, on self-discipline, on keeping a personal mental record of one's conduct – an effective internalization of the forms of femininity and associated behaviors which, though they are presented as natural, must be learned.

The key characteristics of the conduct book female are familiar enough. She is "naturally" chaste, modest, dutiful, and self-effacing – qualities which are presented as necessary to her survival in a social world haunted by predatory masculinity, and ruthless in its rejection of any falling-off from respectability. "An immodest Woman," the Reverend Wetenhall Wilkes fiercely reminds his readers in 1740, "is a kind of Monster, distorted from its proper Form." Less sensational, but promoting a very similar message, John Gregory describes "a native dignity, an ingenuous modesty to be expected in your sex, which is your natural protection from the familiarities of the men."[3] Success in achieving – or performing – this ideal of dignified modesty brings particular rewards. There is a perverse pleasure to be derived from conformity in and of itself (as practiced by Mary Bennet in *Pride and Prejudice*, for example), but its ultimate goal according to the conduct book narrative is, of course, to secure an advantageous marriage, and with it social and financial security, in a highly competitive market. For women, fulfilling social aspirations depended almost exclusively on marrying well. Conduct books describe how the aspirant middle-class girl needs to behave in order to do so, and thereby the kind of feminine behavior that respectable middle-class men should seek and expect in a wife.

This, then, is the individualized disciplinary process, enabled by a burgeoning print culture, which feminist critics such as Mary Poovey and Nancy Armstrong diagnosed as lying at the heart of emergent eighteenth-century definitions of social status which were for them epitomized and brought about by "conduct literature." For these feminist historians of class, sexuality, and the family, conduct books are seen as powerful instruments in the creation of a recognizably modern middle-class social formation, which has its foundations not simply in macroeconomic processes but in the strict, and restrictive, differentiation of gender roles within the domestic economy. As Armstrong puts it in her still influential Foucauldian formulation from 1987, "the modern individual was first and foremost a female" – an assertion which importantly challenges masculinist versions of history while demonstrating the insidious limitations of that feminine identity.[4]

Wollstonecraft's analysis in *Rights of Woman* anticipates in many respects this twentieth-century feminist critique. But her first publication, *Thoughts on the Education of Daughters*, was received by its contemporary audience as a judicious and unsurprising addition to the literature of female advice and instruction. Soon after it appeared, several chapters were reprinted in three consecutive issues of *The Lady's Magazine*, and the following year a pirated edition appeared in a compendium with *Instructions to a Governess* by the influential seventeenth-century French educationist François Fénelon, and the anonymous *Address to Mothers*.[5] This recycling is typical. Successful examples of advice writing enjoyed repeated reissues across many years, in reprints both legitimate and illegitimate, as individual texts and within compendia, as a whole and in part. The quotation above from Wilkes's *Letter*, for example, comes from a passage which is lifted unacknowledged from a much earlier text, Richard Allestree's *The Ladies Calling* (1673); and both of the texts singled out for attention by Wollstonecraft in *Rights of Woman*, Gregory's *Father's Legacy* and Fordyce's *Sermons*, went through multiple editions and were excerpted in numerous anthologies of "improving" reading.

Given the buoyancy of this market with its promise of a reasonable financial return, it's hardly surprising that Wollstonecraft should choose advice literature for her first foray into print and, she hoped, financial independence. *Thoughts* was followed in 1788 by *Original Stories from Real Life ... Calculated to Regulate the Affections and Form the Mind to Truth and Goodness*, and in 1789 by *The Female Reader ... for the Improvement of Young Women*. Modern critical opinion differs on the extent to which these early publications simply reiterate conduct book orthodoxies or anticipate the later, radical Wollstonecraft. For Kathryn Sutherland, for example, *Thoughts* is "a conventional conduct book, in which the arguments and topics of a hundred-year tradition of such manuals by men and women weigh heavy," whereas for Gary Kelly it exemplifies the way in which female-authored texts within that tradition provide "the context for Revolutionary feminism."[6] An accurate characterization, perhaps predictably, lies somewhere in between and depends on a more nuanced engagement with the spectrum of advice writing and with the continuities between "conduct books," the project of female education, and proto-feminist tracts than is suggested by the homogenizing label "conduct literature."

The full title of *Thoughts on the Education of Daughters: with Reflections on Female Conduct, in The More Important Duties of Life* brings out something of those continuities – or contradictions – in its juxtaposition of education, conduct, and duty. To modern eyes, the emphasis on duty looks unacceptably restrictive; for a contemporary audience, education as preparation for a woman's "important Duties" as wife and mother was entirely expected. It's a position explicitly endorsed by Wollstonecraft: "To prepare a woman to fulfil the important duties of a wife and mother, are certainly the objects that should be in view during the early period of life."[7] Comments of this kind no doubt contributed to the approval *Thoughts* received in *The English Review*: "These thoughts are employed on various important situations and incidents in the ordinary life of females, and are, in general, dictated with great judgment."[8]

Other instances where that "hundred-year tradition" of female advice literature might be seen to "weigh heavy," as Sutherland puts it, include Wollstonecraft's advocacy of a particularly modest and asexual version of adult womanhood in her chapter on "Matrimony": "There are a thousand nameless decencies which good sense gives rise to ... It has ever occurred to me that it was sufficient for a woman to receive caresses, and not bestow them."[9] The phrasing echoes Milton's description of Eve's domestic modesty in *Paradise Lost*, a portrait beloved of advice writers; the sentiment recalls Gregory's notorious advice to his daughters "never to discover to [a man] the full extent of your love, no not although you marry him."[10] But within the advice tradition, this emotional reticence is part of a complex coping strategy, a strategic response to women's frequently disappointing experience of marriage – as recognized, for example, in another popular publication, Sarah Pennington's *An Unfortunate Mother's Advice to her Absent Daughters* (1761), which painfully describes the "chearful Compliance" needed to tolerate unacceptable male behaviors.[11]

It is at points like this that the contradictions and even radical potential within conduct literature become most apparent. Marriage is the goal; the alternative – to be "fashionably educated, and left without a fortune," as one of Wollstonecraft's chapter titles puts it – is deeply unattractive; but marriage is itself all too often a disappointment. For the woman, as Wollstonecraft recognizes, her "sphere of action is not large." The response in *Thoughts* is to emphasize the importance of a rational, as opposed to a merely "genteel," education as a means to intellectual resilience: "those who reflect can tell, of what importance it is for the mind to have some resource in itself." And one effect, it is implied, might be a more successful marriage, since "[a] woman may fit herself to be the companion and friend of a man of sense, and yet know how to take care of his family."[12] What Wollstonecraft's "conduct book" is still fending off here is the potential for female education to become a justifiable end in itself.

Wollstonecraft's overriding concern in *Thoughts*, to help women become "independent of the senses," draws on the more purely educational end of the advice tradition, specifically that of radical Dissent to which she had been introduced through her association with the Newington Green group of Unitarian Dissenters.[13] Her title evokes both John Locke's influential *Some Thoughts Concerning Education* (1693) and *Thoughts on Education* (1747) by the Dissenter James Burgh. Burgh recognized the "great consequence to the youth of both sexes, that they be early led into a just and rational way of thinking of things," but his implicit subject is dominantly male.[14] Wollstonecraft takes his principles of moral and spiritual discipline and tests them against the realities of women's lives. Contemporary educational theory is addressed in detail in the following chapter in this volume. Suffice it here to stress the concern, particularly among female educationists, to present mental improvement as a means of escape from fashionable uselessness, and the importance of understanding its continuities with a broader spectrum of instructional writing for women – as demonstrated very clearly in the eclectic, potentially disruptive, but ultimately still conformist advice offered in *Thoughts*.

That eclecticism is again evident in Wollstonecraft's instructional anthology *The Female Reader* (1789). But also evident is her increasing preoccupation with definitions of sexual difference and gendered behavior. *The Female*

Reader begins with quotations from John Gregory, this time his Enlightenment text, *A Comparative View of the State and Faculties of Mankind* (1765), and from the influential female educationist Hester Chapone's *Letters on the Improvement of the Mind* (1773). The brief extract from Gregory implies an endorsement of difference: "As the two sexes have very different parts to act in life nature has marked their characters very differently, in a way that best qualifies them to fulfil their respective duties in society." The passage from Chapone offers an immediate critique of some of its unintended social consequences, contrasting men's pride in their "power ... wealth, dignity, learning, or abilities" with women's desire simply that men "be in love with their persons, careless how despicable their minds appear."[15] Intended to "imprint some useful lessons on the mind, and cultivate the taste at the same time," Wollstonecraft's anthology includes extracts from several examples of what we would categorize as "conduct literature," including not just Gregory's *Father's Legacy*, but George Savile, Marquis of Halifax's much-reprinted *Advice to a Daughter* (1688), and Sarah Pennington's *Unfortunate Mother's Advice* alongside passages from, among others, the Bible, periodical writings, Shakespeare, and the poetry of William Cowper and the leading Dissenter Anna Laetitia Aikin (later Barbauld). As her Preface is keen to point out, Wollstonecraft was concerned to organize the texts in *The Female Reader* into thematic groups, "carefully disposed in a series that tends to make them illustrate each other."[16] The overall effect is to invite the (female) reader to reflect on the relationship between rational improvement and moral responsibility – and on what it means to be a human, and not simply a gendered, subject.

These questions are the legacy of the diverse intellectual influences, including that of "conduct" writers, on Wollstonecraft's intellectual development, and they shape *A Vindication of the Rights of Woman*. "Education," "female conduct" and "the more important duties of life" are still Wollstonecraft's subject but the language has shifted significantly, reflecting her membership of the radical circle around the publisher Joseph Johnson, her engagement with French Revolutionary ideas, and the confidence derived from her attack on Edmund Burke's "libertine imagination" in her *Vindication of the Rights of Men* (1790).[17] Wollstonecraft's second *Vindication* is to be "a treatise ... on female rights and manners" rather than desultory *Thoughts*. And the new clarity with which she sees women as first and foremost human rather than gendered beings crystallizes in her eloquent, but carefully nuanced critique of those male writers on female education who, "considering females rather as women than human creatures, have been more anxious to make them alluring mistresses than affectionate wives and rational mothers."[18]

The writers singled out as having thus "rendered women objects of pity" are Milton, Rousseau, Gregory, and James Fordyce. Of the two conduct book writers, Gregory and Fordyce, the former is aligned with Milton and Rousseau as Wollstonecraft confronts three of her key influencers. Fordyce, on the other hand, appears nowhere in Wollstonecraft's own advice writings and is used to exemplify the most extreme version of a discourse of sexual difference which she has come to see as pervasive in advice writing for women. Gregory is treated with "affectionate respect" in *Rights of Woman*; but now Wollstonecraft identifies a protective timidity governing his address to his daughters, which means he is ultimately judged to "support opinions which ... have had the most baneful effect on the morals and manners of the female world." The father's fear that his daughters might be hurt leads him, she suggests, to encourage in them a "system of dissimulation," a "desire of being always women" which is "the very consciousness that degrades the sex" and compromises the Enlightenment principles she otherwise admired in him. But her vitriol is reserved for what she calls the "sentimental rant" of Fordyce's *Sermons to Young Women*. Wollstonecraft makes her point by quoting one of its most objectionable passages, addressed to men in the voice of "Nature": "[Women] are timid, and want to be defended. They are frail; O do not take advantage of their weakness. Let their fears and blushes endear them." Wollstonecraft is clear that Fordyce's predatory, sexualized language is very different from the sympathetic esteem with which Gregory addresses his daughters, writing as he does from within a wider discourse of advice and education which shows the "respect for the understanding" which Fordyce so spectacularly lacks.[19] But both texts, she suggests, invite women to focus primarily on their gendered identity and relationship to men, rather than on their shared humanity.

In her post-Revolutionary advice treatise, Wollstonecraft exposes the contradictions inherent in earlier advice texts in order to articulate something much more explicitly radical: "I do not wish [women] to have power over men; but over themselves."[20] Her analysis of Gregory and Fordyce anticipates in many ways the twentieth- and twenty-first-century feminist critique of "conduct literature." But her careful distinctions between them are also a warning against too readily homogenizing forms of advice writing, and a reminder that responsible reading, of any kind of text, is a form of defense against its potential effects, as well as a means to appreciate its sometimes unexpected value.

Notes

1 Mary Wollstonecraft, *A Vindication of the Rights of Woman*, in *The Works of Mary Wollstonecraft*, edited by Janet Todd and Marilyn Butler (London: W. Pickering, 1989), 5: 147.
2 *OED*. "Conduct book": first citation 1856(?).
3 Wetenhall Wilkes, *A Letter of Genteel and Moral Advice to a Young Lady* (Dublin: printed for the author, 1740), 77; Dr. [John] Gregory, *A Father's Legacy to his Daughters* (London: W. Strahan, T. Cadell; Edinburgh: J. Balfour, W. Creech, 1774), 43.
4 Nancy Armstrong, *Desire and Domestic Fiction: A Political History of the Novel* (New York: Oxford University Press, 1987), 66.
5 *The Lady's Magazine*, 18 (1787), 227–30, 287, 369–70.
6 Kathryn Sutherland, "Writings on Education and Conduct: Arguments for Female Improvement," in Vivien Jones, ed., *Women and Literature in Britain 1700–1800* (Cambridge: Cambridge University Press, 2000), 41; Gary Kelly, *Revolutionary Feminism: The Mind and Career of Mary Wollstonecraft* (Basingstoke: Macmillan, 1992), 29.
7 Mary Wollstonecraft, *Thoughts on the Education of Daughters* [1788] in *Works*, 4: 25; Mrs. *Wollstonecraft's Thoughts on the Education of Daughters. With Reflections on Female Conduct, in the More Important Duties of Life. To Which Is Added Fenelon* [sic] *Archbishop of Cambray's Instructions to a Governess, and an Address to Mothers* (Dublin: W. Sleator, 1788).
8 Quoted in *Mrs. Wollstonecraft's Thoughts*, sig. [4]r.
9 Wollstonecraft, *Thoughts*, 32.
10 John Milton, *Paradise Lost*, Book 8, line 601; Gregory, *Father's Legacy*, 39.
11 Lady Sarah Pennington, *An Unfortunate Mother's Advice to Her Absent Daughters; in a Letter to Miss Pennington* (London: S. Chandler; York, C. Etherington, 1761), 59.
12 Wollstonecraft, *Thoughts*, 32, 26, 20, 21.
13 Ibid., 12.
14 [James Burgh], *Thoughts on Education* (London: G. Freer, M. Cooper, 1747), 52–53.
15 Mary Wollstonecraft, *The Female Reader: or Miscellaneous Pieces, in Prose and Verse* (1789), in *Works*, 4: 67.
16 Ibid., 55.
17 Mary Wollstonecraft, *A Vindication of the Rights of Men*, in *Works*, 5: 46.
18 Wollstonecraft, *Rights of Woman*, 73.
19 Ibid., 166, 168, 169, 163, 166.
20 Ibid., 131.

CHAPTER 29

Theories of Education

Frances Ferguson

Mary Wollstonecraft came to write about education in much the same way that John Locke and Immanuel Kant did: she wrote after having taught. Running a school with her sisters Everina and Eliza for a time and working as a governess to the daughters of the Kingsborough family in Ireland prompted her to set down her ideas about the work that a teacher should perform and the difficulties that the teacher might face.[1] While Locke and Kant recommended that parents choose their children's tutors carefully and pay them well, Wollstonecraft's experiences led her to outline her pedagogical ideas in *Thoughts on the Education of Daughters* (1787) and to produce instructive fictions in *Original Stories from Real Life* (1788).[2] She took a broad view of education, and imagined that it did not merely concern the teaching of particular subjects such as spelling or math. In her extensive survey, education offered an opportunity to develop moral and political skills for daily living, even in the confines of a household. As Wollstonecraft observed in *A Vindication of the Rights of Woman*, education was essential if women were to be able to be good mothers and wives, and not to tyrannize children and servants out of a sense that they were themselves tyrannized.[3]

Wollstonecraft's thinking was by no means shop-worn, but the tendency of her thinking resonated with prominent educational writings of her time, and she championed many of the same positions that others advocated. Educational writing expanded at a rapid rate during the eighteenth century, as writers addressed themselves to a wide variety and great number of teachers and pupils. John Locke had, in *Some Thoughts Concerning Education* (1693), published the advice he had privately given to his friend Edward Clarke on the education of his son.[4] Locke's object and audience, that is, differed from earlier treatises that concerned the education of a prince. He aimed to advise a father on the education of a child whose future was not so readily identifiable, and who needed to learn how to interact with people without being imperious. This broadening of the audience of fathers and sons, however, was as nothing by comparison with the massive change that Rousseau produced in *Emile* (1762), an educational novel and treatise which he addressed to the mothers of France and sketched as a massive life-lesson plan that would conduct boys to manhood and girls to womanhood.[5]

For Rousseau, education began in infancy. Though he advised against swaddling, which he took to confine the internal organs,[6] he recommended breast-feeding, which would provide the youngest baby with both good health and the sense that it could move securely in the world.[7] He also suggested that infants might have and express moral feelings, and, in particular, indignation at felt injustice.[8] Locke and Rousseau suggested that moral understanding arose early. Yet they were at pains to avoid condemning children for unintended crimes, and argued that moral assessments should be made from a child's standpoint, with a clear sense of what a child might be thinking in a situation that looked quite different to an adult. Locke treated the act of stealing apples from an orchard as a symptom of high spirits; Rousseau observed that no very young child has an idea of property (and therefore can't be understood as stealing).[9] Rather than scanning a child's behavior for evidence of innate depravity, in the manner of sterner educators, they imagined that education was a matter of coordinating children's general human aptitudes with the ideas that would enable them to activate their moral impulses.

While Locke and Rousseau emphasized the importance of a child's being educated for self-government, they continually counseled against a child's becoming a petty tyrant and developing into a greater tyrant with age. Rousseau, like Locke, advised against allowing a child to become domineering – to servants or anyone else. Locke made the point largely by highlighting the force of parental example: a father should not behave tyrannically toward his son lest the son detest him and long for the father's death. Locke thus brought out an analogy between a monarch and a domestic ruler, and suggested that the punishment for fatherly tyrants was the loss of their children's love. Rousseau, however, followed the example of François Fénelon, whose instructive novel *Télémaque* (1699) featured conversations between the young Telemachus and the intermittently appearing figure of Mentor – in actuality the goddess Minerva.[10] Mentor/Minerva, like the tutor in *Emile* after him/her, is virtually omnipresent, though he/she exercises authority by encouraging Telemachus to see his own anger and imperial ambitions as mistakes rather than by dictating specific moral and political behaviors. Instruction takes place in conversation.

Fénelon's idealized figure of the tutor – a god willing to cast off divine prerogatives but standing ready to perform acts of rescue whenever they might be necessary – strongly informed Rousseau's presentation of Emile's tutor, a personage who seemed more like a constantly available instruction manual than a person, always ready to be relied on but never obtruding his views. The imaginary conversation between a wise adult and her young charge, on Fénelon's and Rousseau's model, became a standard format for instructive writing.

Thus, when Wollstonecraft in 1791 deployed the swollen title *Original Stories from Real Life; with Conversations Calculated to Regulate the Affections, and Form the Mind to Truth and Goodness*, she was participating in an educational mode that Rousseau and other English followers of Rousseau had made familiar. For Wollstonecraft, as for Anna Laetitia Barbauld and her brother John Aikin, along with Thomas Day and Maria Edgeworth, fictitious episodes and imaginary conversations made it possible to affirm that "knowledge should be gradually imparted, and flow more from example [that directly addresses the senses] than teaching."[11]

Wollstonecraft's commitment to an education that unfolded in stages was one she was not so much inventing as endorsing. Locke had, after all, advocated a similarly gradual and experience-based education, and Rousseau had made a virtual fetish of the notion that no idea should be introduced before a child was capable of grasping it. Anna Laetitia Barbauld featured the idea of serial development when she followed her recurrent title *Lessons for Children* with age-specific audience instructions: ... *For Children of Two to Three Years Old* (1778); ... *For Children of Three Years Old* (1778); and ... *For Children from Three to Four Years Old* (1779).[12] Moreover, Barbauld, like Wollstonecraft, featured discussions that did not center on the alphabet or rules of grammar but on the elements of daily life – the cat in the room with the mother and child, the respective aptitudes of a cat and a child, with a cat catching mice and a child reading.

The broad outlines of educational thinking that ran from Locke through Rousseau to British writers – and particularly to British Dissenters – were highly consistent: the instruction of children needed to be as transparent as possible. It needed to proceed in language that children could understand, without resorting to the baby talk that made a parent or teacher into a kind of parody of the child. It needed to base itself on experiences that the parent or teacher might readily share with the child, so that it began for very small children in one room in a family home, as Barbauld's *Lessons* did. Rousseau's *Emile* and Barbauld's *Lessons* aimed to encourage a child to deduce concepts from a conversation with an adult. Emile would learn about property by seeing a practical demonstration of what happened when no one recognized any land as property and ruined an owner's gardening by tilling and planting without regard for anyone's earlier labors. When Emile sees his own work overturned by Robert the gardener, he comes to realize that he had earlier destroyed the work of Robert's labors. Property is a concept that depends, in this account, on work rather than possession and on the right to preserve the difference one's work makes.[13]

The emphasis on actual experience, and on concepts derived from conversations about it, however, faced one real difficulty in Rousseau – namely, that it depended on a child's being exposed only to experiences and ideas that were themselves untainted. Rousseau's tutor was a nervous governor, one who needed to restrict Emile's acquaintance with other persons until Emile commanded a full stock of virtuous conceptions. Rousseau's version of early education was an education in which the pupil and the tutor were almost entirely isolated from society.

Barbauld explicitly criticized this aspect of Rousseau's thinking, imagining that his sequestering the pupil with the tutor alone contradicted Rousseau's very insistence on arriving at ideas and actions through experience. Rousseau's plan to shield Emile from society looked to her like an example of a theoretical position on the nature of society obtruding itself into Rousseau's pedagogical fiction and interfering with his practical suggestions. In reaction against this aspect of Rousseau's writing, Barbauld and other British educators began to focus, as Wollstonecraft did, on encouraging a child to sift experiences rather than on editing potential experiences in advance. Education from experience, they thought, must deal with the full range of experiences that a child encountered. While children might be innately sinless, the world was not. It was inevitable that they would continually encounter imperfect examples. Children were therefore encouraged to begin judging other people's actions and their own at an early age.

In her "What Is Education?" Barbauld so strongly emphasized the idea that education should be a matter of practical and immediate instruction that she advised a friend who had consulted her about his son's education to avoid committing himself to any one pedagogical plan.[14] Instead, she said, he as a parent should recognize that he is a walking, talking example to his child. She emphasized the point not by urging her friend to live up to his precepts but by urging him to reduce his doctrinal armory. Her striking example concerned lying. Parents regularly enjoin children never to tell lies, she observed, but they also permit themselves all manner of social lies, and do such things as sending word that they are not home when an unwelcome caller arrives at their door. Her point was not so much the predictable one that parents should never lie, any more than children should. Instead, she made a suppler observation: prescriptions are themselves made to be evaluated in the face of actual circumstances. She ending by not only urging tolerance for social lies but also asking parents to consider the occasions on which they are encouraging their children to lie and thus committing small acts of domestic tyranny in suborning children's testimony.

The understanding that education goes on unremittingly in the experience of daily life was central to Barbauld's thinking: "The moment [the child] was able to form an idea his education was already begun; the education of circumstances—insensible education."[15] And it was this sense that a child learns in every moment that led her and other Dissenting writers to imagine that conversation was a particularly effective means of teaching. Stories that look heavily didactic to twenty-first century readers were just as didactic as we take them to be, but they were clearly designed to feel lightly instructive to their contemporaries. They carried a number of significant assumptions. Wollstonecraft's Mrs. Mason, of *Original Stories from Real Life*, or various adult figures in stories from Aikin and Barbauld's *Evenings at Home*, prized observation, and observation that needed to be valued and cultivated because it captured knowledge almost incidentally.[16] Taking a walk was an exercise in paying attention to the world that one would encounter, and children needed to be encouraged to notice as much of their surroundings as possible. Moreover, the conversations between an adult guardian and her young charges implicitly claimed that the world was theirs to understand, that their innate intelligence so thoroughly equipped them to grasp the nature of what they saw that they could usually be counted on to provide answers instead of asking for them. It was in such a context that Wollstonecraft felt obliged to say that Mrs. Mason "allowed [Mary and Caroline] to ask questions on all occasions, a method she would not have adopted, had she educated them from the first."[17]

The basic position, worked out more or less explicitly among the line of educators I've been identifying, is that persons are so fully a part of the natural creation that they can know truth before the age of reason and are well equipped to observe and judge of the world. Wollstonecraft demonstrated the power of the first aspect of this general educational view when she insisted in *Thoughts on the Education of Daughters* (1787) that it was "in [her] opinion, a well-proved fact, that principles of truth are innate" (even if the particular content that fleshes out those principles can only be gained by experience).[18] The second aspect of it – what we might think of as the political theory that generates a series of domestic policy recommendations – demonstrated how thoroughly Wollstonecraft likened the political economy of families to that of just governments: "She who submits, without conviction, to a parent or husband, will as unreasonably tyrannize over her servants; for slavish fear and tyranny go together."[19]

Conversation between an adult and a child or children offered distinct advantages to educators such as Barbauld, Aikin, and Wollstonecraft. Conversation made education take place almost insensibly, because conversation about the things and persons one might encounter on a walk make education a constant exercise in improvisation. And while we might imagine that the conviviality of social conversation might have prompted teachers and students simply to express approval of one another, these educational dialogues did not restrict themselves to mutual encouragement alone. Many of the stories based on real life depicted the interlocutors observing the mistakes that they and others made. Mrs. Mason's young charges, for instance, noticed a boy who had taken a bird's nest, registered the damage he had done, and tried to figure out how to repair it. Conversation steered pupils to amend their own behaviors. Wollstonecraft joined others in portraying the pupils of *Original Stories* as unexceptional and only of "tolerable capacities" (as if to underscore that any child would be able to benefit from the kind of education she sketched).[20] She also made it clear that Mrs. Mason recognized that "Mary had a turn for ridicule, and Caroline was vain of her person."[21] Encountering persons who were disabled or poor and talking about their own reactions made it possible for young women like Mary and Caroline to be corrected, and to correct themselves. As Wollstonecraft put it in *Thoughts*, "Reflections on miscarriages of conduct, and mistakes in opinion, sink deep into the mind; especially if those miscarriages and mistakes have been a cause of pain— when we smart for our folly we remember it."[22] One's commitment to oneself, in other words, did not extend to a narcissistic insistence that everything one did was right simply because one had done it. Rather, benevolence was a "most essential [service]" to "ourselves": "While we are looking into another's mind, and forming their temper, we are insensibly correcting our own."[23]

Conversation offered the chance to understand someone else's understanding, but it also occasioned self-understanding and a recognition of one's place in the world. Children came to see that they had the physical power to injure small animals such as frogs and birds, and the ability to wound other people by calling attention to their infirmities or mocking their clothes or social bearing. When Jane Austen had her character Emma make a witty remark at Miss Bates' expense, she highlighted how little conversation and conversational self-correction Emma had experienced. No young person educated in the style of Aikin, Barbauld, Day, Edgeworth, or Wollstonecraft could have attained Emma's relatively advanced age without having realized her mistake.

These writers understood conversation as a means of accommodating and acknowledging a number of persons in all their variety, and their thinking also translated itself into a distinctive understanding of scientific work. The Dissenting Academies in Britain taught subjects such as chemistry well before Oxford and Cambridge. The kind of thinking that led Joseph Priestley to his experiments with gases might have appeared remote from the world of Anna Laetitia Barbauld's *Hymns in Prose for Children* (1781), one of the most influential texts in Britain and America through the nineteenth century.[24] Yet both shared an understanding of humans as creatures who needed to attend to other parts of the created world and establish a conversation with it. Scientific experimentation was, in that sense, a natural extension of the metrical prose in which Barbauld depicted children greeting and conversing with sun, moon, stars – and the deity.

Wollstonecraft's accounts of the natural world tended toward the transcendental rather than the scientific, but she practiced another variant of Dissenting conversation when she published *The Female Reader*, a collection of literary and political excerpts.[25] Arranged along lines similar to those of William Enfield's best-selling *The Speaker* (1774) and of *The Female Speaker* that Barbauld would publish in 1811, Wollstonecraft's *Female Reader* offered young women the opportunity to enter into conversation even when they felt they had nothing to say.[26] The selections were chosen not merely to be instructive. Rather, anyone reading a particular passage – whether it be a discussion of appearance and cleanliness from publications such as *The Spectator*, a passage from Barbauld's *Hymns in Prose*, or William Wilberforce's Parliamentary speech advocating the abolition of the slave trade – took her place in a chain of endorsement. She was not merely accepting the editor's judgment that a selection was worthy to be included in the volume. She was endorsing it anew in reading it aloud to an audience that might consist of only one other person but might include the assembled students and staff of a Dissenting Academy. It was literature conceived as an installment on conversation, an anthology that implicitly said, "Read and discuss."

Notes

1 Barbara Taylor, *Mary Wollstonecraft and the Feminist Imagination* (Cambridge: Cambridge University Press, 2003), 40–43.
2 Mary Wollstonecraft, *Thoughts on the Education of Daughters: with Reflections on Female Conduct, in the More Important Duties of Life* (London: J. Johnson, 1787).*Eighteenth Century Collection Online.* Gale Document Number CW117758433. *Original Stories, from Real Life; with Conversations Calculated to Regulate the Affections, and Form the Mind to Truth and Goodness* (London: J. Johnson, 1788). *Eighteenth Century Collection Online.* Gale Document Number CW110216892.
3 Wollstonecraft, *A Vindication of the Rights of Woman: with Strictures on Political and Moral Subjects* (London: J. Johnson, 1792), 10. *Eighteenth Century Collection Online.* Gale Document Number CW104687182.
4 John Locke, "Epistle Dedicatory," in *Some Thoughts concerning Education*, 5th edn. (London: A. & J. Churchill, 1705). *Eighteenth Century Collections Online.* Gale Document Number CW3305399622.
5 Jean-Jacques Rousseau, *Emilius and Sophia: or, a New System of Education.* Translated from the French of J. J. Rousseau, Citizen of Geneva. By the translator of *Eloisa* (London: R. Griffiths, T. Becket & P. A. de Hondt, 1762). *Eighteenth Century Collection Online.* Vol. I: Gale Document Number CW3305401367; Vol. II: Gale Document Number CW3305401696.
6 Ibid., I: 17.
7 Ibid., 22.
8 Ibid., 4.
9 Ibid., 148.
10 François Fénelon, *The Adventures of Telemachus, the Son of Ulysses*, 3rd edn., corrected (London: A. & J. Churchill, 1701).*Eighteenth Century Collections Online.* Gale Document Number CW3312302390.
11 Wollstonecraft, *Original Stories*, vii.
12 Although copies of the first printings of Barbauld's *Lessons* have not survived, Mitzi Myers has reconstructed the initial publication dates from Barbauld's letters and early reviews. See Mitzi Myers, "Of Mice and Mothers: Mrs. Barbauld's 'New Walk' and Gendered Codes in Literature," in *Feminine Principles and Women's Experience in American Composition and Rhetoric* (Pittsburgh: University of Pittsburgh Press, 1995), 282. Anna Laetitia Barbauld, *Lessons for Children, from Two to Three Years Old* (London: J. Johnson, 1787) *Eighteenth Century Collections Online*, Gale Document Number CW3320057293; *Lessons for Children, of Three Years Old.* Part I (London: J. Johnson, 1788) *Eighteenth Century Collections Online*, Gale Document Number CW3320057342; *Lessons for Children, of Three Years Old.* Part II (London: J. Johnson, 1788) *Eighteenth Century Collections Online*, Gale Document Number CW3320057425; *Lessons for Children from Three to Four Years Old* (London: J. Johnson, 1788) *Eighteenth Century Collections Online*, Gale Document Number CW3320130790.

13 Rousseau, *Emilius*, I: 148.

14 Ann Laetitia Barbauld, *Selected Poetry and Prose*, edited by William McCarthy and Elizabeth Kraft (Peterborough: Broadview Press, 2002), 321–32.

15 Ibid., 323.

16 John Aikin and Anna Laetitia Barbauld, *Evenings at Home; or, The Juvenile Budget Opened, Consisting of a Variety of Miscellaneous Pieces, for the Instruction and Amusement of Young Persons* (London: J. Johnson, 1792–96). *Eighteenth Century Collections Online*. Gale Document Numbers CW3304230069; CW3304230226; CW3304230383; CW3304230550.

17 Wollstonecraft, *Original Stories*, xii.

18 Wollstonecraft, *Thoughts on the Education of Daughters*, 13.

19 Ibid., 63.

20 *Original Stories*, xii.

21 Ibid.

22 *Thoughts on the Education of Daughters*, 64.

23 Ibid., 66.

24 Barbauld, *Hymns in Prose for Children. By the Author of Lessons for Children* (London: J. Johnson, 1781).*Eighteenth Century Collections Online*. Gale Document Number CW3320716605.

25 Moira Ferguson, "The Discovery of Mary Wollstonecraft's *The Female Reader*," *Signs: Journal of Women in Culture and Society*, 3:4 (1978), 945–57. Wollstonecraft [under the pseudonym Mr. Cresswick, Teacher of Elocution], *The Female Reader; or, Miscellaneous Pieces in Prose and Verse; Selected from the Best Writers, and Disposed under Proper Heads; for the Improvement of Young Women* in *Works*, edited by Janet Todd and Marilyn Butler (London: W. Pickering, 1989), 53–350.

26 William Enfield, *The Speaker: or, Miscellaneous Pieces, Selected from the Best English Writers, and Disposed under Proper Heads, with a View to Facilitate the Improvement of Youth in Reading and Speaking* (London: J. Johnson, 1774); Anna Laetitia Barbauld, *The Female Speaker: or Miscellaneous Pieces in Prose and Verse, Selected from the Best Writers and Adapted to the Use of Young Women* (London: 1811).

Literature

CHAPTER 30

Sentimentalism and Sensibility

Alex Wetmore

In a book review from December 1789 of the novel *Heerfort and Clara*, Mary Wollstonecraft dismisses the work as yet another example of the "sentimental, pumped up nonsense" that circulates in the current literary marketplace.[1] The comment is not an isolated jab, but the product of considerable relevant experience. Before authoring her now-famous *Vindication of the Rights of Woman*, Wollstonecraft wrote book reviews for Joseph Johnson's progressive journal the *Analytical Review*. And, as Mitzi Myers points out, "although Wollstonecraft reviewed books about children, education, women, travel, and even boxing, fiction – sentimental fiction in particular – seems to have been her niche."[2]

By the late 1780s, the British reading public's taste for sentimental fiction was well established. From the 1740s on, this popular sub-genre of the (still relatively new) novel offered audiences a steady supply of largely loose-knit episodic narratives featuring benevolent protagonists indulging in the exquisite tear-soaked pleasures of "sensibility" – a newly fashionable term, cognate with "sentimentalism," which originally referred to "the operation of the nervous system" but gradually took on "spiritual and moral" significance as a designation for heightened emotional responsiveness linked to refined taste and virtue.[3] Some of the most popular sentimental novels from this period include Samuel Richardson's blockbuster *Pamela; or, Virtue Rewarded* (1740), Sarah Fielding's *The Adventures of David Simple* (1744), Laurence Sterne's *A Sentimental Journey through France and Italy* (1768), and Henry Mackenzie's *The Man of Feeling* (1771). Following a dramatic fall from critical and popular favor in the 1790s (more on that to come), critics tended for many decades to treat the genre of sentimental fiction – with its overwrought emotionality, predictable plots, stock character archetypes and earnest morality – as a slightly embarrassing "oddity or problem," as John Mullan notes. The fad for sentimental novels was "less to be explained" by literary historians "than to be explained away."[4]

Despite being the product of, in Deidre Lynch's phrasing, "an emotional regime that is quite alien to us now,"[5] sentimental fiction has been recuperated by more recent critics for its socio-historical significance as part of a broader "culture of sensibility," propelled by a conflux of ideological, economic, medical, religious and literary developments, leading to a widespread break with neoclassical rationalism in the mid-1700s. Scholars including John Mullan, John Dwyer, Adela Pinch, Daniel M. Gross, Mark Phillips, and many others have tied the mid-century sentimental turn in Britain to influential thinkers of the Scottish Enlightenment like Francis Hutcheson, David Hume, and Adam Smith, whose sympathy-centered theories of human nature were informed by the new paradigm of "nerve theory" in medical science, and presented models of subjectivity that were inherently sociable, primarily propelled by instinctive, intersubjective exchanges of feeling.

A new appreciation for the formal complexities of sentimental fiction has also manifested itself in critical reassessments of the period, as scholars have focused greater attention on the remarkable narrative self-awareness of novels of sensibility, along with other structural eccentricities which mark them as products of "an era of radical literary experiment."[6] In addition, recent criticism has sought out a fuller account of the genre's significant role in the history of women's writing. Though the genre was capable of reinforcing troublingly essentialist assumptions about women as innately irrational and emotional, the mid-century fashion for sensibility nevertheless presented unique opportunities for women to claim new authority over matters of taste, manners, and morals. G. J. Barker-Benfield has noted that the emergence of a culture of feeling was initially widely embraced by women as a hopeful development. Whereas the early eighteenth-century neoclassical discourse of gender tended to express misogynistic fears that women's increased public presence would result in the spread of moral corruption and decadent effeminacy, philosophical and literary texts in the sentimental tradition often support women's increased presence and voice in the public sphere as signs of the arrival of a more refined and polite age.[7] In this atmosphere, women wrote sentimental fiction, they were often its protagonists, and generally its presumed readers. As Barbara Benedict notes in *Framing Feeling*, "at this period, women won a place in the world of letters; their concerns were the concerns of writers, and they were writers themselves, forging a literary culture in opposition to the previous neoclassical literary tradition."[8]

* * *

As fiction reviewer for the *Analytical Review* in the late 1780s, Wollstonecraft was centrally positioned to respond to this unprecedented and growing body of literature created significantly by and for women. Far from supportive, though, the typical response in her reviews of sentimental fiction is a mixture of exasperation and disdain. Wollstonecraft bemoans "sweetly sentimental" novels as "misshapen monsters, daily brought forth to poison the minds of our young females."[9] In one review, an annoyed Wollstonecraft even offers a mock recipe for a female novel, whose ingredients include "sad tales of woe rehearsed in an affected, half-prose, half-poetical style" and "exquisite double-refined sensibility."[10]

Such dismissive comments (and *many* more like them from her fiction reviews) anticipate – and are comfortably consistent with – Wollstonecraft's more well-known condemnations of sensibility from her two major political treatises. In *A Vindication of the Rights of Men* (1790), Wollstonecraft calls "sensibility" the "*manie* of the day"[11] and criticizes Edmund Burke's deployment of "sentimental jargon"[12] in his *Reflections on the Revolution in France* (1790) to stoke misguided fears of a golden age of chivalry under attack. In her follow-up, *A Vindication of the Rights of Woman* (1792), the contemporary "mania" for sensibility is once again given particular attention. Claudia Johnson describes *Rights of Woman* as a "militantly antisentimental work."[13] Alongside arguments in favor of women's intellectual equality, educational reform, and the virtues of cultivating reason, Wollstonecraft consistently rails against "false descriptions of sensibility"[14] which have become "entangled" in women's "motives of action," leading them to become "slaves to their bodies."[15]

* * *

Given these statements, it is no surprise Mary Wollstonecraft has earned a reputation as one of sentimentalism's most fervent critics. However, by the 1790s, she was also not alone. Increasingly, as the century wore on, faith in the culture of sensibility's reformative potential transformed into a growing sense of its limitations. The initial promise of "revolution," "freedom," and "subversion"[16] inhered in the fact that sensibility approached selves as products of embodied sense experience, and, as a result, suggested that the characteristic features of gender, class, and ethnicity were a result of environmental conditioning rather than innate essential nature. However, even as the discourse of sentimentalism posed a potential threat to traditional social hierarchies, it also retained the potential to reconstruct the female body as naturally more receptive to nervous stimulation. As a result, the promise for radical social reform stood alongside a danger that the culture of feeling could also reaffirm traditional and stereotypical associations between women, irrationality, hysteria, and passivity.[17]

It is these types of concerns that informed a wave of critiques of sentimentalism in the latter decades of the eighteenth century. Anxieties over the corrupting effects of sentimental novels on young women were widespread, occasionally making their way into novels themselves (e.g. Hamilton's *Memoirs of Modern Philosophers* [1800] and Jane Austen's *Northanger Abbey* [1817]). Tastes were also changing rapidly owing to the polarizing impact of the French Revolution on British culture, which led to widespread suspicion of the ideological motivations behind any expression of heightened emotion. As John Brewer observes, "By the 1790s what had once been a steady murmur of criticism about the widespread cult of sensibility had become a vociferous challenge to the very idea itself."[18] This "crisis over sensibility"[19] could make for strange bedfellows, as Hannah More (a conservative who famously refused even to read *Rights of Woman*) sounds indistinguishable from the progressive Wollstonecraft when she calls the "profusion of little, amusing, sentimental books" among young women "one of the most universal, as well as most pernicious, sources of corruption among us."[20]

Owing to the various attacks on sentimentalism in the turbulent and divisive 1790s, this period is usually considered to mark the beginning of the end of a recognizable and coherent culture of sensibility. By 1796, *The Monthly Magazine* was already referring to the "fashion" for sensibility in the past tense.[21] And while sentimental fiction would still exert a great deal of tacit influence over writing through the decade, sentimentalism's remarkably rapid descent into cultural obscurity and illegibility was complete by the early nineteenth century. This is made clear from an 1826 letter from Lady Louisa Stuart to Walter Scott, where she recounts introducing Mackenzie's once-popular and highly regarded novel *The Man of Feeling* to a group of young women, who laughed at the very same scenes Stuart had found so sincerely affecting in her youth.[22]

* * *

To end here would leave a picture of Mary Wollstonecraft's relationship to sentimentalism that is relatively consistent (and consistently antagonistic), but also woefully incomplete. One reason for this is Wollstonecraft was herself occasionally linked in the 1790s by opponents to a now unfashionable sensibility through her perceived capacity to inspire unnatural political enthusiasm – what Richard Polwhele terms "gallic frenzy" in *The Unsex'd Females* (1798), a blunt satire of women philosophers. Another substantial missing piece, however, is that Wollstonecraft was not merely a critic of contemporary novels, but was also, significantly, a novelist herself. Her literary career is bookended, as it were, by two novels – *Mary: A Fiction* (1788) and the unfinished *The Wrongs of Woman; or, Maria* (1798) – and critics have noted how both these texts waver between, in some sections, attacking the genre of sentimental fiction in a manner consistent with her other works, and, in others, significantly incorporating (and even celebrating) the very same rhetorical and literary conventions of sentimental writing she elsewhere condemns. Despite promising a narrative about a heroine "who has thinking powers," *Mary*'s protagonist is ultimately undone for being a "creature of impulse" and a "slave of compassion" who at one point pens a passionate "rhapsody on sensibility," while *The Wrongs of Woman*'s reliance upon gothic conventions, and highly fraught emotional scenes filled with "rapturous sympathy," emotive bodies, and typographical exuberance place it in undeniably close dialogue with the sentimental genre.[23]

How should we account for instances from Wollstonecraft's two novels (produced at opposite ends of her tragically foreshortened career) where she employs the very same stock tropes and rhetorical devices of sentimental fiction she elsewhere so vehemently resists? Scholars have tried to address this issue in recent years, and their approaches might be broadly categorized into two types: diachronic and synchronic. The diachronic view posits the inconsistencies and tensions in Wollstonecraft's writing as a product of her fluctuating ideas about sensibility and emotion over time. So, for example, Janet Todd in *Mary Wollstonecraft: A Revolutionary Life*[24] and *The Sign of Angellica*[25] traces a relatively linear development that sees *Mary* as still struggling to fully extricate itself from the generic constraints of sentimental fiction, then the two vindications as forceful rationalist-feminist rejections of sentimentalism, and later works like *Letters Written in Sweden* and *Wrongs* as reflective returns to the unresolved problematics of embodied pleasure and desire, compelled by a variety of personal and political changes in intervening years. The synchronic view, by contrast, sees underlying constants across Wollstonecraft's body of work, despite the superficial appearance of conflicts and inconsistency. In this vein Nancy Yousef[26] suggests that Wollstonecraft might appear to waver (sometimes within the same work) because her main contention is not, in fact, with the notion of sensibility itself, but with a particular strain of eighteenth-century moral philosophy – supported by David Hume,[27] among others – that privileges impulse, and therefore severs the realm of sensibility from reason.[28] So long as reason is accorded sufficient importance, Wollstonecraft appears consistently willing to grant sensibility a central and valued role in human nature. Claudia Johnson's excellent book on sentimentalism and the novel in the 1790s, *Equivocal Beings*, also adopts a synchronic view of Wollstonecraft, approaching her writing as united in a common goal of "undomesticating" female subjectivity.[29] *Mary* may integrate conventions of sentimental fiction, but its protagonist often "swerves" (a term Johnson borrows from Eve Kosofsky Sedgwick) into the traditional subject position occupied by the figure of the "man of feeling."[30] Her vindications may attack the unmanly sentimentalism of conservatives like Burke, but they also imply that the progressive alternative of rational republican masculinity might best be occupied, provocatively, by women. *Wrongs* is, for Johnson, the culmination of these consistent efforts as the novel's final image presents Jemima and Maria deciding to raise Maria's daughter, thus expelling "men and manfulness alike from the domestic scene" and "bringing female homosociality into representation."[31] Both diachronic and synchronic approaches to Wollstonecraft's relationship to sensibility have proven fruitful, but in none of these can we find a way back to the invitingly simple image of Mary Wollstonecraft as sentimentalism's unambiguous rationalist-feminist opponent. Instead, a consensus emerges that, the deeper one probes, the more deeply entangled Wollstonecraft's writing becomes with the literature and culture of sensibility, even as sentimentalism's limitations for women remain a constant and prevalent concern.

Notes

1 Mary Wollstonecraft, "Contributions to the *Analytical Review*, 1788–1797," in *The Works of Mary Wollstonecraft*, edited by Janet Todd and Marilyn Butler (Charlottesville: InteLex Corporation, 2004), 7: 190.
2 Mitzi Myers, "Mary Wollstonecraft's Literary Reviews" in Claudia L. Johnson, ed., *The Cambridge Companion to Mary Wollstonecraft* (Cambridge: Cambridge University Press, 2002), 83.
3 G. J. Barker-Benfield, *The Culture of Sensibility: Sex and Society in Eighteenth-Century Britain* (Chicago: University of Chicago Press, 1992), xvii.
4 John Mullan, *Sentiment and Sociability: The Language of Feeling in the Eighteenth Century*, (Oxford: Clarendon Press, 1988), 14.
5 Deidre Lynch, "On Going Steady with Novels," *The Eighteenth Century: Theory and Interpretation*, 50:2–3 (2009), 211.
6 Patricia Spacks, *Novel Beginnings: Experiments in Eighteenth-Century Fiction* (New Haven: Yale University Press, 2006), 15.

7 Harriet Guest, *Small Change: Women, Learning, Patriotism, 1750–1810* (Chicago: University of Chicago Press, 2000), 17.

8 Barbara Benedict, *Framing Feeling: Sentiment and Style in English Prose Fiction, 1745–1800* (New York: AMS Press, 1994), 13.

9 Wollstonecraft, "Contributions," 7: 20.

10 Ibid., 82.

11 "A Vindication of the Rights of Men," in *The Works of Mary Wollstonecraft* (Charlottesville: Intelex Corporation, 2004), 5: 9.

12 M. Wollstonecraft, "Rights of Men," 5: 30.

13 C. Johnson, *Equivocal Beings: Politics, Gender, and Sentimentality in the 1790s*, (Chicago: University of Chicago Press), 23.

14 Wollstonecraft, "A Vindication of the Rights of Woman," in *The Works of Mary Wollstonecraft* (Charlottesville: Intelex Corporation, 2004), 5: 186.

15 Wollstonecraft, "Rights of Woman," 5: 112.

16 Barker-Benfield, *Sensibility*, xvii.

17 Ibid., xviii.

18 John Brewer, *The Pleasures of the Imagination: English Culture in the Eighteenth Century* (London: HarperCollins, 1997), 121.

19 Ibid., 359.

20 Hannah More, *Strictures on the Modern System of Female Education*, 2 vols., (London, 1799), 157.

21 "Question: Ought Sensibility to be Cherished or Repressed?" *The Monthly Magazine*, 2 (October 1796), 706.

22 L. Stuart, "Letter to Walter Scott, 4 September 1826" in W. Partington, ed., *The Private Letter-Books of Sir Walter Scott* (New York: Frederick Stokes, 1930), 273.

23 Mary Wollstonecraft, *Mary: A Fiction*, in *The Works of Mary Wollstonecraft*, edited by Janet Todd and Marilyn Butler (Charlottesville: Intelex Corporation, 2004), 1: 59; Mary Wollstonecraft, *The Wrongs of Woman; or, Maria*, in *The Works of Mary Wollstonecraft* (Charlottesville: Intelex Corporation, 2004), 1: 106.

24 Janet Todd, *Mary Wollstonecraft: A Revolutionary Life* (London: Weidenfeld & Nicolson, 2000).

25 Janet Todd, *The Sign of Angellica: Women, Writing, and Fiction, 1660–1800* (Cambridge: Cambridge University Press, 1989).

26 Nancy Yousef, "'Emotions that Reason Deepens': Second Thoughts about Affect," *Nineteenth Century Gender Studies*, 11:3 (2015), 61–73.

27 David Hume, *An Enquiry Concerning the Principles of Morals* (London, 1751).

28 Yousef, "Emotions," 4.

29 Johnson, *Equivocal*, 69.

30 Ibid., 50.

31 Ibid., 69.

CHAPTER 31

English Jacobin Novels

April London

The first three volumes of Thomas Holcroft's *Hugh Trevor* were published in 1794, the final three in 1797, the year of Mary Wollstonecraft's death. This brief span marks the high point of what conservatives derogatively branded "Jacobin" fiction. While many of the heterodox ideas embraced by Holcroft were in circulation before the 1790s, they had been given fresh impetus by the paper war that followed Edmund Burke's *Reflections on the Revolution in France* (1790). Reformist and radical critiques of what Wollstonecraft labeled Burke's "rhetorical flourishes and infantine sensibility" drew sharp rejoinders from loyalists, initiating a spiraling debate that continued throughout the revolutionary decade.[1] Key to the contention was the shared belief in an untapped audience susceptible to arguments for wide-scale change. Across the political spectrum, writers acted on their commitment to win adherents to their causes by exploiting the novel's appeal to this emergent readership. *Hugh Trevor* testifies to the genre's influence in its assessments of different print kinds and in the transformative energy sparked by the characters' persuasive speech. The formal and thematic repertoire Holcroft deployed in his proselytizing efforts, including the reflexive interest in writing, matches with the practice of other novelists in the Godwin circle. In *Mary: A Fiction* (1788) and *The Wrongs of Woman; or, Maria* (1798), however, Wollstonecraft departs significantly from the standards of her male colleagues. *Hugh Trevor* helps to illuminate the points at which her compliance with Jacobin conventions yields to a different set of preoccupations, many of which she held in common with Utopian authors and with women writers such as Mary Hays, Elizabeth Inchbald, and Eliza Fenwick.

Advocacy of the plain style most strongly identified in the period with Thomas Paine's political treatises is assigned in *Hugh Trevor* to the hero's mentor, author manqué and truth-teller, Turl, who rests his plea for expressive clarity on the principle that "whatever does not enlighten confuses."[2] Verbal idiosyncrasies fall within the supposed departures from intelligibility. Dialect and idiom, for example, occasionally have positive resonances when identified with the powerless – servants, children, the suffering rural poor – but are more often associated with exploitative activities, including gambling or versions of "religious enthusiasm" such as Methodism.[3] Hugh's serial entanglement in the professional cant of the clerical, political, and legal spheres in which he serves as ghost-writer and apologist extends the critique into the upper reaches of the social hierarchy. The contemporary multiplication of print kinds also comes under attack, with their quantity and fragmentary nature – suicide notes, memoirs, letters, pamphlets, newspaper snippets, interpolated individual histories – metaphorically rendering the self-interestedness of bourgeois urban culture. At first glance, censure of this print glut seems to run parallel to negative references to Gothic, satire, libel, invective, and romance. But Holcroft's treatment of genre moves beyond denunciation to multi-layered appraisal: he draws attention to the formal properties of each of these modes in order to highlight their manipulative techniques (and in the case of libel and satire to suggest their authors' base motives). In what amounts to a series of quick exercises in the practice of engaging skeptically with texts, he teaches his readers to check their emotional responses to novels and to replace them with reasoned, critical ones.

The affective correlative to the plain style is candor; its enemy is secrecy. Radical fiction, in general, regards secrets as suspect because they are assumed to benefit individuals at the expense of "the public good," a point thematically central to *Caleb Williams*, Hays' *Victim of Prejudice*, Fenwick's *Secresy*, Inchbald's *Nature and Art*, and Bage's *Hermsprong*.[4] But while proscribed on political grounds, secrets have the essential narrative function of directing the unfolding action in each of these novels. Their individual plot variations depend on the ability of the oppressed to wrest control of hidden information from the socially privileged. That ability is invariably gendered. For the women characters of the Hays, Fenwick, and Inchbald novels, knowledge ends in execution, death, or exile; for the male protagonists of the others, the exposure of secrets brings at a minimum, self-justification, and, in the case of Hermsprong and Hugh Trevor, the trappings of the conventional happy ending: marriage and inheritance. The pathways to success of the latter heroes rely heavily on coincidence, implausible conversions, and pliant heroines. Equivocal status seems also to be key: financial marginalization, either by birth or circumstance, shapes the engagement of Hermsprong, Caleb, and Hugh with the larger world.

While innocent protagonists might seem better suited to the radical commitment to expose worldly corruption, in practice their naivety often

matters less than the social ambivalence that gives them proximity to
wealth and power. A repeated pattern in each of the six volumes of *Hugh
Trevor* evidences the allure of such access: an initially uncomprehending,
perhaps willfully obtuse Hugh represses his principles and, blinded by the
"devil of flattery," accepts a position in the hope that he will make his
fortune and become the welcome suitor of the novel's heroine, the "lovely
chaste Olivia."[5] Through his serial engagement with intellectual, political,
ecclesiastical, parliamentary, and literary spheres, he witnesses vicious
behavior, discovers too late the covert machinations of his employers,
and finds his plans thwarted. After each disenchantment, he visits his
friend Turl, who once again painstakingly details with "unanswerable
truth" Hugh's collusion with systematic venality.[6]

Patterns of repetition such as these are favored by radical novelists
because they offer a mechanism for balancing the fictional imperatives of
suspense and individualized character development with the authors' own
commitment to unmasking conservative ideology. Hugh's periodic returns
to Turl (or Caleb Williams' to the metaphorical and literal imprisonments
that conversely demonstrate Falkland's malevolence) exemplify this at the
level of narrative structure. Echoes of, or direct quotation from, contemporary treatises, especially Godwin's, accomplish this verbally, not only by
aligning novelistic and political writing, but also by generating chains of
idealized mouthpieces (Elford, Turl, and Evelyn in *Hugh Trevor*,
Mr. Raymond in *Caleb Williams*) that recur across radical literature.
Roman à clef elements – as with the depiction of William Shay as Turl –
provide variations on these parallels between the real and the represented
(and subsequently a model for Isaac D'Israeli's and Elizabeth Hamilton's
loyalist parodies of Godwin, Holcroft, Hays, and Wollstonecraft). More
extravagantly, the doubling or even trebling of character groups refracts the
customary focus on uniquely individual traits, sometimes by extending
identities through mother-and-daughter or father-and-son relationships.
Cross-generational ties are occasionally established by like-mindedness, as
in Turl's elderly counterpart in virtue, Mr. Evelyn, the mouthpiece for the
Jacobin argument that the "diffusion of knowledge" will ultimately prove
the "most effectual means of conferring happiness."[7] Pairings of well- and
ill-intentioned men dramatize this radical faith in the necessary triumph of
reason over passion. In an adaptation of *Clarissa*'s Belford and Lovelace,
Holcroft matches Hugh Trevor with Wakefield, the latter guided by the
"mandevilian" assumption that "if you do not prey upon the world, the
world will prey upon you."[8] While both men are ambitious, Hugh is
unaware of the double identity and libertinism that enable Wakefield's

covert manipulation of his erstwhile friend, a knowledge that the less credulous reader infers well before the eponymous hero.

Throughout the novel, Wakefield's devious acts point the possible directions in which Hugh's wavering between self-interest and virtue might take him. But ultimately, it is the villain who is swayed by the hero's resurgent integrity. With Wakefield's sudden enlightenment, Holcroft effects the convergence of the plot's motivating impulse – to demonstrate that "the good of the whole [is] the true purpose of virtue" – with his authorial designs on the reader. Like the reformed anti-hero, we should now be prepared to recognize an unstoppable "progress of mind."⁹ But, curiously, key elements of the clichéd happy ending assigned to Hugh Trevor would not be out of place in the most reactionary of period fictions: his once-lost "wanderer" uncle, father-figure to him when he was a child, suddenly reappears, anxious to renew familial bonds; Hugh's culpably weak mother dies, releasing her husband, Wakefield, to marry Lydia Wilmot; Hugh himself, now "the acknowledged heir of a man of great wealth," marries his beloved Olivia Mowbray.¹⁰ The recovery of family, the restitution of estates, the summary punishment of "bad" mothers, the renewed friendship of the male principals "in the enjoyment of affluence": all are motifs favored by mid-century conservatives like Henry Fielding or Tobias Smollett and revived by anti-Jacobins in the 1790s.¹¹ Hugh's farewell address to the reader seems to offer something of a correction to his apparent swerve toward orthodoxy when he pleads that "Heaven preserve me from becoming indolent, proud, and oppressive! I have not yet forgotten that oppression exists, that pride is its chief counsellor, that activity and usefulness are the sacred duties of both rich and poor, that the wealth entrusted to my distribution is the property of those whom most it can benefit."¹²

But the "yet" here doesn't quite have the weight to qualify the novel's rush toward bourgeois respectability. Comparison of *Hugh Trevor* with other radical novels whose endings similarly retreat from their core principles uncovers interesting differences. *Hermsprong*, for instance, also elevates the hero to the initially despised gentry class. But Bage ameliorates the discontinuity between radical political assertion and conservative plot resolution with the self-conscious irony of the narrator, Gregory Glen, and the residual vitality of the counterviews voiced by the heroine's feminist friend, Maria Fluart. Paired with the hero and heroine, these characters leaven the high seriousness of the protagonists with their acerbic commentary. *Hugh Trevor*, by contrast, has no attractively fallible secondary characters. Instead, Turl's relentlessly edifying "masculine genius" finds its complement in Olivia's feminine "peaceful morality," a gendering of ethical behavior that exacerbates the novel's awkward mix of sensibility and radical politics.[13]

Godwin sidesteps this difficulty by uncoupling the two conventions on which Holcroft's happy ending depends: the dramatic conversion and marriage-as-reward. In the published version of *Caleb Williams*, the quasi-romantic interest, Emily Melvile, is dispatched in the first volume, allowing for the staging of a final courtroom confrontation between the autocratic persecutor and his once-servant. After Ferdinando Falkland hears Caleb's summary narrative of his life, he pronounces himself "conquered" by the "greatness and elevation of ... mind" that Caleb displays, then dies repentant three days later, leaving Caleb to "live the devoted victim of conscious reproach" and undoing any possibility of the novel's expressing delight in the defeat of tyranny.[14] Another alternative to the problems Holcroft and his fellow radicals encounter in combining analysis of present-day social ills with a program for an egalitarian future is simply to abandon realist narrative altogether. Taking its cue from formal utopias such as Jasper Richardson's *Island of Veritas* (1790), William Hodgson's *Commonwealth of Reason* (1795), and Thomas Spence's *The Marine Republic* (1794), the anonymous *Henry Willoughby* (1798) follows the hero from Old World corruption to "Anachoropolis, or the town of retirement," whose inhabitants "enjoy the pastoral life in all its primitive innocence, and Arcadian felicity."[15] The genre shift from London picaresque to utopian perfection is conclusive; smitten with the Mississippi settlement, Willoughby settles there for life.

Radical utopias, however, are rare, and rarer still are novels that resist the transformative possibilities of a sudden conversion or a courtship plot fulfilled. As we have seen, striking changes of hearts and minds are ubiquitous in male-authored fictions that end with marriage not death, inheritance of family estates not exile, restoration of identity not erasure. Women-authored Jacobin novels with a similar commitment to ideological exposé also deploy the conversion motif. But it is usually less dramatic and considerably more qualified by a gnawing awareness of women's systemic oppression. Matters relating to gender, in other words, complement and sometimes actively contest with political ones. In most of these novels, courtship, far from lending emphasis to the resolution of the hero's quest, mutates into revelations of male iniquity, represented as at once universal and unsusceptible to reform. Mary Hays' *Victim of Prejudice* (1799) and Eliza Fenwick's *Secresy* (1795) typically focus on sexual deceit, and both end tragically. Even in Jacobin novels with "happier" endings, such as Inchbald's *Nature and Art* (1796), the final divvying up of rewards entails retreat from an irremediably fallen society.

The critique of young male libertines in these novels runs parallel to their equally negative depiction of father figures whose tyrannical behavior refutes Burke's theorizing of a "natural" patriarchal authority. Across both generations, the leaguing against women often appears ancillary to exclusively male compacts: in *Secresy* and *The Victim of Prejudice*, it is rivalry with other men, and not desire for women, that animates seducers; marriage similarly turns on arrangements between men, with women as the aestheticized objects of exchange. The halcyon childhoods of Fenwick's Sibella and Hays' Mary compound the distorting effects of this misogyny. Despite their contrary educations – Sibella's is of the Rousseau-inspired variety that Wollstonecraft attacks in *A Vindication of the Rights of Woman*, while Mary's in *Victim of Prejudice* reflects the enlightened Mr. Raymond's "cherished notions" of "female accomplishments" – both, when girls, are intellectually precocious.[16] But independent intelligence finally proves irrelevant: with the onset of puberty, their subjection to male definition, in each instance exacerbated by their guardians' withholding of family secrets, proves inescapable. The sexual determinism central to women-authored Jacobin fiction reaches a lurid apogee in the imprisonment and deaths of Hays' paired mother-and-daughter Marys. In other novels, conversely, generational repetitions reinforce the imperative to acquiesce: the daughters in Inchbald's *Simple Story* and Amelia Opie's *Adeline Mowbray*, with the support of compassionate women friends, reject their mothers' independence, accept prevailing social norms, and survive. Inchbald advances a more overtly radical variation on Hays' and Fenwick's familial lineages. Her *Nature and Art*, originally entitled *A Satire on the Times*, shown to Godwin and Holcroft in 1794, and revised in 1795 as *Prejudices in Education*, traces two sets of contrary fathers and sons. But rather than turning in its conclusion, like *Victim of Prejudice*, *Simple Story*, and *Adeline Mowbray*, to individual expiatory deaths or compromises, *Nature and Art* continues to focus on the collective: the inflexible social, political, and economic hierarchies whose baleful power forces Henry's depleted but still virtuous family to retreat to "a hut, placed on the borders of the sea."[17]

The generic, stylistic, and thematic scope of *Nature and Art* dramatically expands the customary Jacobin range: fable, satire, political disquisition, authorial irony, and romance are used to investigate British imperialism, censorship, prostitution, the conscience-salving charities of the rich, and material, sexual, and legal double standards. An important narrative strand involves William's seduction and abandonment of Hannah Primrose, her attempts to maintain their illegitimate child through farm labor, and her descent into prostitution and theft in London. While Hannah's musings on status difference – "'that dishonesty was only held a sin, to secure the property of the rich'" – stop just short of condoning her turn to thieving, they provide a powerful counterargument to the punitive absolutes and pieties hypocritically mouthed by the wealthy.[18] The contrast of privilege and exclusion culminates in a scene in which William, now a judge, sentences Hannah to death. The deliberate theatricality of the courtroom gives a political face to personal failings in terms that align with the novel's division of its assumed audience into the disparaged "superior rank[s]" and the "unprejudiced reader[s] ... who consider all mankind alike deserving your investigation; who believe that there exist in some, knowledge without the advantage of instruction; refinement of sentiment independent of elegant society."[19]

Wollstonecraft's pre-revolutionary novel *Mary* and her unfinished *The Wrongs of Woman* similarly appeal to imagined readers in preparing the ground for the exposure of gender inequities. The Advertisement to *Mary* promises an "artless tale, without episode, [displaying] the mind of a woman, who has thinking powers," tacitly opposing it to the "interesting tales" driven by courtship and marriage plots that the heroine's vapid mother consumes.[20] In practice, however, intense sensibility prevails, with Wollstonecraft's faith in the correction of inequality after death conveyed in the "joy" with which the heroine, at novel's end, greets the thought that "she was hastening to that world *where there is neither marrying*, nor giving in marriage." *Wrongs of Woman* also aims to address "matrimonial despotism of heart and conduct" by focusing on the "finer sensations" that typify "our best novels."[21] But despite eschewing the model of those eventful fictions involving "great misfortunes" that "more forcibly impress the mind of common readers," the novel deploys a favored Gothic setting, the insane asylum, along with such hackneyed devices as libertine husbands, cruel taskmasters, contested inheritances, and surrogate parents and children.[22] Most damagingly, perhaps, despite her rhetorical question, "Was not the world a vast prison, and women born slaves?" the heroine Maria proves incapable of avoiding romance constructions; incarcerated by her husband, Venables, she reverts to projecting on to her fellow prisoner, Henry Darnford, "all the qualities of a hero's mind."[23]

Wrongs of Woman aligns itself ideologically with Jacobin fiction in giving voice to an abused servant, Jemima, and in its descriptions of gender inequality, the different employment prospects for men and women, and

the appalling conditions of hospitals and workhouses. Formally, its hand-
ling of interpolated narratives, including Darnford's account of his American sojourn, and, more strikingly, Maria's deferred "memoirs" to the child
from whom she has been separated by her husband, is noteworthy. The
point at which Maria's "memoirs" to her absent daughter break off,
however, ends what Godwin calls a "fragment" novel. The "half-finished
sentences" that follow, far from initiating a departure from standard
novelistic tropes, in fact multiply them: in one version, escape from the
asylum, a trial scene in which the judge declares his aversion to her "French
principles," a purloined inheritance, "Divorce by her husband—Her lover
unfaithful—Pregnancy—Miscarriage—Suicide"; in another version,
Maria attempts suicide by laudanum after the miscarriage, but is roused,
in the best sentimental tradition, to declare "I will live for my child!" after
Jemima suddenly appears leading the little girl, assumed dead, but in fact
"secreted" by Maria's husband and brother.²⁴ Perhaps to an even greater
degree than other Jacobin novelists, Wollstonecraft's entanglement in the
received conventions that her novels aspire to call into question limits her
success in enlightening her fellow "bastilled" readers.²⁵

Notes

1 Mary Wollstonecraft, *A Vindication of the Rights of Men* [1790], in *Political Writings*, edited by Janet Todd (Oxford: Oxford University Press, 1994), 60.
2 Thomas Holcroft, *The Adventures of Hugh Trevor*, edited by Seamus Deane (Oxford: Oxford University Press, 1973), 123.
3 Holcroft, *Hugh Trevor*, 93.
4 Ibid., 141.
5 Ibid., 121, 127.
6 Ibid., 159.
7 Ibid., 301.
8 Ibid., 223, 221.
9 Ibid., 230, 4.
10 Ibid., 492, 494.
11 Ibid., 496.
12 Ibid., 494.
13 Ibid., 203, 171.
14 William Godwin, *Things as They Are; Or, The Adventures of Caleb Williams*, edited by David McCracken (Oxford: Oxford University Press, 1970), 324, 325.
15 Anon., *Henry Willoughby: A Novel* (London: 1798), 2: 227, 229.
16 Mary Hays, *The Victim of Prejudice*, edited by Eleanor Ty (Peterborough: Broadview Press, 1998), 5.

17 Elizabeth Inchbald, *Nature and Art*, edited by Shawn Lisa Maurer (Peterborough: Broadview Press, 2005), 153.
18 Ibid., 135.
19 Ibid., 80–81.
20 Mary Wollstonecraft, *Mary and The Wrongs of Woman*, edited by Gary Kelly (Oxford: Oxford University Press, 1976), [xxxi], 2.
21 Ibid., 68.
22 Ibid., 74.
23 Ibid., 79, 99.
24 Ibid., 186, 199, 202, 203.
25 Ibid., 155.

CHAPTER 32

Anti-Jacobin Novels

Gary Kelly

The phrase "anti-Jacobin novel," like "Jacobin novel," was created by and has circulated in academic discourse since the 1970s.[1] The phrase barely appears in the print record of Wollstonecraft's day, and other terms were used to locate such fiction within a larger terrain of novelistic practice. A rare instance of "anti-Jacobin novel" occurred in the April 1800 issue of a short-lived magazine edited by the anti-reform propagandist Robert Bisset, who published his own "anti-Jacobin" novel, *Douglas*, the same year. The magazine's essay on "The History of Literature for the Year 1799" continued three recent related projects. It treated current literature largely as opposition between what it called "Jacobin" and "anti-Jacobin." It summarized the principles of political-cultural-literary critique mounted by the *Anti-Jacobin Magazine*, to which Bisset was a contributor. And the essay corresponded to verse satires such as William Gifford's *Baviad* (1791) and *Maeviad* (1795) and Thomas Mathias' *The Pursuits of Literature* (1794, expanded). These aimed, with some justice, to associate political and other kinds of reformism with literary avant-gardism and political with artistic "innovation." In Bisset's *Magazine*, "anti-Jacobin novel" referred to George Walker's *The Vagabond* in discussion of prose and verse "Works of fiction." After treating Charlotte Smith's and Mary Robinson's novels as "Jacobin," the essay turned to their "anti-Jacobin" opponents, including Henry James Pye's *The Democrat* (1795), Charles Lloyd's *Edmund Oliver* (1798), Isaac D'Israeli's *Vaurien* (1797), *The History of Sir George War-rington; or, The Political Quixote* (1797), and Walker's *The Vagabond* (1799), concluding, "As novels have, of late, been frequently employed to make men disloyal subjects and bad citizens, we rejoice to see that good talents are now employed in the same way, to make men loyal subjects and good citizens."[2]

The statement summarized an important context of Mary Wollstone-craft in several ways. It suggested how, by the time of her death in 1797, a discourse was forming that related political ideology to cultural discourse,

political order, and social practice, and represented these in binary, negative and positive, "Jacobin" and "anti-Jacobin" terms. The statement
implied the incorrect belief, still widespread today, that particular meanings and values inhere once and for all in texts or print objects rather than
being created by the objects' users in particular moments, in their own
interests.[3] Accordingly, the statement assumed that reading internalizes
such meanings and values and thereby shapes readers' and nations' character, culture, and conduct. The statement related literature, broadly understood, to the moral character of individual readers, hence to the ethical
character of civil society, and hence again to the stability of the established
political order. And despite the generally low artistic and intellectual
esteem novels were held in at the time, the statement assigned them a
particularly important role in these respects, presumably because of their
wide circulation and the commonplace criticism that most novel-readers
were young and naive and hence susceptible to ideological and other kinds
of seduction, a situation emplotted in many anti-Jacobin novels.

Such binarization of political, literary, and novelistic discourse was
several things at once. It was a marketing device by authors and publishers.
It was a rhetorical move by professional controversialists like Bisset, seeking
payment and patronage. And it was a politicizing slogan used in the power
struggles of Wollstonecraft's day. As followers of the news then would
know, Jacobin in the British context signified a supposed sympathizer with
the French political faction of radical revolutionaries, named Jacobins from
their meeting place attached to the Paris church of St. Jacques. Used in
Britain during the 1790s, "Jacobin" was a smear used against those they set
up as their opponents by those professing to be anti-Jacobins. But many so
smeared rather represented themselves as "reformers" or "reformists" and
differed among themselves. Further, anti-reformists in Wollstonecraft's day
would more likely characterize themselves as "loyalists" than "anti-Jacobins." For the new terms Jacobin and anti-Jacobin overlapped with related
terms long in use. Since the sixteenth century, "reformist" or "reformer"
could mean a proponent of the Protestant Reformation or further radical-
ization of it. In the seventeenth-century English Civil War these terms
could be applied to supporters of Parliament and religious freedom against
the king and the established church, and to supporters of Cromwell's
republican Commonwealth. In the eighteenth century the terms were
applied to those who promoted Commonwealth principles to reform what
they saw as the religious and political "constitution" established by the
Glorious Revolution of 1688. By contrast, from the seventeenth century
"loyalist" typically meant one loyal during the English Civil War to the king

and established church. Polemical use of "reformist" and "loyalist" informed by this historical background was renewed in the 1790s British debate on the French Revolution, by both reformists such as Richard Price in his 1789 *Discourse on the Love of Our Country* and loyalists such as Edmund Burke in his 1790 anti-Price *Reflections on the Revolution in France*. Both reformists and loyalists drew parallels, for better or worse, between the republican French Revolution and the seventeenth-century republican English Commonwealth. Self-styled loyalists accused reformists of extremism, or "enthusiasm," likely to produce civil strife and linked it to French Revolutionary "excesses." Loyalists such as Burke denounced admiration for the Revolution expressed by many English religious Dissenters or Nonconformists (so-called for dissenting from and not conforming to the established church) and portrayed them as a continuing threat to the "established" order of "church and king" – a common loyalist slogan for over a century.

There was substance to this portrayal. By the early 1790s Dissenters were energetically campaigning for relief from civil disabilities imposed on them by the Glorious Revolution, praising the French Revolution for its establishment of religious freedom, and arguing that loyalism was so entrenched that only constitutional reform could secure similar liberty in Britain. Consequently, loyalists deployed the terms "reformist" and "loyalist" to suggest congruence between religious and political ideology and connection between the ideological conflicts of the 1790s and the bloody civil and religious conflicts of the previous century. Loyalists did not displace "reformist" and "loyalist" with "Jacobin" and "anti-Jacobin" but rather used these terms as a scare tactic to suggest a French connection that became more frightening with the rise of Bonaparte. Wollstonecraft herself would have understood the terms Jacobin and anti-Jacobin in the French context and sympathized with neither. She went to Paris in 1792 to join the coterie of the moderately revolutionary and at that time governing faction of the Girondins, and she found herself in peril after the Jacobin *coup d'état* of 1793 overthrew them. She would have recognized Jacobin as a term bandied in Britain against such friends and mentors as Richard Price, berated by Burke in 1790.

The terms "radicalism" and "conservatism" as used in today's academic discourse for what could then have been named Jacobinism and anti-Jacobinism, reformism and loyalism, did not acquire predominant political signification until decades after Wollstonecraft's death. She may have encountered Jacobin and anti-Jacobin applied to this or that novel, and several factors may have enabled her to understand these as currently developing genres or sub-genres. She frequently reviewed novels while working for Joseph Johnson's *Analytical Review*. She had published a reformist novel, *Mary: A Fiction*, in 1788; in 1796 she joined the Holcroft–Godwin circle where novelistic discourse in its relation to ideology was intensely discussed; and at the time of her death in 1797 she was working on a novel, *The Wrongs of Woman*, that exemplified for polemicists such as Bisset what they were beginning to denominate Jacobin novels and to oppose with "anti-Jacobin novels." Nevertheless, Wollstonecraft would likely have understood these as reformist and loyalist forms covered by such existing phrases as "political novel" and "political romance," "philosophical novel" and "philosophical romance," not in binary opposition but part of a larger topography and longer history of the novel in struggles between interests deploying differing political, social, and religious principles and appropriate novelistic practices.

In the 1790s, "political novel" and "political romance" appear in publishers' advertisements, novel titles, and newspaper articles, often referring to both Jacobin and anti-Jacobin novels. But the terms were also applied to earlier works such as Thomas More's *Utopia* (1516), Fénelon's *Télémaque* (1699), Samuel Johnson's *Rasselas* (1759), and Montesquieu's *Histoire d'Arsace et Isménie* (1783). The phrases were also found in novel titles from the mid-eighteenth century, such as *The Castle Builders; or, The History of William Stephens* [...]*: A Political Novel* [...] (1759), and Laurence Sterne's satirical *roman à clef* entitled *A Political Romance* (1759). Examples from the 1790s include *Gregory's Nose: A Political Romance* (1795) and *Azemia* (1798), satirizing various Jacobins and advertised as "a political novel." The 1810s produced several instances. There was *The Reformist!!! A Serio-Political Novel of the Present Day* (1810). There was *Despotism; or, The Fall of the Jesuits: A Political Romance* (1811), an ostensibly historical novel with obvious reference to 1790s controversies. There was *Gulzara, Princess of Persia* (1816), advertised as a "political romance" on current British and French affairs. And there was George Buxton's *Political Quixote* (1820), advertised as a "political romance," burlesquing the reformist periodical *The Black Dwarf*, and, like several anti-Jacobin novels, converging the traditions of Cervantes' anti-romance *Don Quixote* (1605–15) and Samuel Butler's anti-Nonconformist burlesque *Hudibras* (1662–77) to satirize delusive "systems" producing dangerous "enthusiasm." "Political novel" reappeared in the early 1830s amidst intense reform campaigning and the "silver fork" and "Newgate" novels associated with it, applied to such works as W. Massie's *Sydenham; or, Memoirs of a Man of the World* (1830), *The Cabal: A Tale of the Reign of*

William IV (1831), and the novels of Bulwer Lytton. By this time, however, "political romance" was applied not to fiction as such but to political policies and programs denigrated as mere fictions.

In Wollstonecraft's day philosophy of certain kinds was often seen as inherently political for better or worse, and the phrases "philosophical novel" and "philosophical romance" further indicate the various ways such works were conceived, marketed, and received. These phrases were applied to some political novels in the 1790s but also appeared earlier, as in the French materialist philosopher Helvetius' *The Child of Nature Improved by Chance: A Philosophical Novel* (1774). Further, in the 1790s many novelists denigrated as Jacobins called themselves "philosophers," "modern philosophers," or "new philosophers," after the current French term *philosophe* meaning a social critic mediating modern knowledges to a wider public in critique of the established order. Anti-Jacobin novels frequently attacked "new" philosophy and philosophers, as in Elizabeth Hamilton's *Memoirs of Modern Philosophers* (1800), referring specifically to Mary Hays' Godwinian *Memoirs of Emma Courtney* (1796). "Philosophical romance," like "political romance," had also been applied earlier, to such works as More's *Utopia* (1516), Swift's *Gulliver's Travels* (1726), and William Thomson's *The Man in the Moon* (1783), but more often to some philosophy or political program being denigrated as a "romance" in the sense of an extravagant, unrealistic, and impractical fabrication, as in a definition of "philosophical Romance" as "something to Imagination amusing, but in Reality impossible."⁴ In the 1790s, loyalists characterized in just this way the Jacobin philosophy and politics that they fictionalized in their novels, especially those of Wollstonecraft and her circle.

Political, social, cultural, and publishing histories enable further historical and material contextualizing of anti-Jacobin novels. Like most other kinds, such novels were typically three-volume works, costing from ten to twenty shillings (when a laborer might earn ten shillings a week). Many anti-Jacobin as well as Jacobin novels were published by proprietors and/or leading suppliers of commercial circulating libraries. These rented books and hence knew their market and could profit from prompt response to issues and interests of the moment. Whether such novels were bought or rented, cost and custom would largely limit access to the upper and middle, propertied and professional ranks. Most such people had vested interests in order and stability and accordingly could be expected to favor loyalist views. But some of these people felt marginalized by "things as they are" (title of William Godwin's well-known reformist novel of 1794) and would incline to reformism on certain issues. The spectacle of the French

Revolution's radical changes intensified such differences of opinion in Britain, stimulating readers' interests, writers' responses, and publishers' opportunism.

Novels by known English "Jacobins" featuring overt social-political critique of the established order were prominent in the early and mid-1790s while sympathy with the French Revolution as an example for Britain persisted. This novelistic discourse evolved into broader and more general critique in the Revolutionary and Napoleonic aftermath of 1800s and 1810s. As the Revolution became discredited by factionalism, violence, and war with Britain, loyalist opinion consolidated, bolstered by anti-reformist government legislation and loyalist associations and vigilantism. From the late 1790s to the 1820s loyalist anti-Jacobin literature "exposed" any reformist critique as "Jacobinism." As often, convergence of politics and commerce stimulated literary innovation and publishing entrepreneurship. Novels resembled other media of political discourse from pamphlets to newspapers that were secretly subsidized by the government and its supporters. Authors and publishers seeking such patronage in the form of purchases, "places" (jobs), and payoffs could monetize growing anti-reformist political reaction by offering so-called anti-Jacobin novels. These included those mentioned in Bisset's *Magazine* and earlier in this chapter as well as, among others, Elizabeth Hamilton's *Letters of a Hindoo Rajah* (1796), Charles Lucas's *The Infernal Quixote* (1798), Jane West's *A Tale of the* Times (1799), Edward Dubois's *St Godwin* (1800), Sophia King's *Waldorf; or, The Dangers of Philosophy* (1801), and Amelia Opie's *Adeline Mowbray* (1805).

In broader historical terms, the anti-Jacobin novel and its thematic concerns and artistic practices may be located in the emergent discourse of modernity. This was a field of contest between interests differing over the very processes of modernization that stirred the conflicts of Wollstonecraft's day and that created the commercialized novel and assigned it a major promotional role in them.[5] For those like Wollstonecraft, the discourse of modernity would have centered on self-reflexive personal identity enabling "authentic" relations of intimacy, conjugality, domesticity, sociability, and national and humane consciousness. Such a modern subject was then supposedly better able to engage with modernization's relations of risk and trust, abstract systems such as modern institutions and knowledges, new chronotopes or configurations of time-space from the sentimentalized home to the scientized cosmos, and the need to disembed from "unmodern" sites and situations and re-embed in "modern" ones.

Accordingly, many Jacobin novelists depicted protagonists in the process of forming themselves as modern subjects but obstructed by the unmodernity or false modernity of the established order of "things as they are." Anti-Jacobin novelists riposted by abstaining from extensive depiction of subjectivity and emphasizing social relations and "duties" properly restraining dangerous individualism otherwise disruptive of social, political, and cultural order and hierarchy. Jacobin novelists asserted the superiority of intersubjective sexual intimacy, conjugality, and sociability, though damaged by gendered, familial, social, proprietorial, and institutional hierarchies and thwarted by legal and religious sanctions. Anti-Jacobin novels represented such reformist relations as mere sexual and social license that destabilized conjugality and domesticity, corrupted sociability, undermined property, and subverted "patriotic" religious and political loyalties. Nevertheless, anti-Jacobin novels often cashed in on the titillating potential of such representations by portraying while condemning reformist sexuality and conjugality and treating Jacobin reformist initiatives as Gothic and melodramatic improbabilities. Jacobin novelists engaged their self-reflexive protagonists, often disastrously, with relations of risk and trust, abstract systems, and unfamiliar chronotopes of a hostile system of "things as they are." But anti-Jacobins often engaged their naive, inexperienced, or quixotic protagonists with these aspects of modernity influenced or attracted by Jacobin critique of them and fantasy of a better "system." These are often proposed by a seductive Jacobin-Gothic villain, imperiling the protagonist (often female), who is rescued by intervention of a trustworthy, authoritative male figure, in a variation of the popular plot of "virtue in distress." Jacobin novels favored first-person autobiographical or epistolary narration to engage reader sympathy and so developed Richardsonian and Sentimental novel practices. Anti-Jacobin novels countered by using burlesque to obstruct reader sympathy with victims of "things as they are," and continued the ironic, Fieldingesque tradition by embracing third-person authoritative narration (and burlesquing Sentimental tropes), thus implying the need for other kinds of authority in life, society, culture and politics. Jacobin novels emplotted a "concatenation" of situation, character, and incident to illustrate their philosophical principle of a necessary connection between the system of "things as they are" and individual character and destiny. Anti-Jacobin novels riposted by emplotting a relation between character and circumstances that was subject to chance and required intervention and restorative ordering by a *deus ex machina*, sanctioned by divine providence. Jacobin novels depicted protagonists attempting or forced to disembed from unmodern situations (injustice, exploitation, social inequality of gender and class) by escape, aspiration, ejection, or exile to re-embed in

idealized modern situations (equality, justice, self-approbation, social harmony, and so on), but obstructed by unmodernity or false modernity as
"things as they are," implying the need for reform. Anti-Jacobin novels
depicted protagonists deluded by proponents of false, mistaken, or
unachievable idealized modernity but rescued or enlightened by proponents of a realistic and practical modernity based on loyalist principles.

The major distinguishing feature of anti-Jacobin fiction, however, was
tone and mode. Anti-Jacobin novels sought to discredit reformist immediacy and seriousness, developed from Sentimental literature, by using long-
established techniques of burlesque, bathos, and parody and references to
and adaptations of widely known exemplars such as Cervantes' *Don
Quixote*, Butler's *Hudibras*, and Fielding's novels. Ironically, this strategy
left anti-Jacobin novels, like these antecedents, in the parodic paradox:
readers' creation of meanings from anti-Jacobin novels depended, then as
now, on some knowledge of what they were parodying.

Notes

1 To indicate that "Jacobin" and "anti-Jacobin" are discursive signifiers rather
  than historical realities, I use scare quotes here and then largely abandon them
  for stylistic reasons, but they should be understood throughout.
2 *Historical, Biographical, Literary, and Scientific Magazine* (London:
  G. Cawthorn, 1800), 1: 83.
3 See Roy Harris, *The Language Myth* (London: Duckworth, 1981).
4 James Hervey, *Theron and Aspasio . . .*, 6th edn. (London: J. F. & C. Riving-
  ton, 1789), III, 158.
5 I adapt this account of modernity from Anthony Giddens, *The Consequences
  of Modernity* (Stanford: Stanford University Press, 1990) and other works.

CHAPTER 33

Children's Literature

Andrew O'Malley

Mary Wollstonecraft's literary career in the last two decades of the eighteenth century coincides with the emergence and rapid expansion and diversification of a children's text industry in Britain. There had certainly been books produced for children in previous periods: hornbooks and battledores for learning the alphabet, Puritan-penned accounts of the deaths of godly children such as James Janeway's *A Token for Children* (1673), advice and conduct books for the young of the well-to-do entering the social world are but a few examples. Yet it was not until the second half of the eighteenth century that a perceived need for a specialized literature became widespread enough to foster and sustain a significant number of publishers dedicated to its production: most famously John (then Francis, then Elizabeth) Newbery, followed by many others including Thomas Carnan, William Darton, John Marshall, and Benjamin Tabart. Wollstonecraft herself acknowledged how recent, and welcome, a development "new" children's literature was in an early review for the *Analytical Review* of Thomas Day's *The History of Sandford and Merton* (1789): "The importance of books adapted to the understanding of children, has not till lately been forcibly felt in this kingdom."[1] By the time of her death, there were bookstores selling reading material for young readers exclusively; her widower William Godwin would operate one himself. These were stocked with everything from story books, movables (early pop-up books), poetry collections, plays for "home entertainments," and abridged versions of successful novels, as well as devotional works, geographical "tours," historical accounts, science texts, often about botany and zoology, and day planners for young people that included such practical information as London coach times and how to make change at a shop accurately. What this all suggests, as historians of childhood and scholars of children's literature have long noted, is a significant reconfiguration of the place of the child in both the public imagination and in social practice. This reimagining of the meaning of childhood was anything but an

afterthought or footnote to the grander enterprises of the late Enlightenment; it was a serious concern to many of the period's most notable
thinkers and Wollstonecraft was at its forefront.

Paving the way for what J. H. Plumb famously referred to as the late
eighteenth century's "new world" for children was Locke's educational
treatise, *Some Thoughts Concerning Education* (1693).[2] Locke had considered forming children – specifically upper-class boys, but his ideas were
eventually expanded to girls' education and embraced by the lower middle
classes – as rational, independent subjects a necessary investment in the
nation's future. Indeed, the unformed, *tabula rasa* of the infant mind came
to represent the very idea of futurity and potential, and of the possibility of
progress. The child, both as symbol and as actual social actor, became by
the late Enlightenment a figure of unprecedented concern, as both emblem
of promise and newness and as the site on which a world of more rational
institutions and practices could be built. Jean-Jacques Rousseau expanded
on Locke's ideas, proposing in *Emile* (1762) a radical potential to the
uncorrupted child, a figure who offered an antidote to the vices and
stagnation of the *ancien régime*. Given this endorsement by two key
Enlightenment luminaries, it is no surprise that so many important
intellectuals in Britain wrote about the education of the young including
Joseph Priestley (*Miscellaneous Observations Relating to Education* [1778]),
Erasmus Darwin (*A Plan for the Conduct of Female Education in Boarding
Schools* [1797]), and of course William Godwin (*The Enquirer; Reflections
on Education, Manners, and Literature* [1797]).

With some notable exceptions, such as Catharine Macaulay, theoretical
writing on pedagogy and plans for education were primarily the domain of
male writers who claimed them as areas of philosophical inquiry. Also with
notable exceptions, Thomas Day and the prolific Richard Johnson for
example, the actual business of writing *for* children was undertaken most
often by women. Wollstonecraft was a fairly rare example of a female
author who wrote both theoretically about education as well as for the
young readers whom she wished to educate. Since women were already
regarded as naturally fitted to overseeing the early stages of children's
education, children's literature afforded many the opportunity to write
respectably and for profit. It is tempting to consider that Wollstonecraft
and other women writers, like Anna Barbauld or Maria Edgeworth, who
went on to earn well-deserved reputations in fields with greater intellectual
and artistic cachet, were writing for children merely for the paycheck. But
given the importance of education and childhood to the discourse of
Enlightenment, Wollstonecraft and her peers likely considered their

children's writing as a legitimate, albeit circumscribed, opportunity to participate in one of the most important enterprises of the period: the reform of education.

Wollstonecraft had some direct experience with the education of young people on which to draw when she began writing for and about them. With her sister Emily and friend Fanny Blood, Wollstonecraft briefly ran a school in Newington Green; this experience informed the writing of her conduct book, *Thoughts on the Education of Daughters* (1787), a text clearly inspired by Locke, as the title suggests. Alan Richardson's observation that this early work appealed to what was by then "mainstream taste" on the subject of education is fair: "the ideal of a domestic education supervised by parents; the bourgeois distrust of servants ... the banishment of 'improbable tales' and 'superstitious accounts' (like fairy tales) from the children's library." Indeed, Richardson sees *Thoughts* as not only typically Lockean in its advice, but, with its "strong note of piety," even unexpectedly aligned with one of the more conservative pedagogues of the period, Sarah Trimmer.[3]

After the closing of her school, Wollstonecraft worked for a year as a governess in County Cork, Ireland, instructing the two daughters of the Viscount of Kingsborough. While she disliked the experience, it did serve as the basis for the only book for child readers she would ever author, *Original Stories from Real Life* (1788), the Kingsborough girls providing models for the book's ill-behaved Mary and Caroline. The story chronicles the gradual improvement of two adolescent girls educated by a relative, Mrs. Mason, after the death of their mother. Starting by correcting their cruel, fearful, and so irrational, attitudes toward the lower forms of creation, Mrs. Mason eventually opens the girls' minds to the reason and virtue that ultimately allow them to extend a socially productive, empathetic charity to London's poor by the end of the novel. *Original Stories* sold well enough that its publisher Joseph Johnson would commission plates designed by William Blake for the second edition (1790). At least one critic has suggested that Blake's illustrations of angelic children and ecstatic bards subtly undercut the rational moralism of the text, but given how rarely Blake illustrated work for other authors, it seems likely that he took the commission at least partly out of admiration for Wollstonecraft.[4] Johnson's *Analytical Review* also published a substantial and favorable review of the book. It praised Wollstonecraft's experiential method of promoting knowledge and virtue through dialogue, a formula that was used widely in the period and that coincided with the Enlightenment's aversion to received knowledge, rote-learning, and instruction by precept.[5]

Wollstonecraft's reputation as a children's writer rests more or less exclusively on *Original Stories*, which remained in print, on and off, until the middle of the nineteenth century. For much of the twentieth century, however, this reputation was not very good. Twentieth-century scholars of children's book history tended to view this work as a quintessential example of the stern, humorless, and didactic style referred to, usually disparagingly, as "rational moralism." F. J. Harvey Darton, in his monumental, pioneering study, *Children's Books in England* (1932), allows only two paragraphs at the very end of his chapter on "Moral Tales" to a book whose author he regards as "completely dogmatic ... but also completely logical."[6] The second paragraph is more concerned with "[t]he disaster of Mary Godwin's life" than it is with the book she wrote for children.[7] Percy Muir includes Wollstonecraft in what he dubs the "monstrous regiment" of late eighteenth-century didactic writers.[8] Three decades later, Geoffrey Summerfield would offer the opinion that *Original Stories* "has a strong claim to be the most sinister, ugly, overbearing book for children ever published."[9] Summerfield's (and others') hostility to the book is usually directed at the figure of Mrs. Mason, whom he refers to as "Mrs. Nobo-daddy Mason," and her treatment of the girls in her care. Particularly unpleasant to twentieth-century sensibilities were exchanges in which Mrs. Mason points out the children's weakness, dependence, and impoverished reason. In one notorious example, she chastises the girls for trying to kill snails, remarking "You are often troublesome—I am stronger than you—yet I do not kill you."[10]

Critical distaste for *Original Stories* and more generally for the rationalist-moralist tradition it had come to exemplify was informed by Romantic notions of children's (specifically boys') natural creativity and freedom and by the highly gendered opposition of imagination and didacticism, as Mitzi Myers has very ably demonstrated.[11] Myers was among the first to seek to rehabilitate *Original Stories* and to consider Wollstonecraft's educational work as of a piece with her later more explicitly feminist writing. Since then, a number of scholars have taken up and expanded on this work, resituating *Original Stories* and to some extent *Thoughts on the Education of Daughters* at the center of both Wollstonecraft's oeuvre and of the period's debates over female education. Caroline Franklin, for example, sees *Original Stories* and other "girls' fiction" of the period seizing "the opportunity to bring out into the open and even question the gendering of female education."[12] The recent turn in criticism of Wollstonecraft's juvenile writing has effectively reversed Summerfield's assertion that it is characterized by a "tyrannical spirit," some

scholars now even describing *Original Stories* as "activist children's literature."[13] Dolan sees Mrs. Mason as promoting in her young charges a non-
hierarchical empathy with the poor, with the goal of training "readers to
see the social structures that create and exacerbate poverty."[14] For Laura
Kirkley, the rational training of young women that Wollstonecraft emphasizes is designed to allow them to "exercise their reason to recognize and
resist tyranny."[15] It is difficult to imagine a pedagogy more attuned to
radical Enlightenment ideals than this.

Franklin suggests that what twentieth-century critics regarded as "the
most disconcerting features of [Wollstonecraft's] style," including "the
sordid detailing of social realism" in *Original Stories*, actually "point to
the evolution of didacticism into social protest."[16] The harrowing story of
"Crazy Robin," recounted to the girls by Mrs. Mason, is a fictionalized
version of the well-known case of a former miner and farmer reduced to
living in a cave by financial ruin and emotional distress. One of the actual
Robin's visitors was Thomas Spence, the radical pamphleteer, a fact that in
and of itself hints at a subversive intent in including this anecdote in
Original Stories. As Franklin points out, in her descriptions of such
instances of extreme poverty and distress Wollstonecraft manages to "avoid
the clichés of sensibility" while keeping the focus not on "the girls'
emotions" but on "the dignity of the poor and their capacity for endur-
ance."[17] Romantic idealizations of childhood, which became dominant by
the early nineteenth century and whose traces still strongly inform current
ideas about childhood, tended to depoliticize the state of childhood and to
distance it from the cruel realities of the social world. Certainly this
attitude accounts, at least in part, for the modern distaste for *Original
Stories*; Wollstonecraft refused to cushion the impact of her portrayals for
the sake of preserving children's "innocence."

While she would gain notoriety for her radical gender politics later in
her career, Wollstonecraft's work in the children's text industry is marked
most often by agreement with the period's expert consensus on pedagogical matters. She was for a time the main reviewer of juvenile texts and
educational writing for Johnson's *Analytical Review*, offering opinions on
scores of children's books. Although she only published one original
children's novel, she abridged and altered Madame de Cambon's *Young
Grandison* and translated C. G. Salzmann's *Elements of Morality* from
German, a language she taught herself in the process. Wollstonecraft also
expressed strong approval for two of the period's most important writers
for children, whose pedagogical views differed significantly: Maria
Edgeworth and Sarah Trimmer. Like Edgeworth, and Thomas Day, whose

Sandford and Merton she singled out for particularly high praise in the *Analytical Review*, Wollstonecraft was, at least at first, an enthusiastic supporter of the experiential educational method Rousseau espoused in *Emile*, and she praised the Rousseau-inspired *The Parent's Assistant*.[18] Yet she was also able to find common cause with the devoutly High Anglican Sarah Trimmer, who excoriated *Emile* as a *"visionary, fallacious, and dangerous"* system of education in her *Guardian of Education* (emphasis in original).[19] Of Trimmer's Sunday School text, *A Comment on Dr. Watts's Divine Songs*, for example, Wollstonecraft enthused "we really think this mode well calculated to open the minds of the ignorant."[20] Her high regard of Trimmer is also evident in the fact that Mrs. Mason gives Mary and Caroline a copy of Trimmer's *Fabulous Histories* to help them rethink their attitudes toward animals.[21]

Near the end of her life, after the plaudits and infamy the *Vindications* had brought her, Wollstonecraft returned to writing for the young; an incomplete manuscript intended for her daughter Fanny Imlay and with the working title "Lessons" was published in her *Posthumous Works*. While short and fragmentary, this text reveals a decidedly different approach than her earlier writing for children and hints at a substantial revision of her pedagogical outlook, as Godwin remarks in his "Editor's Advertisement": "It is obvious the author has struck out a path of her own, and by no means intrenched upon the plans of her predecessors."[22] The structure of this work is itself not revolutionary; a series of incrementally more complex lessons, spoken in the voice of a mother to her child, with increasingly sophisticated language and syntax to mirror the child's language development had been a format pioneered by Anna Barbauld.[23] The text also portrays the child's improvement as a progression from less to more rational thinking, typical of most of the children's literature produced in the second half of the eighteenth century. What has changed significantly with this work is, as Alan Richardson remarks, the tone: "a unique variant on the maternal voice of the 'new' literature for children, one that includes a rare admission of parental vulnerability that contrasts strikingly with her own Mrs. Mason's seeming omnipotence."[24] The mother here discusses, for example, her own suffering trying to nurse a teething infant: "you used to bite me. Poor mamma! . . . you hurt me very much."[25]

Perhaps more significant than her admissions that she suffers from headaches or from her child's bites is the mother-narrator's repeated comparisons of the girl's dependence and weakness to her own when she was young. She makes such remarks as "My mamma took care of me, when I was a little girl, like you," or "Papa and I were children, like you;

and men, and women took care of us."²⁶ The effect of this regular
reminder that the adult was once a child is to emphasize that the hierarchies that grant the adult power over the child are temporary. One of
Wollstonecraft's preferred sentence structures in "Lessons" is to balance
two independent clauses on either side of a colon to contrast adult and
child knowledges: "You know already, that potatoes will not do you any
harm: but I must pick the fruit for you, till you are wise enough to know
the ripe apples and pears."²⁷ Yet the comparisons this structure produces
yield not only differences but similarities as well: "You do not love physic:
I do not love it any more than you."²⁸ While Wollstonecraft does not
propose equality between child and adult here, she does close the gap
between figures who were by this time increasingly understood as oppos-
ites. The differences she stages between parent and offspring are not the
absolutes that were typical of her peers, but fluid; they do not dissolve but
do point to a kind of child–adult interaction with some of the radical
egalitarian possibilities Wollstonecraft proposed for the sexes.

Notes

1 Mary Wollstonecraft, *The Works of Mary Wollstonecraft*, edited by Janet Todd
and Marilyn Butler (London: W. Pickering, 1989), 7: 124.
2 See J. H. Plumb, "The New World of Children in Eighteenth-Century
England," *Past & Present*, 67:1 (1975), 64–95.
3 Alan Richardson, "Mary Wollstonecraft in Education," in Claudia L. Johnson, ed., *The Cambridge Companion to Mary Wollstonecraft* (Cambridge:
Cambridge University Press, 2002), 26, 27.
4 For an example of the subversive reading, see Orm Mitchell, "Blake's Subversive Illustrations for Wollstonecraft's *Stories*," *Mosaic*, 17:4 (1984), 17–34. On
Blake's likely admiration of Wollstonecraft, see Caroline Franklin, *Mary
Wollstonecraft: A Literary Life* (Basingstoke: Palgrave, 2004), 40.
5 *The Analytical Review; or, History of Literature, Domestic and Foreign, on an
Enlarged Plan*, 28 vols. (London: J. Johnson, 1788–98), 2: 478–80.
6 F. J. Harvey Darton, *Children's Books in England: Five Centuries of Social Life*,
1932 (Cambridge: Cambridge University Press, 2011), 203.
7 Ibid., 204.
8 Percy Muir, *English Children's Books, 1600–1900*, 1954 (London: B.
T. Batsford Ltd., 1985), 97.
9 Geoffrey Summerfield, *Fantasy and Reason: Children's Literature in the Eighteenth Century* (London: Methuen, 1984), 229.
10 *Works*, 4: 368.
11 See, especially, her landmark study "Impeccable Governesses, Rational
Dames, and Moral Mothers: Mary Wollstonecraft and the Female Tradition
in Georgian Children's Books," *Children's Literature*, 14, 31–59.

12 Franklin, *Mary Wollstonecraft: A Literary Life*, 36.
13 Summerfield, *Fantasy and Reason*, 229; Elizabeth Dolan, *Seeing Suffering in Women's Literature of the Romantic Era* (Aldershot: Ashgate, 2008), 171.
14 Ibid., 167.
15 Laura Kirkley, "'Original Spirits': Literary Translations and Translational Literature in the Works of Mary Wollstonecraft," in Robin Truth Goodman, ed., *Literature and the Development of Feminist Theory* (Cambridge: Cambridge University Press, 2015), 20.
16 Franklin, *Mary Wollstonecraft: A Literary Life*, 45.
17 Ibid., 43.
18 See *Works*, 7: 175–76 for her review of *The History of Sandford and Merton*, and 7: 477 for her review of *The Parent's Assistant*.
19 Sarah Trimmer, ed., *The Guardian of Education* (London: J. Johnson, 1801–05), 1: 184.
20 *Works*, 7: 123.
21 *Works*, 4: 371.
22 Ibid., 467.
23 See, for example, her *Lessons for Children Three to Four Years Old* (London: J. Johnson, 1788).
24 Richardson, "Mary Wollstonecraft in Education," 38.
25 *Works*, 4: 470.
26 Ibid., 471, 472.
27 Ibid., 472.
28 Ibid., 472.

CHAPTER 34

Gothic Literature
Michael Gamer

For Mary Wollstonecraft, the word "gothic" would not have denoted a kind of literature, let alone a mode or genre. At best, it would have signaled an architectural style and the epoch and people who produced it. Literally denoting "of the Goths," the word signified "medieval," perhaps vaguely "barbarous": at once "not classical" and "not modern." It also carried political connotations, thanks to the widespread belief that the ancient Goths were the same Germanic invaders who had settled in England during the late Roman Empire. Synonymous with nativist associations of pre-Norman England, it could be associated with various Saxon traits of inclusiveness, fairness, vigor, and forthrightness. Students of popular culture already will have a notion how such a rich yet opaque term could come, with time, to denote a literature. And once established, Gothic's blend of historical fantasy, uncanny phenomena, sexual danger, and extreme situations has never left us.

For these reasons, "gothic" has long functioned in the accounts of literary historians as a retrospective term, something coined after the fact to describe a cultural phenomenon. Reviewers at the end of the eighteenth century (including Wollstonecraft) used different expressions: "Modern Romance," "Terrorist School of Writing," "the trash of the Minerva Press," "the German School," and others. Some of these rubrics evoked a kind of fiction, while others described a looser aesthetic crossing the genres. Most were pejorative, seeking to group together particular texts to denigrate them, usually as either vulgarly popular or unattractively foreign. Among canonical romantic writers responding to the sudden popularity of the Gothic as the eighteenth century closed, the most famous examples are Samuel Coleridge – who condemned Matthew Lewis' *The Monk* and Charles Maturin's *Bertram* as pernicious importations – and William Wordsworth, who in 1800 defined his own *Lyrical Ballads* in opposition to "frantic novels, sickly and stupid German Tragedies, and deluges of idle and extravagant stories in verse."[1] In each case, we see an author seeking to distinguish his own (serious, literary, national) work from that of an (extravagant, vulgar, imported) other. When we recall that both poets in these years penned works that could easily be classed as Gothic ("Christabel," "The Rime of the Ancient Mariner," "Osorio," "Salisbury Plain," 'The Borderers," "Goody Blake and Harry Gill," and "Hart-Leap Well," to name only a few), the cultural stakes become clear. With neither "gothic" nor "romantic" available as literary rubrics in the same way as today, late eighteenth-century writers wielded different vocabularies to distinguish themselves from one another and to mark themselves as authors of taste worth reading. More pointedly, the condemnations of Coleridge and Wordsworth remind us that what we today confidently call "gothic" and "romantic" were not, around 1800, so easy to tell apart.

Gothic writing, then, had at least two phases during Wollstonecraft's lifetime: an earlier, sometimes dilettantish one, followed by the onset of sudden and lasting popularity. The former is marked by its antiquarian interest in reviving medieval and Early Modern literature and culture, the latter by the rise of circulating librarian-publishers like Thomas Hookham and William Lane who, in publishing original works of fiction on a larger scale, transformed Gothic into a popular commodity. Horace Walpole's foundational romance, *The Castle of Otranto: A Gothic Story* (1764), provides an illuminating example for understanding the earlier decades before Gothic's sudden popularity. It at once embodies the issues surrounding "gothic" as a term while illustrating some of the key characteristics of Gothic writing more generally. In Walpole's title, "gothic" is primarily a historical marker, one denoting a distant medieval past. He deploys it much in the same way we might use "dark ages" today. *Otranto*'s first edition takes these historical claims even further by presenting it as a genuine artifact of older days: a translation complete with an intricate provenance:

> The following work was found in the library of an ancient catholic family in the north of England. It was printed at Naples, in the black letter, in the year 1529. How much sooner it was written does not appear. The principal incidents are such as were believed in the darkest ages of christianity; but the language and conduct have nothing that savours of barbarism. The style is the purest Italian.[2]

At the time of its initial publication, reviewers were divided on the work's authenticity, the *Monthly Review* choosing to praise it as "a work of genius, evincing great dramatic powers, and exhibiting fine views of nature."[3]

However, when a new preface to *Otranto*'s second edition announced the work to be a forgery, the journal reversed its judgment:

> While we considered it as [really a translation from an ancient writer], we could readily excuse its preposterous phenomena, and consider them as sacrifices to a gross and unenlightened age.—But when, as in this edition, the Castle of Otranto is declared to be a modern performance, that indulgence we afforded to the foibles of a supposed antiquity, we can by no means extend to the singularity of a false taste in a cultivated period of learning. It is, indeed, more than strange, that an Author, of a refined and polished genius, should be an advocate for re-establishing the barbarous superstitions of Gothic devilism![4]

Beyond the journal's obvious embarrassment there is a palpable, more complex confusion, one captured in words like "strange" and "singularity" and in the reviewer's assumption that no writer "in a period of cultivated learning" would care to write about such times or of the supernatural. The defensive tone is also instructive. It is as if the so-called distant period of "barbarous superstitions" still remains a little too close for the reviewer's comfort. To write of "Gothic devilism" in 1764, evidently, is to risk "re-establishing" it. What the reviewer denies are the pleasures of the historical imagination: that readers might enjoy engaging with the distant past as either a means of escape or a way of understanding belief systems not their own.

Still, more is at issue here than the question of which historical documents are worth translating and which centuries worth reimagining. At the core of the *Monthly*'s response are legible anxieties over *Otranto*'s exuberant sense of play, particularly the energy with which it reassembles historical milieu and juggles anachronisms to create new aesthetic experiences. Walpole was not the first to do this. As Robert Miles and Emma Clery have shown pointedly, Gothic writing existed long before *Otranto* – just as Walpole's famous villa, Strawberry Hill, was in no way the first attempt to appropriate Gothic architecture into a modern domestic setting.[5] We find earlier models in Thomas and Batty Langley's *Gothic Architecture, Improved* (1741), in the poetry of the William Collins, in novels like Smollett's *Ferdinand Count Fathom* (1757) and Thomas Leland's *Longsword* (1762), in new plays like *Douglas* (1757), and in the continuing popularity of older plays like Shakespeare's *Hamlet*, *Macbeth*, and *Richard III*, all of which make ghostly visitations central to their stories. Eighteenth-century critics were genuinely divided on Shakespeare's supernaturalism. Acknowledging the power of key scenes, they nevertheless dismissed theatrical specters either as relics of an earlier time and as impositions on the rationality of modern audiences – impositions that, in the case of younger viewers, could warp their too credulous minds.[6] Thus, when Robert Jephson in 1781 brought *The Castle of Otranto* to the stage as *The Count of Narbonne*, he stripped Walpole's original of its supernatural vestiges, to great critical and audience approval. A decade later, however, the tide was already turning. Adapting Ann Radcliffe's *Romance of the Forest* (1791) as *Fontainville Forest* for Covent Garden in 1794, James Boaden also departed from his original, but this time in the opposite direction. Where Radcliffe's novel famously supplies rational explanations for its supernatural scenes, Boaden's play transforms its original by providing an actual specter, in this case that of the same murdered Cavalier who has haunted Adeline's dreams. Her fainting dramatically closes the third act. If Jephson had removed most of Walpole's marvels in *The Count of Narbonne*, Boaden chose, in the words of his own epilogue, not "to give up the ghost."[7]

Wollstonecraft's years as a professional writer dovetail nicely with those of Radcliffe, who published her first novel in 1789 and her final one in 1797. Like Radcliffe, Wollstonecraft early in her career penned a short novel of one volume, *Mary: A Fiction* (1788); the bulk of her early writing, however, was non-fiction, done either for periodicals or with an eye to the expanding children's book market. Hired by Joseph Johnson in 1788 to review books on education and sentimental fiction for the *Analytical Review*, Wollstonecraft with time appears to have exercised considerable authority within that periodical over what works – at least those falling "under the rubrics of belles-lettres, education, and moral and religious topics" – were reviewed.[8] Wollstonecraft did not just witness Gothic's rise to popularity, then; she commented on it as a reviewer and quasi-editor as her stature grew. Few eighteenth-century authors experience such rapid ascents in responsibility or prestige, and here again the trajectory of Wollstonecraft's career resonates with that of Radcliffe, whose authorial beginnings were also humble and whose prestige increased dramatically as the 1790s progressed. Nowhere is this expressed more eloquently than on the title pages of her novels. Thus, her first three works – *The Castles of Athlin and Dunbayne* (1789), *The Sicilian Romance* (1790), and *The Romance of the Forest* (1791) – all appear under the imprint of Thomas Hookham of Bond Street, a leading circulating librarian of London. After *The Romance of the Forest* became a critical and popular hit, Radcliffe left Hookham for a more prestigious bookseller, G. G. and J. Robinson, who paid her the unheard-of sum of £900 to bring out her next work, *The Mysteries of Udolpho*. The extraordinary success of this novel led Radcliffe to change publishers one final time; *The Italian* appeared under the imprint of Thomas Cadell, arguably the most celebrated publisher in Britain.[9] Tellingly, it was this final novel that Wollstonecraft chose to review for the *Analytical*.

Radcliffe's ascent from Hookham to Cadell provides one important portrait of Gothic's ascent to omnipresence in literary culture at the turn of the nineteenth century. Another comes via dramatists like Boaden, whose greatest fame stemmed from his successful adaptation of Radcliffe, Lewis, and others to the stage. Gothic's greatest impact, however, arguably came not through its authors and adaptors but instead through publishing firms like William Lane's Minerva Press, whose novels regularly accounted for between one-quarter and one-third of Britain's total production during the 1790s. Within Britain's publishing industry, Lane rose to prominence (and notoriety) through his lucrative circulating library, one of the largest in London. Like Hookham, he began to commission his own books, particularly Gothic and sentimental fiction by women and by new authors. These were most frequently purchased by other for-profit libraries, who found a brisk trade in featuring the newest fiction. Their rarity in archives today stems as much from their popularity (they were often read and reread until they fell to pieces) as from their relatively low cultural status. Jane Austen's *Northanger Abbey* affectionately captures this social aspect of Gothic novel reading, her characters haunting local circulating libraries and, in the face of rain or other foul weather, "shut[ting] themselves up, to read novels together."[10]

Put another way, the popular Gothic novels of the 1790s were primarily books to be borrowed not purchased. At best they were ignored by literary reviewers, who, when they spoke of them at all, usually lumped them with other sentimental fictions to be condemned *en masse*. Certainly Wollstonecraft participated in this act of collective disdain, periodically complaining of "the *cant* of sensibility" and at least once calling novels "the spawn of idleness."[11] Those Gothic fictions that she did notice, however, were often treated with more nuance than was customary, as her review of Radcliffe's *The Italian* demonstrates:

> The nature of the story obliges us to digest improbabilities, and continually to recollect that it is a romance, not a novel, we are reading; especially as the restless curiosity it excites is too often excited by something like stage trick. —We are made to wonder, only to wonder; but the spell, by which we are led, again and again, round the same magic circle, is the spell of genius.[12]

Mixed as the notice is, it is one of the few in which Wollstonecraft ever wielded the word "genius." Typical critical demands, such as probability of incident, are balanced by her openness to the power of mood and artifice. Not requiring worlds functioning according to the dictates of pure reason, she instead asks for scenes to ring true psychologically in ways appropriate to character, time, and setting. She may eschew "improbabilities," but she is willing to grant that standards of probability vary across culture and historical period, a view best articulated in her review of Matthew Lewis' *The Monk*:

> The style is formed, and unaffected, ... but the language and manners of the personages are not sufficiently gothic in their colouring, to agree with the superstitious scenery, borrowed from those times. They want the sombre cast of ignorance, which renders credulity probable: still, the author deserves praise for not attempting to account for supernatural appearances in a natural way.

In this she anticipates the later stipulations of Walter Scott concerning supernatural fiction: a terrified hero may see ghosts, but his doing so must accord with his proclivities and the situation at hand.[13] In this she isolates one of the primary pleasures of the Gothic: that of feeling a character's terror, even if occasioned by phenomena in which the reader does not actually believe.

The opening to Wollstonecraft's final novel, *The Wrongs of Woman; or, Maria*, cultivates many of these same effects:

> Abodes of Horror have frequently been described, and castles, filled with spectres and chimeras, conjured up by the magic spell of genius to harrow the soul, and absorb the wondering mind. But, formed of such stuff as dreams are made of, what were they to the mansion of despair, in one corner of which Maria sat, endeavouring to recall her scattered thoughts![14]

The passage ostentatiously invokes Gothic structures to dismiss them – or, at least, to assert the primacy of human consciousness in creating its own scenes of terror. The "mansion of despair" Maria occupies, after all, is very much the product of her own mind. But Wollstonecraft's point is not simply one of replacing the supernatural with subjectivity. The Gothic not only establishes the atmosphere for Wollstonecraft's novel; it provides a suitable language for describing how ideology and gender work in tandem to create the "wrongs of woman." For Wollstonecraft gives her readers not the usual ingénue trapped in a distant castle and historical setting, but a modern English woman imprisoned in a private madhouse by her unscrupulous husband, Mr. Venables. In this, she seeks to tap Gothic's popular readership while denying them the usual comfort of geographical and temporal distance. Instead, *Maria*'s horrors are resolutely of the here and now, belonging at once to Britain and to the present day.

As with most Gothic fictions featuring heroines, *Maria* is replete with traps, and its drama arises out of Maria's ability to recognize and avoid them. Seeing her enthusiasm for schemes of charity, Venables presents himself first as a man of feeling and then as a suitor by contributing to a favorite cause of hers. He is able to seduce Maria into marriage by the means of her own over-cultivated sensibility. The novel's opening is thus set up by the questions similar to those Wollstonecraft treated as an educational writer, where sensibility threatens to trap women by privileging feeling over reason. Here, however, the risks of such instruction are higher, and their effects more recognizably Gothic. In a novel filled with seductions and attempted seductions, every form of feeling becomes a potential snare. Thus Maria, writing to her daughter, looks up to find that, instead of looking for a means of escape, she has been happily indulging in writing a sentimental autobiographical cautionary tale to her. She is similarly transported after Darnford declares his love for her, so much so that she hardly notices the walls of her prison. For her husband Venables, seduction masks a still more dangerous snare, his will to power, which leads to her eventual incarceration and his taking away her child. Wollstonecraft's analysis thus ranges well beyond these critiques of sensibility, women's education, and marriage as an institution. It extends, with the introduction of Darnford's and Jemima's stories, to subjects as broad as imperial capitalism, class, and the nature of same-sex friendships. These are vividly captured in the wide variety of endings that Wollstonecraft sketched for *Maria*, all of which conspicuously draw on Gothic conventions. These range from exile and suicide to climactic trials for adultery; most deny Maria the sentimental solace of Darnford's love.

That Wollstonecraft chose the Gothic to clothe key scenes of her final work suggests more than merely her desire to reach the broadest spectrum of readers. The aesthetic presented her with a language for representing extreme situations and states of mind. Usually set long ago and in distant lands, Gothic fiction and drama regularly rendered visible – at a safe distance – the ties between ideology and oppression, particularly between the sexes. Novels set in thirteenth-century Italy, sixteenth-century Spain, or seventeenth-century France could traffic in attempted rape, forced marriage, or abduction and confinement, thrilling English readers while assuring them of their comparative liberty, safety, and enlightenment. "Consider the dreadful nature of the suspicions you have entertained," says *Northanger Abbey*'s Henry Tilney to Catherine Morland, who has dared him over the circumstances of his mother's death: "Does our education prepare us for such atrocities? Do our laws connive at them?"[15]

In transporting Gothic scenes to present-day England, Wollstonecraft's most startling innovation was to give the lie to such comforting assertions.

Notes

 1 Samuel Coleridge, Review of *The Monk*, *The Critical Review*, 2nd series, 19 (1797), 194–98; and *Biographia Literaria* (London: Fenner, 1817), 2: 254–92. William Wordsworth, *Lyrical Ballads* (London: Longman & Rees, 1800), 1: xix.
 2 Horace Walpole, *The Castle of Otranto* (London: Thomas Lownds, 1765), iii. Though carrying the date of 1765, Walpole's novel was published on Christmas day of 1764.
 3 *Monthly Review*, 32 (February, 1765), 99.
 4 *Monthly Review*, 32 (May, 1765), 394.
 5 As a revived architectural style, Gothic was first popularized by the engravings that appeared in Thomas and Batty Langley's *Gothic Architecture, Improved*, which was first published in 1741 under the title of *Ancient Architecture*. Walpole criticized Langley's attempts to graft Gothic decorations on to classical forms. On gothic writing before 1764, see Emma Clery and Robert Miles, *Gothic Documents: A Sourcebook, 1700–1820* (Manchester: Manchester University Press, 2000), 1–3.
 6 See Robert P. Reno, "James Boaden's *Fontainville Forest* and Matthew Lewis's *The Castle Spectre*: Challenges of the Supernatural Ghost on the Late Eighteenth-Century Stage," *Eighteenth-Century Life*, 9 (1984), 95–106.
 7 James Boaden, *Fontainville Forest: A Play* (London: Hookham & Carpenter, 1794), 69.
 8 Mary A. Waters, *British Women Writers and the Profession of Literary Criticism, 1789–1832* (Basingstoke: Palgrave Macmillan, 2004), 110.
 9 Charles H. Timperley, *A Dictionary of Printers and Printing* (London: H. Johnson, 1839), 814–15.
10 Jane Austen, *Northanger Abbey and Persuasion* (London: John Murray, 1818), 1: 61.
11 Review of *Edward and Harriet, or the Happy Recovery*, *Analytical Review*, 1 (1788), 207; and Review of *Man as He Is*, *Analytical Review*, 24 (1796), 398.
12 Review of Ann Radcliffe, *The Italian*, *Analytical Review*, 25 (May 1797), 516.
13 See Walter Scott, "Horace Walpole," *Prose Works of Sir Walter Scott, Bart* (Edinburgh: Cadell, 1834–6), 3: 313–17.
14 Mary Wollstonecraft, *The Wrongs of Woman*, *Posthumous Works* (London: J. Johnson), 1: 16.
15 Austen, *Northanger Abbey and Persuasion*, 2: 186.

CHAPTER 35

Travel Writing

Pamela Perkins

During her short life, Mary Wollstonecraft managed to visit a wide swathe of Western Europe, spending time in Lisbon, Ireland, France, and Scandinavia. None of these journeys were pleasure travel: she went to Lisbon to help a dying friend, to Ireland and France to attempt to earn money as a governess and, less conventionally, as what might today be called a journalist, and to Scandinavia to untangle the business problems of her lover Gilbert Imlay. She was not unique among women of her class and era in going abroad for work or out of duty to friends and family: her friend Eliza Fenwick, for one, traveled even further afield while trying to establish a career as a teacher, moving from Ireland to Barbados to New York to Canada.[1] Wollstonecraft, however, turned this travel-by-necessity into a literary opportunity, using her Scandinavian journey as the basis for her final book, *Letters Written during a Short Residence in Sweden, Norway, and Denmark* (1796), which, of all her works, was perhaps the one most admired by her contemporaries. As many critics have noted, *A Short Residence* was not a straightforward travelogue: summing up more than two decades of work on the book, Ingrid Horrocks observes that it has been read as "blending discourses of political philosophy, landscape aesthetics, and sentimental travel."[2] Yet in some respects, that generic slipperiness makes the book very much at home in an era when there was no clear answer to the question of what a "typical" travelogue ought to look like. Not only was the nature of pleasure travel changing during the final years of the eighteenth century, becoming more accessible to women and to the middle classes in general (as critics including William H. A. Williams, Alastair Durie, and George Dekker have noted), but also the idea that travel narratives existed mainly or exclusively to convey factual information about unfamiliar lands and cultures was beginning to fall apart. Wollstonecraft, as a woman traveler, as a travel writer, and as a critic of travel herself, was positioned at the heart of one of the later eighteenth century's more lively literary debates.

297

Travel writing has always been something of a baggy monster. Tim
Youngs and Carl Thompson open their recent critical surveys of the genre
for (respectively) Cambridge and Routledge with mildly frustrated
accounts of the challenges posed by trying to delineate "this stubbornly
indefinable form" and to negotiate the lack of "scholarly consensus" about
it.[3] There is no question that late eighteenth-century writers were struggling as well to reach any sort of agreement about what the genre was
supposed to achieve. Granted, in his groundbreaking 1978 study *Pleasurable Instruction*, Charles L. Batten argues that the earlier eighteenth century had been "quite unanimous in its attitudes toward the proper form of
travel literature," assuming that whether "describ[ing] the wilds of Canada
or the refinements of Paris," the goal of the traveler was to create a smooth
"blending of factual information and literary art."[4] Yet these clear generic
parameters were probably always more apparent in theory than in practice,
and even Batten admits that any consensus about them was breaking down
by the last decades of century, with "pleasure" becoming "divorced from
instruction," leaving travel writing to split into the guidebook on the one
hand and sentimental travel, in which the focus is on the subjective
experience of the traveler, on the other.[5] More recent scholarship has also
offered a more nuanced reading of the history of the genre, with Nigel
Leask, for one, documenting the lively, often passionate, debates about the
nature of travel writing taking place in the years around 1800 and making
a very strong case for placing any split between the pleasurable and the
utilitarian later in the nineteenth century.[6] There is no question that some
of the most influential early nineteenth-century readers continued to take
for granted that a travel writer could – and *should* – attempt to mediate
objective information about place through his or her individual taste and
judgment. In an 1802 article in *The Edinburgh Review*, for example, Henry
Brougham noted, as a commonplace, that the finest works of travel writing
are admirable precisely because the factual information that they provide is
reinforced by the pleasure that they give through their "picture ... of the
traveller's mind, and of the impressions made upon it by the scenes
through which he passed."[7] Likewise, a writer for the 1806 volume of
the *Annual Review* thought that travels were "of all books, perhaps, the
best calculated to excite a strong and general interest" in all classes of
readers, because the presentation of their utilitarian content within an
aesthetic framework ensured that they appealed equally to "the mere
lounger, with whom reading is only a creditable kind of idleness" and
"to the philosopher, who derives from books the materials of useful

contemplation."[8] A writer for *The Eclectic* made a similar point but ratcheted up the rhetoric, declaring that the literary work of travelers was "of high importance" to both "the improvement and happiness of the human race."[9] Given such inflated expectations of the genre in terms of both pleasure and utility, it is perhaps not surprising that when, in 1807, a correspondent of *The Monthly Magazine* proposed an informal, nationwide program of "rational instruction" for the lower classes through the establishment of small parish libraries, he was imagining a utilitarian but accessible collection consisting almost entirely of "Books of Agriculture, History, [and] Modern Voyages and Travels."[10]

Yet even as the literary travelogue was becoming established as a relatively high-status genre because of its supposed ability to merge the aesthetic and the utilitarian, Wollstonecraft and other travelers of the day were confronting an increasingly fractured understanding of what constituted either instruction or appropriate forms of literary pleasure. There was for one thing a marked tendency, even in reviews that are celebratory about the genre as a whole, to take sharp issue with individual writers' choices about what information to present and how to present it. At least in part, that was because the growing accessibility of travel meant that writers were less and less able to claim that they were providing a vital contribution to knowledge in writing about the places they visited. The weary sighs with which, by the first decade of the nineteenth century, reviewers were greeting books on the Scottish Highlands[11] or the more accessible parts of the Continent underscore the struggle to reconcile representations of (literally) well-trodden ground with a sense of the importance of the genre. By the end of the century, many of the reviews of travelogues explicitly debate what constitutes informative travel, with some readers insisting that only those explorers who sought out "new" territory could be seen as making valuable contributions, while others attempted to develop a more inclusive vision of travel as a sort of experimental science that would benefit from repeated data-gathering. After all, as a writer for *The English Review* argued in 1784, "science is ... the result of our comparisons of ideas and things with one another" and so "different travellers may go over the same ground, and yet their observations may on the whole be very different."[12]

Wollstonecraft took a different approach in her contributions to this critical debate. She was acutely aware of the challenges of making an original contribution to the genre, opening her review of Samuel Ireland's *Picturesque Tour through Holland, Brabant, and Part of France,* for example, by noting dryly that as "every inch of the continent has been described with scrupulous exactness by flying and loitering, sprightly and *vapourish* travellers," Ireland has set himself a difficult task. Likewise, in her very positive review of Alexander Jardine's *Letters from Barbary, France, Spain, Portugal, etc.*, she explicitly sets the author apart from what she describes as the increasing numbers of contemporary travelers who rely on a "parade of insipid candour" and "the heightened description of a trifle" to make up for their lack of any new or interesting material.[13] In praising Ireland and Jardine, however, Wollstonecraft does not merely assert that they have managed to make original observations about the places that they visited; more importantly, she constructs an expanded concept of what can be counted as useful "facts." In her article on Ireland, she argues that rather than being a mere aesthetic flourish, "picturesque views ... may be termed matters of fact" as they provide "a distinct general idea of a view or building, which can seldom be collected from dry descriptions."[14] Likewise, she sees Jardine's work as being at its strongest when it evinces "the spirit of the first composition" in its accounts of place, implying that it is a traveler's immediate, emotional engagement with his material that is most informative, rather than any later reflections upon or research into what he or she has observed.[15]

That said, Wollstonecraft's explanation of what enables Jardine to stand apart from his competitors might complicate matters. According to her review, his work reveals him to be "a manly Englishman" as well as "a reflecting man," inclined to "reveries" on the social and political systems that he observes with "a calm, penetrating eye."[16] These terms reinforce a predictable eighteenth-century critical tendency to see those travel writers who escape banality or repetitiveness as possessing qualities associated, implicitly or explicitly, with elite, educated men, making the "traveler's mind" that Brougham and others see as being so delightfully pictured in the best travel writing implicitly male. As a reviewer for *The Monthly Magazine* complains in 1789, the travelogue is being compromised as a genre because "the generality" of travelers who publish their work are "unqualified to make useful remarks" on the social, political, and cultural environments of the places that they are visiting and thus unable to provide their readers with anything but an "uninteresting detail of trifling incidents"[17] that is neither useful nor pleasing. The idea that a traveler needed a particular set of intellectual "qualifications" in order to produce a book about his journey (and the pronoun is appropriate in this context) of course recalls Clifford Siskin's arguments about the professionalization of literary work, which Siskin identifies as beginning in the late eighteenth century and gathering force in the early decades of the nineteenth. Notably, a quarter of a century later, another writer for the same review was making essentially the same complaint but in much greater detail, and not coincidentally doing so in a review of a book by a woman. This later reviewer suggests that as travel has become democratized, travel writing has lost any intellectual edge; he grumbles that the present generation of "publishing pilgrims" think "a sufficient supply of clean notebooks" and "clean linen" is all that is necessary to make a travel writer. In addition, he claims, they "regard requisites of a literary kind as superfluous," not only neglecting to study the history and culture of the places they are visiting before setting out, but also failing to exercise taste or judgment about what is worth seeing, relying instead on post-tour plagiarism as they write up their notes for publication. His conclusion is that because of such "unqualified" travel writers, the travelogue is at risk of dissolving into garbled trivialities, offering readers little other than banal observations about the "prodigious organ at Haarlem" or the "wonderfully rich and magnificent" Louvre.[18]

While neither of the *Monthly's* reviewers explicitly limits his complaints to women travel writers, there is a distinctly gendered edge to the criticism. Women, especially of the upper classes, had always traveled, whether they did so simply to get from town to country or estate to estate (a form of female mobility that Katharine Glover suggests has tended to be over-looked in the study of travel)[19] or to join in a version of the Grand Tour, which Brian Dolan has shown attracted a number of later eighteenth-century leisured British women. What was changing in the last decades of the eighteenth century was, as Elizabeth Bohls, Zoë Kinsley, Betty Hag-glund, and others have noted, that increasing numbers of those women were both writing about and publishing those travels, a literary develop-ment which overlaps very neatly with the critical backlash directed against "unqualified" travelers who chose to publish. Nor was it only critics who associated "good" travel and travel writing with a masculine perspective. Leopold Berchtold, who wrote a handbook for would-be intellectual travelers, clearly did not have women in mind when he advised his readers to be prepared to show their "fire-arms to the landlord in a familiar discourse ... and to tell him with a courageous look, that you are not afraid of a far superior number of enemies."[20] More subtly, his advice to seek out local public officials and other prominent citizens to interview about matters of government and policy reinforces gendered concepts of what counts as useful information – precisely what Wollstonecraft was combating in her reviews.

Granted, there are points in her own work as a travel writer at which Wollstonecraft seems to share those gendered views. As many readers have noted, when she relays the praise of a Swedish official who admires her willingness to ask "men's questions,"[21] she is positioning herself within the very masculine tradition of "informative" travel. Doing so would probably have been a very tempting move, as Scandinavia was not a particularly well-known region in Britain at the time and so the field was open for a writer to stake out a place in the safely high-status genre of informational travel. While there had been a handful of published accounts in the years before Wollstonecraft visited – Nathaniel Wraxall's 1775 *Cursory Remarks Made in a Tour through Some of the Northern Parts of Europe*, for example, or William Coxe's 1784 *Travels into Poland, Russia, Sweden and Denmark* – there was still ample room for more factual accounts of the territory, and Wollstonecraft seems, at times, ready to oblige, providing accounts of everything from Scandinavian methods of heating buildings to the legalities of tenancy and land transfer in Norway. Yet at the same time, she attempts to infuse her accounts of the world around her with the passionate immediacy that she found wanting in some of Jardine's social and political observations, and the result is a book that her contemporaries found particularly feminine, notwithstanding the "men's questions" that Wollstonecraft was asking. Famously, William Godwin described it as a work "calculated to make a man in love with its author," while Wollstonecraft's friend Amelia Opie proclaimed herself dazzled by the "interesting creature of feeling, & imagination" that she saw reflected in the narrative.[22] In effect, what Wollstonecraft is doing is challenging any conventionally gendered concept of travel, demonstrating that collecting and transmitting information neither precludes emotional engagement with a place nor requires the writer to avoid subjective impressions and self-revelation.

When Wollstonecraft set out for Portugal in 1785 to help a dying friend, she was traveling for love and duty, not curiosity and pleasure, and she chose not to write about – or at least not to publish – her experiences. Her journey to Scandinavia ten years later was no less utilitarian and perhaps even more emotionally charged, as it was a final, unsuccessful attempt to maintain a relationship with Gilbert Imlay, the father of the infant child who accompanied her. Yet this time she decided to publish. What happened in the interim was that Wollstonecraft read, thought about, and wrote about travel writing in a way that allowed her to translate personal experience into a literary work in which she attempted to explore and confront some of the challenges and pitfalls that she and other critics identified in the genre. *A Vindication of the Rights of Woman* might still be Wollstonecraft's most familiar engagement with feminist theory, but as a traveler, as a critic of travel writing, and as a travel writer herself, she helped to shape a place for women in one of the late eighteenth century's more popular, if contentious, genres.

Notes

1 Isobel Grundy, "Introduction," in Eliza Fenwick, *Secresy; or The Ruin on the Rock* (Peterborough: Broadview Press, 1994), 16–20.
2 Ingrid Horrocks, "Creating an 'Insinuating Interest': Mary Wollstonecraft's Travel Reviews and *A Short Residence*," *Studies in Travel Writing*, 19:1 (2015), 2.
3 Tim Youngs, *The Cambridge Introduction to Travel Writing* (Cambridge University Press, 2014), 2; Carl Thompson, *Travel Writing* (Abingdon: Routledge, 2011), 13.
4 Charles L. Batten, *Pleasurable Instruction: Form and Convention in Eighteenth-Century Travel Literature* (Berkeley: University of California Press, 1978), xi, 30.
5 Batten, *Pleasurable Instruction*, 30.
6 Nigel Leask, *Curiosity and the Aesthetics of Travel Writing, 1770–1840: From an Antique Land* (Oxford: Oxford University Press, 2002), 5–14.
7 Henry Brougham, Review of Joseph Acerbi's *Travels through Sweden...*, *The Edinburgh Review*, 1:1 (1802), 163.
8 Anon., "Voyages and Travels," *The Annual Review*, 4:1 (1806): 1.
9 Anon., Review of John Barrow's *Travels in China*, *The Eclectic Review*, 1.1 (1805), 241.
10 Anon., "Plan for Village Libraries," *The Monthly Magazine*, 24:2 (1807), 28.
11 For example, see Sir Walter Scott's article "Carr's *Caledonian Sketches*," *The Quarterly Review*, 1:1 (1809), 155–69.
12 Anon., Review of *Observations on the Present State of Denmark, Russia, and Switzerland*, *The English Review*, 3 (1784), 331.
13 Mary Wollstonecraft, Review of Ireland's *Picturesque Tour*, in *The Works of Mary Wollstonecraft*, edited by Janet Todd and Marilyn Butler (New York: New York University Press, 1989), 7: 301, 107.
14 Wollstonecraft, *Works*, 7: 301
15 Ibid., 156
16 Ibid., 107–08.
17 Anon., Review of *Letters on Greece*, *The Monthly Review*, 80 (1789), 377.
18 Anon., Review of *Letters from the North Highlands*, *The Monthly Review*, 86 (1818), 311–12.
19 Katharine Glover, *Elite Women and Polite Society in Eighteenth-Century Scotland* (Woodbridge: Boydell & Brewer, 2011), 140.

20 Leopold Berchtold, *An Essay to Direct and Extend the Inquiries of Patriotic Travelers*. (London, Robinson et. al., 1789), 69.
21 Wollstonecraft, *Works*, 6: 248
22 Quoted in Wollstonecraft, *Letters Written in Sweden, Norway, and Denmark*, edited by Tone Brekke and Jon Mee (Oxford: Oxford University Press, 2009), ix.

CHAPTER 36

History Writing
Jonathan Sachs

In the *Vindication of the Rights of Men*, the first published response to Edmund Burke's *Reflections on the Revolution in France*, Mary Wollstonecraft imagines a scene in an uncertain future when London will be in ruins. "The time may come," she observes, "when the traveler may ask where proud London stood? When its temples, its laws, and its trade, may be buried in one common ruin, and only serve as a byword to point a moral, or furnish senators, who wage a wordy war, on the other side of the Atlantic, with tropes to swell their thundering bursts of eloquence."[1] The passage dismisses the Latinate diction and classical citations that characterize Burke's work, and locates the movement of history toward the Americas, where new progressive societies will draw their morals from an old society in decline, much as Britain had taken Rome as its model. The passage thus sits uneasily in a work dedicated to the inevitable improvement of society through the progress of reason. Not everything will improve, Wollstonecraft implies, and some societies out of step with the march of reason may even fall into ruin. The moment thus reveals a tenuous ambivalence in Wollstonecraft's belief in progress, an ambivalence that runs through Wollstonecraft's thinking about history and historical process. The episode also shows Wollstonecraft working in what we might call the future perfect mode, in which she looks back from the vantage point of an unspecified later time to evaluate her own ongoing present. Wollstonecraft's concern with progress and her belief in a better future means that she writes of the past always with an eye to the future and the anticipated norms of later times. This chapter will suggest that the evaluation of the present from the vantage of the future and the tensions that shadow her belief in progress are closely related and salient features of Wollstonecraft's historical writing.

Wollstonecraft's best known works – the initial *Vindication of the Rights of Men* that first brought her national recognition when the second edition acknowledged her authorship in 1790 and the subsequent *Vindication of*

305

the Rights of Woman that cemented her reputation in 1792 and made her
"the first female member of the canon of Western political thought"² –
treat politics from a theoretical perspective, but also a historical one. While
attentive to principle, both *Vindications* are careful to speculate about the
historical development of the principles upon which they rest. Hence, for
example, the second *Vindication* announces itself as the result of "considering the historic page."³ The work itself is, admittedly, more engaged with
attacking contemporary writing on the education of women by men like
Jean-Jacques Rousseau, James Fordyce, and John Gregory. Nonetheless, its
first chapter locates rights and duties in the origin of society and then closes
with a brief account of how monarchy, aristocracy, and priesthood consoli-
date themselves in "the infancy of society."⁴ All of Wollstonecraft's work
combines an interest in the sweep of history with what she repeatedly calls
"the science of politics." Consequently, Wollstonecraft writes as one who
uses her sense of the past to anticipate what the future will bring but also as
one whose confident sense of the future impresses her account of the past.

Given Wollstonecraft's tendency to grasp politics in conjunction with
the movement of history, we should not be surprised that her one full-
length work of historical writing, *A Historical and Moral View of the French
Revolution* (1794) uses a historical frame to articulate a theory of politics.
This work traces the course of the French Revolution from conflicts between
the crown and the nobles through the storming of the Bastille and the
Declaration of the Rights of Man, before concluding with the march on
Versailles in October 1789. The work alternates reflective passages with a
substantial narrative of events compiled by Wollstonecraft from British
sources like *The New Annual Register* and Thomas Christie's *Letters on the
Revolution in France* (1791) and French ones, including Mirabeau's *Courrier
de Provence* (1789–91), the Assemblée Nationale's *Journal des débats et des
décrets* (1789–91), and Lally-Tollendal's *Mémoire* (1790). A tendency to
paraphrase her sources at length perhaps led to the work being overlooked
by scholars until recently, but the *Historical and Moral View* can now be
understood as a central articulation of Wollstonecraft's mature social and
political ideals. One scholar even ventures that it may be "Wollstonecraft's
best work."⁵ The *Historical and Moral View* was widely and favorably
reviewed upon its appearance, with Wollstonecraft praised for her "calm
and philosophical eye"; for being "truly philosophical"; and for writing "not
like an annalist, but like a philosopher."⁶ Such repeated emphasis on the
philosophical qualities of Wollstonecraft's historiography suggest that, as
Jane Rendall first argued, Scottish Enlightenment historiography shaped
Wollstonecraft's understanding of the Revolution.⁷

Though there are certainly differences between them, the work of Scottish historians like David Hume, William Robertson, John Millar, Lord Kames, and others emphasized a personal dimension of historical experience over and against more traditional historiographies focused on the activities and political decisions of great men.[8] Scottish historical writing tended to emphasize progress, especially as associated with the development of civilization in European societies. Such an approach can be characterized, then, by its focus on the concept of civilization, by a related moral philosophy that highlighted the power of sympathy and sociability, and by an awareness of the historical development of the economic conditions of production. As Millar claimed in his influential work on *The Origin and Distinction of Ranks* (1771), "There is ... in human society, a natural progress from ignorance to knowledge, and from rude to civilized manners, the several stages of which are usually accompanied with peculiar laws and customs."[9]

Even in narratives ostensibly framed by politics or titled after great men like William Robertson's *History of the Reign of the Emperor Charles V* (1769), Scottish Enlightenment historiography shifted its focus away from the activities and political intrigues, the wars and conflicts, of kings, princes, emperors, and their advisors and toward the history of societies, economies, improvement, and manners. Hugh Blair, for example, wrote in his *Lectures on Rhetoric and Belles Lettres* that "whatever displays the state and life of mankind, in different periods, and illustrates the progress of the human mind, is more useful and interesting than the detail of sieges and battles."[10] Given this emphasis on manners, sociability, and sympathy, the history of family forms and gender relations broadly considered and the role and social status of women in particular was a fundamental concern for Scottish Enlightenment thinkers and often the measure of civilization through which various societies were evaluated. Millar, for example, devotes the first of six chapters of *The Origin of the Distinction of Ranks* to "the rank and condition of women in different ages," while William Alexander focuses entirely on the position of women in his *History of Women from the Earliest Antiquity to the Present Time* (1779). In this work, he draws on Millar to claim "the rank ... and condition, in which we find women in any country, mark out to us with the greatest precision, the exact point in the scale of civil society, to which the people of such country have arrived."[11]

But how did societies reach the highest forms of civilization? Those writing in the Scottish tradition attempted to generalize about this question, and they considered themselves philosophical because "they believed that explanations in history should refer to general causes, to universally applicable generalisations about individual behaviour and social development, across historical time and the cultural variety of the present."[12] Linking historical development to the mode of production, the Scots understood the movement from hunting and gathering to pastoral to settled agricultural production to, finally, commercial society as an ineluctable series of four stages that societies passed through as they became more sophisticated. Such histories consistently emphasized the slow and gradual changes in manners that formed the backbone of their increasingly self-conscious program of historical studies.[13] Kames, for example, in his *Historical Law Tracts*, says of the transition from private revenge to penal codes that, "A Revolution so contradictory to the strongest propensity of human nature, could not by any power, or by any artifice, be instantaneous. It behoved to be gradual, and in fact, the progressive Steps tending to its completion, were slow, and, taken singly, almost imperceptible."[14] Scottish Enlightenment historians, then, grounded their thinking in a moral philosophy that stressed the power of sympathy and the advanced manners that result from the growth of human sociability. Their histories were largely stories of progress and improvement.

Wollstonecraft's *Historical and Moral View* shares this belief in progress and self-consciously identifies itself with the philosophical tradition of Scottish historiography. The "Advertisement" announces that it will offer "descriptions of manners and things which, though not strictly necessary to elucidate the events, are intimately connected with the main object" and further warns readers that they will encounter "several theoretical investigations, whilst marking the political effects that naturally flow from the progress of knowledge."[15] The "Preface" then states that the work will "guard against the erroneous inferences of sensibility" and take as its guide only reason, judgment, and "the cool eye of observation".[16] On this basis, Wollstonecraft remains optimistic that the spread of knowledge associated with the Enlightenment and considered to be the basis of the Revolution will bring continued progress and an improved future state. As she notes, "at no period has the scanty diffusion of knowledge permitted the body of the people to participate in the discussion of political science; and if philosophy at length have simplified the principles of social union, so as to render them easy to be comprehended by every sane and thinking being; it appears to me, that man may contemplate with benevolent complacency and becoming pride, the approaching reign of reason and peace."[17] Politics, for Wollstonecraft, is a science, one capable of solving social problems and ushering in a future "reign of reason and peace."

Because politics is considered a science, improvements in politics participated in the general spread of science and learning. Identifying such advances specifically with navigation, astronomy and mathematics, and the spread of print,[18] Wollstonecraft suggests that these developments distinguish the advanced European present from past barbarism. The combination of technology and philosophy is crucial. Scottish Enlightenment historians like John Millar notably measured the stages of society and the progress of manners through the position of women in society, and Wollstonecraft also implies this link when she notes that "arts and commerce have given to society the transcendently pleasing polish of urbanity; and thus, by a gradual softening of manners, the complexion of social life has been completely changed".[19] This suggests that Wollstonecraft, like Scottish Enlightenment historians, understood progress in domestic terms: commerce and industry replace war and conflict and thus enable domestic happiness, making the commercial stage of society inseparable from the improved situation of the family. This is a general picture of present and future improvement where theoretical advances in moral and political philosophy (now considered as sciences) combine with advances in technology made possible by other sciences and the distribution of learning through the proliferation of print to reshape public and private life through reason on a newly established basis of equality. The general history of progress that Wollstonecraft wants to associate with the French Revolution, then, conforms to her vision for the improved prospects of women and the famous "revolution in female manners" that she proposed in the second *Vindication*.[20]

Wollstonecraft wrote the *Historical and Moral View* while living in France between December 1792 and April 1795, but it covers only the lead-up to the revolutionary events of 1789 and stops with the October Days, when a group of Parisian women protesting bread prices marched to Versailles and compelled the royal family to return with them to Paris. This was the violent episode upon which Burke focused such venom in the *Reflections*, inspiring his lament for chivalry, his praise of Marie Antoinette, and his prediction that the Revolution would devolve into savagery. Wollstonecraft similarly takes offense at the force of revolutionary violence. The October Days and other violent episodes raise a broader problem for her narrative: if history, spurred by the advance of reason and related developments in technology, tends ineluctably toward improvement, why does the Revolution fail and how can we explain revolutionary violence? Such questions are amplified by Wollstonecraft's writing about the early days of the Revolution while living during the later Reign of

Terror (1793–94) when revolutionary bloodshed was the order of the day. Wollstonecraft's central task in the *Historical and Moral View* was thus to maintain her belief in radical principles despite the Revolution's violent turn.

Wollstonecraft addresses such questions through the issue of pace – should change be gradual or rapid? – and argues that the French Revolution attempts to accelerate progress beyond its natural pace. The Revolution thus seeks to impose on French society a set of politically advanced norms that it is not yet mature enough to incorporate. Wollstonecraft sees the French as a frivolous people with refined manners but corrupt morals and hence dismisses them as "the most unqualified of any people in Europe to undertake the important work in which they are embarked."[21] The tenacity of chivalry and political absolutism corrupted the nobles by enabling licentiousness while preventing the lower classes from the education that would allow them best to consider their interests. As Wollstonecraft explains, "The depravity of the higher class, and the ignorance of the lower respecting practical political science, rendered them equally incapable of thinking for themselves; so that the measures which flattered the foibles, or gratified the weakness of either, were sure to have great influence in producing a schism in the public mind; which gave an opportunity to the enemies of the revolution to impede its course."[22] Again, we see the emphasis on political science and the implied sense that if people developed their reason such that they understood basic political principles, society could not but move in the direction of progress and improvement. But chivalry and the corrupt set of manners associated with it – especially, as the first chapter explains, the French attraction to theatricality – prevents this recognition.

One way of thinking about this problem would be to ask whether, if chivalry blocks the progress promised by advances in freedom, it is acceptable to pursue the rapid destruction of prejudice and outdated social forms. Wollstonecraft's unequivocal answer is no, that change must always be established gradually and that those in power must ensure that the process is not unduly hasty. As she puts it, "in the infancy of society, and during the advancement of the science of political liberty, it is highly necessary for the governing authority to be guided by the progress of that science; and to prevent, by judicious measures, any check being given to its advancement, whilst equal care is taken not to produce the miseries of anarchy by encouraging licentious freedom."[23] If politics is a science, one thing it teaches is timing. The central problem of the French Revolution, then, was not the principles on which it was established, but rather the unfavorable circumstances and unpromising manners created by the *ancien régime* that hindered the gradual introduction of those principles. The French, on account of chivalry, were immature and unprepared for the advances of political science.

The problem then is twofold. First, there is the issue of the French character. "It has been a common remark of moralists," Wollstonecraft notes, "that we are the least acquainted with our own characters. This has been literally the case with the French: for certainly no people stand in such great need of a check; and, totally destitute of experience in political science, it must have been clear to all men of sound understanding, that some such plan alone would have enabled them to avoid many fatal errours."[24] Then there is the issue of the Revolution's leaders. Wollstonecraft declares that, "Contemplating the progress of the revolution, a melancholy reflection is produced by observing, that almost every precipitate event has been the consequence of a tenacity and littleness of mind in the political actors, whilst they were affecting a roman magnanimity of conduct to which they appear to have been as great strangers, as they were destitute of legitimate patriotism, and political science."[25] The two problems are related, furthermore, since it is the very manners of their own society that corrupt French leaders and make them incapable of properly applying the principles of advanced political science. The corruption of the French national character, in other words, necessitated the Revolution, but such degeneracy also prevented the success of the Revolution, even if founded on sound principles.

But is this a problem for the French Revolution or revolution generally? What are the lessons of the French Revolution for the political science of the future and the potential for continued progress? Returning to the fantasy of London in ruins with which this chapter opened, one lesson is that the return to barbarism is not inevitable, but that rule by hereditary riches and rank will surely provoke instability and eventually ruin. Hence the implied warning to Britain in the imagined occasion of senators from the America's swelling their rhetoric with Burkean examples. But Wollstonecraft offers more than a negative warning in the *Historical and Moral View*, and she maintains – an admittedly ambivalent – hope despite the undeniable carnage of the Revolution by using its failure to articulate a firm belief in gradual change. Wollstonecraft criticizes the haste with which the popular will tried to accelerate the course of change and suggests instead a vision of the future where, "if every day extending freedom be more firmly established in consequence of the general dissemination of truth and knowledge: it then seems injudicious for statesmen to force the adoption of any opinion, by aiming at the speedy destruction of obstinate prejudices; because these premature reforms, instead of promoting, destroy the comfort of those unfortunate beings, who are under their dominion, affording at the same time to despotism the strongest arguments to urge in opposition to the theory of reason. Besides, the objects intended to be forwarded are probably retarded, whilst the tumult of internal commotion and civil discord leads to the most dreadful consequence – the immolating of human victims."[26] Violence comes from haste.

Ultimately, then, Wollstonecraft offers an anti-revolutionary reading of the French Revolution, one that thus uses her long view of history, her belief in the inevitable progress that will result from the spread of political science, to argue for gradualism. As Wollstonecraft proclaims in the last paragraph of her final work, "An ardent affection for the human race makes enthusiastic characters eager to produce alteration in laws and governments prematurely. To render them useful and permanent, they must be the growth of each particular soil, and the gradual fruit of the ripening understanding of the nation, matured by time, not forced by unnatural fermentation."[27] But, Wollstonecraft concludes, had her account of the French Revolution not already proven this, her Scandinavian travels would have convinced her that such slow change now transpires with "an accelerating pace."[28]

Notes

1 Mary Wollstonecraft, *A Vindication of the Rights of Man and A Vindication of the Rights of Woman*, edited by Sylvana Tomaselli (Cambridge: Cambridge University Press, 1995), 37.
2 Daniel I. O'Neill, "John Adams versus Mary Wollstonecraft on the French Revolution and Democracy," *Journal of the History of Ideas*, 68:3 (2007), 42.
3 Wollstonecraft, *A Vindication of the Rights of Woman*, 74.
4 Ibid., 85.
5 Tom Furniss, "Mary Wollstonecraft's French Revolution," in Claudia L. Johnson, ed., *The Cambridge Companion to Mary Wollstonecraft* (Cambridge: Cambridge University Press, 2006), 68.
6 *New Annual Register* (1794), 221–22; *Analytical Review*, 20:4 (1794), 338; and for writing "not like an annalist, but like a philosopher" (*Monthly Review*, new series, 16 [April 1795], 394). The work has the further distinction of being the most heavily annotated text in the library of US founding father, John Adams. See O'Neill, "Adams versus Wollstonecraft."
7 Jane Rendall, "'The Grand Causes Which Combine to Carry Mankind Forward': Wollstonecraft, History, and Revolution," *Women's Writing*, 4:2 (1997), 155–72. Also O'Neill, "Adams versus Wollstonecraft."

8 On this personal dimension see especially Mark Salber Phillips, *Society and Sentiment: Genres of Historical Writing in Britain* (Princeton: Princeton University Press, 2000).

9 John Millar, *The Origin of the Distinction of Ranks; or, An Inquiry into the Circumstances Which Give Rise to Influence and Authority in the Different Members of Society*, edited by Aaron Garrett (Indianapolis: Liberty Fund, 2006), 85.

10 Hugh Blair, *Lectures on Rhetoric and Belles Lettres*, 6th edn. (London, 1796), 3: 52.

11 William Alexander, *The History of Women, from the Earliest Antiquity, to the Present Time* (London, 1779), 1: 103.

12 "Grand Causes," 156.

13 See Mark Phillips, *Society and Sentiment: Genres of Historical Writing in Britain, 1740–1820* (Princeton: Princeton University Press, 2000), 187–233.

14 Cited by Phillips, *Society and Sentiment*, 234.

15 Wollstonecraft, *An Historical and Moral View of the French Revolution* (London: Joseph Johnson, 1794), n.p.

16 Ibid., vi.

17 Ibid., 6–7.

18 Ibid., 3.

19 Ibid., 4.

20 *A Vindication of the Rights of Woman*, 117.

21 *An Historical and Moral View*, 510–11.

22 Ibid., 296.

23 Ibid., 460.

24 Ibid., 354.

25 Ibid., 300.

26 Ibid., 68–70.

27 Mary Wollstonecraft, *A Short Residence in Sweden*, edited by Richard Holmes (Harmondsworth: Penguin, 1987), 198.

28 Ibid.

CHAPTER 37

Periodicals

Jacqueline George

Periodical culture was the realm within which Wollstonecraft realized, in her words, a "new plan of life," marked by "a little peace and independence."[1] While not the first female writer to publish criticism, Wollstonecraft has been rightly identified as "the first truly professional woman literary critic,"[2] as she managed to support herself by working as a periodical contributor and editorial assistant for the last ten years of her life. Describing her ambition to her sister Everina, Wollstonecraft declared herself an original species, emboldened by the encouragement of her publisher Joseph Johnson: "Mr. Johnson ... assures me that if I exert my talents in writing I may support myself in a comfortable way. I am then going to be the first of a new genus—."[3] In 1787, Johnson welcomed Wollstonecraft back to London after a series of professional and personal setbacks, including the closing of her school at Newington Green, the death of Fanny Blood, and her dismissal as governess by Lady Kingsborough. Johnson's financial, intellectual, and emotional support would continue to play an integral role in Wollstonecraft's career, but it was his launching of the *Analytical Review* in 1788 that provided Wollstonecraft with the means of making a living via a robust participation in the public sphere. In this way, periodicals served as a proving ground for Wollstonecraft's social and political philosophy, and a means by which she developed her singular feminist voice.

Writing in a 1716 issue of the *Freeholder*, Joseph Addison notes that "no Periodical Author ... must effect to keep in vogue for any considerable time."[4] According to the *Oxford English Dictionary*, Addison's remark is the first use of the term *periodical* to denote a type of reading material, and it suggests the extent to which periodicals have always constituted a dynamic genre that continually reinvents itself in response to changing conditions (including public taste). The *Freeholder* was the third periodical to which Addison contributed over the course of his career, after the *Tatler* and *The Spectator*. And by the time of Wollstonecraft's birth in 1759, several kinds of periodicals, including newspapers, literary reviews, extended essays, miscellanies, epistolary journals, and satiric papers were published at regular intervals, with installments hawked on the streets of her native London, delivered to coffeehouses, vended by booksellers, or sent to the provinces by mail.

Within these issues, one would find disparate content, from lists of military promotions, to short poems and stories by authors both new and familiar, to gossip regarding sexual and political scandals. Although heterogeneous in content, many eighteenth-century periodicals linked themselves to one another through an array of insular references, replies, and innovations developed in response to contemporary social and authorial phenomena. As Manushag Powell has shown, "periodicals in the eighteenth-century are a self-forming and informing genre, ceaselessly invoking their own conventions and antecedents."[5] In addition, contributors to periodicals often employed initials, *noms de plume*, and alter egos, operating within a clannish and not entirely harmonious authorial community that traversed both print and real life. Indeed, because the *Analytical Review*'s essays were either anonymous or only signed by initials, the precise identification of all of Wollstonecraft's contributions remains to this day a matter of debate.[6]

Yet even with the challenges posed by such generic cross-breeding and authorial intrigue, contemporary scholars have documented a wide expansion of the periodical press during the late seventeenth and early eighteenth centuries by traversing archives, reviewing correspondence, and amassing the available production data from contemporary publishers' catalogs. These scholars have argued that a rise in literacy rates, together with the expiration of certain licensing provisions, inspired publishers to broaden the availability of existing periodicals and to create new ones. "The political pamphlets, satiric papers, and news-reporting papers or 'corantos' so widely read during the Civil War," Kathryn Shevelow observes, "were joined toward the end of the century by epistolary journals, miscellanies, and book reviews, among others, also seeking to reach a wide audience and to extend it further."[7] Between 1753 and 1793 alone, the number of newspaper copies circulated increased from approximately seven million to seventeen million, with over 100 different titles published throughout the United Kingdom.[8] During this same period, the most popular journals and literary reviews disseminated thousands of copies daily, a trend that would continue well into the nineteenth century.[9] And in contrast to books, which remained comparatively heavy and expensive, these periodicals were affordable, portable, and (ostensibly) more personally engaged with their readers.

During Wollstonecraft's childhood residence in Beverley (1763–68), she read magazines and newspapers at home or with friends, "learning to consider social issues troubling the nation" at quite a young age.[10] Periodicals also played a role in educating Wollstonecraft about class structure, gender norms, and current events. Janet Todd argues that the "later liberal sophistication of several Wollstonecraft children suggests that they read newspapers when young and possibly discussed politics at home or outside."[11] Periodicals surely made up part of what Caroline Franklin terms the "emancipatory print culture" that allowed an autodidact like Wollstonecraft to acquire the intellectual stimulation she felt to be lacking at home.[12]

Whereas newspapers were devoted to political, economic, military, and social affairs (both chaste and lewd), the popular periodicals of Wollstonecraft's time tended to emphasize readerly instruction and entertainment. The earliest of these publications presented material in the voice of one, unifying authorial persona, and sought to reach the widest audience possible, including women. Writing in a 1711 issue of *The Spectator*, Addison (in the voice of Mr. Spectator) endows himself with a clear responsibility: "Since I have raised to myself so great an audience, I shall spare no pains to make their instruction agreeable, and their diversion useful ... I shall endeavor to enliven morality with wit, and to temper wit with morality, that my readers may, if possible, both ways find their account in the speculation of the day."[13] While this kind of single-authorial persona format remained popular throughout the eighteenth century, it was joined by the "miscellany," or magazine, which presented discrete, self-standing articles about a range of topics. As the inaugural issue of *The London Magazine* makes clear, these publications hoped to "hardly fail of pleasing almost all Sorts of Persons; the Variety herein contain'd being in some Sort proportionable to the vast Variety of Dispositions and Tastes in the World."[14] By 1780, there would be at least sixty magazines published in London, many of which addressed their readers in these kinds of broad, accommodating terms.

Some periodicals targeted specific demographic groups by identifying instructional needs that periodicals could satisfy. Chief among these groups were middle-class female readers who occupied the domestic sphere, an ostensibly "empty" (and therefore risky) realm of leisure: "periodical editors certainly perceived women as an economic interest group that it was advantageous to attract, and this they did by characterizing them as a social group necessitous of the periodical's oversight."[15] Of course, the notion of female readers needing "oversight" did not originate with the periodical, but eighteenth-century magazines distinguished themselves from the well-established, dictatorial didacticism of conduct books and sermons by ingratiating themselves with their readership and creating a sense of collaboration. *The Lady's Magazine,* for example, branded itself as "an Entertaining Companion for the Fair Sex, Appropriated Solely to Their Use and Amusement,"[16] while *The Lady's Monthly Museum* promised "an assemblage of whatever can tend to please the Fancy, interest the Mind, or exalt the Character of The British Fair."[17]

The time, opportunity, and perceived necessity of providing a "companion" for middle-class female readers rendered them an important "economic interest group" to editors.[18] In addition, the publishers of popular periodicals hired women to contribute to and edit particular titles, such as Eliza Haywood's *Female Spectator* (1744) and Frances Moore Brooke's *Old Maid* (1755). That these works were produced by women, for women, enhanced their marketability and, according to *The Lady's Magazine,* their moral integrity: "The entertainment which our readers have received from our last volume, will receive an additional éclat, when they consider it originates from the joint labors of the sex."[19]

These periodicals offered a kind of curriculum for feminine norms and behavior, extending their readers' educations and providing at least a partial entry into the public sphere. Wollstonecraft, of course, was determined to provide the same, and this shared purpose was made explicit in the spring of 1787, when excerpts from *Thoughts on the Education of Daughters* appeared in three consecutive issues of *The Lady's Magazine.*[20] Generically speaking, the homiletic tone of Wollstonecraft's work differs from the *Magazine*'s editorial character because, as Franklin notes, *Thoughts on the Education of Daughters* is essentially a conduct book written in response to other conduct books. Determining that "her predecessors have not taken female education seriously enough," Wollstonecraft's volume articulates "a more rigorous approach,"[21] grounded in reason and suspicious of intellectual indolence.

In stark contrast, Wollstonecraft's *Female Reader* (1789) eschews the form and tone of the conduct book in favor of a diverse and disparate arrangement of voices more akin to the popular magazine. Although identified as the work of "Mr. Cresswick, Teacher of Elocution," *The Female Reader* is not simply an elocutionary manual but a program for moral improvement: "In this selection many tales and fables will be found as it seems to be following the simple order of nature, to permit young people to pursue works addressed to the imagination, which tend to awaken the affections and fix good habit more firmly in the mind than cold arguments and mere declamation."[22] This coupling of passion and reason would become the cornerstone of Wollstonecraft's educational philosophy, and in *The Female Reader* this "awakening" of natural inclinations is realized, in part, through the reading of selections from periodicals including *The Spectator, The Connoisseur, The Mirror,* and *The World.* By placing these selections alongside works of poetry, scripture, and fiction, *The Female Reader* (like the magazine) attempts to engage as many readers as possible. Early engagement with "sentiments they understand" will lead young women to reason, Wollstonecraft argues, more so than rote memorization of impenetrable content.[23]

While the tone of *The Female Reader* is not as demonstrably friendly as *The Lady's Magazine,* it does present itself as a knowing companion who has even a vain reader's best interests at heart: "Exterior accomplishments are not to be obtained by imitation, they must result from the mind . . . If you wish to be loved by your relations and friends, prove that you can love them by governing your temper; good humor and cheerful gaiety will enliven every feature and dimple your cheeks—but this my young friends is not the work of a day."[24] *The Female Reader's* argument rests on the widely held assumption that reading can and should shape moral behavior; however, as many eighteenth-century intellectuals understood, the sheer proliferation of reading material (particularly fiction) could complicate or even sabotage the execution of such a project. As Eliza Haywood notes in *The Female Spectator,* "reading is universally allowed to be one of the most improving as well as agreeable amusements; but then to render it so, one should, among the number of books which are perpetually issuing from the press, endeavor to single out such as promise to be most conducive to those ends."[25]

In addition to anthologies like *The Female Reader,* one of the ways in which readers could make appropriate reading choices was by reading criticism in one of the many periodical reviews available, from the conservative *Anti-Jacobin Review* to the nonconformist *Monthly Review.* Reviews played a key role in the marketing of new titles (particularly those offered by their own publishing houses), while also providing summaries and sizable extracts. When Johnson launched the *Analytical Review* with Thomas Christie in 1788, they afforded themselves a broad mandate, as articulated in the journal's subtitle: "or history of literature, domestic and foreign, on an enlarged plan. Containing scientific abstracts of important and interesting works, published in English; a general account of such as are of less consequence, with short characters; notices, or reviews of valuable foreign books; criticisms on new pieces of music and works of art; and the literary intelligence of Europe, &c."[26] Rejecting the standard,

autocratic model of traditional journalism in which a single editor controlled all content, Johnson and Christie enacted an "alternative democratic form of editorship," in which reviewers also commissioned and
collected articles as well.[27]

For Wollstonecraft personally, the *Analytical Review* served as an
authorial home whose critical stance fit her own Enlightenment sensibility:
"The true design of a literary journal is, in our opinion, to give such an
account of new publications, as may enable the reader to judge of them for
himself."[28] In all, Wollstonecraft contributed at least 200 reviews to the
Analytical, at the same time as she wrote and published her other works.
Consistent with the multi-disciplinary nature of the publication, her
reviews consider children's literature, poetry, sermons, travel narratives,
educational treatises, fiction, and even a work about boxing. She contributed a majority of her reviews between 1789 and 1790, taking on additional editorial responsibilities when Christie traveled to France (in 1789,
1791, and 1792) and after his death in 1796. Wollstonecraft contributed
to the *Analytical* up until her own death in 1797.

Wollstonecraft's reviews pull no punches, making clear both her evaluations of the works under discussion and, often, her own ideas about the
pedagogical role of contemporary literature. Nowhere are these ideas made
more explicit than in her reviews of fiction, in which she argues in her first
review that, when it comes to *Edward and Harriet, or the Happy Recovery*,
the "*cant* of sensibility" can scarcely be "tried by any criterion of reason."[29]
From the start, Wollstonecraft's reviews articulate her concerns about
sentimental fiction, a genre whose ideological significance she clearly
grasped: "Young women may be termed romantic, when they are under
the direction of artificial feelings; when they boast of being tremblingly
alive all o'er, and faint and sigh as the novelist informs them they
should."[30] As Mitzi Myers has shown, Wollstonecraft's reviews evince a
resistance to "the model of femininity" typically represented by novels,
exposing the "linguistic and structural etiquette of powerlessness and
marginalization" that governed it.[31] This powerlessness, Wollstonecraft
argues, is rooted in the neglect of reason and an overindulgence in
imagined, heightened, and (at their core) fabricated passions: "the heart
is depraved when it is supposed to be refined, and it is a great chance but
false sentiment leads to sensuality, and vague fabricated feelings supply the
place of principles."[32]

This is not to say that Wollstonecraft was opposed to sentiment entirely,
but that she thought it should originate within the subject, not culture.
Novels in which "abstract qualities are continually introduced instead of

persons," vexed her to no end, for she feared they would instruct young
female readers in affectation and "artificial virtue."³³ In contrast, she
lauded those works that appeared to her to be original and natural, such
as M. de Saint-Pierre's *Paul and Mary*: "This interesting moral tale, binds
together a number of lively descriptions of nature, where she wantons in all
the wild captivating grandeur of simplicity."³⁴ Similarly, Wollstonecraft
praises Mary Robinson's *Angelina* for characters who are "naturally pour-
trayed [sic] and distinctly marked" with sentiments that are "just, animated, and rational."³⁵ In the *Analytical,* Wollstonecraft advocates for a
self-reflexive mode of reading that animates the imagination while also
prompting the reader to examine (implicitly or explicitly) her own moral
principles.

Just as the conventional use of the first-person plural *we* represented
Wollstonecraft's identity as a professional critic, linguistically inscribing
her within a specific periodical coterie, her day-to-day life granted her
access to an incredible group of artists, writers, and intellectuals who met
regularly at Johnson's residence to chat and dine together: Henry Fuseli,
Alexander Geddes, John Horne Tooke, Gilbert Wakefield, William Blake,
Thomas Paine, and many others. As a "risk-taker of some vision who had
long befriended and published the unorthodox,"³⁶ Johnson would release
2,700 works over his forty-eight-year career, including a wide array of
theological, medical, scientific, and philosophical titles. The unlikely and
sometimes contentious combinations of guests at his home served as a
consistently stimulating community within which Wollstonecraft could
challenge others and be challenged as a peer. Franklin calls this company
"Wollstonecraft's university."³⁷

Critics concur that Wollstonecraft's work for the *Analytical* aided in her
development as a writer, despite Godwin's accusation that such "miscellaneous" employment served to "damp and contract" genius.³⁸ Myers
notes that Wollstonecraft's reviews of poetry and popular fiction "cluster
around the periods when she was herself most intensely involved in
creative activity,"³⁹ while Franklin attributes to the writing of the reviews
the honing of a style that is particularly evinced in *Vindication of the Rights
of Woman.*⁴⁰ And because Wollstonecraft's reviews teach her periodical
readers how to "critique rather than internalize,"⁴¹ they allow her to
advance the educational reform project she began years before at Newington Green – albeit from a very different subject position. No longer
bound by the subordinate rank of teacher or governess, Wollstonecraft
assumed as a periodical writer the kind of reasoned confidence she would
encourage in others. If Wollstonecraft is "the first liberal feminist thinker

to articulate a coherent political platform for the emancipation of women,"[42] then we must surely credit periodical culture for providing a context within which she could develop a strategy for clearly and effectively conveying her convictions.

Notes

1 Mary Wollstonecraft to Joseph Johnson, 13 September 1787, in *The Collected Letters of Mary Wollstonecraft*, edited by Ralph N. Wardle (Ithaca: Cornell University Press, 1979), 159.
2 Mary A. Waters, *British Women Writers and the Profession of Literary Criticism, 1789–1832* (New York: Palgrave Macmillan, 2004), 3.
3 Mary Wollstonecraft to Everina Wollstonecraft, 7 November 1787, in *Collected Letters*, 164.
4 Joseph Addison, *The Freeholder*, 45 (1716), quoted in the *Oxford English Dictionary*, s.v. "periodical," oed.com.
5 Manushag N. Powell, *Performing Authorship in Eighteenth-Century Periodicals* (Lewisburg: Bucknell University Press, 2012), 10.
6 Janet Todd, "Prefatory Note," in *The Collected Works of Mary Wollstonecraft*, edited by Janet Todd and Marilyn Butler (New York: New York University Press, 1989), 7: 14–18.
7 Kathryn Shevelow, *Women and Print Culture: The Construction of Femininity in the Early Periodical* (London: Routledge, 1989), 25.
8 William St. Clair, *The Reading Nation in the Romantic Period* (Cambridge: Cambridge University Press, 2004), 576.
9 Ibid., 572.
10 Janet Todd, *Mary Wollstonecraft: A Revolutionary Life* (New York: Columbia University Press, 2000), 12.
11 Ibid., 13.
12 Caroline Franklin, *Mary Wollstonecraft: A Literary Life* (New York: Palgrave Macmillan, 2004), 4.
13 Joseph Addison, "Uses of *The Spectator*," in *Essays from Addison*, edited by J. H. Fowler (London: Macmillan, 1907), 29.
14 "Preface," in *The London Magazine, or Gentlemen's Monthly Intelligencer*, 1 (1732), i, http://hdl.handle.net/2027/hvd.hxueti
15 Shevelow, *Women and Print Culture*, 34.
16 *The Lady's Magazine; or Entertaining Companion for the Fair Sex*, 6 (1775), http://hdl.handle.net/2027/mdp.39015055410065
17 *The Lady's Monthly Museum, or Polite Repository of Amusement and Instruction*, 2 (1799), http://hdl.handle.net/2027/nyp.33433104825231
18 Shevelow, *Women and Print Culture*, 34.
19 "To the Public," in *The Lady's Magazine*, 6, (1775), v.
20 "Extracts from *Thoughts on the Education of Daughters*, lately published" in *The Lady's Magazine*, 18, (1787), 227–30, 287–88, 369–70.

21 Franklin, *Mary Wollstonecraft: A Literary Life*, 20.
22 Mary Wollstonecraft, *The Female Reader*, in *Works*, 4: 56.
23 Ibid., 56.
24 Ibid., 59.
25 Eliza Haywood, *The Female Spectator*, 1 (1775), 1, http://hdl.handle.net/2027/uc2.ark:/13960/toht2hd5g
26 *The Analytical Review*, 1 (1778), http://hdl.handle.net/2027/chi.25234377
27 Susan Oliver, "Silencing Joseph Johnson and the *Analytical Review*," *Wordsworth Circle*, 40 (2009), 96.
28 "To the Public," *The Analytical Review*, 1 (1788), i. http://hdl.handle.net/2027/chi.25234377
29 Mary Wollstonecraft, "Article XXXIII," *Analytical Review*, 1 (1788), in *Works*, 7: 19.
30 Ibid., 19.
31 Mitzi Myers, "Mary Wollstonecraft's Literary Reviews," in Claudia L. Johnson, ed., *The Cambridge Companion to Mary Wollstonecraft* (Cambridge: Cambridge University Press, 2002), 89.
32 Mary Wollstonecraft, "Article XXXIII," *Analytical Review*, 1 (1788), in *Works*, 7: 19.
33 Mary Wollstonecraft, "Article XIV," *Analytical Review*, 1 (1788), in *Works*, 7: 27.
34 Mary Wollstonecraft, "Article XXIX," *Analytical Review*, 4 (1789), in *Works*, 7: 153.
35 Mary Wollstonecraft, "Article XXIV," *Analytical Review*, 23 (1796), in *Works*, 7: 461–62.
36 Moira Ferguson and Janet Todd, *Mary Wollstonecraft* (Boston: Twayne, 1984), 8.
37 Franklin, *Mary Wollstonecraft*, 58.
38 William Godwin, *Memoirs of the Author of A Vindication of the Rights of Woman*, edited by Richard Holmes (Harmondsworth: Penguin, 1987), 226.
39 Myers, "Mary Wollstonecraft's Literary Reviews," 82.
40 Franklin, *Mary Wollstonecraft*, 91.
41 Myers, "Mary Wollstonecraft's Literary Reviews," 89.
42 Anne K. Mellor, Review of *Mary Wollstonecraft: A Revolutionary Life* by Janet Todd and *Rebel Writer: Mary Wollstonecraft and Enlightenment Politics* by Wendy Gunther-Canada, Signs, 30 (2005), 1719.

CHAPTER 38

Translations

Alessa Johns

Mary Wollstonecraft's works drew on her extensive travels in Portugal, France, Ireland, Scandinavia, and Germany; she dedicated her most important book, *A Vindication of the Rights of Woman*, to the French political figure Maurice de Talleyrand; and she translated texts from three foreign languages. Nonetheless, scholars' evaluations of her writings tend to remain restricted to the British context, seeing her work in terms of national history, literary achievement, and women's rights. Moreover, the consensus that Wollstonecraft's reputation was ruined after William Godwin revealed her out-of-wedlock liaisons in the *Memoirs of the Author of A Vindication of the Rights of Woman* (1798) has prolonged focus on her biography as much as on her writing, which has in turn distracted from her cosmopolitan literary and intellectual legacy. An entirely different view emerges when one considers translations and reviews of her work. These reveal a Wollstonecraft who, contrary to her conflicted British reception in the early nineteenth century, commanded respect both before and after she died; her writings continued to be translated and her ideas embraced. This suggests that the revived mid-nineteenth-century interest in Wollstone-craft among British feminists and suffragists was due as much to the rebound of her ideas from the Continent and America as native rehabili-tation. The transnational ricocheting of Wollstonecraft translations and ideas has, moreover, continued in the twenty-first century, as her work continues to inspire debate globally.[1] Wollstonecraft should consequently be viewed not only nationally but also internationally.

In the late eighteenth and nineteenth centuries Wollstonecraft was well received in most European countries; British reactionary reticence in the 1790s and beyond was extraordinary, not typical. Eileen Hunt Botting has demonstrated how French, German, Dutch, Danish, Swedish, Spanish, Portuguese, and Czech readers received translations of her work apprecia-tively in the century after her death: "the trend in continental Europe was different than in Britain. Like the nineteenth-century United States, where

323

Wollstonecraft enjoyed a steady and increasingly warm reception in both public and private, continental Europeans were comparatively open to receiving and debating Wollstonecraft's life and works as part of their responses to the woman question."[2]

French and German translations of Wollstonecraft's work were by far the most copious in the 1790s and early 1800s – in the revolutionary and Napoleonic period and after. In France, translations were consistent and reviews positive. An edition of *A Vindication of the Rights of Woman* (1792) titled *Défense des droits des femmes*, was sold in Paris and Lyon already that same year. In 1798 *Maria ou le malheur d'être femme* appeared, also in the same year that it was published in Britain. It was translated by Basile-Joseph Ducos, an eminent journalist and editor, who then became a director of national tax collection and a regent of the central bank (Receveur général des finances et régent de la Banque de France).[3] A. J. N. Lallemant, an active translator of English travel literature as well as Sécretaire de la Marine, brought out a French version of *Original Stories from Real Life* (as *Marie et Caroline, ou Entretiens d'une institutrice avec ses élèves*) in 1799. William Godwin's *Memoirs of the Author of A Vindication of the Rights of Woman* appeared as *Vie et mémoires de Marie Wollstonecraft Godwin* in 1802. Another indication of Wollstonecraft's prominence was César Gardeton's misattribution to her of an 1826 French translation of *Woman Not Inferior to Man* (further translated into Portuguese, again misattributed to Wollstonecraft, and reprinted three times for the Brazilian market). Flora Tristan, the French feminist and socialist who visited London in the late 1830s, expressed dismay at not finding an English copy of Wollstonecraft's book available for purchase there.[4] Wollstonecraft's appeal, due to her passionate advocacy of women's education, women's rights, and middle-class virtues, was widespread and deep, and continued throughout the Romantic period.

The anonymous 1792 French translation of the *Rights of Woman* was unusually faithful to Wollstonecraft's text, "with little of the pruning that was standard practice at the time."[5] Two areas of divergence between Wollstonecraft and her translator do stand out: where Wollstonecraft reconciled her Anglicanism and feminism (even as she criticized how religious instruction took place in schools), the French translator harbored vehement anti-clerical ideas and expressed them in a footnote: "the same abuses, born of papism, that infect the catholic schools exist in the English schools . . . Deceive in order to dominate, that, in two words, is the priestly spirit, from the banks of the Ganges to the banks of the Tiber."[6] Where Wollstonecraft advocated for strengthening girls' bodies through exercise, the French translator in his footnotes reinforced traditional gender roles: "it is necessary that a Woman be a Woman in all ways."[7] Political polemic circulated vigorously in France during this volatile period – including feminist writings of Condorcet and Olympe de Gouges, as well as extensive national discussion about education – and in spite of this, or perhaps because of it, there was interest in the translated work of a previously little-known British woman writer.

And there was substantial appreciation too. The first review in the *Chronique de Paris* concluded that Wollstonecraft "defends her sex very warmly and often very rationally. All the flaws of women she traces back to the tyranny of men" (June 1792). The *Journal Encyclopédique* offered a long two-part review that called the *Droits des femmes* "undeniably one of the best written on behalf of women in a long time. Gentle & humane philosophy, cogent logic, sober & always convincing reasoning, incontrovertible principles, pure morals, lucid argument...all those are there for the satisfaction of the human mind" (August 1792).[8]

While the French reception was vigorous and furthered by elevated social figures, that of Germany was even more copious and prolonged. *A Vindication of the Rights of Woman*, translated as *Rettung der Rechte des Weibes*, appeared in 1793, published by the renowned Philanthropist school at Schnepfenthal in Thuringia. This progressive educational institution proved to be the most significant disseminator of Wollstonecraft's ideas, with a press of its own and subscribers all over German-speaking lands. It brought out *Erzählungen für Kinder* (*Original Stories from Real Life*) in 1795 and translated Godwin's *Memoirs* in 1799, as *Denkschrift auf Maria Wollstonecraft Godwin, die Vertheidigerin der Rechte des Weibes*. In addition, Wollstonecraft's English translation of the *Elements of Morality*, by Schnepfenthal founder Christian Gotthilf Salzmann, was edited and published at the institution in 1796 for use as an English language acquisition text. Salzmann himself felt anxious about some of Wollstonecraft's anti-aristocratic pronouncements and claims for women's political representation in *Rettung der Rechte des Weibes*, and he consequently wrote an introduction and added footnotes to the translation by Georg Friedrich Christian Weissenborn so that he might mitigate her arguments. Perhaps partly because of this, as literary critic Emma Rauschenbusch-Clough noted already in 1898, Wollstonecraft's *Vindication of the Rights of Woman* received a very different welcome in Germany from that in Napoleonic-era Britain: Germans did not feel threatened by Wollstonecraft's "new system" and for the most part viewed her educational ideas as "sensible and wise."[9]

Nonetheless, the Schnepfenthal translator Weissenborn himself wished for Germans to absorb the full force of Wollstonecraft's arguments. In addition to rendering Wollstonecraft's works into German and teaching English using her translation of *Elements of Morality*, Weissenborn wrote articles and reviews that conspicuously furthered her ideas. In the first issue of the influential journal *Bibliothek der pädagogischen Literatur*, to cite one example, Weissenborn contributed a long article (that extended into the second issue) titled "How the Female Sex Has Been Set Back up to Now" ("Über die bisherige Zurücksetzung des weiblichen Geschlechts"). The article closely follows Wollstonecraft and, in a bolder strain than Salzmann's paratexts for the *Rettung der Rechte des Weibes*, concludes that women, like men, need the human right to find happiness in the pursuit of a calling they themselves select. "All individuals must be allowed to seek their happiness where they wish, as soon as they can reason." However, given unfortunate nineteenth-century German social constraints, "Women's happiness is restricted solely to domestic pleasures," and "The husband also looms as the head of domestic society, just as he does in civil society." As a consequence, Weissenborn urges women actively to pursue their rights, taking up the role of citizen-mothers to educate their daughters well, since social change can take generations. They should remain firm and resolute. "Just have the courage to be strong, and you will be! Seek to become that, which you ought to be, and one will be obliged to give you what you are owed! Become familiar with your duties: and one will not be able to deny you your rights!"[10]

Wollstonecraft's works were brought out elsewhere in Germany as well. Lengthy excerpts from the *Historical and Moral View of the Origin and Progress of the French Revolution and the Effect It Has Produced in Europe* (1794), advocating more gradual socio-political change, were translated in the respected liberal journal *Minerva* in 1795.[11] Her *Letters Written during a Short Residence in Sweden, Norway, and Denmark* were translated and published in Hamburg and Altona in 1796, as well as in a new translation published in Leipzig in 1800. *The Wrongs of Woman; or, Maria* was rendered as *Maria oder das Unglück Weib zu seyn*, which also appeared in Leipzig that same year. In 1848, German feminist Mathilde Franziska Anneke, having fled to Wisconsin after fighting alongside her husband Fritz Anneke in the failed 1848 revolution, apparently undertook a translation of *Rights of Woman* and printed it in her German-language newspaper, the *Deutsche Frauen-Zeitung*.[12] She joined feminists and socialists, including Susan B. Anthony and Elizabeth Cady Stanton, in agitating for political reform,[13] and she deepened her connection to Wollstonecraft by naming her son after Wollstonecraft's radical son-in-law Percy Shelley.[14]

German reviews were largely laudatory, especially of the *Vindication of the Rights of Woman*. The reviewer from the *Göttingische Anzeigen* found that it distinguished itself with solid thinking on an important subject; Georg Friedrich Seiler in his *Gemeinnützige Betrachtungen* argued that Wollstonecraft was "keen-witted" with a "noble heart." While there were "exaggerations," according to the *Erlanger gelehrte Zeitung*, these were perceived as corrected by Salzmann's footnotes and were therefore not worrisome. The long two-part review in the *Neue Allgemeine Deutsche Bibliothek* agreed with this assessment.[15] A lone unfavorable review in the *Allgemeine Literatur-Zeitung* judged that women themselves would be the most likely to protest against Wollstonecraft's plans for flattening the distinctions between men and women.[16]

Godwin's *Memoirs* received a lavish and long review. It commended Godwin's love of truth in depicting "the interesting life and the great literary achievements of an estimable woman" who belongs "indisputably to the most noteworthy of her nation in recent history" and therefore holds the "highest claims ... on our attention and gratitude." The review summarized each section of the biography separately and minutely, mentioned all of her writings including posthumous ones, and lamented the early death of this "clever unforgettable woman" who possessed a "restless inquiring mind."[17]

The same journal gave Wollstonecraft's Scandinavian *Letters* a mixed review the next year. On the one hand, it recognized that readers might enjoy Wollstonecraft's descriptions of Norway's natural beauty in summertime, but on the other it took issue with the book's limited geographical coverage and its criticism of Hamburg's commercial culture.[18] The reviewer also brought up Wollstonecraft's biography, asking, "What shall one call her?" because she was not officially married to Imlay yet styled herself his wife. The same periodical's review of *Maria* was respectful of Wollstonecraft even if it doubted the merits of the story. The review questioned whether the translated work could in fact be attributed to the clever Wollstonecraft, who had already published a similarly titled but very different story: *Mary: A Fiction*. *Maria*, characterized as an unfinished and carelessly organized work, was, the reviewer surmised incorrectly, rendered into German via a poor French translation, with the Jemima episodes – a "coarse addition" to the text – perhaps shoved in by the German translator.[19] Wollstonecraft's biography, judging from reviews in the *Neue*

Allgemeine Deutsche Bibliothek, would appear to have enhanced her literary reputation as much as it tainted it.

Wollstonecraft's works appeared elsewhere on the Continent as well, sometimes in chain translations. For example, the first German translation of the *Rights of Woman* was used to generate a Dutch translation, *Verdediging van de Rechten der Vrouwen* (1796),[20] as well as a Danish translation, *Et forsvar for kvindernes rettigheder* (1801). A later German translation by Bertha Pappenheim appeared in 1899[21] and led to a version in Czech, done by Anna Holmová: *Obrana práv žen* (1904).[22] A Dutch translation of *Original Stories* appeared in 1798; *Maria* was published in Swedish in 1799. Wollstonecraft's *Letters Written during a Short Residence in Sweden, Norway, and Denmark* (1796) seems to have been her second most popular work on the Continent, judging not only from its three German editions but also its translations into Swedish (1798), Dutch (1799), Portuguese (in abridged form, 1806), and into Spanish in a manuscript translation by the prominent Francisca Ruiz de Larrea de Böhl de Faber.[23] As a result Wollstonecraft's work received sustained, serious, and positive attention on the Continent, with translations of a variety of writings appearing remarkably soon after the original English versions became available, and reviews and renewed editions ensuring the continued circulation of her ideas.

Given Wollstonecraft's regard on the Continent, her British rehabilitation in the mid-nineteenth century would appear to have depended at least as much on her positive Continental and American reception as on native efforts. Early socialists, for example, took Wollstonecraft's ideas into account in a process of transnational "cross-fertilization" involving French, German, English, Irish, Scottish, and American adherents, many of whom traveled and acted internationally in the early nineteenth century to promote progressive reforms.[24] Activists such as Flora Tristan, Jeanne Deroin, Anna Wheeler, Frances Wright, Mathilde Franziska Anneke, Fredrika Bremer, Anna Jameson, Margaret Fuller, and others in the first decades of the nineteenth century all advanced Wollstonecraft's agenda and have in fact been characterized by Bonnie S. Anderson as the "First International Women's Movement."[25] Men as well as women participated in the emancipatory project in Britain, in America, and on the Continent, as, for example, the avid interest of continental male translators suggests and as the recent work of Arianne Chernock on British men's feminism attests.[26]

In sum, the generally positive reception of Wollstonecraft's translations in the late eighteenth and early nineteenth century on the Continent, the persistence of her ideas in European discourses of education and women's roles, as well as her lionizing in the United States – all of these made themselves felt in British intellectual and progressive circles via mediators and networks. They translated the arguments into the Victorian era to press for women's education, work opportunities, married women's separate property rights, divorce, and the franchise, seeking thoroughgoing social, political, and economic reform. Wollstonecraft's writings have continued to be exchanged and debated in Europe and globally in the late twentieth and twenty-first centuries. The significance of a national British figure like Mary Wollstonecraft can consequently be seen more clearly from a networked, mediated, international vantage point.

Notes

1 See Veena Poonacha, "Framing Gender Identities in Education Philosophy: Jean Jacques Rousseau and Mary Wollstonecraft," *Indian Journal of Gender Studies*, 23:3 (2016), 415–36; "Zahrā Khānum Tāj al-Saltana and Mary Wollstonecraft: A Comparative Study of 'Memoirs of Tāj al-Saltana' and 'A Vindication of the Rights of Woman,'" *International Journal of Persian Literature*, 2:1 (2017), 161–79; Eileen Hunt Botting, "The Problem of Cultural Bias: Wollstonecraft, Mill, and Western Narratives of Women's Progress," in *Wollstonecraft, Mill, and Women's Human Rights* (New Haven: Yale University Press, 2016), 155–203; Eileen Hunt Botting and Charlotte Hammond Matthews, "Overthrowing the Floresta-Wollstonecraft Myth for Latin American Feminism," *Gender and History*, 26:1 (2014), 64–83; Dasa Duhacek, "Mary Wollstonecraft in Serbia," *Women's Studies Quarterly*, 35:3/4 (2007), 292–25; Geetanjali Singh Chanda with Norman G. Owen, "Tainted Goods?: Western Feminism and the Asian Experience," *Asian Journal of Women's Studies*, 7:4 (2001), 90–105.
2 Eileen Hunt Botting, "Wollstonecraft in Europe, 1792–1904: A Revisionist Reception History," *History of European Ideas*, 39:4 (2013), 503–27, at 511.
3 Laura Kirkley, "*Maria, ou Le Malheur d'être femme*: Translating Mary Wollstonecraft in Revolutionary France," *Journal of Eighteenth-Century Studies*, 38:2 (2015), 239–55, at 242. See also Isabelle Bour, "The Boundaries of Sensibility: 1790s French Translations of Mary Wollstonecraft," *Women's Writing*, 11:3 (2004), 493–506.
4 Botting, "Wollstonecraft in Europe," 518, 519.
5 Isabelle Bour, "A New Wollstonecraft: The Reception of the *Vindication of the Rights of Woman* and of *The Wrongs of Woman* in Revolutionary France," *Journal for Eighteenth-Century Studies*, 36:4 (2013), 575–87, at 577.
6 Mary Wollstonecraft, *Défense des droits des femmes* (Paris: Buisson; Lyon: Bruyset, 1792), 424–25: "Les mêmes abus, nés du papisme, qui infectent les collèges catholiques, existent dans les collèges Anglais . . . Tromper pour

dominer, c'est en deux mots l'esprit sacerdotal, des rives du Gange aux rives du Tybre."

7 Wollstonecraft, *Défense*, 461: "Il faut qu'une Femme soit Femme de toutes les manières."

8 Translations quoted from Bour "New Wollstonecraft," 586.

9 Emma Rauschenbusch-Clough, *A Study of Mary Wollstonecraft and The Rights of Woman* (New York: Longmans, Green, & Co., 1898), 191, 193.

10 Georg Friedrich Christian Weissenborn, "Über die bisherige Zurücksetzung des weiblichen Geschlechts," *Bibliothek der pädagogischen Literatur*, 1:1 (1800), 81–99 and 1:2 (1800), 195–210, at 204, 205, 209: "Es muss jedem Menschen erlaubt seyn, seine Glückseligkeit zu suchen, worin er sie suchen will, sobald er den Gebrauch der Vernunft hat." "Die Glückseligkeit des Weibes ist allein auf häusliche Freuden beschränkt." "Auch in der häuslichen Gesellschaft ragt der Mann als das Haupt hervor, wie in der bürgerlichen." "Habet nur Muth stark zu seyn, und Ihr werdet es seyn! Suchet das zu werden, was Ihr seyn sollet; und man wird gezwungen seyn, Euch das zu geben, was man Euch schuldig ist! Lernet Eure Pflichten kennen: und man wird Euch Eure Rechte nicht vorenthalten können!"

11 "Über die Franzosen und ihre Regierungs-Veränderung," *Minerva*, 1 (1795), 157–76.

12 Gerhard K. Friesen, "A Letter from M. F. Anneke: A Forgotten German-American Pioneer in Women's Rights," *Journal of German-American Studies*, XII:2 (1977), 34–46, at 37.

13 Botting "Wollstonecraft in Europe," 519; Charlotte L. Brancaforte, *Mathilde Franziska Anneke: An Essay on Her Life* (Madison: University of Wisconsin, 1998); Maria Wagner, *Mathilde Franziska Anneke in Selbstzeugnissen und Dokumenten* (Frankfurt: Fischer Taschenbuch Verlag, 1980), 127, 420. Only one issue of the *Deutsche Frauen-Zeitung* (Vol. 1, Number 7 [15 October 1852]) has survived; I thank the University of Wisconsin, Madison for making a copy available.

14 Martin Henkel and Rolf Taubert, *Das Weib im Conflict mit den Socialen Verhältnissen: Mathilde Franziska Anneke und die Erste Deutsche Frauenzeitung* (Bochum: Verlag Edition Égalité, 1976), 132.

15 *Neue Allgemeine Deutsche Bibliothek*, 9:1, Pt 1 (1794): 126–32, and 17:1, Pt 2 (1795): 66–71.

16 *Göttingische Anzeigen von gelehrten Sachen*, 155 (28 September 1793); Georg Friedrich Seiler, *Gemeinnützige Betrachtungen der neuesten Schriften* (1793); *Erlanger gelehrte Zeitung* (October 1793); *Allgemeine Literatur-Zeitung* (October 1794); all quoted in Rauschenbusch-Clough, 196–97.

17 *Neue Allgemeine Deutsche Bibliothek*, 50:8, Pt 2 (1800), 507–19, at 507, 519.

18 *Neue Allgemeine Deutsche Bibliothek*, Vol 63:4, Pt 1 (1801), 246–48.

19 *Neue Allgemeine Deutsche Bibliothek*, Vol 67:5, Pt 2 (1801), 330–31.

20 The translation is lost, but was reviewed in the periodical *Vaderlandsche Letteroefeningen*, 7:1 (1797), 343–49. Given that the title announces "notes and a foreword by Christian Gotthilf Salzmann," it can be inferred that the

translation drew on the German version. Laura Kirkley argues that quotations in the review suggest that the tone of the whole translation followed the German version; see Kirkley, "Feminism in Translation: Re-Writing the *Rights of Woman*," in Tom Toremans and Walter Verschueren, eds., *Crossing Cultures: Nineteenth-Century Anglophone Literature in the Low Countries* (Leuven: Leuven University Press, 2009), 189–200. See also Petra Broomans, "Mary Wollstonecraft in Scandinavia: Her Letters in the Netherlands," in Suzan van Dijk, ed., *I Have Heard About You: Foreign Women's Writing Crossing the Dutch Border: From Sappho to Selma Lagerlöf* (Hilversum: Verloren, 2004), 248–53.

21 See Elisabeth Gibbels, *Mary Wollstonecraft zwischen Feminismus und Opportunismus: Die discursiven Strategien in deutschen Übersetzungen von "A Vindication of the Rights of Woman."* (Tübingen: Gunter Narr Verlag, 2004), 98–116.

22 See Botting "Wollstonecraft in Europe," 523–25.

23 The Portuguese translator was Henrique Xavier Baeta; see Maria de Deus Duarte, "A Treasure Hunt in Europe at War, or "a passage in the history of a heart"? The Translation of Mary Wollstonecraft's *Letters Written During a Short Residence in Sweden, Norway, and Denmark* into Portuguese," in Alison E. Martin and Susan Pickford, eds., *Travel Narratives in Translation, 1750–1830: Nationalism, Ideology, Gender* (New York: Routledge, 2012), 181–96. For the Spanish manuscript translation, see Guillermo Carnero, "Francisca Ruiz de Larrea de Böhl de Faber y Mary Wollstonecraft," *Hispanic Review*, 50:2 (Spring 1982): 133–42. A long excerpt was also reprinted in the *Schleswig-Holsteinische Provinzialberichte*, 10:2 (1796), 236–50.

24 Botting "Wollstonecraft in Europe," 519; see also Barbara Taylor, *Eve and the New Jerusalem: Socialism and Feminism in the Nineteenth Century* (New York: Pantheon Books, 1983), esp. 59–70.

25 Bonnie S. Anderson, *Joyous Greetings: The First International Women's Movement, 1830–1860* (New York: Oxford University Press, 2000).

26 Arianne Chernock, *Men and the Making of Modern British Feminism* (Stanford: Stanford University Press, 2010); Alessa Johns, *Bluestocking Feminism and British-German Cultural Transfer, 1750–1837* (Ann Arbor: University of Michigan Press, 2014), esp. 39–87; see also Kirkley "Feminism in Translation"; and Bour "Boundaries."

Suggested Further Reading

PART I LIFE AND WORKS

1 Biography

Gordon, Charlotte, *Romantic Outlaws: The Extraordinary Lives of Mary Wollstonecraft and Mary Shelley* (London: Hutchinson, 2015).

Holmes, Richard, *Footsteps: Adventures of a Romantic Biographer* (Harmondsworth: Penguin, 1986), 90–132.

Pennell, Elizabeth Robins, *Mary Wollstonecraft Godwin* (London: W. H. Allen, 1885).

St. Clair, William, *The Godwins and the Shelleys: The Biography of a Family* (London: Faber, 1990).

Wardle, Ralph, *Mary Wollstonecraft: A Critical Biography* (Lincoln: University of Nebraska Press, 1951).

Woolf, Virginia, *The Common Reader 2* (London: Hogarth Press, 1986), 156–63.

2 Correspondence

Brant, Clare, *Eighteenth-Century Letters and British Culture* (London: Palgrave Macmillan, 2006).

Favret, Mary, *Romantic Correspondence: Women, Politics and the Fiction of Letters* (Cambridge: Cambridge University Press, 1993).

Gilroy, Amanda and Verhoeven, W. M., eds., *Epistolary Histories: Letters, Fiction, Culture* (Charlottesville: University of Virginia Press, 2000).

Horrocks, Ingrid, *Women Wanderers and the Writing of Mobility, 1784–1814* (Cambridge: Cambridge University Press, 2017).

How, James S., *Epistolary Spaces: English Letter-Writing from the Foundation of the Post Office to Richardson's "Clarissa"* (Abingdon: Ashgate, 2003).

Taylor, Barbara, *Mary Wollstonecraft and the Feminist Imagination* (Cambridge: Cambridge University Press, 2003).

Whyman, Susan E., *The Pen and the People: English Letter Writers 1660–1800* (Oxford: Oxford University Press, 2008).

3 Family

Ayres, Brenda, *Betwixt and Between: The Biographies of Mary Wollstonecraft* (New York: Anthem Press, 2017).
Carlson, Julie A., *England's First Family of Writers: Mary Wollstonecraft, William Godwin, Mary Shelley* (Baltimore: Johns Hopkins University Press, 2007).
St. Clair, William, *The Godwins and the Shelleys: A Biography of a Family* (Baltimore: Johns Hopkins University Press, 1989).
Sunstein, Emily, *A Different Face: The Life of Mary Wollstonecraft* (Boston: Little, Brown, & Company, 1975).
Todd, Janet, *Death and the Maidens: Fanny Wollstonecraft and the Shelley Circle* (London: Profile Books, 2007).
Mary Wollstonecraft: A Revolutionary Life (New York: Columbia University Press, 2000).
Tomalin, Claire, *The Life and Death of Mary Wollstonecraft* (New York: Harcourt, 1975).

4 Joseph Johnson

Braithwaite, Helen, *Romanticism, Publishing and Dissent: Joseph Johnson and the Cause of Liberty* (Basingstoke: Palgrave, 2004).
Bugg, John, ed., *The Joseph Johnson Letterbook* (Oxford: Oxford University Press, 2016).
Chard, Leslie F., "Bookseller to Publisher: Joseph Johnson and the English Book Trade, 1760 to 1810," *The Library*, 5th series, 32 (1977), 138–54.
"Joseph Johnson: Father of the Book Trade," *Bulletin of the New York Public Library*, 79 (1975), 51–82.
"Joseph Johnson in the 1790s," *Wordsworth Circle*, 33 (2002), 95–100.
Raven, James, *The Business of Books: Booksellers and the English Book Trade* (New Haven: Yale University Press, 2007).
Smyser, Jane Worthington, "The Trial and Imprisonment of Joseph Johnson, Bookseller," *Bulletin of the New York Public Library*, 77 (1974), 418–35.
Tyson, Gerald. P., *Joseph Johnson: A Liberal Publisher* (Iowa: University of Iowa Press, 1979).

PART II CRITICAL FORTUNES

5 Early Critical Reception

Botting, Eileen Hunt, "Wollstonecraft in Europe, 1792–1904: A Revisionist Reception History," *History of European Ideas*, 39:4 (2013), 503–27.
Janes, R. M., "On the Reception of Mary Wollstonecraft's *A Vindication of the Rights of Woman*," *Journal of the History of Ideas*, 39:2 (1978), 293–302.
Jump, Harriet Devine, *Mary Wollstonecraft and the Critics, 1788–2001*, 2 vols. (London: Routledge Press, 2003).

Kaplan, Cora, "Mary Wollstonecraft's Reception and Legacies," in Claudia L. Johnson, ed., *The Cambridge Companion to Mary Wollstonecraft* (Cambridge: Cambridge University Press, 2002), 246–70.

McInnes, Andrew, *Wollstonecraft's Ghost: The Fate of the Female Philosopher in the Romantic Period* (London: Routledge Press, 2017).

Smith, Abigail M., "The reception of the life and work of Mary Wollstonecraft in the early American republic," unpublished Ph.D. dissertation, University of Aberdeen (2009).

6   Nineteenth-Century Critical Reception

Botting, Eileen Hunt, "Wollstonecraft in Europe, 1792–1904: A Revisionist Reception History," *History of European Ideas*, 39:4 (2013), 503–27.

Botting, Eileen Hunt and Carey, Christine, "Wollstonecraft's Philosophical Impact on Nineteenth-Century American Women's Rights Advocates," *American Journal of Political Science*, 48:4 (2004), 707–22.

Botting, Eileen Hunt, Wilkerson, Christine Carey, and Kozlow, Elizabeth N., "Wollstonecraft as an International Feminist Meme," *Journal of Women's History*, 26:2 (2014), 13–38.

Bour, Isabelle, "The Boundaries of Sensibility: 1790s French Translations of Mary Wollstonecraft," *Women's Writing*, 11:3 (2004), 493–506.

"Une Maria inédite: La réception de The Wrongs of Woman De Mary Wollstonecraft en France," *XVII–XVIII*, HS3 (2013), 133–41.

Kirkley, Laura, "Feminism in Translation: Re-Writing the Rights of Woman," in Tom Toremans and Walter Verschueren, eds., *Crossing Cultures: Nineteenth-Century Anglophone Literature in the Low Countries* (Leuven: Leuven University Press, 2009), 189–200.

7   1970s Critical Reception

Brody, Miriam, *Mary Wollstonecraft: Mother of Women's Rights* (Oxford: Oxford University Press, 2000).

Carlson, Julie A., *England's First Family of Writers: Mary Wollstonecraft, William Godwin, Mary Shelley* (Baltimore: Johns Hopkins University Press, 2007).

Gordon, Charlotte, *Romantic Outlaws: The Extraordinary Lives of Mary Wollstonecraft and Mary Shelley* (New York: Penguin Random House, 2015).

Gordon, Lyndall, *Vindication: A Life of Mary Wollstonecraft* (New York: Harper Collins, 2005).

Todd, Janet, *Mary Wollstonecraft: A Revolutionary Life* (New York: Columbia University Press, 2000).

8   Recent Critical Reception

Halldenius, Lena, *Mary Wollstonecraft and Feminist Republicanism* (London: Pickering & Chatto, 2015).

Johnson, Claudia L., ed., *The Cambridge Companion to Mary Wollstonecraft* (Cambridge: Cambridge University Press, 2002).

Myers, Mitzi, "Sensibility and the 'Walk of Reason': Mary Wollstonecraft's Literary Reviews as Cultural Critique," in Syndy McMillen Conger, ed., *Sensibility in Transformation* (London and Toronto: Associated University Presses, 1990), 120–44.

O'Neill, Daniel, *The Burke–Wollstonecraft Debate: Savagery, Civilization, and Democracy* (Pennsylvania, Pennsylvania State Press, 2007).

Romantic Narrative: Shelley, Hays, Godwin, Wollstonecraft (Baltimore: Johns Hopkins University Press, 2010).

Steiner, Enit Karafili, ed., *Called to Civil Existence: Mary Wollstonecraft's A Vindication of the Rights of Woman* (Amsterdam: New York: Rodopi, 2014).

Taylor, Barbara, *Mary Wollstonecraft and the Feminist Imagination* (Cambridge: Cambridge University Press, 2003).

PART III   HISTORICAL AND CULTURAL CONTEXTS

The French Revolution Debate

9   Writing the French Revolution

Craciun, Adriana and Lokke, Kari, eds., *Rebellious Hearts: British Women Writers and the French Revolution* (Albany,: SUNY Press, 2001).

Baker, Keith Michael, "Fixing the French Constitution," in *Inventing the French Revolution Essays on French Political Culture in the Eighteenth Century* (Stanford: Stanford University Press, 1990), 252–305.

Doody, Margaret, "English Women Novelists and the French Revolution," in *Les femmes en Angleterre et dans les colonies américaines au VXVIIe–XVIIIe siècles: actes du colloque tenu á Paris le 24 et 25 octobre* (Lille: Université de Lille III, 1975), 176–98.

Furniss, Tom, "Mary Wollstonecraft's French Revolution," in Claudia L. Johnson, ed., *The Cambridge Companion to Mary Wollstonecraft* (Cambridge: Cambridge University Press, 2002), 59–81.

Jones, Vivien, "Mary Wollstonecraft's French Revolution," in Claudia L. Johnson, ed., *The Cambridge Companion to Mary Wollstonecraft* (Cambridge: Cambridge University Press, 2002), 59–80.

Macaulay, Catharine, *Observations on the Right Honourable Edmund Burke's Reflections on the Revolution in France* (London: C. Dilly, 1790). Reprinted by Online Library of Liberty, http://oll.libertyfund.org.

Ozouf, Mona, *Festivals and the French Revolution*, translated by Alan Sheridan (Cambridge: Harvard University Press, 1991).

Rancière, Jacques, *The Names of History: On the Poetics of Knowledge*, translated by Hassan Meletry (Minneapolis: University of Minnesota Press, 1995).

Smith, Olivia, *The Politics of Language, 1791–1819* (Oxford: Clarendon Press, 1984).

Williams, Helen Maria, *Letters Written in France*, edited by Neil Freistat and Susan S. Lanseer (Peterborough: Broadview Press, 2001).
Woodward, Lionel D., *Une Anglaise Amie de la Révolution: Helène-Marie Williams et ses amis* (Paris: Librairie Ancienne Honoré Chamption, 1930).

10 Radical Societies

Andrews, Donna T., "Popular Culture and Public Debate: London 1780," *The Historical Journal*, 39:2 (1996), 405–23.
Davis, Michael T., *London Corresponding Society, 1792–1799*, 6 vols. (London: Pickering & Chatto, 2002).
Guest, Harriet, *Unbounded Attachment: Sentiment and Politics in the Age of the French Revolution* (Cambridge: Cambridge University Press, 2013).
Mee, Jon, *Print, Publicity, and Popular Radicalism in the 1790s: The Laurel of Liberty* (Cambridge: Cambridge University Press, 2016).
O'Shaughnessy, David, "*Caleb Williams* and the Philomaths: Recalibrating Political Justice for the Nineteenth Century," *Nineteenth-Century Literature*, 66:4 (2012), 423–48.
Thale, Mary, "The Case of the British Inquisition: Monday and Women in Mid-Eighteenth-Century London Debating Societies," *Albion*, 31:1 (1999), 31–48.
"Women in London Debating Societies in 1780," *Gender & History*, 7:1 (1995), 5–24.

11 Radical Publishers

Andrew, Donna T., "Popular Culture and Public Debate: London 1780," *Historical Journal*, 39 (1996), 405–23.
Barrell, John, "Divided We Grow," *London Review of Books*, 25:11 (June 5, 2003), 8–11.
Braithwaite, Helen, *Romanticism, Publishing and Dissent: Joseph Johnson and the Cause of Liberty* (London: Palgrave, 2003).
Chernock, Arianne, *Men and the Making of Modern British Feminism* (Stanford: Stanford University Press, 2000).
Guest, Harriet, *Unbounded Attachment: Sentiment and Politics in the Age of the French Revolution* (Oxford: Oxford University Press, 2013).
Mee, Jon, *Print, Publicity, and Popular Radicalism in the 1790s: The Laurel of Liberty* (Cambridge: Cambridge University Press, 2016).
Taylor, Barbara, *Mary Wollstonecraft and the Feminist Imagination* (Cambridge: Cambridge University Press, 2003).
Thale, Mary, "London Debating Societies in the 1790s," *Historical Journal*, 32 (1989), 57–86.
"Women in London Debating Societies in 1780," *Gender & History*, 7 (1995), 5–24.
Tyson, G. P., *Joseph Johnson: A Liberal Publisher* (Iowa: University of Iowa Press, 1979).

12   British Conservatism

Barrell, John, *Imagining the King's Death: Figurative Treason, Fantasies of Regicide, 1793–1796* (Oxford: Oxford University Press, 2000).

Butler, Marilyn, *Romantics, Rebels, and Reactionaries: English Literature and Its Background, 1760–1830* (Oxford: Oxford University Press, 1982).

Colley, Linda, *Britons: Forging the Nation, 1707–1837* (London: Pimlico, 1992).

Gilmartin, Kevin, *Writing Against Revolution: Literary Conservatism in Britain, 1790–1832* (Cambridge: Cambridge University Press, 2007).

Grenby, M. O., *The Anti-Jacobin Novel: British Conservatism and the French Revolution* (Cambridge: Cambridge University Press, 2001).

Simpson, David, *Romanticism, Nationalism, and the Revolt Against Theory* (Chicago: University of Chicago Press, 1993).

Smith, Olivia, *The Politics of Language, 1791–1819* (Oxford: Clarendon Press, 1984).

The Rights of Woman Debate

13   Jacobin Reformers

Craciun, Adriana, *British Women Writers and the French Revolution: Citizens of the World* (Basingstoke: Palgrave Macmillan, 2005).

Craciun, Adriana and Lokke, Kari, eds., *Rebellious Hearts: British Women Writers and the French Revolution* (Albany: State University of New York Press, 2001).

Garnai, Amy, *Revolutionary Imaginings: Charlotte Smith, Mary Robinson, Elizabeth Inchbald* (Basingstoke: Palgrave Macmillan 2009).

Guest, Harriet, *Unbounded Attachment: Sentiment and Politics in the Age of the French Revolution* (Oxford: Oxford University Press, 2014).

Johnson, Claudia, *Equivocal Beings: Politics, Gender, and Sentimentality in the 1790s – Wollstonecraft, Radcliffe, Burney, Austen* (Chicago: University of Chicago Press, 2009).

Labbe, Jacqueline, ed., *The History of British Women's Writing, Vol. 5, 1750–1830* (Basingstoke, Palgrave Macmillan, 2010).

Taylor, Barbara, *Mary Wollstonecraft and the Feminist Imagination* (Cambridge: Cambridge University Press, 2003).

Walker, Gina Luria, *Mary Hays (1759–1843): The Growth of a Woman's Mind* (Aldershot: Ashgate, 2006).

14   Liberal Reformers

Ascarelli, Miriam, "A Feminist Connection: Jane Austen and Mary Wollstonecraft," *Persuasions: The Jane Austen Journal On-Line*, 25:1 (2004), n.p.

Chalk, Danielle Leigh, "Comparative Gender in Maria Edgeworth's Belinda," *Studies in Literary Imagination*, 47:2 (2014), 131–52.

Chandler, Anne, "Maria Edgeworth on Citizenship: Rousseau, Darwin, and Feminist Pessimism in Practical Education," *Tulsa Studies in Women's Literature*, 35:1 (2016), 93–122.
DeLucia, JoEllen M., "A Delicate Debate: Mary Wollstonecraft, the Bluestockings, and the Progress of Women," in Enit Karafili Steiner, ed., *Called to Civil Existence: Mary Wollstonecraft's A Vindication of the Rights of Woman* (New York: Editions Rodopi, 2014), 113–30.
DeRosa, Robin, "A Criticism of Contradiction: Anna Leticia Barbauld and the 'Problem' of Nineteenth-Century Women's Writing," in Susan Shifrin, ed., *Women as Sites of Culture: Women's Roles in Cultural Formation from the Renaissance to the Twentieth Century* (Aldershot: Ashgate, 2002), 221–31.
Evans, Rachel, "The Rationality and Femininity of Mary Wollstonecraft and Jane Austen," *Journal of International Women's Studies*, 7:3 (2006), 17–23.
Garner, Naomi Jayne, "'Seeing through a Glass Darkly': Wollstonecraft and the Confinements of Eighteenth-Century Femininity," *Journal of International Women's Studies*, 11:3 (2009), 81–95.
Russo, Stephanie, *Women in Revolutionary Debate: From Burney to Austen* (Houten: HES & De Graaf, 2012).
Weiss, Deborah, "The Extraordinary Ordinary Belinda: Maria Edgeworth's Female Philosopher," *Eighteenth Century Fiction*, 19:4 (2007), 441–61.

15   Conservative Reformers

Grogan, Claire, *Politics and Genre in the Works of Elizabeth Hamilton, 1756–1816* (Farnham: Ashgate, 2012).
London, April, "Jane West and the Politics of Reading," in Alvara S. J. Ribeiro and James G. Basker, eds., *Tradition in Transition: Women Writers, Marginal Texts, and the Eighteenth-Century Canon* (Oxford: Clarendon, 1996), 56–74.
Stott, Anne, "Evangelicalism and Enlightenment: The Educational Agenda of Hannah More," in Mary Hilton and Jill Shefrin, eds., *Educating the Child in Enlightenment Britain: Beliefs, Cultures, Practices*. Ashgate Studies in Childhood, 1700 to the Present (Abingdon: Ashgate, 2009), 41–55.
Wood, Lisa, *Modes of Discipline: Women, Conservatism, and the Novel after the French Revolution*. Bucknell Studies in Eighteenth-Century Literature and Culture (Lewisburg: Bucknell University Press, 2003).
"The Evangelical Novel," in J. A. Downie, ed., *The Oxford Handbook of the Eighteenth-Century Novel* (Oxford: Oxford University Press, 2016), 521–35.

Philosophical Frameworks
16   French *Philosophes*

Hont, Istvan, *Jealousy of Trade: International Competition and the Nation-State in Historical Perspective* (Cambridge: Harvard University Press, 2005).

Knott, Sarah and Taylor, Barbara, eds., *Enlightenment and Feminism* (London: Palgrave, 2005).

O'Brien, Karen, *Naratives of Enlightenment: Cosmopolitan History from Voltaire to Gibbon* (Cambridge: Cambridge University Press, 1997).

Tomaselli, Sylvana, "The Enlightenment Debate on Women," in Paul Hyland with Olga Gomez and Francesca Greensides, eds., *The Enlightenment: A Sourcebook and Reader*, reprint of 1985 edition (Abingdon and New York: Routledge, 2003), 400–04.

"The Role of Woman in Enlightenment Conjectural Histories," in Hans Erich Bödeker and Leiselotte Steinbrügge, eds., *Conceptualizing Women in Enlightenment Thought. Penser la femme au siècle des Lumières* (Berlin: Verlag Arno Spitz, 2001).

17   Dissenters

Andrew, Edward, *Conscience and Its Critics: Protestant Conscience, Enlightenment Reason, and Modern Subjectivity* (Toronto: University of Toronto Press, 2001).

Andrews, Stuart, *Unitarian Radicalism: Political Rhetoric, 1770–1814* (London: Palgrave Macmillan, 2003).

Barker-Benfield, G. J., "Mary Wollstonecraft: Eighteenth-Century Commonwealthwoman," *Journal of the History of Ideas*, 50:1 (1989), 95–115.

Barlow, Richard Burgess, *Citizenship and Conscience: A Study in the Theory and Practice of Religious Toleration in England During the Eighteenth Century* (Philadelphia: University of Pennsylvania Press, 1962).

Bradley, James, *Religion, Revolution and English Radicalism: Non-Conformity in Eighteenth-Century Politics and Society* (Cambridge: Cambridge University Press, 1990).

Braithwaite, Helen, *Romanticism, Publishing and Dissent: Joseph Johnson and the Cause of Liberty* (New York: Palgrave Macmillan, 2003).

Clark, J. C. D., *The Language of Liberty 1660–1832: Political Discourse and Social Dynamics in the Anglo-American World* (Cambridge: Cambridge University Press, 1994).

Gillespie, Katharine, *Domesticity and Dissent in the Seventeenth Century: English Women's Writing and the Public Sphere* (Cambridge: Cambridge University Press, 2004).

Haakonssen, Knud, *Enlightenment and Religion: Rational Dissent in Eighteenth-Century Britain* (Cambridge: Cambridge University Press, 1996).

Hickman, Louise, *Eighteenth-Century Dissent and Cambridge Platonism: Reconceiving the Philosophy of Religion* (London: Routledge, 2017).

James, Felicity, and Inkster, Ian, eds., *Religious Dissent and the Aikin–Barbauld Circle, 1740–1860* (Cambridge: Cambridge University Press, 2012).

Keeble, Neil H., *The Literary Culture of Nonconformity in Later Seventeenth-Century England* (Leicester: Leicester University Press, 1987).

Lincoln, Anthony, *Some Political and Social Ideas of English Dissent, 1763–1800* (Cambridge: Cambridge University Press, 1938).

Lovegrove, Deryck, *Established Church, Sectarian People: Itinerancy and the Transformation of English Dissent, 1780–1830* (Cambridge: Cambridge University Press, 2004).

Mee, Jon, *Romanticism, Enthusiasm, and Regulation: Poetics and the Policing of Culture in the Romantic Period* (Oxford: Oxford University Press, 2003).

Ready, Kathryn, "Dissenting Heads and Hearts: Joseph Priestley, Anna Barbauld, and Conflicting Attitudes towards Devotion within Rational Dissent," *Journal of Religious History*, 34:2 (2010), 174–90.

Richey, Russell E., "The Origins of British Radicalism: The Changing Rationale for Dissent," *Eighteenth-Century Studies*, 7:2 (1973–74), 179–92.

Rivers, Isabel, *Reason, Grace, and Sentiment: A Study of the Language of Religion and Ethics in England, 1660–1780*, 2 vols. (Cambridge: Cambridge University Press, 2005).

Seed, John, *Dissenting Histories: Religious Division and the Politics of Memory in Eighteenth-Century England* (Oxford: Oxford University Press, 2008).

Taylor, Barbara, "The Religious Foundations of Mary Wollstonecraft's Feminism," in Claudia L. Johnson, ed., *The Cambridge Companion to Mary Wollstonecraft* (Cambridge: Cambridge University Press, 2002), 99–118.

Taylor, Stephen and Wykes, David, eds., *Parliament and Dissent* (Edinburgh: Edinburgh University Press, 2005).

Valenze, Deborah M., *Prophetic Sons and Daughters: Female Preaching and Popular Religion in Industrial England* (Princeton: Princeton University Press, 1985).

Watts, Michael R., *The Dissenters*, 3 vols. (Oxford: Oxford University Press, 1986–2015).

Watts, Ruth, *Gender, Power and the Unitarians in England, 1760–1860* (London: Longman, 1998).

White, Daniel E., *Early Romanticism and Religious Dissent* (Cambridge: Cambridge University Press, 2007).

Whitehouse, Tessa, *The Textual Culture of English Protestant Dissent, 1720–1800* (Oxford: Oxford University Press, 2015).

18   Jean-Jacques Rousseau

Works by Rousseau

The Confessions: and Correspondence, Including the Letters to Malesherbes, edited by Christopher Kelly, Roger D. Masters, and Peter G. Stillman and translated by Christopher Kelly (Hanover: University Press of New England for Dartmouth College, 1995).

Discourse on the Origins of Inequality (Second Discourse); Polemics; and Political Economy, edited by Roger D. Masters and Christopher Kelly, translated by Roger D. Masters, Christopher Kelly, and Judith R. Bush (Hanover: University Press of New England for Dartmouth College, 1992).

Emile, or, On Education: Includes Emile and Sophie, or, The Solitaries, edited by Christopher Kelly and Allan Bloom, translated by Christopher Kelly and Allan Bloom (Hanover: University Press of New England for Dartmouth College, 2010).

Julie, or, The New Heloise: Letters of Two Lovers Who Live in a Small Town at the Foot of the Alps, edited by Roger D. Masters and Christopher Kelly, translated by Philip Steward and Jean Vaché (Hanover: University Press of New England for Dartmouth College, 1997).

The Reveries of the Solitary Walker; Botanical Writings; and, Letters to Franquières, edited by Christopher Kelly and Charles E. Butterworth, translated by Alexandra Book, and Terence E. Marshall (Hanover: University Press of New England for Dartmouth College, 2000).

The Social Contract; Discourse on the Virtue Most Necessary for a Hero; Political Fragments; and, Geneva Manuscript, edited by Roger D. Masters and Christopher Kelly, translated by Judith R. Bush, Roger D. Masters, and Christopher Kelly (Hanover: University Press of New England for Dartmouth College, 1994).

Secondary Criticism

Botting, Eileen Hunt, *Family Feuds: Wollstonecraft, Burke, and Rousseau* (Albany: SUNY Press, 2006).

Griffiths, Morwenna, "Educational Relationships: Rousseau, Wollstonecraft and Social Justice," *Journal of Philosophy of Education*, 48:2 (2014), 339–54.

Gunther-Canada, Wendy, "Jean-Jacques Rousseau and Mary Wollstonecraft on the Sexual Politics of Republican Motherhood," *Southeastern Political Review*, 27:3 (1999), 469–90.

Reuter, Martina, "'Like a Fanciful Kind of Half Being': Mary Wollstonecraft's Criticism of Jean-Jacques Rousseau," *Hypatia: A Journal of Feminist Philosophy*, 29:4 (2014), 925–41.

Schulman, Alex, "Gothic Piles and Endless Forests: Wollstonecraft between Burke and Rousseau," *Eighteenth-Century Studies*, 41:1 (2007), 41–54.

Taylor, Barbara, *Mary Wollstonecraft and the Feminist Imagination* (Cambridge: Cambridge University Press, 2003).

Trouille, Mary Seidman, *Sexual Politics in the Enlightenment: Women Writers Read Rousseau* (Albany: SUNY Press, 1997).

19   Edmund Burke

Barker-Benfield, G. J., "Mary Wollstonecraft: Eighteenth-Century Commonwealthwoman," *Journal of the History of Ideas*, 50 (1989), 95–115.

Boulton, James T., *The Language of Politics in the Age of Wilkes and Burke* (London: Routledge and Kegan Paul, 1963), 164–76, 231–32.

Bromwich, David, "Wollstonecraft as a Critic of Burke," *Political Theory*, 23 (1995), 617–34.

Burke, Edmund, *The Writings and Speeches of Edmund Burke*, 9 vols., general editor Paul Langford (Oxford: Clarendon Press, 1989–2015).

Furniss, Tom, "Gender in Revolution: Edmund Burke and Mary Wollstonecraft," in Kelvin Everest, ed., *Revolution in Writing: British Literary Responses to the French Revolution* (Milton Keynes: Open University Press, 1991), 65–100.

Gunther-Canada, Wendy, *Rebel Writer: Mary Wollstonecraft and Enlightenment Politics* (DeKalb: Northern Illinois University Press, 2007).

Conniff, James, "Edmund Burke and His Critics: The Case of Mary Wollstonecraft," *Journal of the History of Ideas*, 60 (1999), 299–318.

Halidanius, Lena, *Mary Wollstonecraft and Feminist Republicanism: Independence, Rights, and the Experience of Unfreedom* (London: Pickering & Chatto, 2015).

Jump, Harriet Devine, "A Vindication of the Rights of Men (1790)," in *Mary Wollstonecraft: Writer* (Hemel Hempstead: Harvester Wheatsheaf, 1994), 50–64.

Kelly, Gary, "From the Rights of Men to Revolutionary Feminism," in *Revolutionary Feminism: The Mind and Career of Mary Wollstonecraft* (Basingstoke: Macmillan, 1992), 84–106.

O'Neill, Daniel, *The Burke–Wollstonecraft Debate: Savagery, Civilization, and Democracy* (Pennsylvania: Pennsylvania State University Press, 2007).

Paulson, Ronald, "Burke, Paine, and Wollstonecraft: The Sublime and the Beautiful," in *Representations of Revolution (1789–1820)* (New Haven: Yale University Press, 1983), 57–87.

Sapiro, Virginia, *A Vindication of Political Virtue: The Political Theory of Mary Wollstonecraft* (Chicago: University of Chicago Press, 1992).

20   William Godwin

Butler, Marilyn, "Godwin, Burke, and *Caleb Williams*," *Essays in Criticism*, 32 (1982), 237–57.

Claeys, Gregory, "The Concept of 'Political Justice' in Godwin's *Political Justice*: A Reconsideration," *Political Theory*, 11 (1983), 565–84.

Clark, John P., *The Philosophical Anarchism of William Godwin* (Princeton: Princeton University Press, 1977).

Clemit, Pamela, "Godwin, Political Justice," in Pamela Clemit, ed., *The Cambridge Companion to British Literature of the French Revolution in the 1790s* (Cambridge: Cambridge University Press, 2011).

"Readers Respond to Godwin: Romantic Republicanism in Letters," *European Romantic Review*, 20 (2009), 701–09.

The Godwinian Novel: The Rational Fictions of Godwin, Brockden Brown, Mary Shelley (Oxford: Clarendon Press, 1993, reprinted 2001).

"The Signal of Regard: William Godwin's Correspondence Networks," *European Romantic Review*, 30 (2019).

Fleisher, David, *William Godwin: A Study in Liberalism* (London: George Allen and Unwin, 1951).

Handwerk, Gary, "Of Caleb's Guilt and Godwin's Truth: Ideology and Ethics in *Caleb Williams*," *English Literary History*, 60 (1993), 939–60.

Kelly, Gary, *The English Jacobin Novel, 1780–1805* (Oxford: Clarendon Press, 1976).

Lamb, Robert, "The Foundations of Godwinian Impartiality," *Utilitas*, 18 (2006), 134–53.

Maniquis, Robert M., and Myers, Victoria, eds., *Godwinian Moments: From the Enlightenment to Romanticism* (Toronto: University of Toronto Press, 2011).

Monro D. H., *Godwin's Moral Philosophy: An Interpretation of William Godwin* (London: Oxford University Press, 1953).

Myers, Mitzi, "Godwin's *Memoirs* of Wollstonecraft: The Shaping of Self and Subject," *Studies in Romanticism*, 20 (1981), 299–316.

O'Brien, Eliza, Stark, Helen, and Turner, Beatrice, eds., *New Approaches to William Godwin: Forms, Fears, Futures* (London: Palgrave Macmillan, 2019).

Philp, Mark, *Godwin's Political Justice* (London: Duckworth, 1986).

Scrivener, Michael H., "Godwin's Philosophy: A Revaluation," *Journal of the History of Ideas*, 39 (1978), 615–26.

21 Political Theory

Barker-Benfield, G. J., "Mary Wollstonecraft: Eighteenth-Century Commonwealthwoman," *Journal of the History of Ideas*, 50:1 (1989), 95–115.

Bergès, Sandrine, *Wollstonecraft's A Vindication of the Rights of Woman* (London: Routledge, 2013).

Bergès, Sandrine and Coffee, Alan, eds., *The Social and Political Philosophy of Mary Wollstonecraft* (Oxford: Oxford University Press, 2016). See particularly the contributions by L. Brace, P. Pettit, S. James, L. Halldenius, and A. Coffee.

Coffee, Alan, "Freedom as Independence: Mary Wollstonecraft and the Grand Blessing of Life," *Hypatia: A Journal of Feminist Philosophy*, 29:4 (2014), 908–24.

"Mary Wollstonecraft, Freedom and the Enduring Power of Social Domination," *European Journal of Political Theory*, 12:2 (2013), 116–35.

Conniff, James, "Edmund Burke and his Critics: The Case of Mary Wollstonecraft," *Journal of the History of Ideas*, 60:2 (1999), 299–318.

Gunther-Canada, Wendy, *Rebel Writer: Mary Wollstonecraft and Enlightenment Politics* (DeKalb: Northern Illinois University Press, 2001).

Halldenius, Lena, *Mary Wollstonecraft and Feminist Republicanism: Independence, Rights and the Experience of Unfreedom* (London: Pickering and Chatto, 2015).

"Mary Wollstonecraft and Freedom as Independence," in Jacqueline Broad and Karen Detlefsen, eds., *Women and Liberty, 1600–1800. Philosophical Essays* (Oxford: Oxford University Press, 2017).

"Mary Wollstonecraft's Feminist Critique of Property: On Becoming a Thief from Principle," *Hypatia: A Journal of Feminist Philosophy*, 29:4 (2014), 942–57.

"Representation in Mary Wollstonecraft's Political Philosophy," in Sandrine Bergès and Alan Coffee, eds., *The Social and Political Philosophy of Mary Wollstonecraft* (Oxford: Oxford University Press, 2016), 166–82.

"The Political Conditions for Free Agency: The Case of Mary Wollstonecraft," in Quentin Skinner and Martin van Gelderen, eds., *Freedom and the Construction of Europe*, 2 vols. (Cambridge: Cambridge University Press, 2013), 2: 227–43.

"The Primacy of Right: On the Triad of Liberty, Equality and Virtue in Wollstonecraft's Political Thought," *British Journal for the History of Philosophy*, 15:1 (2007), 75–99.

Mackenzie, Catriona, "Reason and Sensibility: The Ideal of Women's Self-Governance in the Writings of Mary Wollstonecraft," *Hypatia: A Journal of Feminist Philosophy*, 8:4 (1993), 181–203.

Maynor, John, *Republicanism in the Modern World* (Cambridge: Polity Press, 2003).

Neill, Anna, "Civilization and the Rights of Woman: Liberty and Captivity in the Work of Mary Wollstonecraft," *Women's Writing*, 8:1 (2001), 99–118.

O'Neill, Daniel, *The Burke–Wollstonecraft Debate: Savagery, Civilization, and Democracy* (Pennsylvania: Pennsylvania State University Press, 2007).

Reuter, Martina, "Revolution, Virtue and Duty: Aspects of Politics, Religion and Morality in Mary Wollstonecraft's Thought," in Marius Timmann Mjaaland, Ola Sigurdson, and Sigridur Thorgeirsdottir, eds., *The Body Unbound: Philosophical Perspectives on Politics, Embodiment and Religion* (Newcastle upon Tyne: Cambridge Scholars Publishing, 2010), 107–22.

Sapir, Virginia, *A Vindication of Political Virtue: The Political Theory of Mary Wollstonecraft* (Chicago: The University of Chicago Press, 1992).

Skinner, Quentin, "Freedom as the Absence of Arbitrary Power," in Cecile Laborde and John Maynor, eds., *Republicanism and Political Theory* (Oxford: Blackwell, 2008), 83–101.

Taylor, Barbara, *Mary Wollstonecraft and the Feminist Imagination* (Cambridge: Cambridge University Press, 2003).

22 Feminist Theory

Guest, Harriet, *Unbounded Attachment: Sentiment and Politics in the Age of the French Revolution* (Oxford: Oxford University Press, 2013).

Jones, Vivian, ed., *Women and Literature in Britain, 1700–1800* (Cambridge: Cambridge University Press, 2000).

Knott, Sarah and Taylor, Barbara, eds., *Women, Gender and Enlightenment* (Basingstoke: Palgrave Macmillan, 2005).

Todd, Janet, *Feminist Literary History: A Defence* (London: Polity, 1988).

Wolfson, Susan J., *Borderlines: The Shiftings of Gender in British Romanticism* (Stanford: Stanford University Press).

Legal and Social Culture

23 The Constitution

Burke, Edmund, *Reflections on the Revolution in France* (Harmondsworth: Penguin, 1986).

Hodson, Jane, *Language and Revolution in Burke, Wollstonecraft, Paine and Godwin* (London: Ashgate, 2007).

Kelly, Gary, *Women, Writing and Revolution* (Oxford: Oxford University Press, 1993).

Kramnick, Isaac, *The Rage of Edmund Burke* (New York: Basic Books, 1977).

24 Property Law

Barker, Hannah, *Family and Business during the Industrial Revolution* (Oxford: Oxford University Press, 2017).

Brewer, John and Staves, Susan, eds., *Early Modern Conceptions of Property* (London and New York: Routledge 1995).

Erickson, Amy Louise, *Women and Property in Early Modern England* (London and New York: Routledge, 1993).

Skinner, Gillian, "Women's Status as Legal and Civic Subjects: 'A Worse Condition than Slavery Itself?'" in Vivien Jones, ed., *Women and Literature in Britain 1700–1800* (Cambridge: Cambridge University Press, 2000), 91–111.

Sonenscher, Michael, "Property, Community and Citizenship", in Mark Goldie and Robert Wokler, eds., *The Cambridge History of Eighteenth-Century Political Thought* (Cambridge: Cambridge University Press, 2006), 465–94.

Staves, Susan, *Married Women's Separate Property in England, 1660–1833* (Cambridge: Harvard University Press, 1990).

25 Domestic Law

Akamatsu, Junko, "Revisiting Ecclesiastical Adultery Cases in Eighteenth-Century England," *Journal of Women's History*, 28 (2016), 13–37.

Bailey, Joanne, *Unquiet Lives: Marriage and Marriage Breakdown in England, 1660–1800* (Cambridge: Cambridge University Press, 2003).

Doggett, Maeve, *Marriage, Wife-Beating and the Law in Victorian England* (London: Weidenfeld & Nicholson, 1992).

Dolan, Frances E., "Battered Women, Petty Traitors, and the Legacy of Coverture," *Feminist Studies*, 29 (2003), 249–77.

Probert, Rebecca, *Marriage Law and Practice in the Long Eighteenth Century: A Reassessment* (Cambridge: Cambridge University Press, 2009).

The Legal Regulation of Cohabitation: From Fornicators to Family, 1600–2010 (Cambridge: Cambridge University Press, 2012).

Stone, Lawrence, *Road to Divorce: A History of the Making and Breaking of Marriage in England* (Oxford: Oxford University Press, 1990).

Temkin, Jennifer, *Rape and the Legal Process* (Oxford: Oxford University Press, 2002).

Wright, Danaya C., "The Crisis of Child Custody: A History of the Birth of Family Law in England," *Columbia Journal of Gender and the Law*, 11 (2002), 175–270.

26 *Slavery and Abolition*

Andrew, Donna T., *Philanthropy and Police: London Charity in the Eighteenth Century* (Princeton: Princeton University Press, 1989).

Carey, Brycchan, *British Abolitionism and the Rhetoric of Sensibility: Writing, Sentiment, and Slavery, 1760–1807* (Basingstoke: Palgrave Macmillan, 2005).

Clapp, Elizabeth J and Jeffrey, Julie Roy, eds., *Women, Dissent, and Antislavery in Britain and America, 1790–1865* (Oxford: Oxford University Press 2011).

Ferguson, Moira, *Subject to Others: British Women Writers and Colonial Slavery 1670–1784* (London: Routledge, 1992).

Hersch, B. G., *The Slavery of Sex: Feminist-Abolitionists in America* (Urbana: University of Illinois Press, 1978).

Holcomb, Julie L., "Blood-Stained Sugar: Gender, Commerce and the British Slave-Trade Debates," *Slavery & Abolition*, 35:4 (2014), 611–28.

Howard, Carol, "Wollstonecraft's Thoughts on Slavery and Corruption," *The Eighteenth Century*, 45:1 (2004), 61–86

Macdonald, D. L., "Master, Slave and Mistress in Wollstonecraft's *Vindication*," *Enlightenment and Dissent*, 11 (1992), 46–57.

Matthews, Gelien, *Caribbean Slave Revolts and the British Abolitionist Movement* (Baton Rouge: Louisiana State University Press, 2006).

Midgley, Clare, *Gender and Imperialism* (Manchester: Manchester University Press, 1998).

Women Against Slavery: The British Campaigns, 1780–1870 (London: Routledge, 1992).

Oldfield, J. R., *Popular Politics and British Anti-Slavery: The Mobilisation of Public Opinion Against the Slave Trade 1787–1807* (London: Routledge, 1998).

Page, Anthony, "'A Species of Slavery': Richard Price's Rational Dissent and Antislavery," *Slavery & Abolition*, 32:1 (2011), 53–73.

Sinha, Manish, *The Slave's Cause: A History of Abolition* (New Haven: Yale University Press, 2016).

Yellin, J. F., *Women and Sisters: Antislavery Feminists in American Culture* (New Haven: Yale University Press, 1989).

27 *The Bluestockings*

DeLucia, JoEllen M., "A Delicate Debate: Mary Wollstonecraft, the Bluestockings, and the Progress of Women," in Enit Karafili Steiner, ed., *Called to Civil Existence: Mary Wollstonecraft's "A Vindication of the Rights of Woman"* (Cambridge: Cambridge University Press, 2014), 113–30.

Eaton, Barbara, *Yes Papa! Mrs Chapone and the Bluestocking Circle* (London: Francis Boutle Publishers, 2012).

Eger, Elizabeth, *Bluestockings: Women of Reason from Enlightenment to Romanticism* (Basingstoke: Palgrave Macmillan, 2010).

Guest, Harriet, *Small Change: Women, Learning, Patriotism, 1750–1810* (Chicago: University of Chicago Press, 2000).

Kelly, Gary, general ed., *Bluestocking Feminism: Writings of the Bluestocking Circle, 1738–1785*, 6 vols. (London: Pickering & Chatto, 1999).

Myers, Sylvia Harcstarck, *The Bluestocking Circle: Women, Friendship, and the Life of the Mind in Eighteenth-Century England* (Oxford: Clarendon, 1990).

O'Brien, Karen, *Women and Enlightenment in Eighteenth-Century Britain* (Cambridge: Cambridge University Press, 2009).

Pohl, Nicole and Schellenberg, Betty A., eds., *Reconsidering the Bluestockings* (San Marino: Huntington Library, 2003).

Schellenberg, Betty A., *Literary Coteries and the Making of English Print Culture, 1740–1790* (Cambridge: Cambridge University Press, 2016).

Zuk, Rhoda, ed. *Catherine Talbot & Hester Chapone*, vol. 3 of *Bluestocking Feminism: Writings of the Bluestocking Circle, 1738–1785* (London: Pickering & Chatto, 1999).

28 Conduct Literature

Eaton, Barbara, *Yes Papa! Mrs Chapone and the Bluestocking Circle* (London: Francis Boutle Publishers, 2012).

Eger, Elizabeth, *Bluestockings: Women of Reason from Enlightenment to Romanticism* (Basingstoke: Palgrave Macmillan, 2010).

Jones, Vivien, ed., *Women in the Eighteenth-Century: Constructions of Femininity* (London: Routledge, 1990).

Knott, Sarah and Taylor, Barbara, eds., *Women, Gender and Enlightenment* (Basingstoke: Palgrave Macmillan, 2005).

Schellenberg, Betty A., *Literary Coteries and the Making of English Print Culture, 1740–1790* (Cambridge: Cambridge University Press, 2016).

29 Theories of Education

Hanley, Kirstin Collins, *Mary Wollstonecraft, Pedagogy, and the Practice of Feminism* (New York: Routledge, 2013).

Johnson, Claudia, *Equivocal Beings* (Chicago: University of Chicago Press, 1995).

Jones, Vivien, "Mary Wollstonecraft and the Literature of Advice and Instruction," in Claudia L. Johnson, ed., *The Cambridge Companion to Mary Wollstonecraft* (Cambridge: Cambridge University Press, 2006), 119–40.

Myers, Mitzi, "Impeccable Governesses, Rational Dames, and Moral Mothers: Mary Wollstonecraft and the Female Tradition in Georgian Children's Books," *Children's Literature*, 14 (1986), 31–59.

Richardson, Alan, "Mary Wollstonecraft on Education," in Claudia L. Johnson, ed., *The Cambridge Companion to Mary Wollstonecraft* (Cambridge: Cambridge University Press, 2006), 24–41.

Literature

30   Sentimentalism and Sensibility

Barker-Benfield, G. J., *The Culture of Sensibility: Sex and Society in Eighteenth-Century Britain* (Chicago: University of Chicago Press, 1992).

Benedict, Barbara M., *Framing Feeling: Sentiment and Style in English Prose Fiction, 1745–1800* (New York: AMS Press, 1994).

Brissenden, R. F., *Virtue in Distress: Studies in the Novel of Sentiment from Richardson to Sade* (New York: Harper and Row, 1974).

Crane, R. S., "Suggestions toward a Genealogy of the 'Man of Feeling'" *ELH*, 1:3 (1934), 205–30.

De Bruyn, Frans, "Latitudinarianism and its Importance as a Precursor of Sensibility," *Journal of English and Germanic Philology*, 80:3 (1981), 349–68.

Dwyer, John, *Virtuous Discourse: Sensibility and Community in Late Eighteenth-Century Scotland* (Edinburgh: L. Donald Publishers, 1987).

Ellis, Markman, *The Politics of Sensibility: Race, Gender, and Commerce in the Sentimental Novel* (Cambridge: Cambridge University Press, 1996).

Ellison, Julie K., *Cato's Tears and the Making of Anglo-American Emotion* (Chicago: University of Chicago Press, 1999).

Goring, Paul, *The Rhetoric of Sensibility in Eighteenth-Century Culture* (Cambridge: Cambridge University Press, 2005).

Gross, Daniel M., *The Secret History of Emotion: From Aristotle's Rhetoric to Modern Brain Science* (Chicago: University of Chicago Press, 2006).

Guest, Harriet, *Small Change: Women, Learning, Patriotism, 1750–1810* (Chicago: University of Chicago Press, 2000).

Johnson, Claudia, *Equivocal Beings: Politics, Gender, and Sentimentality in the 1790s* (Chicago: University of Chicago Press, 1995).

Lynch, Deidre, "Personal Effects and Sentimental Fictions," *Eighteenth-Century Fiction*, 12:2 (2000), 345–68.

Mullan, John, *Sentiment and Sociability: The Language of Feeling in the Eighteenth Century* (Oxford: Clarendon Press, 1988).

Pinch, Adela, *Strange Fits of Passion: Epistemologies of Emotion, Hume to Austen* (Stanford: Stanford University Press, 1996).

Rousseau, G. S., "Nerves, Spirits, and Fibres: Towards Defining the Origins of Sensibility," in R. F. Brissenden and J. C. Eade, eds., *Studies in the Eighteenth Century III* (Toronto: University of Toronto Press, 1976).

Terada, Rei. *Feeling in Theory: Emotion after the "Death of the Subject"* (Cambridge: Harvard, University Press, 2001).

Todd, Janet, *Sensibility: An Introduction* (New York: Methuen, 1986).

Van Sant, Ann Jessie, *Eighteenth-Century Sensibility and the Novel: The Senses in Social Context* (New York: Cambridge University Press, 1993).

Yousef, Nancy, "'Emotions that Reason Deepens': Second Thoughts about Affect," *Nineteenth-Century Gender Studies*, 11:3 (2015), 61–73.

31 English Jacobin Novels

Gilmartin, Kevin, *Writing Against Revolution. Literary Conservatism in Britain, 1790–1832* (Cambridge: Cambridge University Press, 2007).

Grenby, M. O., *The Anti-Jacobin Novel: British Conservatism and the French Revolution* (Cambridge: Cambridge University Press, 2001).

Haywood, Ian, *The Revolution in Popular Literature: Print, Politics and the People, 1790–1860* (Cambridge: Cambridge University Press, 2004).

Kelly, Gary, *Women, Writing and Revolution 1790–1827* (Oxford: Clarendon Press, 1993).

Mee, Jon, *Print, Publicity, and Popular Radicalism in the 1790s: The Laurel of Liberty* (Cambridge: Cambridge University Press, 2016).

32 Anti-Jacobin Novels

Erickson, Lee, *The Economy of Literary Form: English Literature and the Industrialization of Publishing, 1800–1850* (Baltimore: Johns Hopkins University Press, 1996).

Grenby, M. O., *The Anti-Jacobin Novel: British Conservatism and the French Revolution* (Cambridge: Cambridge University Press, 2001).

Kelly, Gary, *English Fiction of the Romantic Period, 1789–1830* (London and New York: Longman, 1989).

Rooney, Morgan, *The French Revolution Debate and the British Novel, 1790–1814* (Lewisburg: Bucknell University Press, 2013).

Verhoeven, W. M, general ed., *Anti-Jacobin Novels*, 10 vols. (London: Pickering & Chatto, 2005).

33 Children's Literature

Chandler, Anne, "Wollstonecraft's *Original Stories*: Animal Objects and the Subject of Fiction," *Eighteenth-Century Novel*, 2 (2002), 325–51.

Franklin, Caroline, *Mary Wollstonecraft: A Literary Life* (Basingstoke: Palgrave, 2004).

Klemann, Heather, "How to Think with Animals in Mary Wollstonecraft's *Original Stories* and *The Wrongs of Woman; or, Maria*," *Lion and the Unicorn*, 39:1 (2015), 1–22.

Myers, Mitzi, "Impeccable Governesses, Rational Dames, and Moral Mothers: Mary Wollstonecraft and the Female Tradition in Georgian Children's Books," *Children's Literature*, 14 (1989), 31–59.

Richardson, Alan, "Mary Wollstonecraft in Education," in Claudia L. Johnson, ed., *The Cambridge Companion to Mary Wollstonecraft* (Cambridge: Cambridge University Press, 2002), 24–41.

34 Gothic Literature

Barker-Benfield, G. J., *The Culture of Sensibility: Sex and Society in Eighteenth-Century Britain* (Chicago: University of Chicago Press, 1992).
Clery, E. J., *The Rise of Supernatural Fiction* (Cambridge: Cambridge University Press, 1994).
Gamer, Michael, *Romanticism and the Gothic: Genre, Reception, and Canon Formation* (Cambridge: Cambridge University Press, 2000).
Saggini, Francesca, *The Gothic Novel and the Stage: Romantic Appropriations* (London: Pickering & Chatto, 2015).
Sedgwick, Eve Kosofsky, *Between Men: English Literature and Male Homosocial Desire* (New York: Columbia University Press, 1995).
Wright, Angela and Townsend, Dale, eds., *Romantic Gothic: An Edinburgh Companion* (Edinburgh: Edinburgh University Press, 2016).

35 Travel Writing

Bohls, Elizabeth, *Women Travel Writers and the Language of Aesthetics, 1716–1818* (Cambridge: Cambridge University Press, 2004).
Dekker, George, *Fictions of Romantic Tourism: Radcliffe, Scott, and Mary Shelley* (Stanford: Stanford University Press, 2005).
Dolan, Brian, *Ladies of the Grand Tour: British Women in Pursuit of Enlightenment and Adventure in Eighteenth-Century Europe* (New York: HarperCollins, 2001).
Durie, Alastair J., *Scotland for the Holidays: A History of Tourism in Scotland, 1780–1939* (East Linton: Tuckwell Press, 2003).
Hagglun, Betty, *Tourists and Travelers: Women's Non-Fictional Writing about Scotland, 1770–1830* (Bristol: Channel View Publications, 2010).
Kinsley, Zoë, *Women Writing the Home Tour, 1682–1812* (Aldershot: Ashgate, 2008).
Siskin, Clifford, *The Work of Writing: Literature and Social Change in Britain, 1700–1830* (Baltimore: Johns Hopkins University Press, 1998).
Williams, William H. A., *Creating Irish Tourism: The First Century, 1750–1850* (London: Anthem Press, 2010).

36 History Writing

Furniss, Tom, "Mary Wollstonecraft's French Revolution," in Claudia L. Johnson, *The Cambridge Companion to Mary Wollstonecraft* (Cambridge: Cambridge University Press, 2006).

Phillips, Mark Salber, *Society and Sentiment: Genres of Historical Writing in Britain* (Princeton: Princeton University Press, 2000).
Rendall, Jane, "'The Grand Causes Which Combine to Carry Mankind Forward': Wollstonecraft, History, and Revolution," *Women's Writing*, 4:2 (1997), 155–72.
Schama, Simon, *Citizens: A Chronicle of the French Revolution* (New York: Vintage, 1990).

37   Periodicals

Graham, Walter James, *English Literary Periodicals* (New York: Octagon Books, 1966).
Oliver, Susan, "Silencing Joseph Johnson and the *Analytical Review*," *Wordsworth Circle*, 40 (2009), 96–102.
Roper, Derek, *Reviewing Before the "Edinburgh" 1788–1802* (London: Methuen, 1978).
Stewart, Sally, "Mary Wollstonecraft's Contributions to the *Analytical Review*," *Essays in Literature*, 11 (1984), 187–99.
Waters, Mary, *British Women Writers and the Profession of Literary Criticism, 1789–1832* (New York: Palgrave Macmillan, 2004).

38   Translations

Botting, Eileen Hunt, *Wollstonecraft, Mill, and Women's Human Rights* (New Haven: Yale University Press, 2016).
Botting, Eileen Hunt, Wilkerson, Christine Carey, and Kozlow, Elizabeth N., "Wollstonecraft as an International Feminist Meme," *Journal of Women's History*, 26:2 (2014), 13–38.
Favret, Mary A., "A Short Residence: Traveling with Mary Wollstonecraft," in Claudia L. Johnson, ed., *The Cambridge Companion to Mary Wollstonecraft* (Cambridge: Cambridge University Press, 2002), 209–27.
Hufton, Olwen, *The Prospect Before Her: A History of Women in Western Europe, 1500–1800* (New York: Vintage, 1995).

Index

Adams, Abigail, 44
Adams, John, 8
Addison, Joseph, 314, 316
Aikin, John, 29, 35, 248, 251–52
  Evenings at Home, 250
Alexander, William
  History of Women, 307
Arden, Jane, 4, 11–12, 17
Astell, Mary, 59, 190
  A Serious Proposal to the Ladies, 189
Austen, Jane, 120, 124, 252
  Lady Susan, 124
  Mansfield Park, 123–24
  Northanger Abbey, 260, 293, 295
  Pride and Prejudice, 239

Bage, Robert
  Hermsprong, 265, 267
Barbauld, Anna Laetitia
  "Rights of Woman, The", 121
  "To Dr. Aikin", 122
  "What is Education?", 249
  and Joseph Johnson,
    33, 90, 96, 121
  and MW, 120, 122
  and other female writers, 120
  and the Bluestockings, 233
  Evenings at Home, 250
  Female Speaker, The, 252
  Hymns in Prose for Children, 252
  in MW's *Female Reader*, 243
  Lessons for Children, 248
  MW attacks, 121, 151
  on education, 250–51, 286
  on her education, 122
  on Rousseau, 249
  Poems, 30
  reputation of, 282
Beattie, James, 234
Bishop, Mary, 23
Bishop, Meredith, 4, 23

Bisset, Robert, 274, 276, 278
  Douglas, 273
Blackstone, Sir William, 210, 215–17, 220
  Commentaries on the Laws of England, 215
Blair, Hugh
  Lectures on Rhetoric and Belles Lettres, 307
Blake, William
  and Joseph Johnson, 320
  illustrates MW's *Original Stories*, 42, 283
Blood, Fanny, 4, 5, 8, 23, 283, 314
Bonnycastle, John, 33–34
Brooke, Frances Moore
  Old Maid, 317
Bryan, Margaret
  Letters on Natural Philosophy, 106
Bulwer-Lytton, Edward, 174, 277
Burgh, James
  Thoughts on Education, 147, 242
Burke, Edmund
  and ancient constitution, 79
  as Whig historian, 204
  attacks Thomas Cooper, 96
  Catherine Macaulay responds to, 80–81
  chivalric sentiment of, 66, 77, 80, 102, 169
  classical citation in work of, 305
  Letter to a Noble Lord, 91
  MW responds to, 6, 15, 42–43, 77, 164, 166,
    243
  on America, 166
  on civic virtue, 168
  on constitutional continuity, 165–66, 200
  on custom, 167
  on moral conduct, 169, 171
  on patriarchal authority, 269
  on private affection, 173
  on property, 168
  on prudence, 167
  on radical change, 167
  on revolution principles, 201
  on Richard Price, 88, 165, 275
  Philosophical Enquiry, 164, 170

Reflections, 6, 79, 81, 91, 95, 107, 148,
    164–66, 168, 170, 200–3, 209, 259, 264,
    275, 305, 309
  sensibility of, 170, 262, 264
  use of allegory, 79–81
Burney, Frances, 16, 202

Cambon, Mme. de (Maria Geertrudia van de
    Werken)
  Young Grandison, 34, 285
Carter, Elizabeth, 190, 231–33, 236
Chapone, Hester, 230–32, 234, 236, 243
  Letters on the Improvement of the Mind, 193,
    230, 232–33, 243
Christie, Thomas, 318–19
  Letters on the Revolution in France, 306
Clairmont, Charles, 26
Clairmont, Mary Jane (Claire), 26
Coleridge, Samuel, 289
Cowley, Hannah, 6
Cowper, William, 32, 243
  Negro's Complaint, The, 226
  Task, The, 30
Coxe, William
  *Travels into Poland, Russia, Sweden and
    Denmark*, 302

Darwin, Erasmus, 33
  *A Plan for the Conduct of Female Education in
    Boarding Schools*, 282
  Economy of Vegetation, The, 30
  Loves of the Plants, The, 30
Dawson, Sarah, 4, 23
Day, Thomas, 282
  History of Sandford and Merton, The, 281, 285
Diderot, Denis, 139, 142
D'Israeli, Isaac
  History of Sir George Warrington, The, 273
  Vaurien, 273

Eaton, Daniel Isaac, 33, 91, 97, 99
  Politics for the People, 97
Eaton, Susannah, 90, 98
Edgeworth, Maria
  "The Purple Jar", 122
  and Joseph Johnson, 30, 33, 35, 96, 120
  MW on, 285
  on education, 248
  proposes lady's magazine, 120
  reputation of, 282
Enfield, William, 43
  Speaker, The, 252

Fénelon, François, 173, 240
  Les aventures de Télémaque, 173, 208, 247, 276

Fenwick, Eliza, 264, 297
  Secresy, 265, 268
Fielding, Henry, 267
Fielding, Sarah, 234
  Adventures of David Simple, The, 257
Floresta, Nísia, 51, 53
Fordyce, James, 129, 240, 244, 306
  Sermons to Young Women, 238, 244
Fournée, Marguerite, 8, 25–26
French Revolution, 309
  and education, 44
  British conservatives and, 194
  British politics and, 103
  British women and, 79, 112
  British writers' responses to, 127, 278
  causes of, 144
  Charlotte Smith and, 112
  Dissenters' support of, 148, 275
  Edmund Burke on, 90, 164, 166, 200
  Helen Maria Williams and, 81
  justification of, 46
  letter form during, 15
  MW supports ideals of, 51, 183, 185, 238,
    243
  MW's view of, 306, 309–12
  political debate over, 21, 166, 174, 275
  property and, 187, 208–9
  radical societies and, 88–90
  reshapes British culture, 15
  Revd Richard Price on, 3, 165
  Sarah Trimmer and, 121
  violence of, 7, 8, 45
Fuseli, Henry, 7, 33–35, 320
  Nightmare, The, 33
  *Remarks on the Writing and Conduct of J. J.
    Rousseau*, 34

Gardeton, M. César, 50, 53, 324
Geddes, Alexander, 33–34, 320
Godwin, Ann (Hull), 25
Godwin, Mary Jane (Vial) (formerly, Clairmont),
    26
Godwin, Revd John, 25
Godwin, William
  adopts Fanny Imlay, 26
  and Elizabeth Inchbald, 269
  and John Thelwall, 88
  and Joseph Johnson, 35
  and Mary Robinson, 111
  and the LCS, 88
  and the Philomathian Society, 92
  as biographer, 9, 15, 18–19, 25, 36
  bookshop of, 281
  Caleb Williams, 9, 114, 174, 178, 266, 268
  capacity for empathy, 9, 178

Godwin, William (cont.)
character of, 9, 174, 180
Cursory Strictures, 174
diary of, 92
education of, 25
Enquirer, The, 179, 282
intellectual career of, 174
intellectual circles of, 54, 147
intellectual diversity of, 175
letters of, 173, 178–79
life of, 25
Memoirs, 9, 18–19, 36, 47, 50–54, 57, 69,
114, 120, 132, 152, 179–80, 194, 202,
323–25, 327
MW meets, 9, 25, 33, 111
on FB's Scandinavian letters, 302
on human nature, 175, 177
on moral growth, 178
on private affections, 173
on *VRM*, 31, 203
on *VRW*, 6
Political Justice, 26, 88, 96, 107, 173–75,
177–78, 209
Posthumous Works (of MW), 47, 286
publishes MW's work posthumously, 9, 41,
47–48
publishes *Wrongs of Woman*, 9, 52, 271
relationship with MW, 9, 11, 13, 17–18, 25,
179–80, 215
reputation of, 174
St. Leon, 173
Thoughts Occasioned, 175
Gregory, John
*A Comparative View of the State and Faculties of
Mankind*, 243
A Father's Legacy to his Daughters, 238, 240,
243
advice to daughters, 241, 244
MW on, 119, 129, 235, 238, 244, 306
on women, 239, 244
Gregory, Revd. George, 33

Hamilton, Elizabeth
and Joseph Johnson, 96
as conservative reformer, 128, 129,
130
Cottagers of Glenburnie, 130
criticism of, 133
educational works of, 129
fiction of, 131
fictional characters of, 133
Memoirs of Modern Philosophers,
131–32, 260, 277
Translation of the Letters of a Hindoo Rajah,
131, 278

Hardships of the English Laws in relation to Wives,
209
Hardy, Lydia, 91, 93, 98
Hardy, Thomas, 89–91, 93, 98
Harrington, James
Oceana, 208
Hays, Mary
and George Dyer, 112
and MW's letters, 15, 117
Appeal, 30, 115–16
as part of radical circle, 93, 120
friendship with MW, 7, 9, 111, 113
Joseph Johnson publishes, 121
Letters and Essays, 7, 113
loyal to Joseph Johnson, 121
Memoirs of Emma Courtney, 277
MW and Godwin meet at home of, 9, 25,
111
obituary of MW, 114
response to MW, 69
Victim of Prejudice, 116, 265, 268
Haywood, Eliza
Female Spectator, 317
Helvétius, Claude Adrien, 142, 167
Child of Nature, 277
Henry Willoughby, 268
Hewlett, Revd John, 6, 31
Hodgson, William, 99
Holcroft, Thomas, 26, 89, 92, 265–69, 276
Hugh Trevor, 264, 266–67
Hume, David, 233–34, 258, 307
and slavery, 224
Hurdis, James, 33
Hutcheson, Francis, 258

Imlay, Fanny, 7–9, 17, 21, 24, 26, 36, 286
Imlay, Gilbert
and MW's travel to Scandinavia, 8, 25, 46, 69,
297
MW's letters to, 7, 11–12, 16–17, 21, 47,
141, 155, 211
relationship with MW, 7–9, 17, 24–25, 48,
52, 83, 302, 327
Inchbald, Elizabeth, 173–74, 264
Nature and Art, 265, 269
A Simple Story, 269
Ireland, Samuel
*Picturesque Tour Through Holland, Brabant,
and Part of France*, 299

Janeway, James
A Token for Children, 281
Jardine, Alexander, 300, 302
*Letters from Barbary, France, Spain,Portugal,
etc.*, 300

Johnson, Joseph
  and Henry Fuseli, 34, 36
  and Unitarianism, 30
  as intellectual host, 33, 90, 96, 120, 147, 320
  as publisher, 5, 6, 29–30, 35, 95, 121, 283, 318, 320
  bookshop of, 30, 33–34
  employs MW, 6, 95, 202, 257, 276, 292
  Godwin's *Memoirs*, 36
  health of, 35
  member of SCI, 33, 90, 96
  MW meets, 5
  MW meets Godwin at home of, 25, 34
  relationship with MW, 6, 29–32, 34, 147, 314
  tried for seditious libel, 35, 97
Johnson, Richard, 282
Johnson, Samuel, 6, 225
  Rasselas, 276
Jordan, Jeremiah, 35, 96

Kames, Henry Home, Lord, 307–8
  Historical Law Tracts, 308
Kant, Immanuel
  and slavery, 224
  on education, 246
Keith, George, 30
King, Margaret, 24
Kingsborough, Caroline King, Lady, 5–6, 23, 31, 246, 314
Kingsborough, Robert King, Lord, 6, 23, 31, 246, 283

Louverture, Toussaint, 224
Lee, Richard, 97, 99–100
  On the Death of Mrs. Hardy, 98
Lewis, Matthew
  Monk, The, 289, 294
Lloyd, Charles
  Edmund Oliver, 273
Locke, John
  and slavery, 224
  MW and, 164, 211, 283
  on education, 246–48, 282
  on property, 207–8
  Second Treatise on Government, 224
  Some Thoughts Concerning Education, 242, 246, 282
London Corresponding Society (LCS), 88, 97–99
Lucas, Charles
  Infernal Quixote, The, 278
Lyttelton, George, Lord, 231, 235

Macaulay, Catharine
  as contemporary of MW, 59

as historian, 79–81, 83
as writer on education, 282
  History of England, 80
  Letters on Education, 193
  MW on, 60, 193
  Observations on the Right Honourable Edmund Burke's Reflections, 80–81
  on Edmund Burke, 80
Mackenzie, Henry
  Man of Feeling, The, 257
Malthus, Thomas, 33
Mathias, T. J.
  Pursuits of Literature, 104
Maturin, Charles
  Bertram, 289
Michelet, Jules, 78–79, 83
Millar, John, 309
  Origin of the Distinction of Ranks, The, 307
Milton, John, 146, 151, 159, 241, 244
Montagu, Elizabeth, 190, 231–32, 234–35
More, Hannah
  and other women writers, 120
  as advocate of abolition, 190
  as conservative reformer, 128, 190, 194, 222, 233, 260
  Cœlebs in Search of a Wife, 130, 133
  Essays on Various Subjects, 128, 129
  heroines of, 130
  on women, 106
  Strictures on the Modern System of Female Education, 128, 129
  Village Politics, 105

Necker, Jacques, 140, 142–44
  On the Importance of Religious Opinions, 34, 142
Newton, John, 33

Ogilvie, William
  Essay on the Right of Property in Land, 209
Opie, Amelia (Alderson), 18, 93, 98, 302
  Adeline Mowbray, 269, 278

Paine, Thomas
  Age of Reason, 89
  Agrarian Justice, 208
  and Joseph Johnson, 33, 89, 320
  and LCS, 89
  and William Godwin, 34
  as republican, 182
  Common Sense, 208
  on rights, 204
  plain style of, 264
  response to Edmund Burke, 164, 202
  Rights of Man, 89, 95–96, 104, 202–3

Paine, Thomas (cont.)
  trial of, 97, 104
Pennington, Sarah
  *An Unfortunate Mother's Advice to her Absent
    Daughters*, 242–43
Philomaths, 88, 92–93
Pitt, William, 102
Polwhele, Richard
  satire of, 192–95
  Unsex'd Females, The, 104, 106, 132, 191–92,
    261
Price, Revd. Richard
  A Discourse on the Love of Our Country, 89,
    148, 165, 199, 203, 275
  and Joseph Johnson, 90, 147
  as rational dissenter, 167
  as republican, 182
  Edmund Burke on, 167, 200, 275
  friendship with MW, 147, 166, 204, 226
  in political debate, 166
  influence on MW, 148, 205
  supported abolition, 226
Priestley, Joseph
  and MW, 147, 167
  and Rational Dissent, 147
  Burke on, 167
  Essay on a Course of Liberal Education, 30
  experiments with gases, 252
  Fuseli's portrait of, 33
  house burned down, 150
  Joseph Johnson publishes, 33
  Letters to the Right Honourable Edmund Burke,
    203
  Misc. Observations Relating to Education, 282
  on education, 150
  on social passions, 152
  relationship with Joseph Johnson, 30, 34, 36,
    90, 96
Pye, Henry James
  Democrat, The, 273

Radcliffe, Ann, 16, 292
  Castles of Athlin and Dunbayne, 292
  Italian, 293
  Mysteries of Udolpho, 292
  Romance of the Forest, 292
  Sicilian Romance, 292
Rancière, Jacques, 78, 80
Reveley, Maria, 26
Richardson, Samuel, 230–31, 279
  Clarissa, 14, 266
  Pamela, 257
Robertson, William
  History of the Reign of the Emperor Charles V,
    307

Robinson, Mary
  and MW, 111, 114
  Angelina, 320
  as figure of scandal, 194
  confessional narrative style of, 194
  Letter to the Women of England, 115–16
  MW praises, 320
  Natural Daughter, The, 115
  novels of, 273
  pays tribute to MW, 114
  poetry of, 194
  Polwhele on, 194
  Walsingham, 194
Roscoe, William, 31, 34, 147
Rousseau, Jean-Jacques
  Confessions, 155–57
  Discourse on Political Economy, 208
  Edmund Burke on, 167
  Emile, 139, 155, 158, 208, 247–48, 282, 286
  Emile and Sophie, 155
  friendship with Diderot, 142
  influence on MW, 140, 142, 155, 157, 161
  Julie, or the New Heloise, 155–60
  Letter to D'Alembert, 155, 158
  Letters Written from the Mountain, 155
  MW on, 34, 66, 102, 119, 130, 142, 155–56,
    158–60, 192, 244
  on education, 247–49, 306
  paradoxes of, 156–57, 161
  primitivism of, 102
  Reveries of the Solitary Walker, 155
  Second Discourse, 142, 155
  Social Contract, The, 155–56

Salzmann, Christian Gotthilf, 325, 327
  Elements of Morality, 34, 285, 326
Savile, George, Marquis of Halifax
  Advice to a Daughter, 243
Scott, Sarah, 231
Scott, Sir Walter, 294
Shelley, Mary (Godwin), 9–10, 21, 53, 284
  Frankenstein, 10, 27
Shelley, Percy Bysshe, 27, 54, 327
Skeys, Hugh, 5, 23
Smith, Adam, 139, 208, 258
  Theory of Moral Sentiments, The, 141
Smith, Charlotte, 16, 32, 93, 111, 273
  Desmond, 112–13
  Young Philosopher, The, 114–16
Smollett, Tobias, 267
Society for Constitutional Information (SCI), 33,
  89, 92, 97–98
Society for Effecting the Abolition of the Slave
  Trade, 225
Southey, Robert, 8

Spence, Thomas, 97, 99, 285
 Marine Republic, The, 268
 Pig's Meat, 97
 Rights of Infants, 99
Sterne, Laurence
 A Sentimental Journey, 257

Talleyrand, Charles Maurice de, 6, 15, 323
Thelwall, John, 88, 90, 93, 98
Thoughts on the Education of Daughters
 emphasis on duty in, 241
Tocqueville, Alexis de, 199–200
Tooke, John Horne, 33–34, 89, 93, 320
Trimmer, Sarah, 285
 A Comment on Dr. Watt's Divine Songs, 286
 Fabulous Histories, 286
 Guardian of Education, 286
Turgot, Anne-Robert Jacques, 144

Voltaire (François-Marie Arouet), 140–42, 167
 Essay sur l'histoire-générale, 141
 L'Homme aux quarante écus, 141
 L'Ingénu, 141

Wakefield, Gilbert, 320
 Reply to . . . Bishop Landaff's Address, 35
Walker, George
 Vagabond, The, 273
Walpole, Horace
 Castle of Otranto, The, 290–91
Warrington dissenting academy, 30, 152
Wedgwood, Josiah
 "Am I Not a Man and a Brother", 226
Weissenborn, Friedrich, translator, 325–26
West, Jane
 as conservative reformer, 128
 heroines of, 130
 Letters Addressed to a Young Man, 129
 Letters to a Young Lady, 129
 novels of, 130
 on English Jacobins, 131
 on MW, 132
 on women, 129–30, 133
 reception of, 133
 Tale of the Times, 130, 133, 278
Wilkes, Revd. Wetenhall, 239–40
Williams, Helen Maria
 as historian, 79, 81, 83
 Letters from France, 81–82
 MW on, 81
Wollstonecraft, Charles, 22–23
Wollstonecraft, Edward, 22
Wollstonecraft, Edward Bland (Ned), 22–23
Wollstonecraft, Edward John, 3, 21
Wollstonecraft, Eliza, 4–5, 23, 246

Wollstonecraft, Elizabeth (Dickson), 3, 22
Wollstonecraft, Everina, 4–5, 23, 29, 32, 34, 156, 246, 314
Wollstonecraft, Henry Woodstock, 22
Wollstonecraft, James, 22
Wollstonecraft, Lydia, 22
Wollstonecraft, Mary
 A Vindication of the Rights of Men, xxiii, 6, 15, 31, 34, 42, 77, 95, 148, 164, 202–5, 207, 227, 243, 259, 305
 A Vindication of the Rights of Woman, xxiv–xxv, 6–7, 12, 15, 17, 28, 34, 36, 43–44, 46, 48, 50–53, 57, 59–61, 64, 66–68, 77, 89–91, 93, 96, 99, 111–13, 115, 119–25, 130–32, 141, 146, 149–50, 155–57, 159–61, 164, 171, 179, 189, 191, 200, 202, 204, 210, 216, 227, 238, 240, 243, 246, 257, 259–60, 269, 286, 303, 306, 320, 323–25, 327–28
 alliances with liberal female reformers, 119–25
 alliances with radical female reformers, 111–17
 An Historical and Moral View of the Origin and Progress of the French Revolution, 7, 44, 64, 77, 81, 83, 140, 142–44, 155, 170, 306, 308–9, 311, 326
 as travel writer, 8, 297
 attempt to rescue Fanny Blood, 5
 author of conduct literature, 242
 biographies of, 58, 68–70
 Cave of Fancy, 66
 childhood, 3, 22
 correspondence, 19
 correspondence with Gilbert Imlay, 7–8, 18
 critical reception, 1970s, 59
 critical reception, recent, 64–71
 critique of conduct literature, 242–44
 critique of property law in *Wrongs of Women*, 211
 critique of sentimental literature, 259–60
 death, 9, 26
 departure for Paris, 7
 disagreement with Edmund Burke, 167–68, 203–4
 disagreement with Edmund Burke about virtue, 168–70
 early biographies of, 59, 62
 early publications, 5
 employment with Lady Kingsborough, 5, 23
 employment with Sarah Dawson, 4, 23
 engagement with French *philosophes*, 139–40
 establishes school, 5, 23
 experience as an educator, 5, 246, 283
 her unique form of republicanism, 185
 influence of eighteenth-century Republicanism, 183

Wollstonecraft, Mary (cont.)
  influence of Dissenters, 146–52
  influence of French economic theorists,
    143–44
  influence of historical focus on her political
    vision, 305–7
  influence of Jean-Jacques Rousseau, 155–62
  influence of Mary Astell, 190
  influence of Rousseau's gender politics,
    158–60
  influence of Rousseau's penchant for paradox,
    156–57
  influence of Voltaire, 141–42
  *Letters Written during a Short Residence in
    Sweden, Norway, and Denmark*, xxiv–xxv,
    8–9, 12, 16–18, 24, 46, 52, 64, 69–70, 95,
    141, 152, 155, 179, 186, 261, 297, 326,
    328
  literary relationship with Joseph Johnson, 5, 6,
    7, 29, 95–97
  marriage to William Godwin, 9, 26
  Mary: A Fiction, xxv, 6, 42, 276, 292, 327
  nineteenth-century republications, 51, 53
  obituary, xxii
  Original Stories from Real Life, 6, 10, 24, 31,
    42, 120–22, 155, 157, 241, 246, 248,
    250–51, 283–85, 324–25, 328
  posthumous reviews, 48
  reactions of female conservatives, 132
  relation to Jacobin fiction, 271
  relation to Scottish Enlightenment theories of
    history, 308–9
  relationship with Gilbert Imlay, 6–9, 25
  rescue of Eliza, 4
  response to conduct literature, 238
  reviews of her work, 6, 8, 47
  suicide attempts, 8–9, 25
  The Female Reader, xxiv, 42, 65, 238, 241–43,
    317
  Thoughts on the Education of Daughters, xxiv, 5,
    31, 41, 87, 95, 152, 238, 240–42, 246, 250,
    283–84, 317
  translation of Christian Gotthilf Salzmann's
    Elements of Morality, for the Use of Children,
    34, 285, 325
  translation of Jacques Necker's *Of the
    Importance of Religious Opinions*, 34
  translation of Maria van de Werken de
    Cambon's *Young Grandison*, 34, 285, 325
  translations of MW's work, 323–28
  travels to Scandinavia, 8, 25
  use of gothic tropes, 294–96
  use of the language of slavery, 227–28
  work as a periodical writer, 314, 319–21
  Wrongs of Woman; or, Maria, xxv, 9, 15, 24,
    47, 52, 64, 70, 114, 149, 157, 207, 210,
    212, 261–62, 264, 270, 276, 294, 326, 328
Wollstonecraft, Sarah (Garrison), 23
Woodhouse, James, 234
Wordsworth, William
  Lyrical Ballads, 289
Wraxall, Nathaniel
  *Cursory Remarks Made in a Tour through Some
    of the Northern Parts of Europe*, 302

For EU product safety concerns, contact us at Calle de José Abascal, 56–1°,
28003 Madrid, Spain or eugpsr@cambridge.org.

www.ingramcontent.com/pod-product-compliance
Ingram Content Group UK Ltd.
Pitfield, Milton Keynes, MK11 3LW, UK
UKHW020402140625
459647UK00020B/2607